# The
# Iron Redskin

# The
# Iron Redskin

## THE HISTORY OF THE INDIAN MOTORCYCLE

### HARRY V. SUCHER

**Haynes Publishing**

First published in 1977
Reprinted 1978, 1982, 1984, 1987, 1988, 1990, 1992, 1994
This expanded and redesigned edition published in February 2010

A catalogue record for this book is available from the British Library

ISBN 978 1 84425 500 9

Library of Congress catalog card no. 2007943098

Haynes North America Inc., 861 Lawrence Drive, Newbury Park, California 91320, USA

Published by Haynes Publishing, Sparkford, Yeovil, Somerset BA22 7JJ, UK

Tel: 01963 442030 Fax: 01963 440001
Int. tel: +44 1963 442030 Int. fax: +44 1963 440001
E-mail: sales@haynes.co.uk
Website: www.haynes.co.uk

Printed and bound in Britain by JF Print, Sparkford

**Editor's note**

*The Iron Redskin* was first published in 1977 and since then has been reprinted many times, sometimes with minor updates to the later chapters.

Otherwise the text remains in its original form and so it may be helpful for readers to note that Chapter 11 was last revised in the 1980s and Chapter 12 was a new chapter supplied by the author in the mid-1990s. Any references to the present in these later chapters are therefore contemporary.

We are indebted to the following people who contributed photographs for the colour section in this new edition: Roland Brown, Marc Gallin, Garry Stuart, Chuck Vernon and Indian Motorcycle.

Finally, we would like to thank Bob Stark for his invaluable help in sorting through the new pictures and writing captions, checking the late author's 'new' Chapter 12 and writing the Postscript in order to bring the Indian story up to date.

# Contents

# Foreword

We have always wanted to know more about the Indian motorcycles and the factory located in Springfield, Massachusetts.

This book was prepared by Harry V. Sucher after many years of research, starting from when the factory first opened, to the people who were involved in making the Indian the best motorcycle ever built, to the day the factory closed its doors for the last time.

You will read about such great names as E. Paul du Pont, Jim Wright, and Joe Hosley. In the racing end of the research and development department there was Red (Pop) Armstrong and Jimmy Hill.

I feel very honored to have been a part of the Indian motorcycle organization. I started racing for them in 1936 and continued with them through the good and bad years until they eventually closed their doors.

Again, I feel honored that Harry came to me and asked if I would write this introduction for his book on the Indian motorcycles.

As you read from page one on, you will see how the management and the factory changed through the years, you will also read about the competition riders that rode for Indian, that helped in all types of competition and finally became my good friends. To name just a few, there was Cannonball Baker, Fred Ludlow, and Red Armstrong. Some of the records these old timers set then are still standing today.

Floyd Clymer, my one time boss, and the man responsible for getting me started with Indian, was also a great racer and hill climber. Another was Hap Alzina who did so much for me throughout my whole racing career.

It was always nice to visit the Indian factory in Springfield, and to see its acres of floor space. This book will give you, in detail, a year to year description of the good and bad times the Indian factory really had. It will also tell you about the Indian competition riders including myself.

E. Paul du Pont, who owned the Indian factory during the time I raced for them, was a great man. He gave me much encouragement throughout my racing career.

Also, Jim Wright and Joe Hosley were two of the finest men to work at the Indian factory throughout some of the best years the factory ever had.

Red Armstrong and Jimmy Hill were the backbone of the racing and engineering department. It was a real pleasure to have been able to race and work with them.

As you read on you will find that there were over three thousand Indian motorcycle dealers throughout the world who did some great work for the Indian factory.

Another man that did so much for Indian was Fritzie Baer of Springfield. He later moved to Laconia, New Hampshire to manage the Belnap recreation area. He also helped to run the two hundred mile national championship in 1938 and then again after the war in 1946. They also held the one hundred mile national there.

*Ed Kretz*

**Ed Kretz**
Monterey Park
California

# Author's preface

The motorcycle has sometimes been called the stepchild of the automobile. There have been times in its long history that it has been treated as an orphan in the transportation world. Developed coincidentally with the automobile, the simple and readily available pedal cycle frame was a handy test bed for inventors working on prototypes of small internal combustion engines. As an essentially small and lightweight vehicle, its speed with even low powered engines could be frightening when compared with contemporary four wheelers. This factor, coupled with the propensity for its exposed machinery to be noisy, often brought forth maledictions from the public, many of whom were downright hostile to the presence of powered road vehicles in an era when the horse reigned supreme. In fact, the vested horse interests fought a long and determined battle against any form of powered transport during the pioneer decades of railroad and automobile.

The motorcycle further suffered in its earlier years from a rather crude form of power transmission in the form of a belt that ran to either the front or rear wheel from the engine shaft. This lack of a controllable clutch or indirect transmission, coupled with rather inflexible engines due to their crude carburetion, created something of an all-or-nothing situation that made the machine a rather frightening projectile. In the hands of a novice, disaster was imminent. Even self-taught riders who survived their early experiences found something ever new to learn about the handling qualities of their usually temperamental steeds.

The inherent uncertainties of early day motorcycling offered a vicarious attraction to intrepid individuals. Men who went on to distinguish themselves in many diverse fields were pioneer motorcyclists. The most famous include Sir Arthur Conan Doyle, the creator of Sherlock Holmes, playwright George Bernard Shaw, aviators Alliott Verdon Roe, Charles A. Lindbergh and Clarence Chamberlain. Colonel T.E. Lawrence and President Dwight D. Eisenhower are also included, to name a few.

In addition, the pioneer motorcyclist was perforce something of a mechanic. Reliability could never be taken for granted. The uncertain metallurgy of the time had yet to produce valves that were not continually subject to burning and warping. Piston rings could not be expected to hold their expansion for any length of time. Primitive lubrication systems were prone to fail at some point, usually after a brisk run. The timer and coil or make and break ignition systems were even more temperamental. These factors all added together made for the zestful uncertainty that a top overhaul might have to be undertaken somewhere along the route of even a mild excursion.

As an essentially cheap vehicle, initially conceived to offer low cost transportation to those who could not afford the generally high prices asked for early automobiles, the immediate economic limitations precluded progressive refinements in design. The cheap, but often troublesome, belt drive persisted in many motorcycles until well after the close of the first World War. Variable speed gearboxes and really dependable clutches were consequently tardy in development. Carbide or acetylene lighting systems as used on early cars suffered a reduction in dependability when translated into miniature detail for motorcycles. The vibrations imparted to these lights by primitive suspension systems then in vogue, or even the absence of any springing whatever, could make a night ride a harrowing experience. The crudity of having to run alongside a machine to start it, or the inclusion of a bicycle type pedaling gear for the same purpose, limited the motorcycle to those of better than average physical fitness. Later the almost universal fitting of a kick or jump starting crank geared to the transmission called upon the rider for much physical exertion, and with a large, high-powered machine, definite athletic ability was required.

Through its nearly seventy-five years of commercial manufacture the motorcycle has been singularly vulnerable to the uncertain winds of economic change. In times of general prosperity, the great majority of the motoring public will choose the obvious comfort and superior weather protection of an automobile. In times of economic depression, manufacturing, production and marketing conditions will impose severe problems for all makers of fabricated products. Coupled with these inexorable drawbacks, another impediment to efficient motorcycle production is that its small size does not lend itself readily to mass assembly methods. Frames, forks, wheels, and other chassis parts must be hand fitted from their component parts. Two, or at the most, three, fitters only can work one machine at any given stage of production. It is not surprising that in the face of these formidable handicaps nearly one thousand motorcycle manufacturers in various parts of the world have come and gone since the beginning of the twentieth century. In reviewing these facts, transportation experts have at various times actually predicted the demise of the motorcycle. But through difficult times it has survived, its thread of continuity preserved by those intrigued with its appeal as an economical means of transportation, its unique appeal to the iconoclastic sporting rider, and for its irreplaceable role in traffic patrol and law enforcement.

Only within the past decade has the motorcycle at long last come into its own. Certain farsighted manufacturers have now placed on the market a very wide range of machine types suited to every class of rider and every conceivable use. Due to modern refinements of design, such as improved suspension, steering geometry, braking, and, lately, electric starting, the general appeal of the motorcycle has been enhanced. With these engineering advances, together with an almost unfailing reliability due to enhanced quality control, the machine of today has become a most satisfactory vehicle. Due to high volume production, low cost motorcycles requiring a minimum of maintenance and offering fantastic operating economy are providing millions of people in emerging nations with economical transportation, improving their economic status.

At the same moment, the sporting and recreational aspect of motorcycling has grown to amazing proportions in the world's more economically favored nations. More and more of these people from all walks of life have discovered the zestful adventure and unfettered freedom that only two wheels can provide. As a universal vehicle for both utility and pleasure, the motorcycle has come into its own.

The current popularity of motorcycling has prompted a growing interest in the historical aspects of its development. The names and individual accomplishments of the pioneers who participated in it are being rediscovered. The history of the motorcycle becomes explicitly interwoven with that of the various manufacturers who remained within the industry long enough to make substantial contributions to technical progress and consequent expansion of motorcycle sales. Those firms which were able to survive for a time and even prosper in the face of the difficulties attendant upon motorcycle production and sales, together with those responsible for their design, engineering and management, well deserve to be remembered. This is the story of one of them.

# Acknowledgements

It gives me great pleasure to recall the names of many of those who have contributed to the pleasure and enjoyment of nearly five decades of motorcycling activity; unfortunately, I cannot claim total recall and some may not be mentioned. During the vintage and classic eras there was usually a strong feeling of camaraderie among most motorcyclists, and experienced riders seemed ever willing to help the beginner with technical advice or even a hand with roadside repairs in case of a breakdown, which was then not uncommon. Perhaps this happy state of affairs was heightened by the fact that there were so few of us!

From an earlier time I remember Nelson Bettencourt, John and Jean Burdette, Cyril Duarte, Orrin Hall, Harley Jensen, Hap Jones, Al Lauer, Armando Magri, Frank J. Murray, Angelo Rossi, Joe Sarkees, LeRoy Talbot, and Carol and Glenn Tarwater.

During the years when I was engaged in collecting and restoring old Indian machines there was Bruce Aikin, the late J. Worth Alexander, Maury Biggs, Dewey Bonkrud, Dr. Earl Chalfant, Johnny Eagles, Russell Harmon, the late R.J. Hicketheir, the late Elmo Looper, Charles Myles, Lysle Parker, Gene Rhyne, Sam Pierce, Irving Seaver, Ernest Skelton, Robert Stark, Charles Vernon, Gerald and Ted Williams and Kenneth Young.

It is equally difficult to list the names of all those Indian enthusiasts who have contributed to the writing of this work. Much information has been garnered from dozens of interviews and literally hundreds of conversations and communications from former dealers, factory personnel, and past and present Indian owners who have cooperated in this endeavor in the hope that the essential facts of Indian history may be collected and preserved for posterity. Many of these enthusiasts have contributed valuable historical data in the form of photographs, letters, factory literature and communications, and contemporary news items.

Most of these people are happily still with us, but, inevitably, a few have subsequently taken their last ride. Among the more prominent are Hap Alzina, Floyd Clymer, Jud Carriker, Ray Garner, and Guy Urquehardt.

Distinguished non-motorcyclists no longer with us who contributed significant historical revelations of Indian history include the Honorable Fiorella La Guardia, former United States Congressman and one-time Mayor of the City of New York, William C. Durant, founder of General Motors Corporation and later President of Durant Motors Corporation. The Honorable George B. Sucher of Peoria, Illinois, and Lt. Col. Jacob G. Sucher, former Chief Ordinance Officer at the United States Army Arsenal at Benicia, California: I must also thank Senora Francisca (Luz) Villa, widow of the late General Pancho Villa of the revolutionary Army of the Republic of Mexico.

I am also appreciative of the encouragement given me in this endeavor by Arthur Segal, former President of the Antique Motorcycle Club of America; Frank Conley, Secretary of the Classic and Antique Motorcycle Club; and Jeff Clew and Arthur Mortimer of the Vintage Motor Cycle Club of Great Britain.

I am greatly indebted to the late Howard I. Chapelle, distinguished naval architect and marine historian and Curator Emeritus of Transportation of the United States National Museum who, along with members of his staff, made available for my research, certain material dealing with early motorcycle history in the United States.

I will be forever gratelul to certain surviving executives of the Indian Motorcycle Company for their reminiscences, together with their contributions of documentary and photographic material and other data, without which the story would not have been complete. Thomas Callahan, (Tommy) Butler, with Indian's sales and marketing department from 1914 to 1924; Leslie D. (Dick) Richards, publicity manager from 1920 to 1924; Theodore A. (Ted) Hodgdon, who filled various positions in the advertising department from 1926 through 1932; Ralph B. Rogers, President of the company from 1945 through 1949, and its last surviving chief executive.

Ed Kretz, Fred Ludlow, and the late Joe Petrali generously added much of the color of the competition days of the golden age of motorcycle racing, as did former race mechanics the late Red' Fenwicke and Joe Walker.

I am also indebted to William and Shirlee Bagnall, former publishers of the Motorcyclist magazine for permission to use much historical material from past issues of that publication, as well as to the latter for her reminiscences of the life and times of her father, the late Hap Alzina.

I also wish to thank Helen Hedstrom Carlson and her husband, David A. Carlson, for their contribution of many details of the life and times of the former's father, Carl Oscar Hedstrom.

I also wish to acknowledge the generosity of Skip Marketti of Harrah's Auto Museum, Reno, Nevada, in providing material and photographs of the Indian Arrow project.

Mention must also be made of the work of George Hays and Ronald Mugar, who prepared many of the photographs for publication.

Lastly, I am grateful for the aid of my wife, Margery, who undertook much of the arduous task of research, and who typed and edited the manuscript. While not a motorcyclist herself, she kindly tolerates a garage full of greasy motorcycles.

This book is edicated to the memory of George M. Hendee, Carl Oscar Hedstrom, Frank J. Weschler, and Charles B. Franklin who were responsible for Indian's best days, and with an appreciation to Ralph B. Rogers who brought modern sales and marketing methods to a stagnant domestic motorcycle industry.

*Harry V. Sucher*

**Harry V. Sucher**
Garden Grove
California

# Prologue

It will be no surprise to the thousands of Indian enthusiasts that during the decade and a half since the first edition of the Indian history appeared, interest in the marque has markedly increased. A survey by the author in 1975 noted that at least 35,000 machines from all years had survived. Another survey a decade later suggested that this number had increased to nearly 50,000.

This increase is not only due to the large numbers of enthusiasts who are restoring machines, but also to the efforts of both individuals and commercial firms who are fabricating such formerly scarce components as tool boxes, chainguards, lighting and ignition components, and other small miscellaneous fittings. Steel mudguards for later Chiefs and Scouts are also being made, as are rubber items such as bumper blocks, footboard mats and hand grips. This has prompted the restoration of partially intact machines once considered hopeless projects.

These projects have encouraged commercial operators to proceed with the remanufacture of later models, which have been further aided by the more recent availability of replica transmission gears and both beaded edge and drop center type tires with authentic appearing tread patterns.

Fuel tanks for all models and sheet metal parts for older models are still in critical supply, but it is hoped that these may shortly become available. One prominent commercial restorer has stated that it is economically feasible to make new casting molds for cylinders and cylinder heads, crankcases, gear housings and primary drive housings. He also mentioned possibilities for making jigs for replica frames and forks, although at this time the present supply seems adequate. All that is required is sufficient demand to overcome the inflated cost of the tooling required.

There has been, through the years, much speculation concerning a revival of the Indian motorcycle. But market surveys subsequently conducted by Charles Manthos, as well as Carmen De Leon who later acquired the make's trademarks, showed that there is no mass market for an obsolete machine. The inflationary cost of setting up a production line and the acquisition of necessary tooling for the possible sale of 4 to 5 thousand machines renders such impractical.

Perhaps one of the factors that has been responsible for the growing interest in antique motorcycles is that motorcycling of late has itself harked back to an aura of nostalgia. Many buyers of mature age now able to afford today's expensive machines are inspired by the longings of their youth, and are attracted to machines that bring back such memories.

Under such conditions, it is scarcely logical to assume that Indian enthusiasts would take kindly to some modern machine badge-engineered to have the Indian script on its tank sides. Then too, the timeless appearance and style of the immortal designs of Hedstrom, Gustafson, and Franklin has an ageless grace whose historic appeal cannot be displaced.

Not the least of the old Indians charm are their mechanical functionality. Their basic simplicity and freedom from excess bits and pieces that often characterized competing makes, offers their restoration a minimum of complexity.

Possessing an indefinable style, verve, and legends of their sporting accomplishments, Indian's secure place in transportation nostalgia again emphasizes the time honored slogan, "Old Indians Will Never Die!"

**H.V.S.**

# Chapter 1

# IN THE BEGINNING

Like many another significant invention, the development of the motorcycle resulted from the cumulative efforts of a large number of experimenters. The most successful prototypes were built by those who incorporated the better features of the inventions of their predecessors, coupled with their own innovative abilities.

Development of the internal combustion engine in the United States was pioneered by Elwood Haynes and the Duryea Brothers who, working independently, had developed gasoline powered road wagons to the point of commercial sale by 1894. These vehicles were powered with heavy, low-speed engines of mostly the one and two-cylinder horizontal type and they were water-cooled, there being no small, lightweight air-cooled engines available domestically. Commercial development of motor bicycles lagged from the want of suitable engines during this period, although a few prototypes were built, powered by light steam power, electric motors, and even a strange device fitted with spring activated clockwork.

The first American experimenter of note was E.J. Pennington, of Trenton, New Jersey. In 1894, he built a rather curious machine consisting of the usual pedal cycle frame, but with large diameter tires. A two-cylinder engine was placed on an outrigger frame carried behind the rear wheel, and drove the wheel through connecting rods fastened to an axle crank. While presumably air cooled, the cylinders had no cooling fins. Although the machine could be made to run, Pennington prudently restricted his demonstration runs to short fields, where limited travel would not give the engine time to overheat and possibly seize. He envisioned his creation as the forerunner of a vast manufacturing empire devoted to its production, and attempted to sell stock in a projected company. When Yankee skepticism precluded success, he took his machine to England in 1895, where he interested a bicycle financier named H.J. Lawson. Lawson paid Pennington £100,000 for his patents and formed the Great Horseless Carriage Company, selling stock to numerous individuals. Predictably, the venture collapsed in 1899.

In the meantime, a world wide bicycle boom flourished unabated. The trade press on both sides of the Atlantic kept the public informed of both advances in bicycle technology and progress in the continuing experiments with powered machines. In June of 1898, the Waltham Manufacturing Company of Waltham, Massachusetts, makers of the popular Orient bicycles, announced their intention of marketing motor bicycles. They had adapted their heavyweight pedal model for the fitting of a small, single cylinder De Dion type engine built in France by Aster, and called it the Orient-Aster. These machines were first marketed in the spring of 1899. The Marsh Cycle Company of nearby Brockton built a similar machine, powered with a De Dion type engine, which was first offered for public sale in January of 1900. Following the debut of the Marsh, Colonel Pope announced that development of prototype motorcycles was being conducted in his factory in Hartford. All of these early American machines were of the now familiar clip-on type, with belt drive.

**Opposite: *George M. Hendee, Founder and first President of the Hendee Manufacturing Company.* (Archives of the Hendee Manufacturing Company)**

While these infant enterprises were being launched, the bicycle-orientated public was being introduced to motorcycling through the use of motor powered pacing machines, as a feature of bicycle racing that was being conducted on numerous board tracks throughout New England and the Eastern seaboard. The use of pacing machines originated in France, where two riders on tandem bicycles preceded solo contestants to form a partial vacuum and cut the winds, thus making for faster times and giving a better indication of the pure speed capabilities of the riders. The early French motor powered pacing machines, which came into use about 1896, were of the solo type and were fitted with large capacity slow speed engines which were thought to offer more flexibility of control. Later machines were often tandems, fitted with small De Dion type engines, with the forward rider attending to the steering and adjusting the speed control to accommodate the following contestant. The rear rider acted as engineer, to look after the usually temperamental engines. A former professional bicycle rider named Kenneth Skinner, of New York, imported several De Dion type engines during the winter of 1898,

*Engineer's drawing of an 1898 De Dion Bouton single cylinder motorcycle engine.*

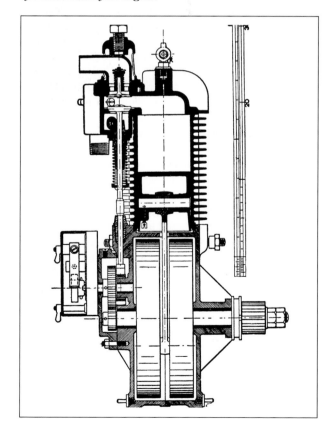

which he fitted to pedal tandem pacers. These machines were first employed in New York's Madison Square Garden, in the spring of 1899. The main objection to the use of these early machines was their unreliability. They would frequently break down during a race, to the consternation of the riders and the disappointment of the spectators. Several machines were kept on hand so that a replacement could be substituted. One of the most reliable motor tandems of the 1900 season was one constructed by a young bicycle builder named Oscar Hedstrom, who rode as engineer, and piloted by Albert Hinshaw, a one time professional bicycle rider.

George M. Hendee was born October 19th 1866, in a suburb of Boston, where his family was engaged in retail trade. Of Spanish origin, George became attracted to bicycling in the heyday of the high wheeler, and persisted in this endeavor until he won the National Amateur High Wheel Championship of the United States in 1886. He held this title until 1892, when he turned professional to compete in racing versions of the newly developed safety bicycle. He was a well known competitor on many of the larger tracks of the eastern circuits, before retiring from the sport in 1895. He continued on in the bicycle field as a sales representative for various manufacturers, where his wide acquaintanceships in the trade were very helpful. He was married in 1894, but the union was dissolved in 1895, by separation. A tireless promoter of the bicycle as a medium of mass transport, he was also keenly interested in the development of the motorbicycle, as its logical extension. In 1897, he decided to enter the field of bicycle manufacture, and selected the city of Springfield, Massachusetts as his site of operations. This was a most logical choice, as New England was then the leading industrial area of the United States. A large number of diverse industries were located in Springfield, including the Springfield Armory, which manufactured the famous Springfield rifle. There were naturally large numbers of highly skilled workers and artisans there whose background made them readily adaptable to many types of industrial employment. With his accumulated savings and $5,000 borrowed from a Springfield bank, Hendee rented a portion of a modest factory known as the Ford Building, located on Worthington Street, and commenced manufacturing operations in the summer of 1898. His initial models were known as the 'Silver King', with accompanying ladies' models appropriately named 'Silver Queen'. The early models were largely assembled from proprietary components secured from wholesalers. As sales increased, machine tools were purchased, together with a small forge, which made for more economical production of parts. The small force of production workers were under the charge of a shop foreman, enabling Hendee to

*Early motor powered pacing machine used on French Velodromes.* (Le Tempes)

spend most of his time travelling the New England and north eastern states, soliciting orders from retailers. By 1899, his sales volume was such that he was able to take over the entire Ford Building, and in the spring of 1900 he purchased the property.

During this period there was much public interest in professional bicycle racing in the New England area. There, a number of very successful indoor six lap board tracks were established in such cities as Providence, Worcester, Boston, Springfield, as well as others in some of the smaller towns. Most of the larger bicycle manufacturers entered paid professional racers to advertise their machines. Not to be outdone, Hendee put in training an athletic young bicycle mechanic named Jacob (Jake) De Rosier, who had joined his company in 1899. De Rosier was a young French-Jewish immigrant who had moved to New York from France with his family a few years before.

Under Hendee's skilful tutelage, he won many races on the New England circuit.

Hendee also undertook race promoting and was said to have had a financial interest in the Springfield Coliseum, a second track which opened in 1900. As a part of his interest in racing activities, Hendee on occasion attended some of the many meets held in New York's Madison Square Garden during the seasons of 1899 and 1900. It was here that he first observed the use of motor pacing tandems, and was duly impressed with the performance and reliability of the machine built by Oscar Hedstrom.

Carl Oscar Hedstrom (he preferred to drop the name Carl), the son of Andrew and Caroline. was born in the little village of Smolend, Sweden on March 12th, 1871. He was the second of three children, the other two being girls. The family emigrated to the United States in 1880 and settled in Brooklyn, where the elder Hedstrom found employment in the building trade. Young Oscar attended the public grammar schools and as he grew up, he showed a marked aptitude for mechanics. Like most active young boys of his day, he became interested in bicycling. While still a schoolboy, his father bought him a 'Victoria' machine with a patent spring fork. He graduated from the eighth grade at the age of sixteen, and apprenticed himself to a small factory in the Bronx that manufactured watch cases. It was here that he learned the use of machine tools, pattern making, forge and foundry work, and the rudiments of metallurgy. He won his ticket as a journeyman in 1892, and was successively employed in several small machine shops in the New York area. His main interest, however, was bicycling, especially after the advent of the safety bicycle, and with his natural mechanical aptitude he soon mastered the intricacies of its design and construction. In his spare time, he began building bicycles in his home workshop, that were of lighter weight and more durable construction than the usual production type machines. He soon took to this avocation on a full time basis, and within a short time his custom-built machines found favor with many professional racing men in the New York area. He also built a number of tandem pacing machines. When Kenneth Skinner imported several small De Dion type engines from France in 1899, Hedstrom obtained one, and set about studying its design and construction. He was able to modify some of those used by Skinner and others to improve their reliability,

which was then sadly lacking. He soon established a reputation for himself as an engine tuner, and modified a number of pacing tandem engines for the increasing number of such machines that were coming into use. His theories on design culminated in his building a pacing tandem in the summer of 1899 that was far and away a great improvement over any other previously used on the eastern and New England circuits. He teamed up with Albert Henshaw to operate this machine on the Madison Square Garden track, during the 1900 season. The ultimate fate of this historic machine is unknown, but, fortunately, one photograph survives. It will be noted that an all-chain countershaft drive was fitted in place of the more usual belt and pulley arrangement. This machine attracted much attention from both racing men and promoters, including George M. Hendee, who was by this time promoting races himself in the newly opened Springfield Coliseum. He offered Henshaw and Hedstrom bonus prices for bringing their machine to Springfield for certain of his programs.

Sometime during the Fall of 1900, Hendee approached Hedstrom concerning an idea he had been nurturing for some time; the designing of an improved model of a motor bicycle suited for commercial production. Hedstrom had apparently been thinking along the same lines, as he readily agreed to undertake such a design, with improvements over contemporary machines such as he had employed in his powered tandems. In order to obtain the use of the necessary facilities, he rented shop space in the tool room of the Worcester Cycle Company, in Middletown, Connecticut, and set to work. Some

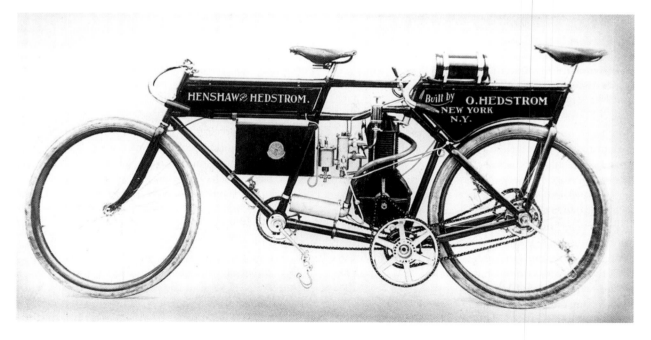

accounts of the matter have stated that the site of his operations was in the old Keating Wheel Works, also in Middletown, and it is entirely possible that at one time or another he utilized both locations. At any rate, his first task was to design a suitable engine, which he based on the well proved De Dion principle. His engine, however, was of entirely new design, for which he had crankcases and cylinder barrels cast from patterns which he made himself. Aside from fitting an improved timing and ignition system, he designed and built a concentric type carburetor that offered enhanced combustion efficiency and flexibility of engine control. The new machine was ready for road testing early in the spring of 1901. The cycle parts consisted of an ordinary roadster type pedal cycle with diamond frame construction. The wood rimmed wheels were shod with 1½ inch x 28 inch single tube pneumatic rubber tires. The single cylinder engine was set in the frame with its crankcase just above the chainwheel bracket, the rearwardly inclined cylinder head taking the place of the seat tube, a short extension of which was fastened to the top of the cylinder head. The ignition timer ran off the crankshaft, as in De Dion practise, the current being supplied by three dry cell batteries carried in a cylindrical canister, along with the spark coil, and clamped to the front down tube. A two-section fuel tank was fitted to the rear mudguard, being curved along its lower edge to conform to its arc. The upper edge was more pronounced in curvature, leading to the later descriptive name of 'camel back'. The smaller chamber of the fuel tank held lubricating oil, which flowed down to the engine by gravity, through a sight glass. The exhaust

pipe led down to a canister type muffler, bolted to the underside of the crank bracket.

The most significant departure from contemporary belt transmission was the all-chain drive. This consisted of a double chain arrangement from the engine sprocket to a countershaft placed in the hanger bracket, which also carried the pedal chainwheel, both the pedal and engine drive chains being carried to sprockets on either side of the rear wheel hub. There was no clutch, the drive being engaged at all times. A standard New Departure coaster brake was fitted for stopping power when back pedalled, and remained at rest when the engine was in operation.

The engine controls consisted of two short levers placed well forward on either side of the top tube, just behind the steering head lug. One of these advanced and retarded the ignition timer. When pulled to the limit of its rearward travel, it lifted a spring-loaded compression release in the cylinder head, to stop the engine. The other lever adjusted the throttle valve on the carburetor. Both controls exerted their action through light rods. The engine displaced about 13 cubic inches, and was rated at 1¾hp by Hedstrom. It developed sufficient power to propel the 98lb machine with a rider of average weight, at speeds up to about 25mph. The machine was handsomely finished in deep blue paint, with the pedal cranks, head fittings, control rods, handle bars, wheel spokes and other small parts nickel plated. The machine was started by pedalling a short distance with the exhaust valve lifted, which was then dropped when sufficient speed was gained to crank the engine.

Hedstrom tested the machine for several weeks on the country roads surrounding Middletown, and made

**Left:** *Motor powered racing tandem built by Carl Oscar Hedstrom in 1900.* **(Archives of the Hendee Manufacturing Company)**

**Right:** *A 1903 model originally donated to the United States National Museum by Bernard E. Andre, pioneer dealer of Charleston, West Virginia, and later restored to authenticity by the Indian factory.* **(The United States National Museum)**

numerous demonstration runs in the presence of Hendee, who made a number of trial runs on it himself. A photograph of Hedstrom alongside the machine is still in existence, its authenticity of location attested to by the name of a now forgotten photographer who stamped the word Middletown on the back of the picture.

The now famous test of the new machine on the Cross Street Hill in Springfield with its formidable 19° gradient was arranged by Hendee, who invited members of the newspaper and bicycling press to view the proceedings. The rather large gathering present were duly impressed with the machine's initial public demonstration. It started easily, showed good acceleration, and the all-chain drive provided unusual hill-climbing ability as the machine was stopped and started again at several points along the gradient. This, in combination with the flexibility of the engine due to Hedstrom's positive throttle and ignition controls, was quite a revelation to those who were formerly familiar only with the previous belt-drive machines whose engines generally ran (if at all) on the all-or-nothing principle. Some early articles in the trade press describing the event as the initial meeting of

Hendee and Hedstrom were, of course, fabrications, but their impression lasted in the minds of many for years to come. The late John J. O'Conner, an early day motorcycle journalist, and a later Indian employee, once wrote several romanticized versions of the test in his florid Victorian prose. He told the author in 1954 that he somewhat embellished the story for dramatic effect, as was often the journalistic practise in those days.

In 1930, E. Paul du Pont, then President of the Indian Motorcycle Company, presented a similar machine that had been long stored in the factory, to the Smithsonian Institution, where it is presently on view. It has been described by some motorcycle historians as the 'First Indian', but in reality it was built in 1903. It bears the number 150 on its crankcase. As the initial production runs were unnumbered until 1903, its true date of manufacture is thus established. It was also for a time fitted with a torpedo type fuel tank on the top tube, as offered as an accessory fitting in 1907, but it is now fitted with the correct camel back type.

The fate of the original machine was unknown for many years, as few, if any, of surviving Indian employees

Left: *Carl Oscar Hedstrom with the first prototype Indian Motorcycle taken at Middletown, Connecticut early in 1901.* (Archives of the Hendee Manufacturing Company)

Above right: *Carl Oscar Hedstrom.* (Helen Hedstrom Carlson)

IN THE BEGINNING

ever recall having seen it. What must be considered authentic knowledge of its ultimate fate came to light in 1954, when Erle Armstrong and Emmett Moore, one time Indian employees, interviewed Hedstrom at his home in Connecticut. His mind still clear at 84, Hedstrom stated that the original machine was ridden only a few times after its initial showing, and was shortly afterwards dismantled to provide parts for another prototype.

At any rate, Hendee and Hedstrom executed that famous agreement to form the Hendee Manufacturing Company as a partnership, with Hendee as President and General Manager, and Hedstrom as Chief Engineer and Designer. The trade name of INDIAN was selected by the founders as that best typifying a wholly American product in the pioneer tradition.

Hendee at once planned production of the new machine at the Worthington Street bicycle plant. Capitalizing on the favorable publicity that resulted from the initial public demonstration, he at once contacted various business and professional men within the local Board of Trade, of which he was already a member (this being the 19th century version of the modern Chamber of Commerce) and soon raised $20,000 through the sale of shares in the new company. Loft space was constructed above the bicycle production area, and with the aid of a couple of assistants, Hedstrom commenced building his machines.

As the bicycle plant had no foundry, an arrangement was made with the Aurora Automatic Machinery Company of Aurora, Illinois, to supply engine castings and carburetor components. As part of the agreement, Aurora was given the rights to use these castings in their own machines, which they had just undertaken to manufacture, and which were sold under the trade name of Thor. After 1907 they added a twin cylinder machine to their line, and manufactured motorcycles until 1915 when production was discontinued. This company is still in existence, manufacturing washing machines, vacuum cleaners and other household appliances.

During the Summer and Fall, about six motorcycles were built by Hedstrom, of which two were sold. To demonstrate the machine's capabilities, Hedstrom took his second prototype around the New England velodrome circuit that Fall and Winter. Clad in black racing tights, he rode around the course during the half time intermission, running at both slow and fast speeds, turning in circles, and otherwise demonstrating its speed and manoeuverability. Public response to his efforts was reported as being very favorable.

One of these 1901 models was shipped to England for exhibit at the annual Stanley Bicycle Show, where motorcycles had also been featured for several seasons. Its qual-

ity construction and then advanced engineering features were said to have attracted much favorable comment. This historic machine still exists and is presently owned by Mrs. Viola Bennett of Oakland, California. It seems that after the exhibition, it was purchased by an engineer named McDermott, who later came to California bringing with him the Indian motorcycle. After his death, the machine ultimately was acquired by the late Gordon Bennett of Oakland, who later restored it to new condition. J. Worth Alexander, a pioneer motorcyclist and a lifelong Indian enthusiast, who is familiar with the earlier models and who has examined the machine, stated that the machine is in authentic original condition and shows evidence of very little use. The authenticity of the machine is further proved by the fact that no engine numbers appear on the crankcase, none being affixed to those of the first production run.

In the spring and summer of 1902, Hedstrom continued to exhibit a machine at both indoor and outdoor bicycle races and various bicycle club competitions, with the result that by the end of the year, 143 models were sold to the public. These demonstrations, combined with an advertising program covering the leading bicycle journals of those days, resulted in more orders than the infant company was able to fill.

# Chapter 2

# THE GOLDEN DECADE 1903–1913

By 1903, the name of Indian had become well established as one of the more prominent makes within the infant industry. Indian's participation in various sporting events was rewarded with valuable publicity. There were a number of trade publications catering for bicyclists, and most of them by this time featured a department devoted to reporting motorcycle news. In turn, all of the more substantial manufacturers of motorcycles bought advertising space in these papers, which in turn stimulated editorial attention to the new industry.

In 1903, the Indian team again won the Fort George Hill Climb, as well as several other less spectacular events. These victories served to further publicize the ruggedness and controllability of Indian machines.

In the late Fall of that year, members of the New York Motorcycle Club, newly formed from the ranks of the New York Bicycle Club, together with members of the nearby Alpha Motorcycle Club, met in Brooklyn to form the Federation of American Motorcyclists. Of the ninety-two motorcyclists present, forty-four contributed $2.00 each for membership dues. In spite of the small attendance, the meeting was optimistically called a convention, from the fact that two clubs were represented. During the following year, several other clubs were persuaded to become affiliated. As the American Motorcycle Association later grew out of this early organization, the AMA records state that this meeting represented their own actual founding. In truth, however, the Federation of American Motorcyclists did not really have the strength to make itself felt until about 1908, when sufficient motorcycles were then in use to give some effect to the organization. The newly-formed FAM spon-

sored the National Endurance Run the next summer, from New York to Boston. Hedstrom and Hendee again repeated their victory of the previous year. About a dozen dealerships had by this time been established in the larger Eastern cities, and sales totaled 77.

The outlook for increased production in 1904 was very promising, and plans were made to augment the facilities of the Worthington Street plant. In order to purchase more tooling, additional shares were sold to investors in Springfield. By that summer, motorcycle sales were paying for their cost of manufacture, and the operation was additionally supported by the continuing sales of 'Silver King' bicycles. In that year Hendee changed the trade name of the bicycle to Indian, in order to consolidate the name of their products.

The management of the firm during the early years was under the close personal supervision of the two founders. Hendee, as President and General Manager, was in charge of advertising and sales promotion. Hedstrom, as Chief Engineer and Designer, was in personal charge of the engine building shop, assisted by half a dozen skilled mechanics. The building of the cycle components was under the charge of senior employees of the bicycle department, who acted as foremen for such subdivisions of the work as frame assembly and brazing, wheel assembly, and in the fabrication of small component parts. A small office force took care of the paper work and accounting. Hendee, a tireless

**Opposite: *Engine details of J. Worth Alexander's 1910 single. The position of the brake pedal is non-standard.* (George Hays)**

production for increased growth of the company. This policy was in direct contrast to the practice of many of his less experienced competitors, who relied on advertising and solicitation of dealers in trade publications rather than on personal contact.

Both partners continued to take an active part in scheduled competition events, and were often joined by Jake De Rosier, whom Hedstrom had been training in all the then known rudiments of motorcycle racing. An apt pupil, De Rosier soon became one of the leading competition riders of the day.

In 1904 further laurels were added to the Indian name when two machines were exhibited at the St. Louis Exposition, held to celebrate the one hundredth anniversary of the Louisiana Purchase. Indian was the only motorcycle to be awarded a Gold Medal for mechanical excellence.

The original design of 1901 had been carried on through the 1904 season with a few minor improvements. During this period, however, Hedstrom had been continuing a practise that he was to follow throughout all his future years with the company; that of constant experimentation and improvement of the product. The results of this work were seen in the 1905 models, when the first of several changes were made. A cartridge-type spring fork replaced the solid bicycle type, to give a softer ride and to reduce the danger of broken fork blades from road shocks. The rider could adjust or even eliminate the spring action by adjusting a single bolt that secured the spring. Twist grip throttle and spark controls were now fitted to the handlebars, allowing the rider full control of the engine without removing his hands from the bars. The mechanism was activated by a series of rods working

promoter, spent much of his time in travelling throughout the New England and Eastern states, calling on bicycle and motorcycle dealers, keeping in close touch with previously franchised agents and soliciting new accounts. From his experience in launching his successful bicycle business, he was well aware of the importance of a strong dealer organization to retail the product, as well as its importance in planning and stabilizing future

*Left: Frank J. Weschler.*

*Right: J. Worth Alexander with his authentically restored 1907 single.* (Ronald Mugar)

*Below left. W. Allyn thumbs his nose in mock derision at his 1905 Indian single, as the disabled machine is towed out of the Wyoming desert by pure horsepower. This was the first motorcycle registered in that state.* (Leslie D. Richards)

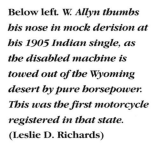

through universal joints. This was a significant safety feature for more positive control of the machine over the poor roads of that day. The introduction of these improvements has made the dating of early machines difficult, as many owners fitted the new forks and controls to earlier models. The cubic displacement of the engine was unchanged, as was the 1¾hp rating, but speed and power were increased by improved cam action and valve timing. Engine longevity was enhanced by the fitting of steel cylinder barrels that were turned on a lathe from solid forgings.

Another improvement was the introduction of a compensating sprocket on the engine shaft. This consisted of a set of circular bronze friction discs, whose tension could be adjusted by the rider. These gave a much smoother drive and did much to eliminate chain breakage. In this year Hedstrom experimented with a 42° V twin engine of about 26 cubic inch displacement, which could be fitted to the standard diamond type frame. Several engines were built for test purposes, and two were used by Hedstrom and De Rosier in races and hill climbs, but were not offered for sale to the public until the following year.

In the spring of 1905, a man joined the Indian staff as a bookkeeper and office manager who was to play a very significant role in company affairs for the next two decades. Frank J. Weschler was born in Westfield,

Massachusetts in 1879. He was educated in the local grammar schools and, after two years of high school, enrolled in a local business college where he learned the rudiments of bookkeeping, accounting, and banking. After graduation he was successively employed as a bookkeeper and became keenly interested in the growth and development of the automobile. He later transferred this interest to the motorcycle industry, and developed an almost fanatic loyalty to the Indian company. He has been described as a short, stocky individual with a serious bearing that was tempered by a keen sense of humor. The worthy measure and depth of his character, and his sincere personality, inspired respect and confidence in his associates, and his innate sense of honesty and fair dealing won him a host of loyal friends, both within the Indian company and throughout the industry. A devoted family man, he was also a devout Catholic, and was later active in the local and regional affairs of the Knights of Columbus Lodge. As a paradox to his position of leadership in the industry, he never learned to ride a motorcycle, and his only personal contact with actual machines was an occasional ride as a passenger in a company-owned sidecar outfit.

The year of 1905 ended triumphantly with sales of 1,181 machines, nearly double the figure of 586 distributed in 1904. Nearly one hundred new dealers were added to the company roster.

As might have been suspected, the very successful Indian machine had several imitators. Aside from the contemporary Thor machines built in Aurora, which used Hedstrom's engine castings by prior agreement, and, incidentally, closely copied the cycle configuration as well, there were also the Royal and the America. The latter featured a large automotive type steering wheel in place of the usual handlebars. Cheaply built of inferior materials by small firms with little capital and scant engineering background, both makes mercifully passed from the scene after a few dozen examples were produced.

In 1906, in addition to the new twin cylinder model, an enlarged single cylinder engine replaced the original 1901 type. It was designed along the same lines, but its cylinder displacement was increased to 19 cubic inches and was rated at 2¼hp. Orders from dealers were now running

*T.K. (Teddy) Hastings somewhere in Scotland at a checkpoint during the 1907 International Six Days Trial. His chain driven twin was an easy winner. (Archives of the Hendee Manufacturing Company)*

ahead of production, with 1,698 machines produced by the close of the year. Working space was now at a premium in the modest Worthington Street factory.

With an eye to focusing public attention on the new models, the founders cast about for new competition worlds to conquer. The transcontinental speed record had previously been a spectacular advertising medium for the automobile industry, as Winton, Packard and Franklin had already dispatched machines coast to coast, over almost impassable tracks which could scarcely be dignified by the term road. The first motorcycle to make the trip had been a Duck, made by the short-lived Dyke Manufacturing Company of Stockton, California. Its intrepid rider, George A. Wyman, had made the crossing from San Francisco to New York City in fifty days, in the early summer of 1902.

President Hendee selected two veteran motorcyclists to make the trip in the summer of 1906, on the new twin cylinder machines. They were Louis J. Mueller of Cleveland, Ohio, and George Holden of Springfield, Massachusetts, Indian's first franchised dealer. The machines were shipped by train to the San Francisco

THE GOLDEN DECADE 1903–1913

*The Indian Tri-car, manufactured in limited quantities during 1908.*

*The Indian Quick Delivery Van, first offered during the 1908 season.*

dealer, George 'Hop' Hopkins, in late July and he readied them for the arrival of the riders. The two left the bay city on August 10th. They reached New York on September 12th, after an exhausting journey for an elapsed time of 31 days, 12 hours and 15 minutes for the 3,476 mile trip. The record was authenticated by impartial automobile club officials, and was not broken for several years. The machines were reported as functioning perfectly, requiring only routine maintenance en route.

As rival factories were springing up all over the country with the growing popularity of the motorcycle, Hedstrom decided that another spectacular demonstration of Indian prowess was in order. Speed trials for automobiles had already been held for several seasons at Ormond Beach, Florida, where the hardpacked sands at low tide offered a safe and unobstructed race course. Hedstrom prepared a special machine for racing against cars at these events, the contest being the early day equivalent of the modern drag race. In one five mile heat, he turned the remarkable time of 5 minutes, twenty-seven seconds, only slightly behind a powerful racing car named the 'Bullet' driven by Alexander Winton. He made equally good showings against the formidable Oldsmobile 'Torpedo' models. While the matches were informal and no official records were recognized by the then infant FAM, the publicity value was incalculable, as the results were widely reported in the newspapers.

Many new dealers were securing Indian franchises, and in 1907 C. Will Risdon, a pioneer Los Angeles motorcyclist, established the first Indian dealership in southern California.

The small size and high performance capabilities of the motorcycle were now coming under the scrutiny of law enforcement officials as another form of conveyance, and the Metropolitan Police Force of New York City purchased two Indian twins. These were at first employed to catch runaway saddle and wagon horses on the city streets, a very real hazard in the congested traffic conditions existing even then in the heart of the larger cities. It was largely for this reason that the Indian management standardized the left hand throttle control, as it left a presumably right handed officer free to wave, point, signal, or even shoot, while keeping his machine under positive control.

As the demand for increased production of new Indian machines was increasing, it became evident to the founders that new and larger quarters were needed if the company was to continue its expansion. There was also the problem of delays in production, as the Aurora Company was often unable to produce engine castings and carburetor parts on schedule. Hedstrom's plan was to set up his own forge and foundry to overcome this difficulty, but this operation could not be accommodated on the already overcrowded Worthington Street plant.

A site available for a new factory was located in a building situated in an area of Springfield, known as the Highland Community. This edifice was a four-storey building with heavy exterior red brick walls, the insides of which were buttressed at intervals to support massive oak joints carrying heavy oak floors and interior partitions. It was situated on a roughly triangular plot of land at the junction of State Street and Wilbraham Road, the front entrance facing State Street. The west end of the

# Twin-Cylinder Indian

(5 h. p.)  38.61³

Price, with mechanical inlet valve          $260

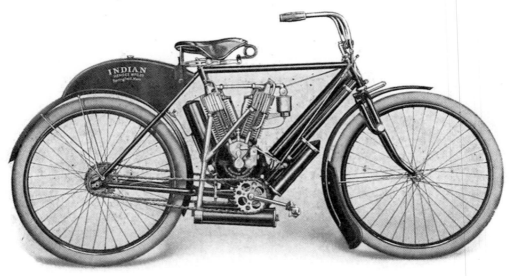

## SPECIFICATIONS

**MOTOR**—Hedstrom improved, air-cooled, 5 h.p., 38.61³ twin motor. Stroke, 3¼ inches; bore 2¾ inches.

**CARBURETER**—Hedstrom improved automatic compensating carbureter.

**CONTROL**—Indian patented, leverless, double grip, twist-of-wrist system. Right grip controls electrical spark and exhaust valves; left grip controls throttle.

**MUFFLER**—Indian improved muffler, absolutely silent. Fitted with Indian cut out, operated by foot.

**SPEED**—Five to sixty miles per hour, according to gear.

**FRAME**—Best seamless steel tubing, 1⅛ top, 16 ga., 1¼ bottom, 14 ga. All joints internally reinforced. Height, 22 inches.

**FORK**—Indian patented improved convertible double cushion fork; may be made rigid by tightening one nut. Seamless steel tubing. Fork crowns and hinge joints are drop forgings.

**WHEELS**—Twenty-eight inches; 36 spokes front and rear; spokes in rear wheel on motor drive sprocket-side laced in. Mudguards front and rear; front guard with splasher.

**WHEEL BASE**—Fifty-one inches.

**TRANSMISSION**—Indian roller gear drive from engine to countershaft. Gears entirely covered by gear case. Option: Chain drive, ⅝-inch pitch roller chains.

**GEAR**—Pedaling, 50 inches; motor, 5 to 1, with 27-tooth sprocket, for gear and chain drive Option: 31 and 23-tooth sprockets.

**BRAKE**—Corbin-Indian duplex motocycle coaster-brake.

**SADDLE**—Imported Brooks B-100 motocycle saddle with compound springs. Options: B-100-4, B-90-4, for heavy riders.

**TIRES**—G. & J. improved detachable 2¼ inches. Rims, hollow, steel, finished to match frame.

**BATTERY**—Indian special dry cells. Good for from 800 to 1500 miles, dependent on care afforded. Option: Three regular No. 6 dry cells.

**COIL**—Hedstrom formula torpedo spark coil.

**SPARK PLUGS**—Hedstrom mica plugs.

**TANKS**—Gasolene capacity, 5 quarts, sufficient for about 75 to 100 miles. Oil capacity, 1 quart. sufficient for 200 miles.

**TOOL BAG**—Indian improved square bag, containing all necessary tools, oil can and repair outfit.

**INLET VALVES**—Mechanically operated. Option: Automatically operated.

**MAGNETO IGNITION**—$40.00 extra.

**OIL GAUGE**—This gauge is fitted at the base of the motor, whereby the rider can determine at all times amount of oil in base.

**WEIGHT**—One hundred and thirty-five pounds, full road equipment; stripped, 120 pounds. Shipping weight, 200 pounds.

**FINISH**—Royal Indian Blue; all bright parts nickled on copper. Options: Black or Indian red.

**TANDEM ATTACHMENT**—With handle-bar, but without saddle, $15.00 extra.

*The improved twin model, marketed in 1908.*

# Twin-Cylinder Indian

(7 h.p.)  60.32³

Price  .  .  .  .  .  .  .  .  .  $360

## SPECIFICATIONS

**MOTOR**—Hedstrom improved, air-cooled, 7 h.p., 60.32³ twin motor   Stroke, 3¼ inches; bore, 3⁷⁄₁₆ inches.

**CARBURETER**—Hedstrom improved automatic compensating carbureter.

**CONTROL**—Indian patented, leverless, double grip, twist-of-wrist system.   Right grip controls electrical spark and exhaust valves; left grip controls throttle.

**SPEED**—Five to sixty-five miles per hour, according to gear.

**FRAME**—Best seamless steel tubing, 1⅛ top, 16 ga., 1¼ bottom, 14 ga.   All joints internally reinforced.   Height, 22 inches.

**FORK**—Indian patented improved convertible double cushion fork; may be made rigid by tightening one nut.   Seamless steel tubing.   Fork crowns and hinge joints are drop forgings.

**WHEELS**—Twenty-eight inches; 36 spokes front and rear; spokes in rear wheel on motor drive sprocket-side laced in.

**WHEEL BASE**—Fifty-one inches.

**TRANSMISSION**—Chain drive, ⅝-inch pitch roller chains.

**GEAR**—To order.

**BRAKE**—Corbin-Indian duplex motocycle coaster-brake.

**SADDLE**—Imported Brooks B-100 motocycle saddle with compound springs.   Options: B-100-4 B-90-4, for heavy riders, or racing saddle style.

**TIRES**—G. & J.—improved detachable 2¼ inches.   Rims, hollow, steel, finished to match frame.

**BATTERY**—Indian special dry cells.   Good for from 800 to 1500 miles, dependent on care afforded.   Option: Three regular No. 6 dry cells.

**COIL**—Hedstrom formula torpedo spark coil.

**SPARK PLUGS**—Hedstrom mica plugs.

**TANKS**—Gasolene capacity, 4 quarts; oil capacity, 1 quart.

**TOOL BAG**—Indian improved square bag, containing all necessary tools, oil can and repair outfit.

**INLET VALVES**—Automatically operated.   Option: Mechanically operated.

**MAGNETO IGNITION**—$40.00 extra.

**OIL GAUGE**—This gauge is fitted at the base of the motor, whereby the rider can determine at all times amount of oil in base.

**WEIGHT**—For racing, 120 pounds.   Shipping weight, 220 pounds.

**FINISH**—Royal Indian blue; all bright parts nickeled on copper.   Options: Black or Indian red.

*The noted 'monkey-on-a-stick' racer marketed in 1908.*

building faced a smaller triangle of land known as Winchester Park, which in later years was the site of a fire station. In those days this was a newly-settled section of the city, its growth being stimulated by the increased industrial expansion in Springfield.

The original portion of the brick building at 837 State Street, which was later incorporated as a part of the Indian factory, was built by an educational organization known as the Springfield Institute, a private foundation supported by public donations. It purchased the State Street property in 1886, and built the building which still bears the legend on the cornerstone: 'Industrial Institute – 1887–1895.' In 1895, the City of Springfield announced its intention to add industrial training to its public school curriculum, and made immediate plans to build its own premises on nearby Elliot Street. In the meantime, it purchased the Industrial Institute building and conducted classes there until the Elliot Street building was completed a year later. It leased a part of the building to the Hendee Manufacturing Company in the Fall of 1906, and afterwards sold them the entire premises in 1909.

The Hendee Manufacturing Company occupied half of the building early in 1907, where Hedstrom set up his forge and foundry, transferring much of the tooling from the Worthington Street plant. Motorcycle frames, forks and certain other small parts were fabricated at the

Worthington Street plant for some time thereafter. Bicycle manufacture was also continued there until this production terminated in 1930.

The 1907 sales year opened with high hopes for continuing success, with numerous additions to Indian's ever-growing roster of dealers. The line of machines included the improved 2¾hp single and the 3½hp twin, both having automatic inlet valves. A larger fuel and oil tank was added to both models, the latter now fitted with a hand pump to allow the rider to force more oil into the engine as conditions warranted. The primary chain drive from the engine sprocket to the countershaft was replaced by a roller gear drive, together with improved friction discs. Total sales for the year were 2,176 units. There was a moderate business recession during this year, but the demand for motorcycles increased, due no doubt to the continuing demand for mechanical transportation at a time when the mass-produced cheap car was as yet unavailable.

In 1907 a man joined the engineering staff whose contributions in later years was to have a significant effect upon Indian's fortunes. Charles Gustafson was born in Minnesota in 1869, his parents having emigrated from Scandinavia to the United States shortly after the American Civil War. A self-taught mechanic and practical engineer, he progressed through various mechanical occupations, and became employed in 1906 by the Reading-Standard Motorcycle Company of Reading, Pennsylvania, a relatively small firm which entered the

*Indian's first racing star, Jake De Rosier, posed with a prototype 1908 racing machine.*

industry during the pioneer era. During his tenure there he had designed a simple V-twin engine, with mechanically operated valves. This engine, said to be based on the design of the contemporary French Peugeot, had an atmospherically operated intake valve in its original form. Gustafson's engine in both single and twin cylinder types formed the basis of Reading-Standard production until the company's final demise in 1924. Gustafson's position with Indian was to assist Hedstrom in the engineering department. A couple of years later his teenage son, Charles Jr. joined the firm as his father's assistant.

A significant event of 1907 was the inception of the Tourist Trophy races in the Isle of Man. This venue had been chosen because there was much opposition on the English mainland to the closing of public roads for speed events. For much the same reason, H.F. Locke-King had been inspired to build Brooklands, a speed course on private land, which was opened the same year. It was the Isle of Man, however, that offered the more practical solution. The Island was autonomously governed by its own parliament, and as tourism and vacation resorting was the mainstay of the Island's economy, the officials had already closed certain sections of the road for auto racing since 1905. The first Tourist Trophy Race was staged in the summer of 1907 and provided events for both single and twin cylinder machines. It was run over the so-called short

*Carl Oscar Hedstrom (wearing cap) with his factory racing team at Daytona Beach, Florida, in the winter of 1909. Left to right Walter Goerke, who later became a dealer, Robert Stubbs, and A.G. Chappie.* **(Archives of the Hendee Manufacturing Company)**

course of 15 miles on roads adjacent to Douglas. The winner of the twin-cylinder event was Rembrandt Fowler, riding a Peugeot-engined Norton. The second place was captured by a young pioneer motorcyclist named William H. (Billy) Wells, on a German Vindec of which he had recently acquired the English distribution rights.

Another significant motorcycling event of 1907, held in England, was the running of the first Thousand Mile Reliability Trial, which was later to become the International Six Days Trial. The contest was held on public roads, with many check points to be passed at fixed times, reliability rather than speed being the basis of the competition. Among a large field of entrants was one T.K. (Teddy) Hastings, a member of the Crescent Motorcycle Club of the Bronx, New York, on an Indian twin. He made the trip to England at his own expense. Out of a possible 1,000 points, his score was a remarkable 994. The reliability of the Hedstrom engine was an instrumental factor in his victory, coupled with the all-chain drive which was of distinct advantage in hilly country. The impact of Hasting's victory was not lost on both the English motorcycling public and press, and much was made of it on both sides of the Atlantic. Hastings later went to Australia and became an Indian dealer in Melbourne.

The 1908 Indians were offered with several optional new features in engine design, although the original bicycle type diamond frame of 1901 was still retained. Mechanical intake valves were available as an optional extra, the atmospheric type being fitted as standard. The intake valve was placed in the top of the cylinder head and was activated by an arm resembling a hacksaw frame. It ran off a double nosed cam on the engine shaft that also worked the exhaust valve. Another option was the fitting of a German Bosch magneto, although the coil and timer type was still cataloged as standard.

The 1908 line was augmented by the addition of two racing machines, which were offered with either single or twin cylinder engines. The camel back fuel tank was replaced by a torpedo-shaped tank, clipped to the top frame tube. The saddle was fitted to an extension of the top tube and extended rearward over the back wheel, enabling the rider to assume a crouched position that considerably lowered wind resistance. It was popularly known as the 'monkey-on-a-stick' model. This machine, in both single and twin cylinder types, was successfully entered in several races and hill climbs by both Hedstrom and De Rosier. It was also ridden by B.A. Swenson, a former professional bicycle racer from Provincetown, Rhode Island, known as the 'Terrible Swede', in the New York to Chicago race of that year. He lowered the time to 33 hours 26 minutes for the 978 miles, setting up a new record. A three-wheeled forecar with a commercial body was also offered.

This year also saw De Rosier's emergence as a formidable competitor on the larger board bicycle tracks or velodromes that were beginning to feature motorcycle races. In July, a new six lap velodrome was opened at Paterson, New Jersey, and as a headline event the National Championship Races of the National Bicycle and Motorcycle Show and the Federation of American Motorcyclists were scheduled. For these races, Hedstrom built a special machine for De Rosier. It featured a lengthened frame with a torpedo type between-the-rails fuel tank, the engine being carried in a loop in front of the pedal bracket. The extended wheelbase and lowered center of gravity made for much better handling. In addition, Hedstrom experimented with various combinations of fork rake and trail to improve the steering.

The Paterson track was very narrow, with 48° banking on the turns. The referee consequently ruled that only two riders could compete at one time. De Rosier defeated John King of Newark, riding an Excelsior, in the 10-mile feature race for the dual championship. He then made an exhibition run against time, covering the mile in 56 seconds. This was the first event to establish board track records, and the FAM now recognized a new class of professional rider and accepted De Rosier's times up to 10 miles as the class records.

De Rosier remained at the Paterson track all summer, riding against time in exhibition runs and against any competition that could be arranged. On August 23rd he set a new quarter mile record, turning a lap and a half in 13 ⅕ seconds, for a speed of 68.2mph. On the same day he won the three mile event, with a time of 3.01, which broke the record of 3.03 made the preceding month by Paul Derkum of Bakersfield, California on a mile horse track at Fresno, riding a Reading-Standard. This was the beginning of board track speeds moving ahead of dirt track competition.

T.K. Hastings again journeyed to England in 1908, to compete in the Six Days Trial, his expenses this time being defrayed by President Hendee. He repeated his performance of the preceding year, gaining further overseas publicity for Indian. William H. Wells was again duly impressed by Hastings' repeat victory, and approached Hendee regarding the securing of the Indian import rights for the United Kingdom. After some correspondence, Hendee made a trip to England during the summer, and the agreement was consummated. Hendee also aided Wells in financing the new venture, as well as supplying the funds for the construction of an attractive showroom, at 178 Great Portland Street, London. Wells launched an extensive sales campaign, and it was reported that the initial shipment of twenty-five machines, mostly twins, were sold almost immediately. During the next two years he also established a number of satellite dealerships in several large cities in the British Isles.

In deference to his success in England and his dedication to Indian, Wells was given an honorary seat on Indian's Board of Directors in 1911, a position he held until the company was reorganized as the Indian Motocycle Company in November 1923.

All in all, 1908 was a very successful year, with President Hendee announcing 3,257 machines sold and that over 400 franchised dealers were active in the United States alone, as well as several additions to their overseas outlets.

In anticipation of an increasing demand for Indian motorcycles in 1909, the first of a number of subsequent additions was planned for the State Street factory. The original building and adjacent land had already been purchased by the company that Spring, with funds raised from the sales of additional shares. The floor area

was doubled by the addition of another wing that faced State Street. Frame building and all other motorcycle operations were now conducted on these premises, and all bicycle manufacturing activities were carried out at the Worthington Street plant.

To assist with the planned expansion of the sales campaign, Edward Buffam, a former sales manager for a small Massachusetts shoe manufacturing concern and a crony of Hendee's from his bicycle racing days, was hired as Assistant Sales Manager.

In 1909 President Hendee also added new members to the Indian racing team. These included Walter Goerke, Robert Stubbs, A.G. Chappie, who later was to gain additional fame as a racing star on Flying Merkel machines, and Erle 'Red' Armstrong, so named for his thatch of flaming red hair and who had formerly been a profes-

sional bicycle racer. The latter would hold many important positions within the company until the end of its days in 1955.

The 1909 Indian line was entirely redesigned. The loop frames with lengthened wheelbase, as featured in the racing machines built for De Rosier, replaced the former diamond bicycle type, but the single-bladed cartridge type spring fork was retained. The fuel tanks were of the streamlined torpedo type, clipped between the upper and lower tank rails. The oil was carried in a rectangular half gallon tank, clipped to the forward side of the seat tube. In addition to the improved 2¾hp single, two twin cylinder models were offered, one a 7hp 61 cubic inch Big Twin and a 5hp 38 cubic inch Light Twin. Both were of the time-tried 42° type, again with the option of standard coil and timer or Bosch magneto, at slightly higher cost. Mechanically operated valves were now standard. The rocker gear for the intake valve was redesigned for lightened weight and smoother action, a push rod now being fitted in place of the previous hacksaw type that had proved somewhat cumbersome and subject to rapid wear. The experiments of the previous year with steering geometry proved fruit-

ful, as the machines handled much better at high speeds, a case in point that racing improves the breed.

In order to subject the new models to more searching tests, Hedstrom took several members of his racing team to Daytona Beach that winter for the annual speed trials, together with about a dozen various machines.

The increasingly popular Tourist Trophy Races on the Isle of Man were coming into their third season in 1909. Hedstrom had not originally planned to take a team to the island that year, due to the pressure of design and development work. However, Billy Wells, an inveterate speed enthusiast, expressed his intention of entering a team of all British riders, and Hedstrom finally offered to come to England a short time before the start of the races, to assist in the preparation of the machines. Wells fielded a team of three Indian riders headed by G. Lee Evans. Ill luck dogged their efforts, however, as two of the riders were forced out in the early part of the race with tire trouble. Evans closely followed Harry Collier on a Matchless twin during the final stage of the race and came in second, some four minutes behind him.

In the meantime, board track racing was becoming the most popular motorcycle sport in the United

*The Hedstrom aero engine of 1911, a frank copy of the popular French Gnome-et-Rhone, at the United States National Museum.* **(The Smithsonian Institution)**

*A different angle of the Hedstrom aero engine.* **(The Smithsonian Institution)**

*The short-lived 1910 belt drive model with planetary gear drive.*

States. Jack Prince, an engineer from New Jersey who had been prominent in the building of bicycle tracks, began the construction of larger dromes for use with motorcycles, and was later to build a large number of tracks from coast to coast during the ensuing decade. He opened the Coliseum track in Los Angeles in the spring of 1909, and De Rosier, together with an aspiring amateur named Fred Huyck from Chicago, came west, seeking fame and fortune. The Coliseum was the largest board track built by Prince up to that time, having 3½ laps to the mile. De Rosier brought with him two new machines and six new specially tuned racing engines designed for him by Hedstrom. During the first few weeks of competition, he broke all existing records up to 20 miles. His competition was Paul Derkum, on a Reading-Standard, Ron Mitchell, on an NSU, Al Lingenfelder, on a Thor, and Bob Samuelson, a private entrant on an Indian. De Rosier's superb equipment and superlative riding skill enabled him to beat all comers, and he lowered the mile mark to 47⅓ seconds. He continued to lead the field by setting all records up to 100 miles, turning the latter in 97 minutes riding the same machine the entire distance.

*The 1910 Big Twin with two-speed transmission.*

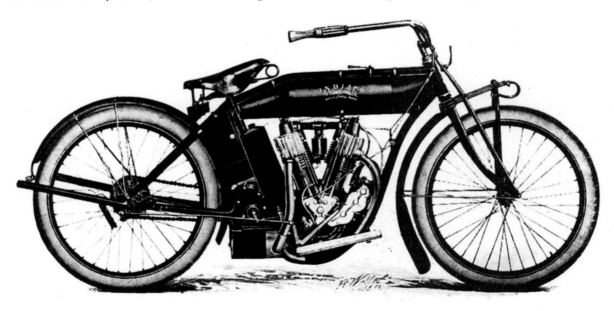

Meanwhile, amateur Indian riders such as 'Fearless' Charles Balke, and Ray Seymour, appeared at the Coliseum, along with Morty Graves and his Flying Merkel. Graves was subsequently given factory support, as were the Indian riders whose machines were tuned in the shop of C. Will Risden. In July, Graves beat De Rosier's best distance records, when he entered the Six Hour event. In this type of race, the competition was divided into two hour heats run over a three day period, the riders being allowed to change machines or engines if necessary, which it very frequently was. Graves won the first two hour heat with a distance of 134 miles. Ray Seymour, on a Reading-Standard, lowered the mile record to 47 seconds flat, and Al Lingenfelder, on an NSU, broke De Rosier's 15 and 25 mile records by four and six minutes respectively.

Back at Springfield, Prince opened a new ⅓ mile bowl named the Springfield Stadium, which was partly financed by Hendee in order to provide competition facilities on Indian's home ground. The track was exceedingly fast, as it was built exactly circular instead of to the usual oval section. De Rosier returned home to win all of the professional events held at the initial opening in August, his main competitor being Fred Huyck, of Chicago. De Rosier rode his specially-built racing machine to a new mile record of 42⅖ seconds. His speed was calculated at 84 miles per hour, a phenomenal accomplishment in 1909! Other riders entering competition for the first time were Indian factory employees Charles Gustafson, Jr., and Charles Spencer, riding as private entrants.

In the Fall, Spencer, who was soon to join Indian's racing team, inaugurated a new type of distance event in the form of a 24 hour run, pit stops being made only to refuel or to change wheels in case of tire trouble. In company with Gustafson, Spencer covered 1,089 miles, the former making a distance of 1,043. During the night portion of the run, no artificial light was available. The two rode almost in company until a series of chain failures on Gustafson's machine gave Spencer the lead.

During 1909, dirt track racing on horse tracks at numerous county fairgrounds became popular. While the FAM had not yet grown sufficiently in scope to sanction these events or have officials on hand to oversee the proceedings and tabulate records, such races served well as a local showcase for motorcycle sport. The dirt tracks could never be as fast as the boards, but they gained in popularity in ensuing years and ultimately grew to the stature of sanctioned events after the board tracks passed from the scene in the late 1920's.

1909 ended as a very successful year for Indian, with increased sales of 4,771 machines, due to increased advertising, phenomenal racing victories, and enhanced production capacity of the enlarged factory. Sales to law enforcement bodies increased, the standard left hand throttle control being an important inducement for such use.

In December, a new department of publicity was instituted, and John J. 'Long John' O'Conner, a one-time professional bicycle racer and later a pioneer motorcyclist, was hired as its head. He possessed a flair for journalism and his flamboyant Victorian prose was to be read widely by motorcycle enthusiasts for the next four decades.

1910 marked the year when the motorcycle at long last came into its own. The pioneer, clip-on days of flimsy machines was now passed, and the more substantially-built machines were by this time offering an acceptable degree of reliability. The automobile, which was assuming more or less its final form, was as yet too costly for the man of modest means. The motorcycle reigned supreme as the best bargain in point to point transportation. World wide interest in powered two wheelers was such that the thrust of the great bicycle boom, which had begun two decades earlier, was somewhat dulled in all but the least developed countries of the world.

In the United States, the vast distances and generally poor roads existing in most of the sections of the country made mandatory a rugged type of machine with substantial power, whose design was already crystallizing as the heavyweight V-twin. While lightweight single cylinder machines were built and sold in fair numbers, the ratio of heavy to light machines sold by this time was running about four to one.

**Right:** *Herbert Le Vack with the 1911 8-valve 61 cu in factory racer with which he posted numerous records at Brooklands after World War I. He made a final run at 107.5mph in November 1921.* (The Archives of the Hendee Manufacturing Company)

**Below left:** *Volney Davis with the single speed 5hp Light Twin on which he made two transcontinental crossings.*

The Indian line for 1910 showed extensive changes and improvements in a wide range of eight models, and all could well be described as prototypes of the modern motorcycle. They were the result of much testing and experimentation on the part of Hedstrom and his engineering staff during the preceding two years. The loop frame of 1909 was strengthened somewhat, and the cartridge type forks of 1905 were replaced by the soon-to-be-famous cradle spring successor, that featured trailing link suspension supported by a quarter elliptic leaf spring with its scrolled end extending forward over the wheel. A no less important improvement was the use of chrome vanadium steel in the fabrication of frame tubes and forgings, the front spring being of specially treated material. Positive engine pump lubrication was not built into all of the various engine models, the system being activated by gears which had been subjected to extensive testing the year before on the factory-owned racing engines.

Another advanced feature was the offering of a two-speed gearbox with a clutch, that was an optional extra on the 4hp 30.50 cubic inch single and the new 7hp 61 cubic inch twin that had been refined the previous year in the board track racing machines. All the single speed chain drive machines were fitted with clutches as standard.

Other models included two versions of the 19 cubic inch 2¾hp single with magneto ignition as standard, with battery and coil optional, at a $25.00 price reduction. The 4hp single was offered with the same options. A new 38 cubic inch 5hp twin was added to the line as a single-speed model.

The biggest surprise was a flat belt drive version of the 4hp single, the first time such a drive had ever been fitted to an Indian. While the reversion to a belt drive was construed by many enthusiasts as a retrograde step in Indian design policy, Hedstrom advanced two reasons for its introduction. Most of the contemporary American manufacturers offered one or more, if not all, of their models with the belt, its obvious advantage being that it was a soft type of transmission that smoothed out both the torque of the engine and road shocks from the rear wheel. Many Indian dealers had lately informed the factory that the inclusion of a belt drive model would put them in a better competitive position. There was also the fact that most of the British and foreign machines still used the belt, and some of the export staff reasoned that such a model could broaden Indian's appeal overseas. In truth, the system fitted to the 4hp model was a decided improvement over most of the contemporary designs, as it featured a large engine pulley with a self-contained planetary gearset that nullified many of the disadvantages of the belt passing around a very small engine pulley. Its high cost of manufacture, however, made its selling price the same as that of the all chain drive models.

Few American customers were attracted to the model as most Indian customers were already sold on the all-chain drive as originally fitted. Billy Wells, who visited the factory in 1910, was not impressed with it. He was reported as informing Hedstrom that English buyers of Indians were attracted to the make because it had chain drive. Production was suspended after about 450 were built, and no known survivors exist today.

A serious technical omission in the 4hp and 7hp single and twin cylinder models offered with the optional two-speed gearbox was the lack of kickstart mechanism. Riders were forced to push start the machines in the absence of any pedaling gear. Most adopted the expedi-

ent of starting up by placing the machine on the stand and pulling the rear wheel back against compression. However, the two-speed models found favor for use in hilly country and in difficult colonial conditions.

Indian's competition program for 1910 was inaugurated by De Rosier's appearance at the newly built one mile board track at Playa del Rey, near Los Angeles, where he won back his 100 mile title lost to Morty Graves the previous year at the Coliseum. He turned the first 50 miles in 39.13 minutes, but was forced to push his machine across the finish line for a loss of five minutes, still beating Graves' time of 1.26.14.

The Wandemere Speedway at Salt Lake City, Utah, was rushed to completion that summer by Jack Prince, and De Rosier arrived there late in June, with two new racing machines and half a dozen improved engines supplied by the factory, to continue his battle for Indian supremacy. His most serious competitor was a local amateur, Frank Whittle, who rode Flying Merkels. Meanwhile, Graves, Ray Seymour, Charles 'Fearless' Balke and Al Ward appeared to round out the amateur class, and drew large

*Pictures of Indian entrants in the 1911 Isle of Man TT.*

crowds with their exciting contests that often resulted in blanket finishes.

Late that Fall the same riders headed west to the Los Angeles Coliseum, where numerous time trials were scheduled. De Rosier turned the mile in 42 seconds flat, at a speed of 85.71 mph. Whittle shipped his Merkels out from Salt Lake City to contest De Rosier's records. He failed in this up to the 17 mile mark, but made startling inroads in distances after that point up to the 35th mile, when his engine disintegrated after much full throttle running. Whittle then lost four of his records to Graves when the latter, also Merkel mounted, made a 20-mile dash that took every mile record en route. Graves held these records for about three weeks until Balke, with factory sponsorship, took his Indian around the oval for some very fast times that resulted in breaking all of Graves' records by December 31st.

Dirt track racing continued as a popular local sport on the fairground circuits, but actual records were not preserved due to the then lack of FAM recognition of such events. The machines used were mostly single cylinder 30.50 models, as the 61's of the board track type were considered at the time as being too fast, and too difficult, to handle on dirt.

With an eye to enhancing Indian's racing prestige, Hedstrom set about designing the first of his four and eight valve 30.50 and 61 inch single and twin cylinder racing engines, which showed a marked increase in power over his more conventional two-valve-per-cylinder types. These engines were tested in various racing

*Oliver R. Godfrey (right) being led in triumph from the finish line by Billy Wells after the 1911 TT.* **(The Archives of the Hendee Manufacturing Company)**

frames by Charles Gustafson, Jr., and Charles Spencer, who in this year joined Indian's professional racing team. They were said to have been designed to counter the threat of Excelsior's formidable big valve machines.

In contemplating an expected increase in sales, the factory space was again enlarged by the addition of a new wing to the State Street plant. This structure was built behind the original Springfield Institute building, and extended along the Wilbraham Road frontage. This was also designed by Hedstrom and carried out the original architectural motif of a fortress-like exterior. Shortly before the new factory addition was finished, a spur track from the main line of what was then the New York, Long Island and New Haven railroad, was extended across State Street into the middle of the property. This termi-

nated in the great courtyard of the plant, and greatly facilitated shipping and receiving.

A notable long distance ride that summer was made by enthusiast Volney Davis, on a 5hp twin. He started from San Francisco and made a roundabout 6,200 mile trip to New York City. He then made the return trip to San Francisco on the same machine, for a total distance of 10,400 miles, much of which was over trackless waste, primitive trails, and sometimes along railroad tracks. Davis reported that no serious mechanical trouble was encountered en route, except for numerous tire failures.

By 1910, over sixty police departments were using Indian machines, the latest large city to purchase them being Sacramento, California. Many commercial users were added to the list, such as public utility companies, Rural Free Delivery carriers, messengers, department stores and others.

By this time, two factory branches had been opened to aid in parts and service delivery, one being in Chicago, the other in San Francisco. 1910 also marked the first year

*A rare photograph of the paddock at Douglas after the 1911 TT races, showing Oliver Godfrey (with raised arms) and Carl Oscar Hedstrom (in hat). The winning machine, no 26, is in foreground, with Moorhouse's third place machine (no 31) at rear.* **(The Archives of the Hendee Manufacturing Company)**

that the famous Indian red color was used in place of the navy blue, which had been used on all production machines since 1901. Another optional color was light green. The word INDIAN in block letters on the fuel tank was replaced by the larger gold Indian script, with the legend Hendee Manufacturing Company in small block letters, also in gold, underneath it.

Indian sales rose impressively during the year, with two hundred more dealers added to the roster. Billy Wells increased his orders for the United Kingdom, and added more sub-dealers in other towns and cities outside of the London area. 1910 production totaled 6,137 units.

The Indian line for 1911 followed closely that of the previous year, but with detailed improvements. The 19

**Below:** *J. Worth Alexander's 1912 single speed twin with a then-popular tandem seat.* **(Ronald Mugar)**

**Bottom:** *The 1912 belt drive Indian single with the then conventional pulley drive idler.*

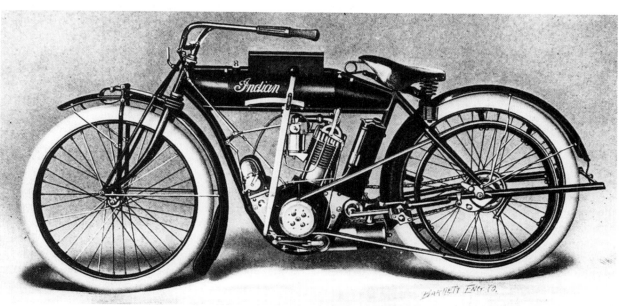

cubic inch singles were dropped due to a dwindling demand for low-powered machines. A somewhat heavier clutch was designed for all chain drive models, and a forward mounted kickstarting mechanism was fitted. This comprised an extra sprocket mounted on the engine shaft, connected by chain to a larger one fixed to the forward engine plates, and activated by a pedal crank.

The 4hp belt drive model was retained, but a simpler and more conventional drive was fitted, with the then commonly used small engine pulley driving a large one on the rear wheel, and a lever operated belt tensioner. There was still feeling that a demand existed for this type of machine, but the somewhat complicated and expensive planetary drive was dropped, as manufacturing costs could not be recovered on small production volume.

In February 1911, De Rosier resumed his competition activities, the record assaults continuing with his breaking all marks up to 90 mph. In time trials, he turned a 41⅕ second mile for a speed of 88mph at the Los Angeles Coliseum. De Rosier planned a 100 mile ride, but ran out of fuel during the 92nd mile and did not try for another attempt.

By Spring, the entire competition picture had changed. The leading amateur riders had by this time all been hired by various motorcycle manufacturers and were supposedly competing for trophies. However, they were now riding as professionals and were paid by retainers, with bonuses for record time or racing victories. After breaking numerous records, De Rosier decided to make a trip to Europe in the Summer. He subsequently entered various competitions at Brooklands, sponsored by Billy Wells.

Racing at home continued at the new Elmhurst speedway in Oakland, California. Two new tracks were opened in Denver, the Tuileries Park and the Lakeside. The initial races were inaugurated with many former dirt track stars making their first bid for fame and fortune on the faster board courses. These included Joe Wolters, riding an Excelsior, and Indian riders Erle Armstrong, Glen 'Slivers' Boyd, and Eddie Hasha. A new racing circuit was instituted with newly opened tracks at Buffalo, Cleveland, Chicago and Detroit. At the latter, named Riverview, Wolters appeared with a newly designed big valve Excelsior that defeated the entire field and set a new mark of 89mph. His Excelsior proved unbeatable until Ray Seymour and Eddie Hasha entered ensuing meets on the new eight valve twins and regained all records within a two week period. Hasha's mile time was lowered to 39⅗ seconds.

With the increasing sales of Indians and the general healthy condition of the motorcycle market, Hedstrom drew up plans for a contemplated five-story addition to the factory that would encompass the balance of the State Street property. Indian dealerships in the United States alone now numbered over twelve hundred. To aid these dealers in their publicity, and to implement expanding advertising coverage, R. L. Harriman, a former advertising executive with farm journals, was hired as Advertising Manager.

In 1911, Hedstrom inaugurated the first of subsequent excursions on the part of the Indian company into products not related to motorcycle manufacture. During this period, aviation was fast becoming of great public interest. The activities of Glenn Curtis and other pioneer aviators were being well publicized, and aviation in general was now in its romantic period. Once the basic problems of airframe design had been mastered, the most pressing problem was then the development of reliable engines. With his inherent mechanical curiosity, Hedstrom had been following aviation progress with interest. Together with Charles Gustafson, he had been studying the design of contemporary aircraft engines. Their interest soon reached the point where, during that summer, two prototype engines had been built and tested. Surprisingly enough, their design was not original, but a frank copy of the then well-known French Gnome-et-Rhone, which had been designed and built in France since 1907. The engines operated on the then popular rotary principle, where the cylinders and crankcase, along with the propellor, revolved about a fixed crankshaft attached to a bracket bolted to the forward bulkhead in the airplane's fuselage. After a prototype had passed successful bench tests, Hendee suggested that limited production of the engines be undertaken. The company issued a catalog describing a 50hp seven cylinder engine, with a $2,000 price tag. One of these engines was fitted to a Farman type biplane piloted by Earl Ovington in a flight between Long Island and New York City, as an attempt to inaugurate an airmail service. One such engine is presently on display in the Smithsonian Institution. Some aviation authorities have claimed that this engine was the one used by Ovington. Howard I. Chapelle, Curator Emeritus of the Museum, reported that it is one of three manufactured, and that it is a new and unused example. No company records exist today regarding aircraft engine production nor any reference to licensing arrangements with the French manufacturers.

To consolidate Indian's leading position in the competition sphere, Hendee and Hedstrom decided to attempt an all-out effort to win the Isle of Man TT races, which were coming into their fifth season. In January, these plans were made known to Billy Wells, who responded with immediate enthusiasm and promised to engage the best available riders he could find in England to represent Indian. After some correspondence in the matter,

An Indian sidecar outfit runs in second place in a match race at Brooklands, about 1912. Note the rough surface of the concrete. (The Archives of the Hendee Manufacturing Company)

Hedstrom stipulated that De Rosier would be one member of the team, with the balance of the riders selected by Wells. Additional interest was forthcoming in the TT by virtue of the fact that the organizers now planned to utilize the mountain circuit, which was 37½ miles in distance and would entail five laps, for a total of 187 miles. Best of all, a twin cylinder class would comprise the Senior race, but with piston displacement limited to 585cc. The mountainous character of the course, now necessitating the ascent of Snaefell, would make almost mandatory the fitting of change speed gearboxes. The English trade press was jubilant that at long last the contest would be a good test for touring machines of substantial design.

Hedstrom immediately set to work on the project, with the help of members of the racing staff, and six standard machines were modified for the event. The cylinders were sleeved to bring the displacement down to the required dimensions, other modifications including dropped handlebars and forward placed controls, so the riders could assume a crouched position.

Hedstrom, De Rosier, and three mechanics set sail for England in June, well over a month before the races, to allow ample time for tuning the six machines and to enable the contestants to familarize themselves with the course. Wells selected Oliver Godfrey and A. J. Moorhouse, two promising young Indian enthusiasts and expert riders, along with a young Irishman from Dublin, Charles Bayley Franklin. Godfrey was later to become associated with a large motorcycle dealership in London. Moorhouse was to die tragically at Brooklands a year later when his Indian went over the banking.

Franklin was born in Dublin in 1880 to parents of comfortable, middle class circumstances. After attending public school, where he showed interest in science and mathematics, he enrolled in the Dublin College of Science, where he majored in electrical engineering. Upon graduation in 1908, he secured a position in the engineering department of Dublin's municipal government. He became interested in motorcycling during the pioneer period and owned several early makes of machines. A keen student of motorcycle design, he became attracted to Indian in 1910, when Wells awarded a franchise to a Dublin dealer. He became a regular competitor in local club events, where his early competition successes and riding ability soon caught Wells' attention.

The main interest in the TT races was, as usual, the Senior event for larger capacity machines, and in this year there was an unusually large field of 67 riders, competing on twenty different makes of machine. One third of the entrants rode single geared machines, and well over three-quarters had belt drive.

The Indian team consisted of five machines, with De Rosier billed as the leading rider. Always with an eye for publicity, he wore as his racing attire running shoes and black theatrical tights. He also covered his chin with heavy bandages to protect it from hitting the tank rail, when riding in a prone position.

An eyewitness to the races, the late G. S. Davison, has left us an account of the contest in his book, The Story of the TT. 'The weather was fortunately bright and sunny, as the mountain course was mostly a farm track and could have been extraordinarily hazardous in wet condition. De Rosier took the lead on the first lap, closely followed by

Charlie Collier on a Matchless twin and Godfrey, on another Indian. Indians ridden by Franklin and Moorhouse were lying fourth and sixth, so only two British machines were among the first half dozen competitors.

Collier took the lead in the second lap, with the rest of the Indian team close behind. In the fourth lap he sustained a puncture, and, although according to his lap time he lost only four minutes, he dropped back to third place. He also ran out of fuel several times, but managed to pull into second place behind Godfrey and just ahead of Franklin and Moorhouse, at the finish. As Collier had taken on extra fuel, which was against the rules, the Indian team lodged a protest. The stewards disqualified his entry, and Indians were designated as the winners of the first three places in the now immortal Godfrey, Franklin and Moorhouse combination. De Rosier had

*Oliver R. Godfrey with an Indian factory racer at Brooklands.* **(The Archives of the Hendee Manufacturing Company)**

been highly touted as a probable first place winner, but he was obviously not at home on rough road courses and he finished with the last of the pack. The winning times were 3.56.10, 3.59.52 and 4.5.34, respectively. Godfrey's average speed was 47.6mph, not a bad showing considering the hazards of the course.

The British contestants were not a little chagrined at having been beaten by foreigners, but the reliability of the Hedstrom engines, coupled with their rugged two speed gearboxes, with gearing carefully selected for the course, made their victory an almost foregone conclusion. The English motorcycle press made much of the results in relation to the general unsuitability of single geared machines.

The Indian company quite naturally made capital of the victory, glossing over Collier's formidable challenge on his rugged Matchless. All in all, Indian's performance was very creditable indeed. De Rosier did not return to Springfield with the Indian team following the TT races, and remained in England under the sponsorship of Billy

**Right:** *The probable sole surviving 1912 factory 30.50cu in racer of a group of about 50 offered for public sale in that year, now owned by Russell Harmon. This machine has been clocked at speeds of nearly 100mph.* (Ronald Mugar)

**Below:** *Dewey Bonkrud's 1913 Big Twin with three-speed transmission.* (Ronald Mugar)

Wells, to undertake a number of match races at Brooklands that summer.

De Rosier's chief rival was Charlie Collier, still smarting from his second place disqualification in the island race. As De Rosier was the acknowledged champion of the United States, and Collier had already made several unbeaten records at Brooklands, there was much public interest in the forthcoming match races between the two, scheduled for July. De Rosier prepared one of the factory 61 cubic inch twins, installed in the usual short wheel based board track frame. No change speed gears were fitted, the drive being direct through a countershaft, without a clutch. Collier's machine was, of course, one of his own Matchless models, with a 61 cubic inch overhead valve JAP V twin fitted with direct belt drive.

The two champions were to race over distances of two, five and ten laps and were escorted by a starter's car for flying starts. The initial two lap race was a close contest. De Rosier allowed Collier to take a slight lead, taking advantage of his slipstream nearly the whole distance. Just before the finish, he pulled ahead with a burst of acceleration, and won by only a length at 80.59mph. In the five lap event, De Rosier employed the same tactics, but blew a tire in the fourth lap at nearly 90mph. With superb riding skill he was able to halt his machine without a fall, but, of course, was forced to retire.

The third two mile event was equally exciting. The two contestants ran closely for nearly the entire distance when, on the last lap, a spark plug wire came loose on Collier's engine. He managed to replace it while running

at reduced speed, but in the meantime De Rosier had built up a substantial lead. By a heroic effort, Collier nearly caught up with him, but De Rosier won at 84.5mph. The contest was an interesting comparison of two varied styles of racing. Collier's habit was to attempt an early lead and hold it all the way. De Rosier's strategy was to nurse his engine carefully until the last lap, and employ the slip stream technique, wherever possible.

In a reorganization of Indian's now expanding executive staff, Frank Weschler was named company Treasurer. J. D. Stephens, recently hired as Office Manager, was promoted to Assistant Treasurer.

In the spring of 1911, construction was started on the planned addition to the factory, but this was not entirely completed until the following year. Large towers at the corners and along the intermediate parts of the structure contained stairwells and elevators, with the bays in between housing the various manufacturing and assembly departments. These structures now formed a quadrangle, which enclosed a large courtyard. Much new tooling was ordered from Brown and Sharpe of Providence, Rhode Island, and several new large hydraulic presses were installed, to operate the various dies, many of which were made by Hedstrom himself for specialized components. The Indian company, in fact, possessed some of the most sophisticated tooling of the time, for general manufacture. A new steam plant was ordered from Babcock and Wilcox, with two large, coal-fired steam engines turning huge pulley wheels on three-inch shafts and carrying massive leather primary driving belts, which drove the overhead shafting throughout the

Right: *The famous Indian cradle spring frame introduced in 1913.*

# THE INDIAN CRADLE SPRING FRAME

OVER 250 inches of supple, highly tempered, chrome vanadium springs, between the saddle and road, make this the most luxurious riding motorcycle ever sent upon the highway. There are eight leaves to each spring group, the maximum length being 23 inches. The universal use of flat leaf springs for body suspension on high class motor cars, and the rigid testing of this system for eighteen months previous to its adoption by the Indian engineers, constitute its credentials. Since its announcement the words "motorcycle comfort" have held a new significance among riders.

Following the successful use of automobile type leaf-springs in the Indian fork for several years, their application to the rear wheel comes as a logical development. The new Indian Cradle Spring Frame is the greatest comfort device ever applied to a motorcycle, giving the rider the sensation of a steady, forward gliding motion.

The application of this original, distinctive, and exclusive suspension to a motorcycle frame is another triumph for Indian ingenuity. Two sets of leaves are mounted on either side of the rear wheel to a horseshoe shaped anchorage forward and to a hinged arch stay aft. Each spring has a maximum working zone of 3 inches in a vertical plane. It is practically impossible for these springs to hit "bottom" save under the most extraordinary conditions.

The lower rear end of the frame is hinged, allowing the rear wheel and suspension to work in an arc according to road irregularities. Each spring has double scrolls which come into action successively on light and heavy jolts, while rubber bumpers take the recoil.

This radical new departure in motorcycle springing systems, from the antiquated spiral principles handed down from bicycle days, marks a tremendous forward step in the quest of parlor car comfort on the highway. With the advent of the Indian Cradle Spring Frame, rigid types become obsolete.

With the new frame a much lower riding position is obtained, the saddle of the regular being 33 inches from the ground, and on the T.T., 31½ inches. From saddle to footboard is 30½ inches on the regular, and 30 inches on the T.T. In addition to reducing fatigue to a minimum, the spring frame has the further very advantageous quality of lengthening the life of the machine by nullifying vibration and its ravages of crystallization.

The famous Indian cradle spring frame introduced in 1913

MAIN OFFICE AND WORKS

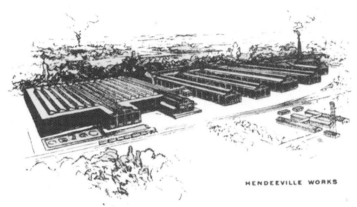

HENDEEVILLE WORKS

# HENDEE MANUFACTURING COMPANY

## SPRINGFIELD, MASSACHUSETTS, U. S. A.

(Largest Side Car Manufacturers in the World)

BRANCHES AND SERVICE STATIONS:

| | | |
|---|---|---|
| 457 Peachtree St. ATLANTA, GA. | 1930 Grand Ave. KANSAS CITY, MO. | 366-368 Euston Road LONDON, N. W., ENG. |
| Michigan Ave. at 13th St. CHICAGO, ILL. | 501 Sixth St., South MINNEAPOLIS, MINN. | 109 Russell St. MELBOURNE, AUSTRALIA |
| 2208 Commerce St. DALLAS, TEXAS | 234 Van Ness Ave. SAN FRANCISCO, CAL. | 12-14 Mercer St. TORONTO, CAN. |

*The Indian factory complexes in 1913, showing both the State Street and Hendeeville plants.*

plant, to run the various machine tools. Generators supplied a self-contained electric plant for lighting the entire factory complex. The executive offices were also remodeled, with rich oak paneling on the walls.

Plans were also underway to add additional factory space by the acquisition of additional facilities in East Springfield. A large, single-storey building was laid out, sufficient land being purchased for anticipated future expansion. This facility later supplied all the forgings used in fork and frame manufacture.

The considerable sum of money for these activities was raised through the sale of additional shares, which were mostly taken up by prominent Springfield investors and bankers. While Indian's production was continually increasing through the ever growing demand, the net profits per unit to the manufacturers were not great, as the Indian machines were always costly to produce. As Chief Engineer, Hedstrom always insisted on the use of high quality materials, along with the fitting of the best available proprietary fittings bought from trade supplies, such as magnetos, lighting sets, tires, saddles and other parts. While the Indians were not the cheapest machines on the market, both Hedstrom and Hendee felt the necessity to keep Indian's selling cost well within competitive bounds, as compared to the three dozen odd other manufacturers then engaged in motorcycle manufacture. At the same moment, the continuing sales of substantial blocks of shares to outside investors had, by 1911, removed the financial control of the company from the hands of the founders.

The 1912 range of machines was continued much the same as for the previous season, except for minor detail improvements. There were two big twin 7hp and two single cylinder 4hp models, mainly differentiated by the option of single speed, all chain drive with auxiliary pedaling gear for starting, or the two-speed gearbox with chain starting device. To capitalize on the recent TT victory, the machines were cataloged as TT models.

The resultant sales of these machines added numerous new dealers to the roster. Among them was one Jud Carriker of Santa Ana, California, a young pioneer motorcyclist who previously had a dealership for Pope cycles. Carriker had quite a local reputation as an engine tuner, and the following year was made Pacific Coast Racing Manager, all competition engines used in the west being sent to him by the factory for final adjustment and tuning.

In 1912, a repair department was added to the factory, which enabled callers to have their machines overhauled or repaired by factory personnel. Myron Warner was for a time the foreman in charge. Now nearly 90 years of age, he has lately been reported as living in retirement in Poway, California.

This year also saw the retention by President Hendee of one Erwin G. Baker, to take a two-speed 7hp model on a demonstration tour of Cuba and Central America. This remarkable man, whose name was later to be featured prominently in the motorcycling and automotive world during the ensuing three decades, was born in Indianapolis, Indiana in 1882. His father was a skilled machinist employed in a local railroad shop, and for a time it was planned that young Erwin was to follow his father's trade. As a young boy he became interested in athletics, participated in the usual boyhood sports, most particularly wrestling, boxing and tumbling. He developed remarkable powers of physical endurance, keeping regular hours, eating nutritious foods and abstaining from alcohol and tobacco. When he was nineteen years old he toured the midwestern states with a vaudeville troupe that featured tumbling and weight lifting acts. As

*The 1913 single geared Big Twin. This model was a popular seller due to its high power output and reasonable price, and was favored by utility riders not requiring high speeds.*

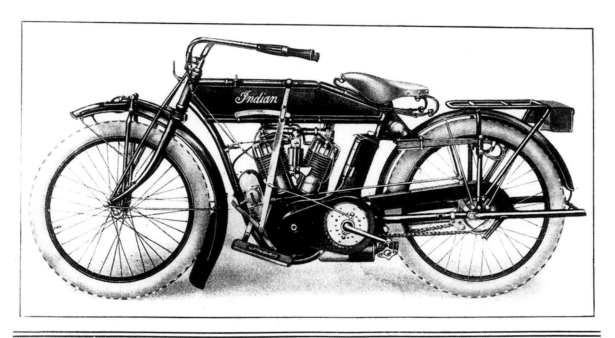

# SPECIFICATIONS

## 7 H. P. Twin-Cylinder 61.  Regular Model  -  $250.00 f. o. b. Factory

a further measure of his physical prowess he trained himself to go with as little sleep as possible, sometimes sleeping in a kneeling position against his bed.

He next took up professional bicycle racing, and entered a motorcycle race in 1908 on an Indian, as a last-minute entrant to fill out a card, using a stock machine which he purchased second hand the year before from a local dealer. He became an Indian enthusiast overnight and won numerous local endurance races. He was generally known as 'Bake' to his many motorcycling friends, the appellation 'Cannonball' not being applied until years later by a newspaper writer, following some of his exploits.

Baker was always a freelance operator and undertook his various endurance runs under contract. He would require a fixed sum for an appearance, with stipulated bonuses for attaining certain fixed times for the bettering of existing records. His earlier feats were usually undertaken on Indians, but he also rode Aces and Hendersons. In later years, he transferred his activities to cars. His last long distance transcontinental ride was made on an Indian four in 1941 when he was sixty years of age. He passed away at his Indianapolis home in 1960. His last act was to commission his old friend of pioneer motorcycling days, August E. 'Blick' Wolters, to restore his favorite mount, a 1912 Indian. His historic machine is presently on view at Bill Tuthill's Museum of Speed at Daytona Beach, Florida.

Board track racing continued to draw large crowds in the larger cities all over the country. New tracks were built in Milwaukee, Omaha, Houston, Cleveland and Atlantic City. The fastest was probably the Elmhurst, at Oakland, California, a full half mile oval with 40° to 43° banking, where many speed records were made. Racing features included match races between cars and motorcycles and even airplanes! Many race promoters were grossing huge sums of money, $10,000 daily gates being not uncommon.

The Chicago built Excelsiors, with their 2¼ inch big valve engines, continued to challenge Hedstrom's newly developed eight valve specials. Super-X star Joe Wolters gunned the latest version of one of these machines around the Riverview Exposition oval in Chicago, for a new drome record of 89mph. As the Indian racing star, De Rosier was then appearing in Europe, so the first of the improved eight valve factory engines were supplied to Eddie Hasha and Ray Seymour. Hasha immediately set about attacking Wolters' record, and on May 1st reached a record mile in 39⅗ seconds at 95mph at the newly-opened track at Playa del Rey, then a seacoast resort suburb south of Los Angeles.

On July 4th, before a capacity crowd at Omaha, Glen 'Slivers' Boyd won his famous nickname when, on the 43rd mile of a 50 mile match race, he blew a rear tire. The wheel locked and spun him to the bottom of the apron where, trapped under the machine, he slid for nearly 100 feet. He was hospitalized for two weeks while physicians removed over 200 splinters from various parts of his anatomy. The largest was in his thigh and was over 14 inches long. Boyd carried this with him for some time afterwards, to prove to skeptics that the story was true.

Board track racing continued throughout the season, but no new records were established until December 30th when Lee Humiston, a rising Excelsior star, rode a specially tuned big valve machine around the Playa del Rey track for a 36 second mile, the first 100mph run over the boards ever made.

One of the most sensational races of the season was run at Elmhurst, on November 12th, with the famous grudge race between Charles 'Fearless' Balke, now riding for Excelsior, and Indian's new professional, Ray Seymour. The fifty-mile race was run at a dead heat for most of the distance, with Seymour pulling ahead slightly at the finish for a wheel's length win. A sell out crowd of hysterical fans were on their feet for most of the event.

A team of Indian riders was entered in the 1912 TT races by Billy Wells, but without factory sponsorship, as Hedstrom and his design staff were otherwise occupied. The event proved a disaster. Oliver Godfrey, the previous year's first place winner, was a non-starter due to engine trouble. James Alexander was the best performer in eighth place. Franklin, plagued by tire trouble, finished twelfth. Franklin somewhat redeemed his loss later that summer when, with factory sponsorship, he established a new record at Brooklands of 300 miles in 280 minutes. His short wheelbase track type machine was fitted with one of Hedstrom's new eight valve 61 cubic inch board track engines, one of eight sent over a couple of months previously to Billy Wells. This was a remarkable feat of endurance considering his time in the saddle and the uneven condition of some parts of the track. Four of these engines were later given to the noted Edinburgh Indian dealers, Jimmy and Alfie Alexander, who raced them at various meets up to the time of the European war.

An interesting sidelight on the continuing controversy concerning the expenditures for racing was the offering for sale in 1912 of a number of factory racing machines to the public, although these were not listed in the regular catalogs. It is said that Hendee gave forth the opinion that if a few such machines were sold it could emphasize the fact that they were indeed of some commercial sales value. It is reported that most of these, about twenty-five in all, were of the single cylinder 30.50 cubic inch four valve type. One is known to survive, owned by Russell Harmon. He secured it some years ago from the original owner, who purchased it through a Kansas dealer for $275.00.

In the spring of 1912, Indian's management decided to develop a spring frame to be fitted to both single and twin cylinder models. While motorcycle sales were soaring, there was the competitive threat from both the cheap car and from the newly-developed cycle car. The latter were characteristically flimsy creations, sold at prices competitive to the twin cylinder sidecar outfit and were advertised as superior to the motorcycle in regard to the stability of four wheels, passenger comfort and better weather protection. Most makers fitted various makes of motorcycle engines bought from the latter trade. The Indian company had been approached by several makers in regard to supplying engines and transmissions, but wisely decided to concentrate on their own activities, as orders for motorcycles were still running ahead of production.

The spring frame, as devised by Hedstrom, was surprisingly modern in concept. The lower chain stays were made movable by their fitting as a swinging arm, hinged below the gearbox hanger. The suspension was provided by a pair of quarter elliptic scroll-ended leaf type springs, their forward ends bolted at a U-shaped bracket on the upper frame, just behind and below the saddle. The position and action of the swinging arm was such that the length of the chain was practically constant. This mechanism provided enhanced rising comfort, as a

*Some of the Indian executive and managerial personnel in 1913* **Honest Injun.**

deflection of about five inches was possible if the spring leaves were kept well greased. There was some lateral deflection of the rear wheel under extreme conditions, however, due to the small diameter of the chain stays and the unit added substantial weight to the rear of the machine, and was rather expensive to manufacture.

Another projected improvement was enhancing the effectiveness of the rear brake by increasing the diameter and width of the drum, to allow the fitting of a larger brake band.

1912 also saw the beginning of a series of disagreements between Hendee and Hedstrom as managers, and the Board of Directors, concerning financial matters of the company. While sales had dramatically increased each year, the Directors were concerned with the profit picture, which they considered was not in keeping with Indian's growth. Hedstrom's insistence on expenditures for the best available materials and accessories was questioned, as well as the vast expenditures on the development of racing machines and the upkeep of an expensive racing team, individual members of which were now earning up to $20,000 a year in salaries and bonuses. There was also the matter of the continuing factory

# SOUTH AFRICAN DAREDEVILS
# RIDE IN A WOODEN BOWL

TAKING their lives in their hands at every performance, Altona Edwards,

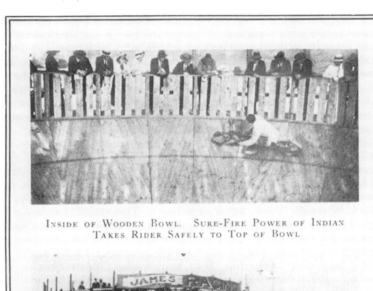

INSIDE OF WOODEN BOWL. SURE-FIRE POWER OF INDIAN
TAKES RIDER SAFELY TO TOP OF BOWL

SHOWING OUTSIDE CONSTRUCTION OF THE BOWL.
INDIAN MACHINES USED EXCLUSIVELY

It has a very bumpy surface, the track being built in thirty-two sections, in order to carry it from place to place.

Mr. Edwards is using a three and a half horsepower INDIAN for his work and induced the young fellows on his team also to use INDIANS, which they find best suited for performance purposes, both on account of speed and strength. Mr. Edwards told Williams Hunt & Company, South African agents for the INDIAN, that he would ride no other machine but an INDIAN, as his life depended on it. He puts on twelve and fourteen performances a day during the season.

It is a well known fact that the INDIAN is the preferred machine for trick riders and other public performers. In Los Angeles, where 100,000 moving picture actors are engaged in producing picture plays, the INDIAN is used almost exclusively in war plays and other productions in which it is desired to use numbers of motorcyclists. The success of the machine in this sort of work comes from its careful construction and the excellent materials used.

George Botha and Will Wilson, stage a motorcycle pursuit race and other motorcycle and bicycle riding exhibitions in a huge wooden bowl at every fair sized town and dorp in South Africa to which the James Carnival Company tours. The track is 45 feet in circumference, 15 feet high and banked to an angle of 75 degrees.

expansion, the 1911 projection now running close to a million dollars as it continued into 1912.

The founders argued that the quality integrity of the products must be maintained to continue public confidence and that the extensive racing program was necessary to maintain Indian's name in the motorcycle sporting world. They pointed to the increase in profits from $289,000 in 1910 to $476,000 in 1911, an ample proof of their business practices. The year ended with a record of 19,585 machines produced, and record profits of $502,000.

By this time the company had established numerous factory branches, to facilitate the supply of machines and spare parts to dealers in various parts of the country. In addition to the first factory branches established in Chicago and San Francisco, there were now outlets in Atlanta, Georgia, Kansas City, Missouri, Dallas, Texas as well as in Toronto, Canada.

1913 opened with high hopes for greatly expanded production, as orders were still running well ahead of deliveries. By January, the new facilities were in full use. Hedstrom oversaw all production operations in the two factories, as well as being in full charge of design and engineering. He had been ably assisted in these activities by Charles Gustafson, Sr., along with another production supervisor who had risen from the ranks, Theron L. Loose.

Aside from the spring frame and improved braking system, Hedstrom had also improved the design of the standard Hedstrom carburetors. Engine power in all models had been materially improved since the two previous seasons, due to redesigned valve and cam action. To improve the idling capabilities and to give the engines more flexibility, a new jet chamber was added to the carburetor body, which was fitted to all models after midyear.

Apart from the general technical excellence and advanced design features of Indian products, the quality of manufacture as supervised by Hedstrom was closely scrutinized. All assembly operations were also under strict control. All engines were tested on a dynamometer and every hundredth machine was removed from the assembly line, for road testing.

Another design innovation planned for the next season was an electric starting system and developmental work was undertaken at the suggestion of President Hendee. He reasoned that such a device fitted to the 7hp big twins would enhance their appeal, particularly to sidecar enthusiasts, and would place such outfits in a more competitive position in regard to the light car or cycle car. Self-starting mechanisms were now much in the news due to Charles Kettering's recent perfection of automotive self-starters. What with the ever-increasing power being built into motorcycle engines, it was becoming generally recognized that considerable muscular effort was necessary to spin the motor with the usual kickstarter. With the cooperation of the engineers of the Standard Electric Company in nearby Pittsfield, work was undertaken on the project in January, 1913.

The system, activated by a pair of six volt storage batteries fitted on either side of the seat post under the saddle, consisted of a 1½hp starting motor attached by brackets to the forward engine plates, in place of the standard kickstarter sprocket. The starter was a motor-generator of the multi-polar type, with four poles that were compound wound. The drive to the engine sprocket was by chain, with a small cone-type clutch to absorb shocks. The starter was unique for its day in being of the inverted commutator type, which allowed very compact construction, together with a large brush contact surface. The motor worked under a compound field, utilizing both series and shunt winding. A controlling switch was fitted, which enabled it to work as either a starter or generator. A magnetic regulator was fitted, which operated as a voltage control device to prevent overcharging of the batteries.

The system worked well on the three or four prototype models tested during the ensuing months, but Hedstrom and others of the company's engineering staff were dubious concerning its ultimate success because the batteries at that time were never wholly reliable in their ability to hold sufficient charge. Added to this difficulty was their sensitivity to vibration of the machine, especially over the generally rough roads of the period. President Hendee, however, was adamant in his enthusiasm, and plans were made for production of a limited number of electric starting 7hp twins for the 1914 season, the model being named the Hendee Special.

The most far-reaching event of 1913 was the resignation of Hedstrom from the company, on March 24th. There has been much subsequent speculation and many reasons advanced by would-be company historians through the years as to the reason for his momentous decision, which came as a complete surprise to most of the factory personnel, dealers, and Indian owners. Some have stated that he was 'just tired'. Others have cited his frustrations in carrying out his design and production activities as well as his dedication to Indian's extensive competition program, in the face of constant criticism and interference from the Board of Directors. It has also been suggested that a serious disagreement occurred between himself and Hendee over the expenditure of over $100,000 for the development of the Hendee Special, which did not have his approval. But there is no evidence that this incident caused any lasting enmity. A more valid and perhaps more serious reason has recently come to light that logically explains why he would suddenly leave the company when its fame and fortunes were at the highest pinnacle of success and prosperity.

The Board of Directors, who had lately come to control the fortunes of the company through their majority ownership of its stock, were not motorcycle enthusiasts, but hard-headed businessmen and investors who were primarily concerned with profits. While naturally enthusiastic concerning Indian's ever-increasing sales and consequent expansion of production facilities, they were constantly preoccupied with production efficiency and the elimination of any procedures that would jeopardize the dividends on their holdings. Sometime during the spring of 1912, a new course of financial planning was decided upon which, while illegal today under strict laws governing corporate financial practises, was widely practised by many business concerns in the earlier days of the century. This procedure was known as 'watering' the stock, and was undertaken to increase its monetary value artificially in the eyes of the investing public without regard to its value in relation to actual company assets. The watering operation was undertaken through the issuance of glowing

*Indian entrants in the first of the series of desert races held in the Southwest. Photographed at Tucson are (from left) Smith, Weitzell and Derkum.* **(The Archives of the Hendee Manufacturing Company)**

reports of company activities and business volume in various newspapers and financial publications, to stimulate public interest in the stock as a growth investment. The value of the shares was then reported as rising, and prospective purchasers were charged increasingly higher prices for the common shares, the preferred variety, with fixed dividends being, of course, held by the members of the Board through their position as majority shareholders. This operation in later years, and through the swashbuckling days of Wall Street, became known as 'bull pool' speculation, and had much to do with the ultimate inflated value of some stock shares on the general market leading to the 1929 debacle.

At any rate, much publicity was subsequently released concerning Indian's growing prosperity, with news items about the increasing value of its general assets. The actual value of Indian's holdings after 1912 is difficult to determine today, although there is evidence that they probably amounted to about seven million dollars. Bull pool announcements, however, ultimately pegged the figure to thirty-five million dollars.

1913 production was planned for 35,000 units, about 43% of the contemporary domestic market. As Indian's sales had been rising dramatically since 1910, both at home and overseas, it could be made plausible to the public that the value of its assets was considerable. It was hoped that a large issue of common shares would bring in enough additional capital to provide a surplus for reinvestment.

Hedstrom, Hendee and Treasurer Weschler were adamant in their opposition to this proposal, as they considered such practise dishonest, but as the former were now minority shareholders and Weschler had only the position of an executive employee, their objections were overruled by the majority.

It is possible that Hedstrom may have anticipated this situation as far back as 1910. In that year he purchased a tract of land near Portland, Connecticut, on the banks of the Connecticut River, where he built a fine house. He had married Julia Anderson in the spring of 1898, and their first child, a daughter named Helen, was born May 10, 1901, just as he was concluding his experiments with his first motorcycle. A second child, a boy, passed away when he was five years old. His wife and daughter moved to Portland, and Hedstrom stayed in Springfield during the week and travelled to Portland for the weekends in his Mercer touring car.

When the news of Hedstrom's resignation became public, he received many lucrative offers of employment from other manufacturing firms, both within and without the motorcycle industry. He refused them all, however, and elected to live the life of a country squire on his suburban estate, spending his time hunting, fishing, and tinkering in an elaborate workshop that he had built behind his house. He also experimented with high-speed racing launches on the Connecticut River and joined a local yachting club.

In the Fall of 1913, the first of a series of desert races through the southwest was scheduled. Billed as an endurance event, these were to take place over what was aptly described as the worst roads on the North American continent. The course selected was between San Diego, California and Phoenix, Arizona, and was approximately 445 miles in length. It was mostly over isolated desert tracks, first traveled by the covered wagons of the pioneer immigrants, the only really passable roads being on the last leg from Caliente to Phoenix, a distance of 94 miles. Aside from the formidable conditions of the desert tracks, contestants risked hunger, thirst, and heat prostration in case of a breakdown. There was also the threat of possible annihilation at the hands of roving bands of renegade Apache Indians who still inhabited parts of this region, as well as from Mexican guerrillas who often raided the ranches north of the border to steal cattle.

The first race was to take place on October 31st, November 1st and 2nd, with overnight stops at Yuma, 116 miles from San Diego, and Caliente, 116 miles to the east, the 90-odd miles to Phoenix being the last leg. Eighteen riders representing Excelsior, Harley Davidson, Indian and Thor were flagged off at 2 minute intervals from the public square in San Diego at 5:30am. The Indian team was headed by Cannonball Baker, other members being Paul Derkum, Harry Weitzell, Ray Smith, Paul Keating, Lorenzo Boido, who was only sixteen years old, Robert

Young and Ellison Wilson. All rode stock 7hp two-speeders, except Weitzell, who was single-geared.

All went well during the first fifty miles as the roads were in fair condition. Ahead lay the dreaded Mammoth Wash, the sandy graveyard of many wagons of the early pioneer immigrants, which was covered with shifting dunes. Baker was eliminated here by engine trouble. Derkum managed to work up to 6th place, from the tail end of the pack.

The contestants were given permission to cross on the railroad bridge over the Colorado River, avoiding the long wait for the cable ferry. Derkum was the first to reach Yuma, making the 116 miles in 7 hours, eleven minutes, his time attesting to the severe conditions of the course. He reached Phoenix first, followed by Ray Smith and Harry Weitzell on their Indians. John Leng, Excelsior and Roy Artley, on a Thor, placed next, with Lorenzo Boido, Indian, 6th, trailing by Art Holmes and Frank Meock on Harleys. Derkum's win was credited to the fact that he cemented small section car tires to his rims in place of the standard motorcycle type, which were more prone to fail under desert conditions.

Indian's competition program continued through the 1913 season, with many important victories on both the boards and horse tracks.

Gustafson and Theron L. Loose, who had been promoted as Plant Superintendent, were able to maintain efficient production assembly and quality control established by Hedstrom.

*Two Indian touring enthusiasts somewhere in the Rocky Mountains in 1913.*

# Some of the Leading Indian Racing Men of the Country

"BILLY" TEUBNER

P.J.C. DERKUM

RUSSELL COES

CHARLES "FEARLESS" BALKE

"SPECK" WARNER

"MARTIE" GRAVES

J.U. CONSTANT

RAY SEYMOUR

ERWIN G. BAKER

W.D. MOTT

H.C. GOULD

GEO. EVANS

J.H. KELLY

MOREWITZ

C.G. BUCKNER

JOE BARRIBEAU

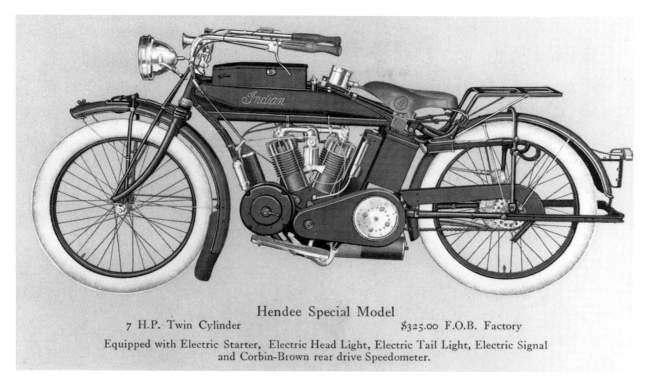

Hendee Special Model

7 H.P. Twin Cylinder                                      $325.00 F.O.B. Factory

Equipped with Electric Starter, Electric Head Light, Electric Tail Light, Electric Signal
and Corbin-Brown rear drive Speedometer.

Total production for 1913, projected for 35,000 units, actually reached 31,950, an all-time record for the company, and approximately 42% of the total domestic production. About 25% of this number was exported to foreign countries.

The conversion of Indian's outstanding shares was undertaken by a large banking and investment firm in New York city which is still in existence. This firm today denies all connection with the episode, but in 1959, a son of one of the principals involved, in return for the author's promise of anonymity, stated that the concern did indeed finance the transaction. The sum involved in the conversion was 13 million dollars, considerably short of the 35 million dollar figure envisioned by Indian's Board of Directors, but, according to the report, still considerably more than what actually represented Indian's assets. Hedstrom's reported sale of his holdings amounted to about $650,000, appreciably less than was reported in contemporary accounts of the transaction. Hendee continued to hold the office of company President, and Charles Gustafson was then elevated to the position of Chief Engineer.

The actual details of Indian's financial status during its earlier days were never officially divulged. The founders were known to be reticent concerning

**Left:** *Some leading Indian racing stars of 1913.* **(The Western Motorcyclist and Bicyclist)**

*The ill-fated electric starting 'Hendee Special' model, developed in 1913 for the 1914 sales season.*

company finances, and confided only with close company associates and trusted employees. Such executives or clerical help who might later have been able to pass on such information have long since passed away. The only office files containing partial information regarding the company's financial affairs mysteriously disappeared some years ago. It is for this reason that Indian's history in this area can be only partially reconstructed from information gathered from sources outside the company.

There was some concern among certain Indian dealers and riders about Hedstrom's resignation in relation to possible alteration in design of the machines or changes in company policy. While no announcements regarding the matter were made, Indian's sales force hastened to assure all concerned that no radical changes were to be forthcoming.

In the spring of 1913 Indian's star racing team member, Jake De Rosier, for some unaccountable reason, rode a big valve Excelsior machine in an informal match race at the Paterson, New Jersey track. When the news of this reached President Hendee, who could not tolerate company disloyalty, De Rosier was immediately fired. Shortly afterwards he was injured in a match race at Los Angeles and died a year later from his injuries.

# Chapter 3

# THE GREAT DECLINE
# 1914–1923

The Hendee Manufacturing Company emerged in 1914 as the giant of the world's motorcycle industry, in view of its record production of the preceding year. The State Street and East Springfield factories were now operating at full capacity, with over twelve acres of floor space, thirty-five separate departments, and an assembly line nearly seven miles long, manned by nearly three thousand employees. Ways and means were sought to enhance production, in order to supply the growing roster of world-wide dealers, which now numbered nearly three thousand.

In January, the company announced that 100,000 twin cylinder machines had been built and sold since the initial models were offered in 1907.

An intensive advertising program was launched, with more than 300,000 pieces of literature being distributed through various channels during the first two months of the year. In addition, various advertising aids were made available to the dealers, for publication in local newspapers and other media. To augment the advertising staff, formerly managed by President Hendee, R.L. Harriman, who was formerly employed by the Marketing Department of a large Boston department store, joined the staff.

In addition, much attention was given to the company's ever-growing export business. Two shiploads of machines alone were ordered by J.H. Rhodes for sale in the eighty dealerships in Australasia. Additional outlets in South America and South Africa placed orders in excess of 50% over the preceding year.

The 1914 season marked a growing public interest in the sidecar market. While the Model T Ford and other makes of low-cost cars were appearing in increasing numbers, their average selling price of about $850.00 was double that of a V-twin sidecar outfit. Many family men, not otherwise interested in the sporting side of motorcycling, were turning to these units for transportation. Accordingly, plans were made to produce 4,500 sidecars.

A five model range was offered for 1914, each being a refinement of the previous season. These included the 61 cubic inch 7hp twins in both single geared and two-speed models, with like offerings of the 30.50 cubic inch singles, all models being fitted with the spring frame introduced in 1913. The 5hp light twin was dropped in order to economize production. The electric-starting 'Hendee Special' did not live up to its expectations. While the starting mechanism worked well, the best of the then available batteries could not maintain sufficient charge to furnish more than a couple of dozen starts before becoming completely exhausted. Two extra batteries were provided with each machine in a futile attempt to overcome the difficulty. It was reported that Billy Wells had the two Specials on the stand at the Stanley Show in London removed during the second day, due to the embarrassment of repeated battery failures. Factory production of the Specials was halted in March; all subsequent big twins were then being assembled without the electrical equipment. Most of the owners of these machines ultimately removed the electric starting device, and, in most cases,

**Opposite:** *Factory testers put a sidecar machine gun mount prototype military model through its paces in the woods adjacent to Springfield. This rare picture was surrepticiously snapped by Leslie D. Richards in 1916.*

the factory supplied units of the standard kickstarting mechanism, at no charge. No known examples of the Hendee Specials as such are known to have survived. The technical failure of the Special in no way hampered sales of the standard big twin, as its sterling reputation was already well established. The financial loss to the company was considerable, due to the then relatively large sums expended for its development during the preceding year.

Indians were everywhere in the news. The Mexican revolutionary general, Doroteo Aranga, better known in history as Pancho (or Francisco) Villa, learned to ride an Indian during one of his periods of enforced exile in the United States. Although his brief association with Indians did not give him time to become a proficient rider, his enthusiasm led him to seriously consider the employment of a number of 7hp two-speed twins for dispatch carrying and liaison duties on his forthcoming military campaigns against the Federal forces in Northern Mexico. He was subsequently advised against their use for this purpose by veteran riders, who cited the roughness of certain parts of the area and the lack of proper maintenance facilities.

*Thomas Callahan Butler.* (Horton Studio)

In June another 300,000 pieces of advertising literature was placed in the mails. The company's 1914 advertising program made it the largest motorcycle advertiser in the United States, with exposure that reached an estimated 17 million readers. To aid in these expanded sales and advertising campaigns, more staff members were added to the managerial departments. James B. MacNaughton, a former newspaper man, joined the Sales Department as assistant to Edward Buffam. Jack Priest, also a former newspaper executive, joined the Advertising Department, and, in collaboration with R.L. Harriman, edited the new company magazine *Honest Injun* which was mailed every other month to Indian owners and any other interested people.

That Spring, Indian's Engineering Department was augmented by the addition of Charles B. Franklin. While Charles Gustafson had been capably managing the department and overseeing production with the assistance of Theron L. Loose, he was somewhat handicapped by his inability to perform the drafting work necessary for the creation of new designs. The top management also rightly decided that the addition of new blood might bring forth fresh ideas, especially needed in the face of the growing threat of stronger competition from Indian's up-and-coming rival, Harley-Davidson. Franklin's appointment was due in large part to the intercession of Billy Wells, who had been informing President Hendee of his continuing spare-time studies in advanced motorcycle design. This also marked the first time that a professionally trained engineer joined Indian's design staff, as neither Hedstrom nor any of his assistants had enjoyed any formal engineering training. It is reported that Franklin's enthusiasm at the prospect of a job with Indian was such that he immediately resigned from a lifetime civil service position, when the news of his appointment was telegraphed to him by President Hendee. Together with his wife, Nancy, he arrived in Springfield in March, and rented a small second story apartment within walking distance of the factory.

Franklin's first assignment was to produce designs for a small two-stroke utility type machine. The management had decided late in the preceding year that such a model would add to their coverage of the market, attract novice riders, and offer further competition to the many foreign-built lightweights exported to the more underdeveloped countries. There was also a growing market in the United States for utility machines, the most promising of which was the introduction of a cheap, two-stroke machine by the Cleveland Motorcycle Company, of Cleveland, Ohio, which was provisionally priced at $125.00.

The new machine was designated as the Model K, and was cataloged as the 'Featherweight'. A small machine, weighing 130lbs, it was powered with a 13½ cubic inch two-stroke engine, rated at 2hp and patterned on the contemporary 269cc Villiers designed by Charles Marston in England in 1912, which was widely fitted to utility type machines during the next decade. The 'Featherweight' had a light frame with a fuel tank clipped above a single top tube. The forks were of the single-bladed bicycle type with the cartridge spring suspension, as fitted to the 1905 models. The machine had a light pattern clutch and three-speed gearbox and was listed at $150.00. Pioneer motorcyclists reported that it was pleasant to ride and very easy to control, and under favorable conditions could achieve a top speed of 35mph on the flat. It was definitely underpowered, however, and possessed feeble powers of acceleration. While the model sold in limited numbers, its introduction met with some resistance from not a few dealers, whose inherent preference was for the more powerful V-twins upon which their sales orientation was based. The earlier models had the design fault of a hardened phosphor bronze connecting rod bearing that induced rapid wear of the piston pin; this was corrected in later production. While the engine possessed ample cylinder dimensions for the work intended, it appeared that further development of its porting arrangements was in order to provide more power. This was undertaken later in 1915. But after continuing disappointing sales during the first half of the 1916 season, production was discontinued. It is certain that the 'Featherweight' could have made the grade with more development, but dealer resistance and the increasing production costs due to inflationary conditions brought on by the European war, mitigated against its commercial success.

A new member of the Sales Department, who joined the company in the Spring of 1914, was Thomas Callahan Butler, Jr., who was born in Palatka, Florida, in 1889. As a young man he showed a marked interest in science and mathematics, and attended a technical college in Georgia. He later matriculated at the famous Virginia Military Institute. He became interested in motorcycling during the pioneer period, and in 1912 became the southern distributor for Excelsior motorcycles. Possessed of a unique personality, he combined the courtly manners and flamboyant style of an antebellum southern gentleman with the shrewdness and business acumen of a Yankee horse trader. Though his Excelsior dealership was flourishing, he became attracted to the superior design features and general high quality of the Indian. With characteristic impulsiveness, he sent a telegram to Frank J. Weschler, offering to terminate his connection with Excelsior if he were offered a position on Indian's sales staff. Weschler immediately appointed him sales representative for the southern states.

Competition activities for 1914 opened with Joseph O'Conner on a 7hp Indian twin establishing a new world's hour record for motorcycles, on a horse track outside of Phoenix, Arizona, covering 66 miles, 1,100 yards. Cannonball Baker, who was visiting in Arizona at the time, immediately rode the same course on a similar machine for a new record of 66 miles, 1,660 yards.

This year also marked another significant motorcycling event with the formation of the first formal organization of the American Motorcycle Manufacturers Association which, in later years, became known as the American Motorcycle and Allied Trades Association. Its main office was established in Manhattan. Members of the Board of Directors included W.G. Shrack of Angola, New York; Arthur Davidson of Milwaukee; Thomas W. Henderson of Detroit; K.H. Jacoby of Middletown, Ohio, and L.D. Harden of Hartford, Connecticut. According to an article published in *The New York Times* on January 9th, "the Association, having for its particular objectives to foster the interests of those engaged in the business and kindred industries, to reform abuses in the trade,

*Mexican revolutionary Pancho (Francisco) Villa surrounded by his aides poses with a 1914 Hendee Special somewhere in Arizona.* **(El Paso Public Library)**

and to secure freedom for its members from unjust exactions".

An Indian team was again entered in the 1914 TT races, with Billy Wells as manager. Six specially built machines were dispatched to the island in May, along with Paul Derkum, who, by this time, had gained considerable fame as a road racing star and who was selected by Indian management as the team captain. Franklin, already heavily involved in design work at Springfield, had not planned to participate, but at Wells' insistence he was given leave of absence to join the Island contingent. Without Hedstrom's mechanical wizardry, victory again eluded Indian. Oliver Godfrey, the 1911 winner, could manage only second place. Franklin tied for eighth place with Howard R. Davies, on a Sunbeam.

This year also marked the first time that Harley-Davidson offered a serious challenge to Indian's long-time competition supremacy. Heretofore, Harley-Davidson had more or less officially ignored all forms of speed competition, stressing in its sales publicity the production of rugged and dependable utility machines designed for personal transportation and commercial uses. The company had entered a few long distance endurance contests in earlier years, with some success, but up to this time had not instituted a racing department nor hired any professional riders. As motorcycle sales increased after 1910, however, the racing challenges of Excelsior, Indian, Pope and Thor were such that Harley-Davidson felt they could no longer be ignored. Consequently, in 1913 the management hired William (Bill) Ottaway away from the Aurora Automatic Machine Company, where he was in charge of engineering and design and responsible for Thor's considerable competition successes in several preceding seasons. Ottaway was not a trained engineer, but rather a gifted mechanic, engine tuner, and artificer. Upon joining Harley-Davidson, he undertook to modify their original overhead-inlet-side-valve exhaust valve design to deliver more power, as well as the designing of out-and-out racing engines.

Harley's first bid for racing supremacy came in the summer of 1914, in the first of a series of races at the newly-opened dirt track at Dodge City, Kansas. Its suitability for high speed contests came to the attention of the Competition Committee of the FAM during their annual convention in 1913, held that year in Denver, Colorado. It was decided that dirt track racing was to become a recognized part of their competition program. The necessary preparations were made and, on July 4th, the first of the annual 300-mile races was held. To ensure a large field of entrants, the 61 cubic inch engines currently being used on the board tracks were allowed to compete in the formulation of the rules.

Thirty-six entrants on six different makes of machines were at the starting line, Excelsior, Harley-Davidson, Indian, Merkel, Pope, and Thor. Indian fielded a formidable team of eight valve specials, whose engines were an improved version of Hedstrom's original 1911 design. On the board tracks they were capable of speeds up to 100mph. One of them, ridden that spring by George Sidney, had already attained a speed of 93.48mph at Brooklands for the flying kilometer, and fastest time yet recorded at that famous track.

Lee Taylor, on a Merkel, took the lead for the first sixty miles, closely followed by Walt Cunningham, on a Harley. He passed Taylor at the hundred mile mark, and nearly lapped the field, when forced to retire with chain and spark plug trouble at the hundred and sixty-eighth mile. 'Slivers' Boyd forged ahead on his Indian to win at 68mph. While the Harley-Davidson camp had suffered a defeat, the speed of their new racing machines was a sobering lesson to the other contenders that formidable competition was in the making.

Indian's first serious defeat of the season came in September, during the National Championship Races held at Savannah, Georgia. The strong Excelsior team was primed for victory in this classic 300 miler, as their star rider, Bob Perry, had led the field with ease in 1913. Martin Schroeder, on a Harley, led the pack for the first 80 miles, closely followed by Bob Perry, Excelsior, Erle Armstrong, Indian, Ray Weishaar, Harley, and Cannonball Baker, on the stock Indian that he had just ridden across the continent a few weeks before, for a record of eleven and a half days. Lee Taylor came from behind the field at the 200th mile and was never headed after that for a signal Merkel victory.

An important Indian policy instituted in the spring of 1914 was that of mailing a congratulatory letter and a monetary reward to private Indian riders winning some significant club or regional sporting event. Many old time riders treasured these as souvenirs of past victories, and in the old days a check for $25.00, $50.00, or even $100.00 for an important win was a very substantial reward. The plan was said to have been initiated by Frank Weschler, himself a dyed-in-the-wool competition enthusiast in the Indian tradition.

Another important event occurred in 1914, that was to have both immediate and lasting effects upon the industrial economy of the United States. Henry Ford, the eccentric backyard mechanic who had evolved a fantastically efficient concept of mass production of automobiles, announced that he was raising the wages of all production workers from $2.50 for a ten-hour working day, to $5.00. He reasoned that their productivity, in his factories at least, had reached the point where he could

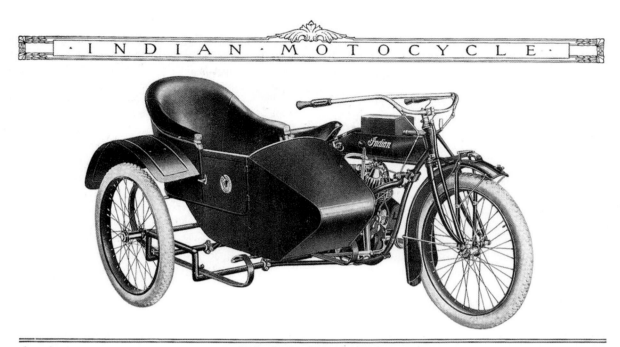

INDIAN SIDE CAR

Price, $70.00

*The Indian sidecar. The body style changed but little between 1913 and 1921.*

not only afford this, but that such an increase could greatly enhance their individual purchasing power. Of course, he cannily envisioned mass purchases of Ford cars by those who had previously been limited to the bicycle or motorcycle. Those who were concerned with the growth of unionism, were jubilant. Industrialists generally were horrified; some stated that the country would soon be dislocated by runaway inflation. Others avowed that Socialism would soon destroy the traditional American heritage of free enterprise and the capitalist system. The effect of Ford's new wage policy was initially local, but it presaged a trend of increased wage scales that forced most industries to revise their economic planning. The effect upon the domestic motorcycle industry was ultimately, critical, as the majority of the manufacturers were lightly financed and often ineptly managed. The burden of revising costing and production schedules, combined with the later problems of inflation brought about by World War I, proved too difficult for many to surmount.

Indians again participated in the San Diego to Phoenix desert races in 1914. Led by Cannonball Baker, the team included Harry Weitzell, Walter House, Paul Frantzen, Lorenzo Boido, and Ellison Wilson. This year the event was scheduled to finish on November 5th, the day before the opening of the Arizona State Fair, which was an annual fixture in Phoenix. A purse of $12,500 was put up

by the fair officials, with 45% going to the winner, 25% to the runner up, the balance being split between the last two finalists.

While billed as the team captain, Baker did not compete, as he had already entered the Borderline Derby, the course of which spanned the desert and mountains between El Paso, Texas and Phoenix. He rode the same two-speed, 7hp twin that had carried him across the continent for a new record, and which he had ridden in the Savannah races two months previously.

The riders were flagged off at two-minute intervals from the city plaza in San Diego, at dawn on the morning of November 3rd. An almost fatal adventure befell Indian rider, Paul Frantzen, who followed Roy Artley and George Currier of the Excelsior team out of San Diego. He left the main track to follow an alleged shortcut through the sand hills south of Holtville. He fell off, injured his right knee, and rolled over a high bank. He was nearly buried in the resultant sand slide. Unable to lift his machine, he started walking in the fierce noonday heat, looking for help. Sand worked into his boots and rubbed his feet raw, so he discarded them, going barefoot over the hot sand and sharp rocks. Later that evening he collapsed from exhaustion, but was awakened about midnight by the bawling of cattle. He managed to revive somewhat and followed the sound, only to find that he had stumbled into a camp of Mexican guerrillas who had been raiding ranches adjacent to the border. The desperados gave him some water, and discussed whether or not they should cut his throat. They finally put him on a horse and led him to a nearby railroad station, where he eventually caught a train to Yuma. To this day his machine is still buried somewhere in the sand hills.

Two other Indian riders, Weitzell and House, became lost in the same Holtville desert. Weitzell plunged into a hole and it took him over two hours to dig his machine out. He started up and almost immediately met House, on foot after his machine had nearly buried itself in loose sand. He took House aboard and the two found the latter's machine. Weitzell tied a rope around the steering head and managed to pull it out. Fortunately, the engine was undamaged, and the two limped into Yuma, after drinking the last of their water.

George Currier, on his Excelsior, led the race until within 18 miles of Yuma, when a rock perforated his engine's crankcase. Seventeen year old Alonzo Boido won, followed by Art Holmes and sixteen year old Harry Crandall, on Harleys. The time for the 405 mile race was 14 hours, nine minutes, a record that stood for five years.

Production for 1914 did not quite reach that of the previous record year. The Board of Directors questioned production efficiency for what they considered the somewhat reduced profit of $711.000 for the year. However, the onset of the war in Europe inexorably drove up the price of raw materials and certain bought out components which was beyond the control of management. Seven per cent annual dividends were paid to investors holding preferred stock, announcements of 1¾ per cent quarterly dividends being made by Treasurer Weschler, and paid through the Highland Trust Bank.

During the Fall of 1914, President Hendee's close associates noted his somewhat increasingly detached interest in company affairs. He was seldom found in his office, being seen mostly at Board of Directors' meetings. The previous year he had purchased an extensive tract of land on the banks of the Connecticut River, near East Haddam, Connecticut, and was in process of developing it as a country estate. Some of his associates opined that he did not relish the role of President after the resignation of Hedstrom, who had competently handled all production and had overseen all factory operations. Others thought that the constant friction with the Board of Directors was becoming a source of anguish to him, in addition to the fact that he was now less in control of the destinies of the company. At any rate, Hendee delegated more and more managerial authority to Weschler, whose dedication to Indian was now a byword in the industry. The latter, while still bearing the title of Treasurer, in turn delegated most of the duties of that position to his assistant, J.D. Stephens. Weschler was now, in effect, General Manager of company affairs, directing his personal efforts to whatever sphere of its operation required attention.

Production for 1915, aside from limited assembly of the 'Featherweight', was concentrated on two improved twins. One was the well proved 61 cubic inch 7hp model, the other a lighter 42 cubic inch 5hp model. Two-speed gears were standard, but a three-speed gear was now offered as an optional extra, which was based on a prototype model developed by Hedstrom in 1913. An all-electric model was offered in place of the ill-fated Hendee Special, with a Splitdorf magneto-generator providing current for head and tail lamps. The spring frame was modified slightly for more strength, with an additional seat pillar being placed just ahead of the rear wheel, to stiffen the frame.

A special racing machine, produced in very limited numbers, was also cataloged this year. It was of the short wheel base type with a specially tuned engine. The type of drive was optional, either clutch and countershaft or straight countershaft, no gears being fitted. It featured a racing type saddle and high pressure racing tires.

In order to reduce production costs, the complicated and expensive Hedstrom carburetor was replaced with the proprietary Schebler unit, which was by this time fitted as standard by most other makes within the industry. In order not to offend the many die-hard Hedstrom enthusiasts, the former unit was made available as an optional extra. The Hedstrom unit was always shown as fitted in the company catalogs, but few, if any, were to be seen on actual machines after March of that year. The performance of the machines fitted with the Schebler type actually exceeded the previous models, as Gustafson and Franklin had slightly altered the valve timing and cam action of the Hedstrom engines for more power. Prototypes had been subjected to searching tests on the nearby Springfield Coliseum track the preceding Fall, ridden by Erle Armstrong and Charles Gustafson, Jr. Public interest in sidecar outfits continued, and a substantial number of these units were produced, along with optional box bodies for various commercial uses.

With the now growing number of transportation buyers swelling the ranks of Indian's customers, Weschler sought to aid dealers in attracting these buyers by advising them to make their shops more attractive. In a series of articles in the 1915 issues of *Honest Injun*, he

**Right:** *The final form of the Hedstrom designed Big Twin, now fitted with a magneto-generator for 1915.*

## MAGNETO-GENERATOR

Combined ignition and lighting in one instrument, wherein each system is totally independent, long has been the dream of motorcycle builders, and like many other features which have contributed to the improvement of the gasoline cycle, finds its first realization in the Indian Magneto-Generator. This instrument eliminates a separate lighting generator with its driving system, together with the extra weight and complication, and produces both high tension magneto ignition and lighting current from a single, compact machine.

In many respects the Indian Magneto-Generator marks original advancement in electric lighting and ignition for motorcycles. It consists of two units combined in a single instrument, wherein the generator has absolutely no influence over the ignition system.

No matter how slow the motor may be operated, the magneto will give a perfect spark for ignition. A 6-volt battery is floated between the Magneto-Generator and the lamps so that a perfect light will be given when the machine is at a standstill or running at any speed. Should the battery give out through misuse or neglect it is possible to connect the lamps direct with the instrument which will give a perfect light when running at a speed of 18 miles per hour.

The headlight is of 9 candlepower, and the tail light, 2 candlepower, and the use of nitrogen bulbs increases the light 25 per cent.

## LIGHT AND HORN CONTROL BUTTONS

One of the excellent features of this system is a miniature switchboard attached to the rear of the tool box. This switchboard is made of hard rubber, and mounts two switch buttons. The smaller one cuts out the horn, so that when the machine is standing unguarded, the mischievous small boy cannot annoy the neighborhood, and waste battery current. The larger button controls the head and tail lights, and has three positions, viz., full on, dim for city riding, and out, thus rendering the rider able to comply with all state or local ordinances pertaining to light regulation on motor vehicles.

This equipment, including a powerful electric warning signal operated by battery current from a handlebar switch, will be furnished for $30 additional to the list price of any model, when such equipment is ordered with machine.

16

## · I N D I A N · M O T O C Y C L E ·

| MODEL D-1 | DYNAMOMETER TEST—20 H. P. | SPEEDWAY |

Price, $250.00

### WE GUARANTEE THIS MODEL WILL GIVE A SPEED OF 70 MILES
### AN HOUR WHEN IT LEAVES OUR FACTORY

### Specifications

MOTOR—7 h. p. air-cooled. Internal mechanism constructed to meet any special requirement. Piston displacement, 61.00 cubic inches.

CARBURETOR—Automatic.

VALVES—Mechanically operated.

IGNITION—Improved high tension, enclosed magneto.

SPARK PLUGS—Indian mica with snap-on terminals.

MUFFLER—Indian improved with cut-out.

LUBRICATION—Double force feed system. Gear driven pump automatically maintains constant level in motor base for normal running. Auxiliary hand pump for emergency use. Window in motor base indicates oil level.

HANDLEBARS—Indian upright, adjustable. Option, Indian adjustable racing, at no extra charge.

CONTROL—Indian patented, leverless, double grip "twist-of-the-wrist" system. Right grip controls compression release and spark; left grip controls throttle.

CLUTCH—Indian multiple dry plate clutch on countershaft. Operated by lever. Option, this model can also be fitted with regular compensating sprocket in place of clutch at no extra charge.

TRANSMISSION—Indian double roller chain system. Chains, ¼ inch wide, ⅝-inch pitch. Driving chains adjustable.

GEAR RATIOS—According to requirements. In ordering, state conditions machine will be used under and same will be geared accordingly.

TANKS—Gasoline and oil constructed, reinforced by baffle plates. Indian sure-tight gasoline cut-off built into tank. Gasoline tank cap fitted with priming gun.

FRAME—Rigid type. Special steel tubing, reinforced throughout its length.

FORK—Indian Cradle Spring fork. Strongly braced and reinforced. Springs, 5 leaf scroll type, constructed of Chrome-Vanadium spring steel. Nickel steel reinforcements. Fork crown, drop forgings. Option, rigid type fork, without extra charge.

WHEELBASE—53 inches.

WHEELS—28 inches diameter, 36 spokes front and rear.

TIRES—28 x 2¾ inches, or smaller, according to requirements.

GUARDS—Indian beaded mudguards, front and rear.

BRAKES—Indian improved, band type.

STAND—Permanent positioned rear stand, folding type. Locks to rear guard when not in use.

SADDLE—Indian racing.

FINISH—Indian red, all bright parts nickeled over heavy coat of copper.

FOOTBOARDS—Hinged construction to permit folding up.

IMPORTANT NOTICE—Specifications of Tanks, Saddle, Handlebars, Equipment, etc., we reserve the right to control to fit conditions.

11

*Left: The Indian Racing Model in limited production for public sale in 1915. Several of these were later fitted with factory special ohv four and eight-valve engines during the ensuing decade.*

offered suggestions as to display layouts, merchandise distribution, and, above all, the maintenance of clean premises.

On the sporting scene, Harley-Davidson continued their aggressive competition campaign against their chief rivals, Excelsior and Indian. The first major event of the year was the road race at Venice, then a small, seaside resort town southwest of Los Angeles, for a purse of $2,000. Factory teams representing Dayton, Excelsior, Harley-Davidson, Indian, Pope, and Thor were entered. Otto Walker led the Harley contingent, with improved engines developed the previous winter by Bill Ottaway. Walker covered the 300 mile course laid out through the streets at an average speed of 68.3l mph, to win the event. Another Harley rider, Red Parkhurst, was second, Carl Goudy and Bob Perry, Excelsior mounted, were third and fourth. A new Indian rider, the youthful Fred Ludlow, was fifth, and Morty Graves, also Indian mounted, was sixth.

On July 4th, the 300 mile Dodge City Race saw twenty-nine riders entered on seven different makes of machine, Cyclone, Emblem, Excelsior, Harley, Indian, Pope and Thor. Don Johns on his Cyclone set a terrific pace and lapped several contestants during the first 50 miles. His machine had an overhead camshaft engine of very advanced design, from the board of Walter Strand, and was manufactured by the Joerns Motor Company of St. Paul. A relatively new company, its products could well have swept the boards in competition had not the concern been plagued with financial and managerial troubles from the start, precluding further development. Johns was forced to retire in the 101st mile with a broken chain, leaving Excelsior's Carl Goudy and Morty Graves in first and second places. By the 90th lap, the Indian team led by Don Johns, and all of the Excelsiors, were out with engine trouble. Otto Walker led the Harley pack to the finish, with all six places. Walker's time was 76.26mph, nearly nine miles faster than the speeds of the previous year.

Indian partially won back its lost laurels at the new board track at Tacoma, Washington, that August, when Erle Armstrong took first place in the 300 mile feature race at a speed of 79.84mph. Otto Walker, on a Harley, was second and Don Johns, Indian, was third.

The Harleys made a comeback in September at the newly opened Maywood board track, near Chicago, when Otto Walker again led the pack with one of Bill Ottaway's new eight valve racing machines, at a speed of 89.11mph on a very fast track. Indian fielded their professional team, but all dropped out along the way with engine trouble. There were no desert races in 1915, due to continuing trouble along the border with Pancho Villa's guerrilla raiders.

In the Spring of 1915, Indian's top management, headed by Frank Weschler, conferred with the Engineering and Design Departments on the matter of changing the basic design of Indian engines. While the Hedstrom type had well proved its worth during the past decade of continuous improvement, it was decided that it had by this time undergone its maximum economical development. Another factor under consideration was that it was an expensive engine to manufacture and there had been continuous pressure from the Board of Directors to consider ways and means of cutting production costs. It was also a fact that both the standard engines lately developed by Excelsior and Harley-Davidson, and of the same cylinder displacement, had somewhat of an edge in power development. It was becoming well known that many amateur mechanics had experienced some difficulty in adjusting the rather sensitive Indian overhead valve gear and otherwise keeping the engine in proper tune.

Charles Gustafson offered the opinion that a well-designed side valve type could be a simplified improvement, such as the modified Peugeot V-twin that he had perfected for the Reading-Standard Company, and which had subsequently undergone refinement for both enhanced reliability and economical manufacture. Franklin agreed with him, and experimentation with various prototypes was immediately undertaken, over the objections of some of the Scandinavian contingent in the engineering shop who were still loyal to the Hedstrom type.

The new engine was laid out to conform to the then standard 61 cubic inch displacement employed for all American V-twins, but still adhering to the 42° cylinder angle, which was considered to give the best balance.

The new engine, which was designated as the Powerplus, was rated, as was its predecessor, at 7hp with the standard SAE rating. However, it actually developed 16 to 17hp on the dynamometer, a substantial increase over the last Hedstrom models.

In order not unduly to interrupt the normal flow of production, the Powerplus engine was built with the same crankcase dimensions as the last Hedstrom type, so that it could be fitted to the current frames and engine plates without major changes in the standard big twin models. The only other modification was the fitting of a slightly improved three-speed gearbox and a somewhat heavier clutch.

Tommy Butler, who took a lively interest in the development of the new engine, not only from the sales standpoint but for his keen knowledge of motorcycle engineering, was happy to report to both Frank Weschler and the Board of Directors that the new model could be produced much more economically than its immediate predecessors, a critical factor in increasingly difficult times.

Butler's interest in the Powerplus project brought about the close friendship between himself and Franklin, as they shared the same enthusiasm for both Indian and progress in motorcycle design. Some of their associates marvelled at the relationship between the ebullient Butler and the quiet, taciturn Franklin, who had made few close friends within the company, although he was well respected for his obvious abilities as a designer and engineer. Their friendship continued on through the years, with Butler later filling the role of Franklin's biographer after the latter passed away in the Fall of 1932.

In order to provide a public test of the new engine coincidental to its introduction for the 1916 sales season, Cannonball Baker was engaged to undertake the Three Flag run, from Canada to Mexico. Baker suggested that as he was already on the west coast, time could be saved by shipping him an engine to Seattle. He could then use it

*J. Worth Alexander's restored 1916 Powerplus, the first model of a new series of machines. 20,000 of this model were supplied to the US Army as a military model.*
**(Ronald Mugar)**

as a replacement for the standard Hedstrom model presently fitted to his 1914 two-speed model, the same machine he had used on the 1915 transcontinental run. This was done immediately, with Ballou and Wright, the Seattle dealers, readying the machine for the run, scheduled for mid-August.

Baker set out on August 24th from Vancouver, British Columbia, and immediately encountered dense fog in northern Washington. No sooner had he made his way out of the overcast when he was forced to proceed south via a circuitous route, to avoid numerous forest fires. The trip through northern California was equally hazardous, due to the almost impassable roads. Better conditions were found south of Sacramento, when, accompanied on this leg of the journey by Hap Alzina, he made the 48 mile trip to Stockton in 50 minutes, on a paved highway. The primitive road over the Tejon Pass from Bakersfield to Los Angeles was travelled in five hours, for the 129 miles. He arrived in Tijuana, Mexico, at noon on August 27th, making 1,655 miles in three days, nine hours, and 15 minutes. His only stop was in Fresno, where he took a three hour nap.

Baker had nothing but praise for the new engine, both for its faultless performance and its notable increase in power. Much was made of his trip in the motorcycle press, as well as in Indian's subsequent extensive advertising displays.

To demonstrate the prowess of the new model even further, Baker was sent to Australia, where he broke with ease a number of local distance records in the six to twenty-four-hour categories. On the way home, he

stopped at the island of Oahu and made the 90 mile run around the island, over jungle trails, in the then record time of 2 hours 4 minutes.

The 1915 season closed with a net profit to the company of $617,000 with the usual quarterly dividends being paid to the preferred shareholders. Production was lower than the previous year, principally due to the loss of most of the European markets as a result of the war and the German U-boat menace, which dislocated shipping generally.

The 1916 season opened with rewarding public response to the new Powerplus model. Due to its increased power, it was well suited for sidecar use. Large numbers of machines were dispatched to Australia, Africa, Central and South America and Canada, where import of English machines was now curtailed by the war.

Company production was concentrated on two versions of the Powerplus. One was the standard spring frame model, the other a lower priced solid frame model which sold for $250.00. Electric battery lighting was not offered this season as the similarly equipped Hedstrom machine of the previous season did not measure up to its anticipated reliability.

Offered as an optional extra, some 1916 models were equipped with the Splitdorf Mag-Dyno system. This consisted of a head and tail lamp powered by a generator that was integral with the magneto, the lighting coils providing direct current without the need of a battery. This system was fairly reliable, but had the disadvantage that the intensity of the lighting varied with the speed of the engine. Night riders had the option of purchasing the usual acetylene lighting outfits.

Production of the Featherweight two-stroke model was continued until August. Also cataloged for the first time were single and twin cylinder editions of the four and eight valve short wheelbase racing machines, with direct countershaft single-speed drive. The management decided that more of these machines, in the hands of private owners, would help to counteract the formidable challenge of Harley-Davidson on the racing scene, as well as provide a gesture to placate the Board of Directors, in demonstrating that racing machines could have a place in commercial sales.

On the competition side, 1916 was almost a total disaster for Indian. At the second annual running of the Dodge City 300 on July 4th, Indian fielded a strong team captained by Don Johns, with Erle Armstrong, Paul 'Speck' Warner, Gene Walker and Ray Seymour. The Excelsior team was headed by Bob Perry and included Joe Wolters and Morty Graves. Harley-Davidson entered eight riders, headed by Otto Walker, with Ray Weishaar, Paul Gott, Irving Jahnke, Sam Correnti, Clarence Johnson, Floyd Clymer, Harry Crandall and Harry Brant. Bill Ottaway entered both his new eight valve specials along with three of the older, but now modified, pocket valve machines.

*J. Worth Alexander's 1916 33cu in Powerplus single with unsprung frame. Most of these machines were sold for solo or sidecar commercial work. (Ronald Mugar)*

Dodge City officials went all out to make the meet a festive occasion, with the streets decorated with flags and bunting. Two floors of Dodge City's largest hotel, the Harvey House, were set aside as the racers' headquarters. Representatives from the factories of each of the contending manufacturers were on hand, together with those of the Goodyear and Firestone tire companies.

Otto Walker was a non-starter, due to illness. Ottaway then substituted twenty-one year old Floyd Clymer, a native of Berthoud, Colorado, who had won several local events on an Excelsior, but who had lately become a Harley-Davidson dealer in Denver. He had previously enjoyed some notoriety as a 'kid agent' for cars, as well as for an adventurous journey in a Flanders automobile, from Denver to Spokane, Washington, in 1910, in company with his younger brother.

The official starter for the race was T.S. Sullivan, automotive editor of the *Boston Globe* newspaper, who waved off the racers at 11 am. Don Johns, Indian, spurted into the lead, but with a burst of speed Clymer overhauled him on the second lap. Johns dropped back to third place, with Bob Perry, Excelsior, gaining second place, but dropping out in the fifth lap with a broken valve. Clymer continued to widen his lead until nineteen year old Irving Jahnke came up from last place and moved in behind him. Clymer stayed just ahead for the first hundred miles, setting a new speed record for the course of 83.62mph. From then on Clymer and Jahnke alternated in first place until the 150th mile, when the timekeeper announced that their two times were identical.

Don Johns dropped out with engine trouble at the 200th mile. Clymer and Jahnke continued their seesaw run to the finish, with Jahnke coming in first. Clymer dropped out with a blown tire when nearly at the finish. Joe Wolters, Excelsior, was second, Ray Weishaar was third, with Paul Warner and Gene Walker, on Indians, in fourth and fifth places. Morty Graves, Excelsior, was sixth. Jahnke's win was at the record speed of 79.79mph, and he was rewarded with $800.00 in prize money plus a $200.00 bonus for his lap times.

Later that month, another strong Harley team cleaned up at the famous Sheepshead Bay board track at Long Island, New York, winning, first, second, third, fourth, and sixth places. Don Johns, Indian, was the sole member of his team to place, running fifth. Red Parkhurst, the Harley winner, made the fast time of 89mph, in spite of a forced stop to change a spark plug. In the two mile National Championships held on the same course, a Harley team composed of M.K. 'Curly' Fredericks, Bill Brier, and Alvin Barclay took all three first places at average speeds of over 90mph.

This pattern was repeated with continuing regularity all across the nation that year, the contemporary motorcycling press recounting at least fifteen National Championship races where Harley scored victory after victory.

In August, the first Pikes Peak Hill Climb was held, with strong teams from Harley-Davidson, Indian, Excelsior and Thor participating. Indian made an all-out effort to win with eight valve racing engines and three-speed gearboxes fitted to standard frame machines, the first time such a combination had been used in competition. The course was twelve miles in length, rising from 9,000 to 14,108 feet, the top of the peak. The Harley and Excelsior teams used lightweight single-geared machines, which appeared to give an advantage with very low weight. Floyd Clymer, on an Excelsior, won both professional events, with Frank Kunce, on a Harley, winning the State Championship.

Indian could take only small consolation in making a good showing in the 1916 desert races scheduled that Fall because the Mexican border troubles had diminished somewhat due to Pancho Villa's forces withdrawing to the south. The course this year was a new one, being from Springerville, Arizona to Phoenix, a distance of 441 miles.

Cannonball Baker headed Indian's team, which included Alan Bedell, also a transcontinental record breaker, Roy Artley, and Jack Dodds. Joe Wolters, Excelsior's board track star, was there to try his skill on the sand, along with team mates Arguile Davis and Al Meacham. Harry Crandall and R.J. Orput represented Harley-Davidson.

The race was flagged off at Springerville at dawn on November 6th, the riders leaving at two minute intervals. Roy Artley was first into Flagstaff, at 1:38pm, followed by Alan Bedell two minutes later. Jack Dodds limped in at 3:30pm, having had trouble en route with sand in his carburetor. R.J. Orput was somewhere behind, reportedly with a broken fork spring. After the contestants neared Winslow, Baker was closely following Crandall when the latter topped a rise at high speed and took a spill, while landing just over the crest. Baker, who was forced to put his machine into a slide to avoid hitting the now prone Crandall, went off the road into a ravine, and injured his right leg. Both managed to straighten their machines and proceed on course. Al Meacham was the next casualty, buckling his front wheel on a large rock. Bedell took a header over the bars and cut his forehead open, but managed to lift his machine and carry on. Roy Artley came in first, arriving in Phoenix after 13 hours and 12 minutes of riding, on what was aptly described as the worst road in North America. Blood-spattered Bedell was second. Joe Wolters, Excelsior, was third, and Dodds, Indian, was fourth, Indian taking three out of four places.

A final minor victory of the year for Indian was the winning of the first annual hill climb to be held at San Juan Capistrano, a village near one of the historic Franciscan missions, sixty miles south of Los Angeles in nearby Orange County. Local enthusiasts had long eyed a certain 600 foot high hill with an even slope of about 35°, as an ideal competition site, and a large number of riders supported the event. It was won by Paul 'Speck' Warner, a former factory employee and competition rider, who had moved to California the year before. His machine was a standard 1915 Hedstrom-engined three-speed model, slightly modified for hill climbing by lowering the gear ratios.

In November, all of the leading motorcycle manufacturers agreed to suspend competition activities, due to the troubled conditions brought on by the European war, which had been raging for the past two years. The United States policy at first was to remain neutral, but the sinking of the Lusitania in 1915, followed by continuing attacks by U-boats on non-combatant shipping, had finally aroused intense sympathy for the Allied cause. The management of the leading motorcycle manufacturers were in tacit agreement that the continuation of competition activities was now scarcely patriotic in view of the fact that a large number of industrial concerns were engaged in defense projects at the behest of the government, which was now preparing to put the country in a state of preparedness.

There was also the prospect of government contracts being awarded to various motorcycle manufacturers for military machines, as there had been much interest lately on the part of the War Department in experiments with trucks, automobiles and motorcycles for military use. This had come about by virtue of the continuing troubles with Mexico since 1915.

The significance of the Mexican campaign was that it marked the first time that the US Army had utilized powered transport. The results made a profound impression on the senior officers on the General Staff, whose tactical thinking had heretofore been based on cavalry manoeuvers perfected fifty years earlier during the Civil War. As a part of the general preparedness activities, the War Department invited the major motorcycle manufacturers to design prototype two and three-wheelers especially adapted to military use.

Aside from the fact that motorcycle sales generally had enjoyed a marked increase since 1910, 1916 was a year of attrition for the industry. While the so-called big three manufacturers – Indian, Harley-Davidson and Excelsior, were in a fairly sound financial conditon, the second-string ranks, comprising Merkel, Pope and Thor, were not, which was also the case with several minor manufacturers whose sales since the pioneer days had never enjoyed substantial volume.

Although many established big three dealers were jubilant at the diminishing competition, some knowledgeable leaders within the industry rightly viewed this thinning of the ranks with some alarm. It was now apparent in some quarters that a new approach to marketing procedures might be in order, along with some options of smaller utility type machines. The Indian management, now headed by Frank Weschler, had apparently been thinking along these same lines. A new lightweight model was to be offered as an improvement over the ill-fated Featherweight model which had undergone prototype development since the Spring.

Engineered ostensibly by Charles Gustafson, Sr, the titular head of the Engineering and Design Department, the new machine was a creation of Franklin's who was responsible for its execution. It was based on the Featherweight, but had a slightly heavier frame that carried a torpedo-shaped fuel tank clipped to the bottom of the single top tube. The 1905 type single-bladed cartridge type spring forks were retained. The engine, however, was entirely new, being now a four-stroke horizontally-opposed twin of 15 cubic inches rated at 4hp on the SAE rating. It was a frank copy of the contemporarily popular English Douglas, ran very smoothly, and produced more than double the power of its predecessor. Its selling price was provisionally fixed at $165.00, but the rising cost of production ultimately increased this to $180.00, when it was cataloged for the 1917 season.

The new machine, designated as the Model O, received favorable comment from many riders, as it was easy to start, pleasant to ride, and offered acceptable performance as to acceleration and hill climbing. An early criticism was that the rear cylinder was prone to overheat under hard driving, a fault later corrected in subsequent production by modifications to the oiling system.

The Model O suffered the ultimate fate of the Featherweight, however, due in the main to the same factors. Many of the dealers, with indoctrinated loyalty to the powerful V-twin, did not look with favor upon a utility type machine, and were somewhat loath to give sufficient promotion to the newcomer. Some intrepid lady riders favored the new machines, which gave rise to the thoughts in some quarters that riding it was somewhat a threat to masculinity. Then there was the overshadowing stigma from its underpowered predecessor. With aggressive promotion from the factory, the model might have succeeded, but with the prospect of war contracts and subsequent accelerated production of heavyweight

*Erwin G. 'Cannonball' Baker on the Mexican border with one of the first Powerplus models.* **(The Archives of the Hendee Manufacturing Company)**

machines, this support was not forthcoming. The machine was again cataloged in 1918, with minor improvements to the engine, larger footboards and saddle, and an improved front suspension featuring trailing link forks supported by a straight quarter elliptic leaf spring. After disappointing sales early in the following season, production ceased during the late Summer.

During the Summer and Fall of 1916, the Design Department, at the request of the War Department, built a number of various prototype machines intended for military use. Some of them were three-wheeled sidecar types intended as mobile machine gun carriers, while others were especially strengthened outfits for the same purpose.

It was during this preparedness period that the Board of Directors decided that the Company should go all out in an attempt to secure large military contracts to the exclusion of civilian domestic and general export require-

ments. The Directors, with the profit motive uppermost, were of the opinion that much money could be made on a large volume of production without the attendant expenses of advertising and marketing. President Hendee and Treasurer Weschler both argued against this plan. They both warned that virtual abandonment of the civilian market, at home and overseas, would not only be detrimental to future peace time sales, but would result in the dislocation of their carefully built up dealer organization. After several stormy sessions in the Board room, Hendee and Weschler were overruled, and ways and means were planned to secure as much War Department business as was possible.

The man most prominent in negotiating with government officials was a newcomer to the Sales Department, Francis I. (Frank) Long, who had a record of a very successful sales career in the midwest in the agricultural implement and automobile fields. An aggressive and ebullient individual, he was known to boast that he was

**Right:** *The solid frame 'economy model' Powerplus of 1916. At $250.00 it was a transportation bargain of its day.*

# MODEL G
REGULAR
FRAME
BIG TWIN
3 SPEED
PRICE $250.00

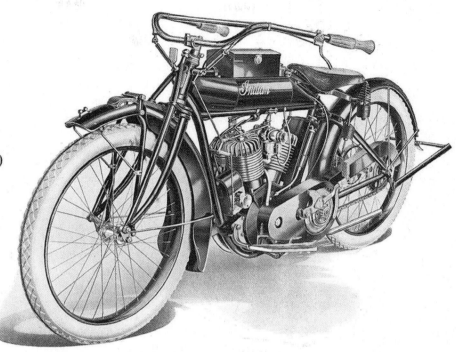

## MODEL G—SPECIFICATIONS

MOTOR—Indian Powerplus type, air cooled cylinders, 3¼" bore, 3³¹⁄₃₂" stroke; piston displacement, 60.88 cubic inches. Normal rating, 7 H. P. Develops 15 to 18 horsepower on dynamometer test. Roller bearing connecting rods and main shaft. Interchangeable, enclosed valves in side pockets. Cams and timing gears all mounted in separate housing outside crank case. Three-ring pistons. High compression. Large valves. One-piece L-head cylinders.

CARBURETOR—Indian-Schebler automatic, compensating type. Variable fuel and air adjustment. Fuel feed automatically regulated to synchronize with throttle range. Automatic auxiliary air valve. Instantaneous acceleration without choking.

IGNITION—Dixie high tension enclosed magneto. Indian spark plugs ⅞" 18 thread. Splitdorf Mag-Dynamo for ignition and lighting supplied at extra cost. See special booklet.

LUBRICATION—Indian worm drive oil pump geared to crankshaft. Adjustable feed. Enclosed in cam housing and quickly accessible. Positive under all conditions.

STARTER—Indian Light Pressure cranker geared to countershaft. Positive, simple and reliable. Will spin motor three or more revolutions on each impulse. Can be operated by a woman.

CLUTCH—Indian Heavy Duty dry multiple disc type. Elektra clutch lining against steel. Smooth engagement with positive drive. Sixty-three inches of contact surface. Clutch quickly adjustable.

HANDLEBARS—Indian truss bar type. Adjustable for all riding positions with positive locking single stem. Cushion grips. Indian universal double grip control. Ignition timing and compression release for starting controlled by right grip. Throttle control by left grip.

TRANSMISSION—Three-speed sliding-gear, progressive system. Ball bearings.

STANDARD SPROCKET EQUIPMENT—Motor, 17 tooth; clutch, 38 tooth; countershaft, 21 tooth; rear wheel, 36 tooth; giving following ratios: 4 to 1, 6 to 1, 10 to 1. Option 40 tooth rear.

CHAINS—Duckworth double roller, ⅜" wide, ⅝" pitch. Both chains independently adjustable and protected by guards.

FRAME—Indian regular construction. Chrome vanadium steel tubing with drop forged connections. Indian Cantilever Comfort seat absorbs road vibration and prevents riding fatigue.

FORK—Indian original Cradle Spring suspension. Chrome vanadium steel tubing with interior reinforcements. Drop forged fittings. Double scroll elliptic leaf springs.

BRAKES—Two, internal and external band types. Internal brake applied by right foot lever; external brake applied by left handlebar lever. Elektra friction lining against steel. Both brakes independently adjustable and powerful enough for all emergencies.

WHEELS—28" single clinch, C. C. rims. 36 spokes front and rear. Knockout axles all around.

TIRES—Goodyear Blue Streak detachable, 28" x 3" all around, diamond anti-skid tread.

WHEELBASE—55 inches.

REAR STAND—Indian hinged type, anti-rattler mountings. Quick acting. No interference with axle adjustment when stand is in use.

MUFFLER—Indian single expansion chamber with tail pipe and cut-out. Individual exhaust tubes from cylinders eliminate back pressure. Exhaust silenced without loss of power.

TANKS—Gasoline tank capacity over two gallons. Positive needle shutoff. Large filler cap with self contained syringe. Oil tank capacity two quarts. Located near motor, insuring fluidity in cold weather.

SADDLE—Indian Cantilever Comfort Saddle.

FOOTBOARDS—Pressed steel with rubber mats. Automatic folding. Large and comfortable.

LUGGAGE CARRIER—Indian Cradle Spring Frame type, furnished at $2.00 extra when ordered with machine.

WHEEL GUARDS—Pressed steel, molded type with beaded edges. Strong and light. Side wings on front, arrest steering splash. Triple rear braces.

TOOL EQUIPMENT—Metal tool box with spring lock and key, mounted over gasoline tank. Full set of tools, tire repair outfit, telescoping pump and clips.

FINISH—Standard Indian red, with nickel or black japan trimmings. Lustrous and durable.

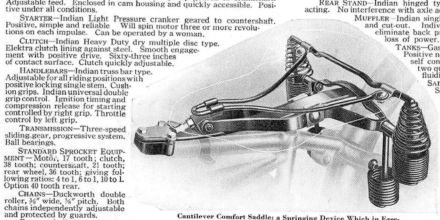

Cantilever Comfort Saddle: a Springing Device Which in Ease-Giving Excels all Attachments of Other Makes. This is Fitted both to Models G and K.

11

the only man in the world who held memberships in the Masonic fraternity, the B'nai-Brith, and the Knights of Columbus, all at the same time. Long possessed a number of strong political contacts in Washington, DC, as well as in his native state of Ohio, with the organization known as the 'Ohio Gang', of which Senator, and later, President Warren G. Harding was a member. Long was also in charge of the factory's Municipal Sales force, which was concerned with selling machines to law enforcement bodies. He was later assisted in this department by W. Stanley Bouton, who was to succeed him in this office.

The opposite condition prevailed with both Harley-Davidson and Excelsior. While these companies wished to participate in the war effort, they were mindful of the more longstanding commitments of peace time, and negotiated contracts for only a limited number of military machines.

Perhaps the most significant event of 1916, was the resignation in August of President Hendee. He had earlier announced his intention of retiring before his fiftieth birthday, which was now coming up in October. Close friends had reported that he was becoming growingly weary with the continuing battles over policy matters with the often hostile Board of Directors, and it was also rumored that he felt his prestige had suffered with the failure of the Hendee Special. Whatever the reasons, Hendee had apparently been planning retirement for some time. A bachelor since 1895, he had married his long-time company secretary, Edith Hale, in 1915, and moved from Springfield to lead the life of a country squire on a large estate at East Suffield, Connecticut. Like his former partner, he refused many lucrative offers from several industrial concerns, preferring to retire from active business life. In the liquidation of his company holdings, it was reported that the sale of his shares amounted to approximately $950,000, a princely sum in the days of honest dollars. Throughout the ensuing years, Hendee was an occasional visitor in Springfield, where he had many friends of long standing but as time passed these visits became less frequent. He always maintained a sustaining interest in Indian affairs, and in later years was known to express anguish at the sad fate that at last befell the great company which owed so much to his early efforts. He became an invalid during his declining years, and passed away in the Summer of 1943. Some years later Hendee's widow married an old family friend, James Moriarty, and at this writing the couple still live on the Hendee estate at East Suffield.

Hendee's last official act, and one which was to have significant bearing on Indians' later fortunes, was the appointment of a very competent man, William G.

McCann, to the post of Export Manager. McCann had already experienced several years of endeavor in the general export business, and enjoyed numerous contacts with various overseas export-import organizations. He was able to carry on in this field on Indian's behalf and to later expand the already lucrative export market that Hendee had so carefully built up during the preceding decade.

With the resignation of Hendee, the Board of Directors elected one of their members, John F. Alvord of New York, as President. He was also president of the Standard Electric Company and of the Edison-Splitdorf Company, manufacturers of automotive electrical equipment and magnetos. He was more of a financier than an industrialist, and spent most of his time at his offices in Manhattan. An infrequent visitor in Springfield, except for his attendance at Board meetings, he relegated most of the management of the company to Frank Weschler.

Negotiations with the government regarding war contracts continued in the Fall of 1916. After testing various prototype machines supplied by the big three manufacturers, Government procurement officers decided to secure standard 61 cubic inch V-twin machines with three-speed gearboxes, having slightly lowered gear ratios, in both solo and sidecar types. The standard sidecar designs were utilized, but with slightly stiffer springs. In the negotiations, conducted largely through Frank Long, Indian contracted to supply an initial order of 20,000 machines. During this time, Harley-Davidson agreed to furnish about 7,000 machines, with Excelsior supplying about 2,500.

The initial problem Indian faced in this contract was the unit price per machine or sidecar. The Army purchasing agents quite naturally were obligated to buy equipment at the lowest possible figure, and the Board of Directors ultimately settled for $187.50 for each machine and $47.00 for a sidecar chassis and body. This agreement almost caused financial disaster for Indian, as the cost of manufacture was steadily rising each month from the continuing inflationary rise in material cost.

A part of the trouble in costing out these contracts lay with Sales Manager Edward Buffam, whose actual financial and industrial experience was at best limited. During normal times since 1910, he had been able to project fairly accurate production schedules, especially as Indian's market penetration was then on the increase. He was also able to rely heavily on his old friend and mentor, President Hendee, who was a shrewd judge of the subject. Buffam's assistant, James B. MacNaughton, was even less qualified in the production field to be of substantial help, and in the end it was Plant Superintendent Theron L. Loose who set up tentative costing schedules, with the aid of Frank Weschler, who by this time had a fair working knowledge of all phases of motorcycle production. In the final analysis the summation of Indian's War Department commitments was nothing short of appalling. The company was now faced with supplying 20,000 machines, together with a large number of sidecar outfits, at a substantial loss.

An important change in company policy as the result of wartime, was the closing of the foundry and the farming out of certain of the component parts to subcontractors. It was found in costing out the various manufacturing processes that specialist suppliers could do the work more economically. Engine castings were made through contract by Brown and Sharpe of Providence, which firm subsequently supplied these parts for many years. Certain forgings, such as frame and fork lugs, and other items were obtained locally, mainly from the Moore Drop Forge Company.

To effect further economies, the Hendeeville plant was disposed of to the Moore Drop Forge Company.

In desperation, Weschler turned to the company's original production genius, Oscar Hedstrom, for help. It was later reported that Hedstrom was loath to leave, even for a short time, the relaxed environment of his Connecticut estate to again encounter company problems. Additionally, he would be involved in supervising the manufacture of a model which was not now of his own creation, and with a company with whose management he was not wholly in accord. After several impassioned pleas from Weschler, however, he at last consented to oversee production matters on a salary basis for a limited time, and accordingly commuted to Springfield for about three months during the Fall of 1916. The chaos he encountered in the Production Department was nothing short of appalling, but it is said that within a matter of weeks he was able to bring the operation under some measure of control.

Hedstrom's temporary return to the fold was widely heralded as being his patriotic contribution to the war effort, the true state of affairs being a carefully guarded secret. A side effect of his short tenure of service was a distinct rise in employee morale, as a majority of the production workers were veterans of the old Hedstrom days and were more than happy to see their old chief once again managing the vast factory. It was no secret within the industry that the war contracts were less than desirable. The conservative management of the family-owned Harley-Davidson company as well as that of Excelsior, faced similar production difficulties, but they had the advantage of a much smaller overall production commitment and continued to supply their civilian market.

Old time factory employees have stated that no design changes were made in the basically standard 61 twin

*An experimental four wheel machine gun carrier at a New York Armory in 1916.* (**Wide World**)

during Hedstrom's short term of management. The only minor change, which came about early in 1917, was the substitution of a two-piece pressed steel fuel tank that was clamped over the frame tubes, in place of the earlier Hedstrom between-the-rails type fitted since 1910, which was more expensive to produce. Another minor modification was the substitution of Bowden type push-pull controls for the articulated rod type that had been used since 1903. While the latter had worked well if kept well lubricated, they were also more costly to produce. The former single-stem bicycle type fork crown was altered to a triple-stem type which was much more rigid, and which prevented flexing, especially in sidecar work.

Hedstrom's main activity was to achieve maximum efficiency of production and in this he was able to bring the cost-per-unit to the point where the company could make a small profit. As the production activities were centered on one model, in addition to the sidecars, production of the Model O was cut back to minor proportions.

The United States declared war on Germany and the Central Powers on April 6th, 1917. While the country's industries had been largely projected toward a war footing, the armed forces were woefully unprepared. The Regular Army numbered only about 50,000 men, who were largely without modern equipment or material. President Wilson immediately launched an impassioned appeal to industry for all-out war production. With a whole-hearted response from the manufacturers in a general climate of patriotic fervor, the American public, in most cases, gave the government its undivided support.

While the production of military motorcycles now reached a new high, under the pressure of the war effort, there came the problem of servicing and maintenance under field conditions. Tommy Butler was given a leave of absence from the company to set up a service organization within the armed forces. With the co-operation of the armed forces recruiting section, about 3,000 motorcycle mechanics were mustered in, and were trained to service and repair not only the Indian machines, but also the Harley-Davidsons and the small number of Excelsiors which were being supplied to the services. Butler was given carte blanche authority to expedite the implementation of these units, and his business cards and official stationery bore the legend 'Special Assistant to President Woodrow Wilson'. All in all, the heavyweight big twin American motorcycles gave sterling service under often appalling conditions of use, as well as sometimes abuse and neglect.

When Indian's contracts were fulfilled by the Spring of 1918, an additional contract was negotiated for a further 25,000 machines. This new agreement was more favorable to the company, as a better price was arranged. Some of the machines supplied were of the solid frame type, which could be produced more economically.

As often occurs in war, much of the material produced never actually reached the front. Many motorcycles were retained for home use. Of the many thousands of military Indians produced, only about 10,000 actually saw service in Europe. Many were subsequently sold as surplus after the Armistice, some being exported to foreign countries.

Many of the wartime machines were retained in government service for some years, and could be seen on various government installations as late as the early 1930's. Even as late as the opening of World War II, crates of new Indians turned up from time to time as nearly-forgotten stocks of stored supplies were unearthed in out-of-the-way places.

In all, more than 70,000 military motorcycles were supplied to the armed forces and government agencies, of which about 41,000 were Indians and 15,000 were Harley-Davidsons, the balance being Excelsiors and a few Clevelands.

In spite of the large number of military machines manufactured for the government, the Indian company emerged from the war in a rather precarious financial condition. The profits per unit had been negligible, and inflationary production costs had risen to unnatural proportions. Worse still, war production had starved out many of Indian's dealers, and not a few had defected to Harley-Davidson, Excelsior, Emblem and Reading-Standard. Perhaps the most crucial shortage was in spare parts, as most of this production had been allocated to the government. Many Indian owners had been put off the road for the lack of some minor replacement.

With the cancellation of all war contracts in January 1919, the company announced that henceforth all production would be directed toward domestic and overseas export requirements, although the first of the winter's production run still carried wartime olive drab paint.

What with the pent up demand for civilian transport of all kinds, the company, still under Weschler's general management, faced the future with nearly an empty treasury and an almost wrecked dealer organization.

The 1919 production program consisted of three models. The now well proven big twin was offered in both standard form, designated the Model N, and electrically equipped, as the NE. There was also the option of either spring frame or solid rear section at a lower

**Right:** *The ill-fated Model K Featherweight of 1916. Its engine a frank copy of the contemporary English Villiers of 1912, it developed insufficient power for US road conditions.*

MODEL K
FEATHERWEIGHT
3 SPEED
PRICE $150.00

# MODEL K — SPECIFICATIONS

MOTOR— Indian single cylinder, two-stroke type. Bore, 2½″, stroke, 2¾″, piston displacement, 13½ cubic inches. Rated horsepower, 2½. Valveless; only three moving parts. Simple, clean, silent, efficient. Maximum road speed developed, 40 miles per hour.

CARBURETOR— Indian automatic, two-stroke type. Throttle gives full range of motor speed from zero to maximum.

IGNITION— Dixie enclosed magneto. Fixed ignition, timed for maximum motor speed. No continuous hand manipulation required.

LUBRICATION— Automatic. Gasoline and oil mixed in correct proportions and drawn into combustion chamber as a unit. Interior of motor amply lubricated by natural functioning of engine without aid of force mechanism. Simple, reliable, economical.

STARTER— Indian Light Pressure type. Simple, positive, reliable, easy to operate. Can be operated by a woman.

CLUTCH— Indian dry plate multiple disc type. Elektra friction lining in contact with steel. Smooth, positive, weatherproof, durable. Adjustable clutch tension for all riding conditions.

HANDLEBARS— Indian upright, adjustable, incorporating motor controls.

TRANSMISSION— Indian three speed gear, progressive system. Rear wheel ratios: 5–1 on high, 9–1 on intermediate, 16–1 on low.

CHAINS— Duckworth double roller, $\frac{3}{16}$″ wide, ½″ pitch.

FRAME— Indian keystone type. Light, strong, graceful lines. Low riding position. Indian Cantilever Comfort Saddle

absorbs all road vibration. Height from saddle to ground, 29″.

FORK— Indian cushion cartridge type. Adjustable for load and riding conditions.

BRAKE— Indian external band brake with foot control. Powerful, quick acting, simple, adjustable.

WHEELS— 26″, 36 spokes front and rear.

TIRES— 26″ x 2¼″, Goodyear detachable.

WHEELBASE— 46¾ inches.

REAR STAND— Indian folding type with anti-rattle mounting. When in use does not interfere with axle adjustment. Snaps to mudguard clip when not in use.

MUFFLER— Indian single expansion chamber type with tail pipe. Silences without back pressure.

TANKS— Gasoline capacity, one gallon. Oil capacity, ½ gallon. Unit combination tank with separate compartments, mounted over motor. Oil tank incorporates ¼ pint detachable measure for measuring correct quantity of oil to be mixed with gasoline for lubricating purposes. Tanks hold enough fuel to travel 100 miles under ordinary conditions.

SADDLE— Indian Cantilever Comfort Saddle.

FOOTRESTS— Indian, rubber covered. Comfortable, roomy. No pedals.

LUGGAGE CARRIER— Standard equipment.

WHEEL GUARDS— Indian molded type, beaded edges.

EQUIPMENT— Toolbox with set of all necessary tools. tire kit, pump.

FINISH— Standard Indian red with nickel trimmings.

16

price, although the latter was not shown in company catalogs. A single cylinder commercial model was also offered, to all purposes a standard spring frame model without the front cylinder. The remaining cylinder was given a longer stroke, for a piston displacement of 33.50 cubic inches. The machine carried the standard three-speed transmission with rather low gearing, for both enhanced pulling power and to promote longevity by preventing over-revving of the engine. This model was intended to haul a sidecar chassis fitted with a commercial box body, and was sold almost entirely as an export model, as its performance capabilities as a solo machine were severely limited. This model was offered for two seasons and for many years later was to continue in commercial service in many countries overseas. Both this and the Standard N model were designed for the fitting of acetylene lighting sets, which had been standard on the previous military models.

The most significant event of 1919 was the undertaking of prototype work on the soon-to-be-famous Indian

*Factory literature showing testers with Featherweight machines on the State Street factory roof during winter weather in 1915.*

Scout, which was wholly the brainchild of Charles B. Franklin. In anticipation of extensive postwar sales, Weschler and others in top company management had decided that an entirely new type of machine was in order, that might attract a wider range of buyers, and which would be lighter, more easily controlled, and, above all, easier to start than the heavyweight V-twin, which by this time had come to dominate nearly all of the domestic production. It was clearly evident from past experience that there was by this time only a very limited market for ultralight machines, but at the same moment the heavyweight V-twin was unsuited to a large portion of a hopefully potential market.

In anticipation of launching a new type of machine, Weschler had previously dispatched Franklin and Butler on a tour of the New England and Eastern area in a Powerplus sidecar outfit, in order to interview dealers

## TESTING FEATHERWEIGHTS ON THE ROOF

HERE'S a picture story of Indian alertness and enterprise during a recent heavy snow storm in Springfield. The roads were impassable but this didn't stop Indian progress for a minute. Here you see a group of Indian testors giving Featherweights a trial spin on the broad factory roof. Thus the good work goes on!

MODEL H
OVERHEAD
VALVE RAC-
ING TYPE
PRICES:
8-VALVE $350.00
4-VALVE $300.00

# MODEL H—SPECIFICATIONS

MOTOR—Indian, special design. Double sets of intake and exhaust valves, mounted in top of cylinder head and mechanically operated. No auxiliary ports. Built in single and twin cylinder types. Piston displacement: single, 30.50 cubic inches; twin, 61 cubic inches. Specially adjusted for racing.

CARBURETOR—Indian automatic.

IGNITION—Dixie high tension enclosed magneto. Indian spark plugs with snap-on terminals.

LUBRICATION—Indian worm driven pump. Positive under all conditions. Supplementary hand pump for special requirements. Sight level indicator in motor base. Mechanical pump feed quickly adjustable to conditions.

HANDLEBARS— Indian dropped racing type, adjustable.

CONTROL—Indian grip control, "twist-of-the-wrist" system.

CLUTCH—Indian dry plate multiple disc clutch on countershaft. Compensating sprocket on direct chain drive without extra charge, optional.

TRANSMISSION—Double roller chains. Independent adjustment.

GEAR RATIO—As specified within range of standard sprocket combinations in stock.

TANKS—Variable capacity, according to specifications within standard stock. Needle valve shut-off in tank. Large filler cap with self-contained priming gun.

FRAME—Indian standard type, chrome vanadium steel tubing with drop forged connections.

FORK—Indian Cradle Spring type, standard. Option, truss fork.

WHEELBASE—53 inches.

WHEELS—28″; 36 spokes front and rear.

TIRES—Goodyear Blue Streak, size to meet requirements.

WHEEL GUARDS—Indian pressed steel racing type.

BRAKES—Indian external band brake with back pedal control. Adjustable.

REAR STAND—Indian folding stand, if specified.

SADDLE—Indian racing.

FINISH—Indian red, nickel trimmings.

FOOTRESTS—Pedals.

NOTE— We reserve the right to make any changes in these specifications that special circumstances may warrant.

17

and riders as to their opinions of various types of machines as well as their personal likes and dislikes concerning different makes. From the results of this survey, Franklin, with some help from Butler, evolved the design of a machine which he had under consideration since 1912, when he had first begun to undertake serious studies in motorcycle design.

Discarding previous concepts, Franklin boldly attacked the problem with an entirely fresh approach to motorcycle design. The engine was a V-twin of 37 cubic inch displacement, with a cylinder angle of 42° and side-by-side valves – essentially a scaled-down version of his successful Powerplus engine. The three-speed gearbox was connected to the engine with a solid primary drive, consisting of three helical pinions running in an oil-tight case, the whole being contained in one unit. All the component parts were of very substantial construction, with large diameter main and upper end bearings and very large valves to provide efficient breathing for good power output. While the cubic capacity of the engine was modest compared to the conventional large displacement V-twin, Franklin reasoned that it was of sufficient power to provide adequate all-around performance to a machine of moderate size and weight, that could be easily handled by the average rider and yet be easy to start.

The frame was of the cradle type, with twin down tubes diverging at the bottom to form a substantial base

*The Light Twin Model O introduced in 1917 as a replacement for the underpowered Model K Featherweight. Generally modern in concept, it featured the early type Hedstrom designed cartridge sprung front fork.*

under the engine and effectively hold the machine together in one solid unit.

The front suspension was similar to that previously fitted to the standard Powerplus models, but was supported by a straight-ended leaf spring, without a scroll. The fuel tank was of a pleasing contour and was carried between the upper and lower top tubes, with two chambers, the larger holding the gasoline, and the smaller forming an oil reservoir to feed the engine's total loss lubrication system.

During that Spring and Summer, several prototype machines were tested under varying conditions of road and weather, in central and western Massachusetts, the testers sometimes venturing into Connecticut and Maryland. The Engineering Department and company officials were well pleased with the results. The small capacity engine was rated at 5hp on the then standard SAE rating, but it actually developed about 12 actual hp. The torque characteristics were such that there was adequate power for serious hill climbing and for top speeds of from 53 to 55mph.

After a few detail changes were made, plans were made to put the Scout into full-scale production for the 1920 sales year, the first machines coming off the assembly lines in late September of 1919.

In order to keep Indian's prowess before the public during the Scout development, Weschler decided that another form of transcontinental record breaking should be attempted, this time with a sidecar outfit. Cannonball Baker was engaged to make the run, using a standard 61 cubic inch machine and with Erle Armstrong as the passenger. Hoping for good weather, the two started

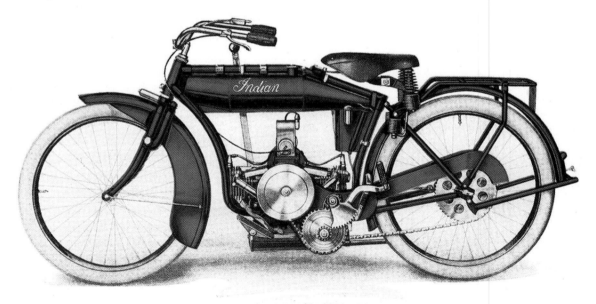

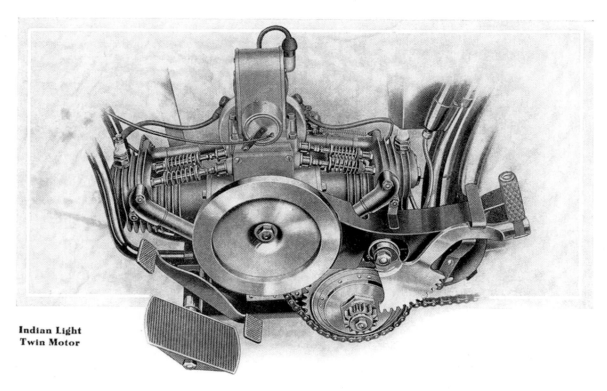

**Indian Light
Twin Motor**

from Springfield early in May. After making good time as far as the Mississippi River, severe rain and consequent muddy conditions were encountered along the almost bottomless roads of the midwest.

Baker managed to flog the outfit through the 'gumbo' until the Kansas plains were reached, but the constant wrenching of the three wheels through the glutinous mud ultimately fractured most of the sidecar chassis tubes. The pair gave up near Emporia, and the remains were shipped back to the factory.

In the meantime, the Board of Directors who had controlled Indian's destinies since 1916, had been showing disenchantment with the company's future. Expected wartime profits had been disappointing, and the substantial cash outlay required for tooling up the planned Scout production with a depleted treasury, and the necessity for raising more capital, did not appear to them to be a sound proposition. Weschler argued that the new model was necessary to expand the company's postwar business, not only as a lightweight machine with a broader public appeal, but also to complement the now archaic Powerplus standard big twin. The matter was somewhat heatedly discussed in several Board meetings, along with the evergreen problem of the scope of expenditures to support continuing competition.

The upshot of the matter was that a new group of investors replaced the Alvord group in December 1919,

*The engine of the Model O opposed twin. Its Douglas antecedents are clearly apparent.*

with Henry H. Skinner, a local Springfield bank executive, as President. As in the case of his predecessor, Skinner gave Weschler virtual command of company operations.

Another important motorcycling event of 1919 was the demise of the Federation of American Motorcyclists. Membership had dwindled after the onset of the war. Production of civilian machines had been curtailed, and there was much public sentiment against sporting events or even Sunday riding during this period. Then, of course, many of the members, as young active men, were in the armed forces. As a result, the FAM's sustaining membership was reduced by half at the time of the Armistice.

The problem was first publicized in the March 6th issue of *Motorcycle and Bicycle Illustrated*, a leading trade magazine of the day managed by H.W. Parsons, who was both owner and editor. The article was written by Leslie D. (Dick) Richards, then Associate Editor.

Richards pointed out the relatively weak condition of the FAM at all levels, and stressed the need of the sport for a strong backbone of both membership participation and efficient management if the organization was to be effective in representing the best interests of motorcycling in general. He suggested that if the FAM could not

*Indian*

INDIAN LIGHT TWIN MODEL O

a machine of light weight, low fuel consumption, moderate cost and sufficient speed and power.

Its speed range is from 6 to 36 miles an hour with a pull conservatively estimated at 2½ horsepower, though dynamometer tests develop a full 4 brake horse power—all that can be put into a true light weight machine.

### SUPER-RESILIENT FORK

A cradle spring front fork similar to that of the Powerplus, but proportionally smaller and without the scroll, is provided. It has five chrome silico manganese steel leaves in the spring. The forks themselves are of heavy construction capable of withstanding strains in excess of any likely to be imposed upon them. This construction gives a very smooth action and excellent shock absorption.

### THE MOTOR

The Light Twin, four-stroke motor is of the long stroke type with outside flywheel and side by side valves. The cylinders, mounted 180 degrees apart, are cast in one piece and are heat-treated, generous cooling ribs being provided and the valve chambers being located on the top to receive the greatest cooling air volume. The bore is 2 inches, the stroke 2½ inches. The piston displacement being 15.70 cubic inches.

All valves are interchangeable and mechanically operated. Located side by side on the top of the cylinders, they are quickly accessible and can be dismounted through removable caps in the cylinder heads.

Cast iron pistons with two rings above the wrist pins are used. The big ends of the connecting rods are of the marine type, being split to permit taking up the bearings for wear by removable shims. The wrist pins are hollow.

The crankshaft is of the double-throw type, being a single forging with cranks set 180 degrees apart. It rides on large bronze bearings and carries the flywheel outside on the left end. All moving parts are individually and collectively balanced to produce the smoothest possible running at all speeds.

Lubrication is by the splash system, oil being fed as required to the motor base by a hand pump located on the one quart oil tank sufficient for 250 miles average running. The two gallon gasoline tank holds sufficient fuel for 160 miles on normal roads.

LIGHT TWIN GEAR SHIFT MECHANISM

The Dixie Magneto is used for ignition, with a fixed spark caring for spark timing automatically. The carburetor is of the two-lever type, with one lever on the handlebar operating the throttle and the other underneath it controlling the air for vaporizing and mixing. A hot air intake pipe is provided to insure even firing at all motor speeds and to thoroughly vaporize the inferior fuel of today, utilizing every particle for power and wasting none.

The gears are shifted by a short, strong arm working over a horizontal quadrant above the top tube. The quadrant is slotted. Gear shifting is a simple, quick operation on the lightweight.

be strengthened, a new group should be formed to take its place.

Further comment was next forthcoming from Irwin D. Allen of Akron, Ohio, then President of the FAM. Allen admitted the growing weakness of the FAM and cited the managerial and financial problems extant in keeping the organization viable, in the face of declining interest from the membership at large. He frankly stated that if riders in general did not wish to support the FAM in its present form, the formation of another body was definitely in order, and that the FAM management would gladly step aside if such were deemed necessary.

During these discussions, Parsons published an editorial advocating immediate action either to reorganize the FAM or institute another body to take its place.

At the annual meeting of the American Motorcycle Manufacturers Association, now known as the Motorcycle and Allied Trades Association, Parsons spoke at length on the FAM's existing weaknesses and the need for a strong body to govern motorcycle competition. He ultimately moved and was seconded, after much general discussion, that the M&ATA take over the functions of the FAM until such time as a new governing body could be organized. Parsons was promptly nominated and elected to serve as the chairman of a committee to carry out this edict.

During subsequent meetings, under the guidance of M&ATA officials, it was decided to form a new organization known as the American Motorcycle Association, which was to be free and independent of trade influence and which was to be managed and governed by a freely elected group of officers from the ranks of the membership.

At the annual motorcycle show held in Chicago, in January 1920, competition control, the most critical of motorcycling activities, was turned over to one A.B. Coffman, as Chairman. An able administrator, Coffman's personality did not suit many of the members, as he was reported as being often arrogant and disagreeable. He was replaced the following year by Douglas Hobart, a former draftsman in Indian's Engineering Department. The competition headquarters were then moved from New York to Hobart's home in Hartford, Conn.

L.D. Richards, to whom much credit is due in the ultimate formation of the AMA, had become interested in motorcycles in the pioneer era when, as a fifteen year old schoolboy in 1910, he purloined a ride on a tradesman's

Indian sidecar outfit. His motorcycling activities were subsequently interrupted when he enlisted in the navy.

After his separation from service in 1917, he purchased a second-hand standard Indian Powerplus model and joined the Crotona Motorcycle Club, which was then one of the larger motorcycle clubs of the day and had extensive quarters in the Bronx. A skilled rider of no mean ability, he was subsequently elected Road Captain. Possessed of natural journalistic ability, he was shortly thereafter invited to join the staff of *Motorcycle and Bicycle Illustrated* by H.W. Parsons. With a keen interest in motorcycle affairs, Richards became a tireless promoter of the industry, and was particularly concerned with sales orientation and development of utility and commercial machines.

He attained considerable notoriety in sporting circles when, in the Spring of 1919, he won the coveted Excelsior-Henderson trophy, as well as the Harley-Davidson trophy, for the highest solo score in the Crotona Motorcycle Club's 24-hour endurance run, a fixture for some years in Eastern competition circles.

The course this year was from the club house in the Bronx through Monticello, Hinghamton, to Albany, thence to Pittsfield and Springfield, Massachusetts, the final return lap to New York City via Hartford, Connecticut, Danbury and White Plains, for a distance of 535 miles.

Unlike many of the competitors, Richards carefully toured the course ahead of time, making a mental note of the hazards if wet weather intervened.

There were factory teams entered by Indian, captained by Cannonball Baker, Harley-Davidson, Excelsior, Reading-Standard, and Thor, along with many private entrants.

Billed as a novice rider, Richards' prior surveys enabled him to negotiate successfully the now muddy roads, as the expected hard rain had started shortly after the riders started. Just outside of Oneonta, New York, Richards led Baker through a particularly muddy stretch of road. He was able to make his way over it, but Baker, who had entered the contest with his usual eclat, and with no prior survey of the course, skidded into a puddle, bent his forks and filled his engine with water, effectively terminating his ride.

Out of a possible score of 1,000 points, Richards ended up with a remarkable 998. Julius Stern, also Indian mounted, was second, with 996.

Baker, with his usual generosity, was effusive with congratulations for Richards, and the two became lifelong friends.

In the meantime, back at the Indian factory, Weschler was busily engaged with his characteristic enthusiasm in planning the next year's production schedule and in rearranging his executive staff. He encouraged loyal and valuable members to stay on, and discharged those whom he felt had either outlasted their usefulness or who had shown by their attitude that they were not in accord with continuing company policies.

Being well aware of the importance of expanding Indian's already profitable export markets, Weschler retained Bill McCann as Export Manager, to which position he had been installed by President Hendee in 1916. McCann had performed sterling service in this regard and had already laid plans to revitalize the overseas business, which had been severely dislocated by the war.

To act as an overseas agent, McCann promoted George Sherman to this post. Sherman was a member of the Advertising Department and a man of recognized abilities in marketing, who had great enthusiasm for Indian's cause. A flamboyant and somewhat theatrical individual, Sherman was credited with building up William Wrigley's burgeoning chewing gum empire in the earlier years of the century, enabling him to amass a multimillion dollar fortune.

Sherman departed for Europe in the Summer of 1919, and eschewing his usual theatrics, negotiated an agreement with the prestigious R.S. Stokvis and Sonen, Dutch import-export firm, to handle Indian distribution and sales in Europe. This company, based in Rotterdam, had extensive trade connections throughout Europe and other countries, and chartered their own fleet of ships to service their various enterprises. By Spring of the following year, their agents had awarded franchises to dealers in the principal European countries.

Billy Wells continued his importation of Indian machines into the United Kingdom, under the original agreement made with President Hendee in 1908. The big standard twins were popular with both solo and side-car riders, the former often fitting sports type handlebars for the TT effect. In anticipation of expanding postwar sales, and in need of larger quarters for both showroom and repair facilities, Wells moved from the original Great Portland Street building to larger premises at 368 Euston Street.

In the reorganization of the factory personnel, Weschler fired John J. O'Conner and Jack Priest, ostensibly because they had been lately spending much of their working time at the bar in the nearby Highland Hotel. It was also alleged that both were in the habit of receiving kickbacks from various local printing plants that had company contracts to produce Indian's vast volume of catalogs and sales literature. Priest moved to New York and re-entered the advertising business. O'Conner went west to Los Angeles, where he subsequently became editor of the *Western Motorcyclist and Bicyclist* magazine, which later became *The Motorcyclist*.

In commenting on the episode in later years, O'Conner told the author that he had acted properly, as he considered himself an independent agent for Indian's advertising media. Whatever the equity of the matter, it was well known in Springfield that O'Conner was often antagonistic toward Weschler's company policies, and that the latter was often critical of both O'Conner's and Priest's working habits.

Edward Buffam, an aging survivor of the high wheel bicycle era and Indian's initial founding, was carried on the company rolls as Sales Manager, with J.B. MacNaughton as his assistant. The two were never the best of friends and were frequently at odds over policy matters.

A newcomer, Francis (Frank) I. Waters, replaced Priest as the head of the Advertising Department. Another newcomer, L.D. 'Dick' Richards, replaced O'Conner. Weschler had been greatly impressed by Richards' opinions respecting the reorganization of the FAM and his journalistic ability as well as by the fact that he was an Indian enthusiast.

Other new young employees were Robert (Bob) Haley, who headed the Order Department, and William (Bill) Carey, who headed the Parts Department. Arthur (Art) Anderson headed the Bicycle Department, but later was transferred to the Sales Department.

Another innovation was the conversion of the former customer service department that was established to repair owners' machines, and was formerly managed by Myron Warner, into a dealers' service facility to provide short educational courses to mechanics staffing Indian's dealerships. These two week courses were held throughout the winter months, and with the payment of a modest fee, the student could select one of several categories of service and repair instruction.

The school was under the management of Erle Armstrong. Once known as 'Red', but latterly known as 'Pop', he endeared himself through the years to a large number of aspiring Indian mechanics, many of whom subsequently acquired dealerships.

It is evident that Weschler had intuitive premonition of the difficult days ahead for the motorcycle industry, and wisely decided to augment the staff by hiring a group of young motorcycle enthusiasts to implement the challenging postwar era.

In addition, a now augmented staff of about fifty clerical workers were distributed throughout the various Departments, to handle bookkeeping, typing, filing, mailing and other ancillary services. The production force at this time numbered about 1,800 men.

The company reorganization was not accomplished without some dissention among the staff. Some, quite naturally, resented the discharging of certain of their friends. Others were not happy in being shifted to other Departments. A few of the senior executives, including Buffam and MacNaughton, resented Weschler's expanded authority. These two were subsequently reported to confer with certain of their acquaintances among the Board of Directors, in an effort to undermine the former's authority or to question his judgment concerning policy matters. These minor unpleasantries were less important, however, than the enthusiasm of most of the new and younger staff members, and the dedication of most of the older employees, who were loyal to Weschler and were sympathetic with his dedication to Indian's cause.

To strengthen Indian's dealer effectiveness, Weschler augmented the crew of the company's traveling representatives, which before the war had been staffed to cover all geographical regions of the country. These men performed the highly important task of maintaining direct liaison between management and Indian's retail

**Above:** *Erwin G. Baker in New Zealand during his record breaking runs in the winter of 1919.* (The Archives of the Hendee Manufacturing Company)

**Right:** *Two typical hard-riding Indian enthusiasts outside the Indian factory in 1918. Leslie D. Richards (left) and Oliver Berkheimer, Bronx Indian dealer on their 1917 Powerplus machines.* (Leslie D. Richards)

sales outlets. Most of these men were dedicated Indian enthusiasts, and were able to lend the dealers much moral support.

In order to attempt to salvage additional profits from the generally unprofitable War Department contracts, Weschler dispatched Frank Long and W. Stanley Bouton on a trip to England and Europe, to ascertain whether or not any of the surplus or condemned Indian military models could be recovered. It was hoped that these machines, if available, could be dismantled for spare parts or remanufactured. Long, through his political connections in Washington, had secured a commission in the Army as a Major, which in turn enabled him to obtain permission for this survey through the proper channels. After duly examining large numbers of machines at various military depots, Long concluded that their generally poor condition would render the trouble and expense of shipping them home economically impractical.

The immediate postwar period saw the greatest interest in motorcycle competition in the United States that had yet been seen. A war weary and somewhat disillusioned people clamored for new thrills and excitement, and all forms of professional and amateur sports were receiving increasing attention from the populace suddenly relieved of the pressures of the war effort.

The Harley-Davidson Company emerged from the war in a relatively much stronger position than either of its chief rivals, Excelsior and Indian, as they had held government contracts to the minimum, totalling only 15,000 machines, and had managed to not only expand civilian production but carefully nurtured and expanded their dealer organization at the expense of their rivals. They almost immediately threw down the gauntlet to their competitors and announced that they were launching an extensive competition campaign. In anticipation of increased sales volume, the management went forward with plans to build a giant factory on Juneau Street, in Milwaukee, which was to be slightly larger than Indian's in Springfield – up to that time the largest in the world.

Many of the old board tracks which had fallen into disrepair through the ravages of time and weather, were refurbished, and new and larger tracks were built in many of the principal cities. Harley-Davidson, which heretofore had not concentrated on board track competition, were now launching an all-out challenge to Indian's leadership. Chief Engineer and Competition Manager Bill Ottaway assembled his famous stable of professional stars, soon to become known as the 'Wrecking Crew', consisting of Fred Ludlow, Ralph Hepburn, Albert 'Shrimp' Burns, and the veteran Otto Walker, together with Leslie 'Red' Parkhurst.

The first big event of the year was the 200 mile Championship race held on June 22nd, 1919, at Los Angeles' Ascot Speedway, before an enthusiastic crowd of 10,000 fans. Indian's entrants included Bill Church, Dave Kinney, Bob Newman, Ralph Sullivan and Ray Weishaar. Excelsior fielded a strong team with Roy Artley, Wells Bennett and M. Tice.

On the rolling start, Weishaar streaked ahead of the field, but soon was overhauled by Hepburn, and the two led the pack in a seesaw contest, the latter, as a newcomer, fighting furiously to prove himself. Hepburn ultimately came in first, to win both the Firestone trophy and the Harley-Davidson cup, as well as the $650.00 winner's purse. The Harley team swept the board to take all six places.

On July 5th, the Nebraska State Championship Meet was held on the rough 1.8 mile oval at Grand Island. Indian's team consisted of Gene Walker, Roy Artley and Waldo Korn. Harley's 'Wrecking Crew' again garnered top honors, with Hepburn winning the 25-mile event. Gene Walker won the 10-miler, with Artley coming in third behind Weishaar.

On July 14th, the Driving Park Mile at Columbus, Ohio, was the scene of another duel between the great Indian team of Jim Davis and Gene Walker and Harley aces 'Shrimp' Burns and 'Red' Parkhurst. There existed a bitter intra-team rivalry between Davis and Gene Walker and as the two ran neck and neck ahead of the pack in the 5-mile race, they began trading punches in the stretch. The referee finally called the race a no contest, much to the consternation of Indian Race Manager, Charles Spencer. It was later reported that the two finally settled the matter under the grandstand, after the races were over.

The big board track contest of the year took place at Sheepshead Bay, Long Island. Otto Walker, on an eight valve Harley, won the two mile dash. Gene Walker, on an Indian, took the 10-mile event at 95mph. Ray Weishaar, on another eight valve Harley, broke Lee Humiston's Excelsior record for the 50-mile event. 'Shrimp' Burns, also Harley mounted, turned the 100 miles in an hour and seven minutes. Indian took the sidecar event, a new post war feature in board track racing, with Teddy Carroll lapping the field to win the 25-mile championship.

Interest in the desert races had lagged during the war. The course was extremely hazardous for both men and machines, and there was the ever-present danger of encountering one of the small bands of Mexican guerrillas who were constantly crossing the border to steal cattle.

In March 1919, Roy Artley on a standard 61 inch Indian twin made a record-breaking run from Los Angeles to San Diego, making 142 miles in 127 minutes.

*Erwin G. Baker with Erle Armstrong as passenger shown during a factory effort to break the transcontinental side-car record in the spring of 1919 …*

*… Confident at the start in Springfield, they were defeated by horrendous road conditions in the midwest …*

*… as attested by the condition of the outfit as shipped back to Springfield.* (Leslie D. Richards)

In May, he decided to attack Lorenzo Boido's 1914 record San Diego to Phoenix run, this time on a new Henderson Four. After two false starts, involving engine failure soon after leaving San Diego, he finally made the 394 miles on the somewhat improved roads, in 13 hours, ten minutes, for a new record.

In the Spring of 1920 he tried again, on this occasion on his Indian twin. Taking a route totalling 416 miles, he established a new record of 12 hours, 28 minutes. This time was not beaten until the mid-1930's, the roads by that time being almost all paved.

The first important postwar road race was held at Marion, Indiana, on September 1st. The course laid out over a country road was five miles long and consisted of two long straights, connected by a series of sharp curves. It was estimated that more than 15,000 spectators lined the course to see the now famous Harley 'Wrecking Crew' win all six places, with 'Red' Parkhurst coming in first, at 66.6mph.

The Indian management and many enthusiasts were much chagrined at Harley-Davidson's postwar supremacy in competition, but their victories had been won at a tremendous cost in both money and effort expended in engineering development and racing team management. Indian had stretched their meager racing budget to the limit in order to meet Harley's challenge. Most of their racing equipment was from prewar days as the pressures of war production had precluded much attention to the competition activities after 1916.

The surviving big three manufacturers, in anticipation of accelerated postwar sales, faced the 1920 season with much optimism. Indian's huge manufacturing complex had an annual production capacity of 35,000 machines. Harley-Davidson was potentially able to equal Indian's production with the building of their new factory, which was completed in April. Excelsior's facilities were somewhat smaller, but it has been estimated that they had the production capacity to turn out at least 25,000 units each year, comprising both Henderson Fours and Excelsior twins. The newly-organised Ace Company in Philadelphia announced an ambitious sales program of 4,000 machines for 1920. A few other manufacturers were still in limited production, such as Cleveland, Reading-Standard, Emblem, Schickel and Iver Johnson, together with a few lesser-known makes.

The motorcycling sensation of the year was, of course, the introduction of the Scout, which was first shown to the public at the National Motorcycle Show held that year at the old Coliseum, in Chicago. There was initially some skepticism within Indian's management regarding the machine's public acceptance, as it was considerably smaller and less powerful than the 61 cubic inch twins that had become more or less the standard American Motorcycle. Then there was the overlying apprehension of failure with the introduction of another small machine, following the marketing problems with the 'Featherweight' and the Model O.

But soon the faith of Weschler, Franklin and Tommy Butler, who worked closely with the Scout, was vindicated after the first few demonstration machines came into the hands of various dealers. The breathing capabilities of the engine, with its oversized valves, made for a surprising power development, and for its then modest cylinder displacement, its performance was nothing short of amazing.

Servicing and overhauling was facilitated by the accessible position of the engine-gearbox unit. It was said that an experienced mechanic could remove the engine, complete a general overhaul, replace it and road test the machine in an eight-hour working day.

As the public response to the Scout was almost immediate, the management planned a large production schedule and a night shift was added in March to enhance production. Large orders came in from Australasia, England, and from R.S. Stokvis and Sonen for the European markets.

The now venerable Powerplus twin was continued, with a generator powered lighting set being carried on a bracket in front of the down tube and driven by a belt, its pulley attached to the inner face of the engine sprocket. In deference to the needs of sidecar enthusiasts, a 74 cubic inch version of the big twin was made available for extra speed and power. Many solo riders ordered these machines for their enhanced performance. These models enjoyed continuing popularity in England, for both solo and sidecar use, the former often being fitted with dropped-type handlebars.

The heavy-duty 33 cubic inch commercial single was also available to special order, although not listed in the regular catalogs and was largely produced for the export market, with a commercial box sidecar.

It was the Scout, however, that occupied the spotlight of general interest. Of all makes and models produced worldwide, it soon became considered in many quarters as the best, all-around, general purpose machine available anywhere. Its performance was such that it was suitable for general law enforcement and highway patrol duties. The State of Massachusetts soon purchased a fleet of 100 Scouts for this work, and during the next few years, the State of Pennsylvania built up a group of about 450 machines, for the same purpose.

On the sporting side, Scouts in the hands of private owners were entered in all categories of speed and endurance contests, which resulted in victories almost too numerous to mention. A noteworthy performance was the breaking of the long-standing 24-hour endurance road record in Australia. On August 28th, 1920, H.A. Parsons covered 1,114 miles in 24 hours, over the varied road course near Victoria. The new record bettered the former mark by over 250 miles. In the process, Parsons set a new record of 579 miles for twelve hours, and beat all records from one hour upwards.

The power of Franklin's new 37 cubic inch engine was such that it found much favor, especially overseas, as a sidecar machine. It could haul a light outfit with a passenger effortlessly, at cruising speeds of 40mph.

The Scout's only domestic competitor was the horizontally-opposed 37 cubic inch twin, announced in the same year by Harley-Davidson. Known as the Sport Twin, it was similar in size and weight to the Scout. Like Indian's Model O of 1917, its engine design owed much to the contemporary English Douglas. A smooth-running machine that was pleasant to ride and handle, it lacked the power development and speed of the Scout and was of somewhat unorthodox appearance, at least to American riders. It was mildly popular in the United States and enjoyed a brief vogue in England and Australia. The author rode one of these machines briefly in the late 1920's and immediately noted its inferior performance as compared to the more popular Scout. After limited production for two seasons, it was discontinued after 1922.

Harley-Davidson renewed their competition challenge to their two principal competitors for the 1920 season. Learning that Indian was planning an all-out assault on existing world straightaway speed records at Daytona Beach, Florida, Harley-Davidson dispatched in February a competition team of Otto Walker, 'Red' Parkhurst and Fred Ludlow, along with team manager R.W. Enos and Hap Scherer of the Advertising Department, to the famous Florida course.

Bad weather prevailed for several days, but with clearing skies, Ludlow made a record one-way run of 103mph on Friday, February 13th, with a modified pocket valve motor.

Parkhurst uncrated a special 68 cubic inch eight-valve machine, and on the 16th made a phenomenal run of 114mph. On the next day, a special bullet-shaped sidecar was fitted to this machine, and with Ludlow as the passenger, the outfit topped 99mph, under difficult conditions of rain and soft sand. There was some doubt in the trade that the 68 cubic inch records would stand, as all previous rulings of the FAM were for engines of 61 cubic inch displacement.

Not to be outdone, the Indian team consisting of Gene Walker and an aspiring amateur named James McBride,

along with competition manager, Charles Spencer and two mechanics, arrived at the beach the following April. They had come to challenge Harley-Davidson's records, together with some International records as well.

For a recapitulation of an eyewitness account of the proceedings, we are indebted to Dr. Joseph Bailey of the Vintage Motor Cycle Club.

In the 61 cubic inch or 1,000cc class, Walker and McBride were each to ride eight valve board track-type models, as well as stock side-valve Powerplus engines mounted in racing frames. For the 500cc or 30.50 cubic inch class, each was to ride a four-valve racing single.

The course had already been carefully surveyed for distances of one kilometer to five miles, the speeds being measured by the Warner electrical timing device, the official apparatus of the AM & ATA and the American Automobile Association. The official timer from the AAA was R. A. Leavell.

The timing apparatus was set up on April 12th for Walker to make a trial run on his eight-valve machine, over the flying mile. The eastern Florida coast at Daytona runs in a northwest to southeast direction, and Walker elected to run up the course to take advantage of the strong southerly wind that was blowing. The run astonished everyone, including Leavell, as the timer showed 113.71mph. To check the results, Walker made another run, with almost the same speed recorded.

Much elated, Walker decided to go for the international flying start kilometer and mile records, with both the 1,000cc and 500cc classes. The strong wind was still blowing, and a tabulation of his kilometer times gives a fair approximation of its strength. With the wind he was timed at 19.32 seconds, or 115.78mph. On the return run he was slower at 23.88 seconds, or 93.67mph, with a mean time for the two runs of 21.60 seconds for a 103.56mph average. With the runs with the 500cc single, it was much the same story, 25.06 seconds, 89.26mph on the first run over the kilometer, 29.36 seconds, 76.18mph on the return. The average times were 27.21 seconds, 82.20mph. It could be argued that both machines were overgeared for the return runs into the wind, but apparently everything else was satisfactory and Walker and the company officials seemed well satisfied with the results.

A couple of days later Walker and McBride had a field day with a succession of flying start one way runs, over the kilometer, mile, two mile, and five mile courses. But of these, only Walker's 108.71mph over the five miles on the 1,000cc, eight-valver and his 85.66mph on the 500cc single would be eligible for international ratification.

McBride's stock Powerplus machine, built up from standard parts, but very carefully tuned, covered the mile at 99.25mph and the five miles at 95.08mph. His 500cc eight-valver recorded 77.69mph for the five miles. These were exceptional speeds, but the wind was still blowing.

These times were widely hailed in the United States by the Indian factory and enthusiasts, especially as much was made of the fact that the twins adhered to the official 61 cubic inch or 1,000cc measurement. They were regarded with some skepticism in England and Europe, however, as being abnormally fast on a beach course. However, only one-way runs were accepted at that time as records, and the Indian camp could scarcely be expected to record the slowest of their two-way runs for certification purposes. As the United States' affiliation with the FICM was ever tenuous at best, Walker's and McBride's accomplishments at Daytona were never recognized in the international record books. Walker's eight-valve engine is presently on view at Bill Tuthill's Museum of Speed at Daytona Beach.

The first championship meet of 1920 was held in Los Angeles' Ascot Park, which drew a record crowd of 25,000 spectators. Albert Burns, who had now switched to Indians, opened the 25-mile National with a terrific burst of speed at the start. He was closely followed by Otto Walker on one of Bill Ottaway's new eight valvers, together with newcomer Bob Newman, on an Indian. Burns rode at a suicidal pace, nearly sliding out several times. At the finish he was well ahead of the pack and set new record times for 5, 10, 15 and 20 miles. His win at 80.89mph on the rough track was a source of jubilation for the Indian camp, after the numerous defeats of the preceding year.

The 50-mile National was another crowd thriller at Ascot, with several spectacular near-fatalities. Ray Weishaar, on a Harley eight-valver, blew a rear tire and made a bruising 200-foot slide to the edge of the track. Miraculously, he was unhurt, but his machine was badly battered. In the 28th mile, Bill Church, on an Indian, led Joe Wolters, riding a new overhead camshaft Excelsior machine, into a too-fast turn. The rear tire blew, skidding Church and his machine across the track in a trail of flaming gasoline. Wolters courageously put his machine down to avoid the prostrate Church. From the stands it appeared that both riders were in the midst of the fire, but fortunately neither rider was seriously injured.

Harley's ace rider, Otto Walker, provided the final thrill of the day when he swooped into a fast turn, trying for second place in the last mile. To avoid hitting the fence, he was forced to down his machine, missing the obstruction by inches. He managed to remount, much to the relief of the spectators and came in third behind Albert Burns and Bob Newman, on Indians.

Another thrilling race meet was held at the old North Randall mile track south of Cleveland, Ohio, on September 19th, when most of the well-known professionals clashed on this country oval.

The first event was the dash for the National One Mile Championship between Gene Walker, Albert Burns and Don Marks on Indians, with Jim Davis, Ralph Hepburn and Fred Ludlow on Harleys. The pack ran in almost a dead heat, until Gene Walker gunned his Indian just before the finish line to win, breaking his own one-mile record in 45²⁄₅th seconds.

The 5-mile sidecar event was a sizzling duel between Floyd Dreyer and Sam Riddle, on Indian Flexi outfits, and Jiggs Price and William P. Governor, on Harleys. Price rode at full bore to pass both Riddle and Dreyer, winding up with the fastest 5 miles ever made with a sidecar up to that time, a 4:33³⁄₅ record.

Gene Walker next blazed through a new 5 mile solo mark of 3:51.

Dreyer and Price staged an almost dead heat battle in the 10-mile sidecar sprint race, but Dreyer's desperate burst of speed was a little short at the finish. Price and his Harley outfit won at a wheel length, for a new national record of 9 minutes, 10 seconds.

The 10-mile solo record was a new mark of 7:53 when Albert Burns, this time riding one of Charles B. Franklin's new side valve racers, nosed out Harley-mounted Jim Davis by a machine's length, at the finish.

In the 25-mile feature, Gene Walker tangled with the formidable Fred Ludlow. Walker maintained a slight lead until he spilled near the finish. Ludlow blasted his Harley into the lead, closely followed by Jim Davis, with Ralph Hepburn just behind. The latter spun out when his rear wheel collapsed, allowing Don Marks, Indian, to come in third.

The final 1920 championship meet was held on October 23rd at Readville, Massachusetts. Indian's Gene Walker clipped a fraction of a mile from his 5-mile record, to win in 3:50⁴⁄₅. Jiggs Price, with his Harley outfit, hung up a new national sidecar record for 2 miles, at 1:49¹⁄₅.

The 10-mile National was mishandled by the officials. Seven riders were allowed to start instead of six, as specified by the rules. The Indian team, through their manager, Charles Spencer, lodged a protest. An elimination heat was ordered, with the seventh man to finish to be scratched. In this heat Gene Walker dropped out due to a fouled spark plug. As he held the 10-mile record, Spencer argued that he should be allowed another try. The officials refused, and the entire Indian team walked out on the event. Ralph Hepburn then proceeded to 'win' the event over his Harley team mates, who now comprised the entire field.

In spite of high hopes on the part of the motorcycle industry for record sales in the first postwar years, public

interest in two-wheelers, in the United States at least, appeared to be waning. The problem was compounded by inflated prices of raw materials and accessory components due to the war, and also by the fact that production labor was demanding higher wages. While the mass-produced cheap car, notably Ford, had heretofore not offered serious competition to motorcycles, its price was now only slightly higher than that of a standard big twin sidecar outfit. Other auto manufacturers announced plans to enter the low-priced field, including the irrepressible William (Billy) Durant, who had formerly put together the massively growing General Motors combine.

As a paradox, the export market for American machines appeared healthy as the low cost car was not yet a reality in either England or Europe, although Ford had already announced an ambitious overseas manufacturing program and had built a factory in England just before the war. In any case, the motorcycle still remained as the most economical mode of transport in every overseas area.

Indian had already made extensive plans for mass production of the well received Scout, and considerable sums of money had been expended for new dies and tooling, much of it designed by Franklin in the Fall of 1919. Production difficulties occurred, however, due to the ever-rising costs of materials, and the continuing demand on the part of the production force for higher wages. The problem was compounded by the inability of Indian's sales organization, still headed by Edward Buffam, to forecast with accuracy sales demand and machine distribution, and of the buying organization to

*Erwin G. Baker at speed somewhere in the Mojave Desert during a transcontinental record attempt in the summer of 1919. Note the shortened mudguards.* (Leslie D. Richards)

*Leslie D. (Dick) Richards.* (Thompson Studio)

correctly estimate or cost out material and accessory requirements.

In an effort to centralize responsibility for both sales and production, and in addition to his general managerial duties, Frank Weschler was authorized by President Skinner and the Board of Directors to directly oversee the activities of the Production Department. This led to some hard feelings on the part of some of the executives formerly responsible, including a growing conflict between Buffam, MacNaughton and Weschler over what exact course of action was to be followed. Weschler put the whole production operation in the capable hands of

*Herbert Le Vack is congratulated by Billy Wells (center, in hat) after winning the 1920 Brooklands Gold Cup race at 70.6mph, in spite of numerous stops for tire changes. The machine is a 61 cu in factory Powerplus racer.* **(The Archives of the Hendee Manufacturing Company)**

Plant Superintendent, Theron L. Loose. At this juncture, Charles Gustafson, Sr. resigned as Chief Engineer. Associates reported that he felt his position had been eroded by Franklin with his now successful Scout, the problem being further compounded by now frequent disagreements between the two over certain details of Scout design. Charles Gustafson, Jr., however, remained with the company for some years, serving in both the Racing and Experimental Departments, where his outstanding mechanical abilities were of continuing value to the company. Franklin was immediately appointed Chief Designer and Engineer.

To add further to the company's woes, the treasury had been seriously depleted by the unprofitable war contracts, along with the loss of many customers and dealers who had deserted to other makes, when machines and spare parts had become unavailable. Various members of the Sales Department were

dispatched across the country on fence-mending expeditions and other attempts to bring some of these former enthusiasts back into the fold. Tommy Butler was sent to Chicago to reorganize the formerly active branch in that city. Among the employees there was a young enthusiast in the Service Department named Ray E. Garner who, a couple of years later, moved to Portland, Oregon, to take over a dealership there. The author's authentically restored 1938 Four was originally sold by Garner to the Portland Police Department.

Leslie D. Richards, who had joined the company in January 1920, as Publicity Manager tackled his new position with much dedication. A part of his job was to write publicity articles for submission to the various trade publications. The general tone of these writings, as turned out by all motorcycle publicity departments in those days, was one of lavish praise for the virtues of the make in question, along with glowingly optimistic reports about the future of motorcycle sales. Another of his duties was to revive Indian's bimonthly house organ, *Honest Injun*, which had languished during the company's post war difficulties. It subsequently reappeared as the *Wigwam News*, and adhered to the same general format as before.

The realities of the actual status of the now contemporary motorcycle market were carefully glossed over or patently ignored, the object being to convey to the motorcycling public and other readers of potential motorcycling interest that all was lovely in the garden. This style of approach had been largely instigated by O'Conner during the several years in which he was associated with Indian, and most of the other competition copy writers had followed suit, although up to that time O'Conner had been the acknowledged past master of this type of prose.

Richards had in a very short space of time become well conversant with the growing problems of the postwar motorcycle industry. A thoughtful man, he almost at once became concerned with the now alarming trend of events, and of the many problems which were now threatening Indian as well as the other competitive makes. Other members of the industry, including executives of Excelsior and Harley-Davidson, were also becoming concerned about generally declining sales, including one Hap Scherer, who was Publicity Manager for Harley.

The pattern of blatantly distorted publicity writings emanating from the various motorcycle factories was countenanced by the trade publications themselves. These magazines, which were wholly dependent upon the industry for their survival, were loath to embark on any sort of independent editorial policies. Nothing critical or objective in the way of results of road tests or comments on even glaring technical faults in newly-introduced machines were ever aired, as the editors feared offending their supporting advertisers. With such ostrich-like policies, prospective buyers and especially newcomers to the sport had no source of honest evaluation of either machines or accessories. As the status of the industry declined, it was more or less tacitly agreed among both manufacturers and journalists that actual production figures were never to be revealed. In this continuing policy, projections, when referred to in this area, were either purposely vague or wildly optimistic.

This veil of silence was at long last journalistically penetrated, not, quite naturally, by the sychophantic motorcycling press, but in the pages of a trade paper published for the benefit of the automobile industry.

This important incident came about in a rather indirect way. Norman G. Shidle was a young automotive enthusiast with a background of technical training and a flair for journalism who, in 1919, had founded a publication called *Automotive Industries*. Aside from his interest in technical advances and production problems of the industry, he had become concerned with matters of sales and marketing.

While design progress and the perfection of mass production techniques had resulted in well over eight million automobiles being registered in the United States by the end of the war, more than two-thirds of all the rest of the world combined, all was not well within a supposedly healthy industry. There had been an alarming number of failures within the ranks of the contemporary manufacturers, many of which were attributed to their inability properly to assess the market demands and otherwise to supply types and models of machines most suited to potential customers.

Shidle sought to point out solutions to these problems in a series of articles in his magazine, in the field of scientific market analysis. It might well be stated that he was a pioneer in an area which, today, is an inherent part of general industrial management. To enhance his knowledge of the subject, he had subsidized a member of his staff, one Raymond Prescott, in studies in advanced economics at Columbia University.

In a continuing series of articles, Shidle sought to alert automobile manufacturers to the need of a thorough market analysis for the planning of new models, or for planning production schedules for those currently in process of manufacture.

Dick Richards, along with his duties of writing Indian publicity, was currently engaged in studying Shidle's and other offerings in the automotive marketing field, and he noted the lack of any exploration of motorcycling problems. After some thought he ultimately wrote to Shidle, commenting on his automotive articles and suggesting that some attention should be paid to motorcycle marketing.

The upshot of the matter was that Shidle attended the 1921 National Motorcycle Show held that year in New York's Madison Square Garden. He arranged for a meeting at a nearby hotel with Richards, Hap Scherer, Advertising Manager of Harley-Davidson, and with representatives of the Advertising staffs of Excelsior and Reading-Standard. His object in conferring with these

people was to obtain from them information concerning past production figures, an enumeration of various types of machines produced, together with their methods of projecting future sales and material purchases to coincide with them. In return, he and his staff would conduct a marketing analysis of the motorcycle industry.

Shidle found that he was working within a rather sensitive area as, with generally declining sales, none of the manufacturers had been revealing production figures or sales projections to the public, still less to their competitors.

In reminiscing about this meeting, Richards recalls that he was somewhat skeptical about Shidle's motives, as being primarily an automotive economist, he had been working within an industry of which a segment was offering stiff competition to the motorcycle.

The motorcycling representatives became convinced of Shidle's sincerity in offering them aid in their marketing efforts, and after prolonged discussion, agreed to furnish him with the necessary information. It was mutually decided to keep the whole affair a close secret, as it was an admitted fact that if the top management of the various companies got wind of the matter, the employees involved would face instant dismissal for divulging production and sales data.

During subsequent discussions of holding further meetings, the Excelsior representative elected to retire from the group, leaving Richards of Indian, Hap Scherer of Harley-Davidson, and an advertising executive of Reading-Standard, whose name is now forgotten. This group had several meetings with Shidle and Prescott, during the Spring of 1921. In order to insure strict secrecy, they met clandestinely in Shidle's office in New York, the motorcycle members making the trip on the pretext of other business commitments.

Shidle's and Prescott's ultimate conclusions regarding declining motorcycle sales generally coincided with the already conceived ideas of both Richards and Scherer, namely that the industry's general emphasis on speed and power, combined with extensive commitments to racing competition, had alienated a large segment of the buying public. The now classic American heavyweight V-twin required much muscular effort to start, was difficult to manhandle in confined spaces, was possessed of an offensive exhaust noise due to inadequate silencing, and generally appealed only to young, athletic men with a penchant for high speed travel.

The emphasis on competition and racing, while lately appealing to large crowds of spectators seeking thrills and excitement, had effectively implanted in the public mind that motorcycle riding was a dangerous undertaking, and few, if any of those buying tickets would ever be

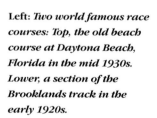

**Above and right:** *Two views of a 1920 61cu in Powerplus model of 1920 as restored by Vintage Motor Cycle Club member Colin Spong. The flat English style handlebars must be noted.* (Colin Spong)

**Left:** *Two world famous race courses: Top, the old beach course at Daytona Beach, Florida in the mid 1930s. Lower, a section of the Brooklands track in the early 1920s.*

interested in motorcycling other than as a gladiatorial contest to be watched but not participated in individually.

The further conclusions were that a potentially vast market of low-powered, low-cost utility machines of light weight and easy starting capabilities had been totally ignored.

Shidle published his conclusions in a two-part article in *Automotive Industries* entitled, 'Where is the Motorcycle Going?', and sent copies for reprinting to the motorcycle trade press. The only editor with the courage to print it was W.J. Parsons of *Motorcycle and Bicycle*

*Illustrated*, the first part appearing in the April 27th issue, the second part on May 4th.

Both Richards and Scherer continued their own market surveys, basing their conclusions on both their own research and that of Shidle and Prescott, but the project remained a secret for the next several months. An interesting sidelight to the Shidle-Richards-Scherer episode occurred the following year, in an article appearing in the September 28th issue of the Chicago-based *Motorcycling and Bicycling*, which was then edited by L.E. Fowler, a professional automotive engineer who had been responsible for the design of the once-popular lightweight two-stroke Cleveland. Its subject was an interview between Fowler and James Ward Packard, the then-retired designer and one time chief engineer of the Packard Motor Car Company.

Packard, who had been a pioneer bicyclist during the high-wheeler days, predicted not only a future revival of interest in bicycling, but an intensified future interest on the part of the general public in ultralightweight motorcycles, provided reliable and easily-started models could be mass produced to sell at modest prices. Prophetic words from the manufacturer of one of America's finest automobiles, whose prophecy was fulfilled by Japanese motorcycle concerns some four decades later!

In the meantime, Indian's sales for 1920 proved disappointing to the management. Weschler had confidently predicted that 30,000 machines would be produced by late summer, but due to financial and production problems, only slightly over 19,000 units came off the assembly lines by September. A huge inventory of raw materials and bought-out components was on hand, mostly purchased at the instigation of Buffam and MacNaughton, whose off-the-cuff guesses of sales projections went wide of the mark.

Added to Weschler's continuing woes, production workers were demanding an increase in wages, a serious drain on the already depleted treasury. The only bright light on an otherwise dark horizon was the growing popularity of the Scout, particularly overseas. At home, interest in this machine was also encouraging and many dealers who had deserted the fold during the war, renewed their franchises.

Beset by numerous problems, the factory did not officially support the first postwar TT races. Billy Wells made his usual offer to aid private entries by Indian owners, but the only serious competitor was Reuben Harveyson, who did not place.

Sales volume for 1920 totalled $3,768,000.00 with only $68,000 reported as profit. The preferred shareholders continued to receive their 1¾ per cent quarterly dividends.

While the Scout had an encouragingly widened sales appeal and attracted many new converts to motorcycling, especially in the export field, it possessed a serious lack in its original form by not being fitted with electric lights. Franklin had apparently followed the current English custom of expecting night riders to furnish their own lighting in the form of proprietary acetylene units, which in those days appeared to offer more dependable illumination. This deficiency was corrected in the Fall of 1920 for the 1921 sales season, by fitting a Splitdorf generator and lighting system. This proved generally satisfactory, if careful attention was paid to care of the battery.

What with the overwhelming enthusiasm for the Scout, many riders, dealers, and overseas agents began importuning the factory to design a larger, heavyweight V-twin along Scout lines, with more speed and power, which would have a special appeal for sidecar work. Many of the Indian executives seconded the idea, as the venerable Powerplus, now generally known as the 'Standard', still had the high and spindly old-fashioned look of prewar days, in common with the current big twin Harley and Excelsior models.

Franklin was therefore set to work designing an enlarged Scout type which was ultimately to be known as the Chief.

Some of the factory executives were opposed to the idea of launching a new model in the face of difficult times, especially as the present Standard model was a steady seller and had a wide following overseas. Butler and Richards were particularly adamant in their opposition, pointing out that sales efforts should be directed toward continuing attention to the very popular Scout, and citing the high costs involved in tooling up for the new model. Dealer pressure prevailed in the end and the soon-to-be-famous Chief was announced in the Fall of 1921.

The new heavyweight was in essence a slightly enlarged Scout, with a 61 cubic inch 42° V-twin engine, laid out with the now familiar helical gear drive and unit construction with the gearbox. The engine was basically similar to the Standard, except for the primary drive. In order to economize on manufacture, many Standard components were utilized, such as front forks and suspension system, wheel and brake assemblies, footboards and saddles. The principal new components were the frame, which was solid, like the Scout, new wider mudguards, and a pleasantly streamlined fuel tank, with integral oil reservoir for the total loss lubrication system. A separate generator and battery provided electric lighting as standard. The engine was sufficiently powerful to give a top speed of well over 90mph and gave good performance even when attached to a sidecar, the top speed then being over 70mph. In this latter guise it was a popular vehicle for bootleggers transporting illicit spirits, as the unpopular Prohibition Law had already been in effect for a year.

Attendant to the development of the Chief and detail improvements to the 61 inch and 74 inch Standards, the Engineering Department developed, in collaboration with the American-La France Company, a compact chemical fire fighting unit that was contained on a standard sidecar chassis. This unit was intended to provide a high speed, light duty fire engine that proved to be popular with many small town municipal engine companies, as well as private industrial concerns that maintained their own fire fighting units. It is certain that many such firms purchased these moderately priced sidecar outfits to effect a downward revision of their fire insurance premiums.

Both the Indian and Harley-Davidson factories entered the 1921 competition season with some misgivings. Harley-Davidson had expended vast sums in developing new equipment and for salaries and bonuses for their racing team for the postwar events, yet had experienced an equally disappointing postwar sales response. Added to this was their indebtedness incurred from the building and equipping of the vast Juneau Street factory, all of which had not yet been utilized due to the unexpected drop in sales response.

Excelsior had already decided against further factory participation in racing, a decision made by President Ignatz Schwinn after the tragic death of their racing star, Bob Perry, at Los Angeles Ascot Speedway on January 4th, 1920. Excelsior's Engineering Department had designed and built half a dozen extremely potent overhead camshaft racing engines, based somewhat on the fabulously successful but short-lived Cyclone of 1915. While testing one of these machines on the very fast course, Perry lost control, and went out over the banking, being killed instantly. Schwinn, reportedly an eccentric individual, was said in his grief to have immediately gone into the racing shop and smashed the remaining cammers with a sledge hammer.

The big classic of the year was the 1921 300-mile National at Dodge City, where all of the factory teams converged on July 4th. While Excelsior officially did not sponsor a team, Waldo Korn was on hand with one of the last overhead camshaft machines.

The Indian team consisted of M.K. 'Curley' Fredericks, Albert 'Shrimp' Burns, Johnny Seymour (no relation to Ray), Don Pope, 'Speck' Warner, Floyd Dreyer, and Hammond Springs, all riding Charles Franklin's newly-developed and very potent side-valve Powerplus type machines, known as pocket valvers, none of the previously appearing eight-valvers being entered.

For Harley-Davidson, Ralph Hepburn was to ride the only eight-valver, with team mates Jim Davis, Otto Walker, Ray Weishaar, Fred Ludlow and Walter Higley riding two cam pocket valve machines.

The lap record set in 1920 at 93mph was soon bested by Burns, and equalled by Waldo Korn on his Excelsior.

This last running of the famed Kansas prairie event was almost a one-man show for Hepburn. He gained an early lead and streaked ahead of the entire field for the first 100 miles, running wide open all the way, for a record time of one hour and seven minutes, 5.4 seconds. Hepburn stopped at the pits for fuel and oil, and was passed by Otto Walker, who held the lead for three laps until the flying Hepburn overhauled him. At the 200th mile he had made another record of 2 hours, 7 minutes, 5 seconds. By this time the furious pace was taking its toll of both men and machines. Many riders were dropping out with overheated engines as the continuous full bore running in the hot Kansas sun caused many a warped valve. Hepburn's machine continued to run faultlessly, however, and at the checkered flag he had broken all existing records up to 300 miles. His 85.7mph average

*Indian racing star Gene Walker leads Albert 'Shrimp' Burns on a dirt track county fair ground course in 1920. The lady spectator appears ecstatic. (Leslie D. Richards)*

topped even the existing board track records, the latter courses being generally acknowledged as naturally much faster than the dirt.

Johnny Seymour on his Indian came in second, but he was 12 miles behind. The balance of the Harley pack came in last.

Hepburn repeated his Dodge City victories at Portland, Oregon, on August 6th and 7th, being the winner of six of the seven main events. The only Indian placing in this meet was ridden by Johnny Seymour, who came third in the 10-mile race.

There were many board track events that summer, as Jack Prince had been building racing dromes since the preceding Fall at Beverly Hills, Redwood City, just south of San Francisco, and at Cotati, a small rural village 45 miles north of San Francisco and a few miles south of the author's home town of Santa Rosa.

As a young boy interested in motor sports, the building and opening of this track was an inspiration for much of the author's youthful excitement. Prince usually financed his tracks by soliciting local investors in the purchase of shares, together with the sale of 'lifetime' passes at $100.00 each. Lumber was plentiful and common labor was cheap, and Prince, together with a couple of foremen and about a dozen overseers, supervised the actual construction, which was undertaken with local labor. Prince, ever a nattily dressed man, drove about the site in a handsome black buggy with red wheels, drawn by a beautiful sorrel horse.

The Cotati oval was a 1¼ mile course, averaging 100 feet in width and it was gently banked on the straights, rising to between 45 and 50 degrees on the curves. The two grandstands, with a capacity of about 2,500, were placed on either side of the straights, their lower tiers raised sufficiently to provide a full view of the course. The surface was laid with 2 inch x 4 inch lumber set on edge and supported by a heavy framing of 8 inch x 10 inch stringers, placed on 8 foot centers. Horizontal studs of the same dimensions supported the structure from below, each stud resting on a short baulk of timber buried in the ground to resist movement.

The lower lip of the oval ended in a flat apron about 10 feet wide, as an escape route for a disabled machine. The upper edge of the oval was surrounded by a low railing of 2 inch x 12 inch planks, presumably to prevent a motorcycle rider or race car driver from flying out over the banking. A tunnel was dug under one edge of the track to admit contestants and service vehicles. It was said that the structure contained a freight car load of nails and spikes to hold it together.

The opening event at this track, on July 4th, 1921, was an automobile race which featured some of the leading drivers of that time, such as Tommy Milton and Ralph de Palma. It was followed by another contest on July 28th, featuring some lesser stars, but included an up-and-coming driver, Peter de Paola.

On August 28th the first motorcycle races were held and featured most of the leading professional riders of

the day. These races, attended by the author, comprised a number of events from one to fifty miles.

Ralph Hepburn was again the star, and established a new 1.25 mile record for 42.4 seconds. He also won the 25-mile feature in 16 minutes, 29.7 seconds. Johnny Seymour, on an Indian, was second, being beaten by only 4 seconds.

To anyone yet living who was fortunate enough to recall the days of the boards, the total picture was a thrilling spectacle that can never be forgotten. The eager anticipation of the spectators, the bunting-draped stands, and the music of the American Legion Band, all combined to set the stage for a holiday atmosphere. This, combined with the odor of raw lumber, and the pungent perfume of burned castor oil, was the incense of high adventure of any speed enthusiast.

Due to the restricted width of the course, each event was limited to six riders. The usual board track racing machines were built, with low weight as the criterion and were usually well under 300 pounds. No power absorbing clutches or gearboxes were ever fitted, the drive being direct to the rear wheel via a solid countershaft sprocket, whose shaft was fixed through a bracket fitted just behind the engine plates.

The engines had only rudimentary controls, as the spark position was fixed and the throttleless carburetor was set in the wide-open position. The only means of rider control was by a kill button near one handlebar grip, which enabled the rider to short-circuit the magneto.

While this enabled the motor to be stopped at will, holding the button off too long would result in the lubricating oil fouling the spark plugs.

The wheels were usually of 23 inch diameter carrying 28 inch x 2½ inch special racing tires built by Goodyear or Firestone, inflated with about 100lbs of air. The front suspension was made very stiff to avoid bouncing of the wheel, and generally offered less than an inch of travel.

The machines were started by being towed behind a sidecar outfit, which, in keeping with the spirit of the event, was generally stripped down to resemble a racing vehicle. The passenger faced aft and held one end of the towrope, the other end being wrapped once around the racer's handlebar and held in the rider's hand. At a speed of about 50mph the rider let go of the rope and released the kill button, the sidecar outfit then simultaneously swerving down to the escape apron.

When all the contestants had been thus brought into action, the starter waved his flag to position the riders for a flying start as they circled the track to warm up their machines.

The excitement of the race was heightened by the noise of the engines, as all had open exhausts with very short stacks, which usually emitted flames and sparks at speed. The pungent smell of castor oil pervaded everything.

For the actual techniques employed in team racing, both on the boards as well as the dirt tracks, we are indebted to the reminiscences of Fred Ludlow, octage-

**Left:** *Friendly rivals Roy Artley and Fred Ludlow at the Los Angeles Ascot track in 1920. The two were doubly related in law, as they married sisters.*

**Right:** *Gene Walker leads the pack at a Labor Day race at Cleveland, Ohio, in 1920. One of the era's greatest riders, he was seldom beaten in any contest. This was in the days before footing on the turns was allowed.* **(Leslie D. Richards)**

narian survivor of America's golden age of motorcycle racing and legendary winner of five national championships of one, five, ten, twenty-five and fifty miles at Syracuse, New York, during one race on September 19th, 1921.

One of the first principles of team racing was that of riding pace. By prearrangement, one team member would pull out ahead, his body and machine splitting the air, leaving an area behind him into which another rider could follow without requiring quite as much power. The exact area of this partial vacuum was sometimes behind a machine, or at one side or another – sometimes difficult for a follower to find, although it was always there.

The rider setting the pace was constantly checking his engine for excessive heat. The following riders were at once both carefully pacing each other and attempting to keep an eye on the lead rider's observations as to his own engine's condition. When the engine heat reached its maximum safe operating temperature, but before any risk of seizure was imminent, the leader would then drop back behind the following rider, into his slipstream. The star rider was usually encouraged to attempt to gain first place at the finish, but if his engine overheated, or the competition's tactics upset the slipstreaming sequences, the rider in first position near the finish line was expected to make a win, if possible.

Top racing teams spent a vast amount of time practising between races, to perfect their track manoeuvers, test new or experimental equipment, or to break in new team or substitute members.

Aside from the importance of team strategy on the tracks, stops at the pits, whether scheduled or unscheduled, together with communication between the riders and pit attendants during the race, were important for victory.

When a rider coasted to the pits for a stop, hopefully only for fuel and lubricants, he was expected to know just at which point he should kill his engine on the course so that he could stop at the proper point, no brakes being available on track machines. As he rolled to the proper stopping place, a husky mechanic was stationed to grab his handlebars to kill the last of his momentum and simultaneously hoist the machine on low blocks previously set in proper position. As the rider was helped out of the saddle, two other mechanics with speed wrenches began removing the front and rear wheels respectively for changing, while a fourth opened the tank caps and commenced filling both fuel and oil reservoirs with pressure hoses. A fifth mechanic was already changing both spark plugs. Another attendant would hand the rider either a drink of water, fruit juice or a soft drink, according to his choice, and at the same time install a clean pair of goggles over his helmet. Well drilled pit attendants could perform these operations in about 65 seconds. In a 300 mile event, two such stops were required.

Communication between the pit boss and the riders was achieved by each team member having an individual color incorporated on his jersey. A set of flags corresponding with these colors, but with white centers, was placed in the pits. If a rider's flag was held out with the time marked in colored chalk in the white center it meant that the pace was to be held steady. If the flag was held out with no signal, this indicated that the mechanic in charge wanted to listen to the rider's engine. On the next lap the engine was blipped with the kill button, as the pits were passed. On the following lap, the rider would either be signaled with a flag, or a message held out on a small black board such as the word lean, or heat.

The pit crew at most race courses set up a 20 foot tower so that an observer could watch the backstretch or turns for any rider who had been forced to retire. An auxiliary crew with a sidecar outfit could then be quickly dispatched to either make an emergency repair, or bring the stalled machine and rider in, as the occasion warranted.

While this latter manoeuver could be readily observed by the spectators, the intricacies of the necessary team activities were generally not observed, most thinking that the contests were simply duels of raw speed and horsepower. What the public most definitely did not know was that the teams with the fastest machinery were often beaten by teams with less potent equipment, whose internal organization had been refined by intensive practise.

Ludlow toured the country in a Harley-Davidson sidecar outfit, giving racing films shows to various clubs and other organizations with an interest in racing. Some time later he was summarily fired from the Harley-Davidson organization, at which time he became a cycle mechanic in C. Will Risdon's Indian agency in Los Angeles. He joined the South Pasadena Police Department as a motorcycle officer in 1923, and a year or so later transferred to a similar post in the Pasadena Police Department. He then switched his allegiance to Indian, and, as shall be seen, went on in later years to bring further laurels to himself and the Redskin camp.

As popular as the board tracks had become by the early 1920's, interest was soon to wane. Stockholders who invested money in construction shares never seemed to profit from their holdings, and it was generally the promoters who made the substantial profits.

The sport was extremely hazardous for the riders, and many of the stars were killed or seriously injured. An almost certain fatality was the result of flying out over the banking.

One of the most spectacular accidents occurred at the track at Newark, New Jersey, when Indian star Eddie Hasha, in company with other riders, died when they came off the banking and landed in the stands, killing several spectators.

The general atmosphere of some of the tracks was less than desirable with much illegal betting, along with the sale of bootleg liquor. Some of the tracks were invaded by groups of prostitutes, who openly solicited customers in the stands or at the gates, during the races.

After an appalling series of fatal accidents, the local press in various cities and towns openly campaigned against the sport, often referring to the sites as Murderdromes.

The sport gradually died a natural death when wind and weather finally caused the tracks to deteriorate, and when encroaching subdivisions and industrial demands finally forced their closing. As a somewhat gladiatorial and savage type of sport, the board tracks finally did, as shall be seen, arouse much public sentiment against motorcycling in general.

The 1921 competition season was no less a disaster for Indian than that of 1916 and both the factory management as well as many riders and dealers were disconsolate concerning Harley-Davidson's triumph. The latter company's victories, however, cost them dearly. While actual monetary figures were, of course, never officially disclosed, it was rumored throughout the trade that Harley-Davidson's Racing Department had spent nearly $200,000 for the season. Indian's meager finances during that year allowed for but minimal expenditures for competition, and it was readily apparent to knowledge-

*Leslie D. Richards poses with his winning 1917 Standard Powerplus model and the trophies won in the Crotona Motor Cycle Club's 24 hour run.* **(Leslie D. Richards)**

able factory and dealer personnel that victory could only belong to the manufacturer that was willing to spend the most money. The expenditure of such large sums of money during a period of generally declining motorcycle sales became an open question.

*Typical machine park at an Indian dealers' annual picnic in the 1920s. This event was sponsored by Providence, Rhode Island dealer Ben 'The Terrible Swede' Swenson, who had one of the most active franchises.* **(Leslie D. Richards)**

While Harley-Davidson's financial position was at that time much better than Indian's, their management was known to have been concerned with the rising costs of competition. In November, President Walter Davidson officially announced that henceforth there would be no factory participation in racing, and that only a few special machines would be built and sold to selected riders.

Motorcycle competition was somewhat subdued in 1922, due to the withdrawal of both Harley-Davidson and Excelsior, terminating official sponsorship. The Indian company was not in a strong enough financial position to field as many riders as it had in the immediate postwar seasons, but Weschler was still adamant in stretching his meager racing budget to the utmost, to keep the flag flying.

Some of the racing stars of both Harley-Davidson and Excelsior continued their racing careers by signing up with Indian. The great Ralph Hepburn was one, and repeated his previous year's victory win at the last running of the Dodge City 300-mile classic on an eight-valve special, whose cam action and carburetion had been improved by Franklin and extensively tested by Charles Gustafson, Jr.

Hepburn and Jim Davis, who had also joined the wigwam, toured the California board track circuit that

*Fun and games at the annual Indian Company picnic in 1921. In the tug-of-war event between the managerial and production staff, Vice President Weschler provides his bulk as anchor man. Charles Franklin (fourth from right) does his part standing.* **(Leslie D. Richards)**

**Right:** *Indian Company executives and Department heads after the 1921 reorganisation.*

summer. The latter established a new world's record of a mile in 32.53 seconds thundering around the Beverley Hills oval at the astonishing speed of 110.75mph. Hepburn attempted to beat this time and came fractionally close for a time of 32.64 seconds.

A month later, both Hepburn and Davis competed against the veterans of Harley's famous 'Wrecking Crew' at the San Carlos track, near Redwood City. Otto Walker, Ray Weishaar, and Fred Ludlow, riding their 1920 Harleys, put up a terrific battle, but Hepburn was the star of the day with his winning of the 50-mile feature race. Spectator interest was enhanced by the appearance of auto racing star, Barney Oldfield, who presented Hepburn with a special gold medal, inscribed to 'The Master Rider of the World'.

Hepburn was by this time in great demand by race promoters everywhere. At the New York State Fair at Syracuse on September 16th, he won the 10-mile State sidecar championship, on a factory outfit raced previously by Floyd Dreyer.

Hepburn finished his triumphant 1922 season at San Luis Obispo, California, where, on a very fast dirt oval, he broke the world's record for such courses in a 39.6 second mile. Running a 25-mile distance, he made additional records at 5, 6, and 10 and 25 miles. These times are still carried as 61 cubic inch class records in *All Sports Record Book*, by Frank G. Menke, a noted sports authority.

HENDEE MANUFACTURING COMPANY—SPRINGFIELD, MASS. U.S.A.

1921

### OFFICERS

HENRY H. SKINNER . . . . . . . President
WILLIAM E. GILBERT . . . . . Vice President
FRANK J. WESCHLER . . Vice Pres. & Treas.
LINDLEY D. HUBBELL . . . . . Vice President
PARMLEY HANFORD . . . . . . Secretary
JOHN D. STEPHENS . . . . . Asst. Treasurer

### BOARD of DIRECTORS

WILLIAM F. BARTHOLOMEW
HOWARD R. BEMIS
EDWIN A. CARTER
CHARLES E. CHILDS
WILLIAM E. GILBERT
LINDLEY D. HUBBELL
HENRY H. SKINNER
FRANK J. WESCHLER

FRANK J. WESCHLER
Vice President & Treasurer in Charge
of Finance and Sales

JOHN D. STEPHENS
Asst. Treasurer

PARMLEY HANFORD
Secretary

LINDLEY D. HUBBELL
Vice President in Charge of Operations

EDWARD BUFFUM
Sales Manager

THOMAS C. BUTLER, JR.
Mgr. Chicago Branch

U. ALBERT HICKS
Asst. Mgr. Chicago Branch

ARTHUR A. ANDERSON
Mgr. Bicycle Department

WILLIAM A. PRENTICE
Sales Department

EDWARD W. CABBITT
Sales Department

JAMES B. MCNAUGHTON
Sales Promotion Manager

FRANCIS M. WATERS
Advertising Manager

LESLIE D. RICHARDS
Publicity Manager

CHARLES B. FRANKLIN
Chief Engineer

THERON L. LOOSE
General Superintendent

CHARLES F. EVANS
Chief Inspector

WILLIAM G. MCCANN
Export Manager

WILLIAM H. WELLS
Mgr. London Branch

THOMAS J. RITCHIE
Export Department

ROGER MILLS
Export Department

W. STANLEY BOUTON
Service Manager

EARL ROBBINS
Asst. Service Manager

HAROLD R. GORDON
Purchasing Agent

DWIGHT L. MOODY
Asst. Purchasing Agent

WILLIAM B. CAREY
Mgr. Parts Department

ROBERT HALEY
Mgr. Order Department

JOHN W. LEAHY
Chief Accountant

J. T. CRONIN
Mgr. Credit Department

Hepburn next transferred his interest to car racing, and was ultimately killed in 1946 when he crashed a Novi front drive special at Indianapolis, during the qualifying trials. Hepburn, then 50 years old, had been warned by other drivers that his reflexes were now too slow to cope with the hazards of racing.

The Indian Scout continued to put up fantastic endurance records, in both factory sponsorship and in the hands of private riders. Cannonball Baker was engaged to take a Scout on another transcontinental run, this time aimed at proving its economy. In November he started from New York City, reaching Los Angeles 179 hours and 28 minutes later, at an average speed of 20mph. The Scout consumed only 40 gallons of gasoline and 5 gallons of lubricating oil for the 3,368 mile trip.

Floyd Clymer, who had recently dropped his Harley-Davidson franchise in Denver and taken over an Indian agency, rode a stripped down Scout to the top of Pike's Peak. Undaunted by the warnings of experienced mountain guides that he would not be able to reach timberline, Clymer performed the impossible by riding the Scout to a point two miles further than ever reached by horse or burro!

The problems at the Indian factory continued during the 1922 season. Even with the knowledge of declining motorcycle sales, the management was still unsure of just what production figures to plan for. The problem was compounded by the fact that, due to Edward Buffam's previous inaccurate sales estimates, the company had a $2,500,000 inventory of raw materials and accessories on hand that was far too great a burden to be carrying for the actual production of the previous two years. General Manager Weschler had been able to secure financing from local bankers on short term notes to carry on factory operation, but the interest charges on these, and the indebtedness on the excessive inventory, were diminishing the company's dwindling cash reserves. Matters were now becoming serious as Indian had lost over $912,000 the previous year.

In the meantime, Dick Richards had been continuing his sales and market analyses, based on data garnered from Norman Shidle and Raymond Prescott. He prepared a series of charts depicting future sales estimates based on his findings, along with raw material requirements for projected production. He also advocated the concentration of production on the Scout, whose popularity was the only factor enabling the company's survival, together with the development of lighter utility models. He ultimately approached Weschler with his findings, and after some study of his conclusions, the latter relieved him of his publicity duties and instructed him to pursue his studies on a full time basis, providing him with a private office, secretarial help, and an expense account to facilitate the work.

When the word of a new approach to Indian's most vexing problems got around the office, much interest was stimulated, and there was a noticeable increase in company morale. Richards prepared a series of charts showing projected orders and consequent sales, with material requirements for anticipated production. Weschler immediately ordered the production executives to follow the recommendations.

Both Buffam and MacNaughton, however, were antagonistic to this new turn of events, which they considered a threat to their authority, and old-time employees have recounted numerous instances of their hostility and obstructive tactics directed toward Richards.

In order to better implement the new procedures, Weschler relieved Franklin of his duties as Chief Engineer and replaced him with Colonel Lindley D. Hubbell, who had just retired from the Army and had been in command of Springfield's Arsenal. While this was a technical demotion for Franklin, the change was much to his liking, as it left him free to direct all his efforts toward design matters, leaving production supervision to Hubbell.

In the midst of Weschler's efforts to enhance production efficiency, MacNaughton conferred with some members of the Board of Directors concerning production problems, and with apparent intent to undermine both Weschler's and Richards' sales and production efforts. MacNaughton persuaded the Board to authorize the hiring under contract of a firm of industrial efficiency experts from New York, who were supposedly able to solve production problems. Representatives of this company came to the factory, redistributed machine tools, relocated personnel, and generally turned the production lines into chaos. When it was shown that production was actually hampered by their misguided efforts, Weschler obtained authority from the Board of Directors to terminate their contract.

With much of company capital tied up in surplus material inventory, the treasury was depleted to the point that it now became difficult to meet the payroll. With local banks now wary of extending the company more credit, Weschler was forced to seek short term loans outside of Springfield. After some difficulty, he was able to raise additional money from banks as far south as Atlanta, and as far west as Chicago in order to meet running expenses, making frequent train trips to effect these arrangements.

**Right:** *The 61cu in Powerplus Standard model, updated in the Fall of 1922 for the 1923 sales season. Featured are valanced mudguards with flat steel stays in place of the former rods, and a strengthened rear suspension.*

# Indian Standard

PRICE $370

T**HE** name INDIAN STANDARD is justly and most appropriately fitted to the Cradle Spring Frame model with the famous Powerplus Motor.

Entering its seventh year of leadership the Cradle Spring Frame is a feature in itself which has claimed matter of fact recognition for its comfortable riding qualities. The Powerplus Motor, Two Unit Electric System, ammeter and switch and many other distinctive features of this model have naturally been continued.

Prominent among the new features are the new Splitdorf Magneto and large crown mud guards, both front and rear. The guards provide increased protection to the rider and machine against road splashings as well as ample clearance for attaching skid chains or to allow for mud caked wheels. They also add to the beauty and general appearance of the model. Naturally the fork crowns have been enlarged as a part of the improvement.

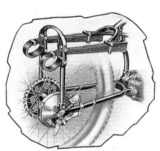

CRADLE SPRING FRAME

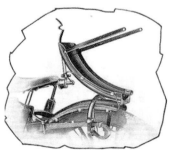

HINGED MUD GUARD

# *Indian Chief*

PRICE $435

WHILE the INDIAN CHIEF was designed primarily to meet the requirements of sidecar service, nevertheless, as a solo mount where the qualities of power, speed and stamina are required, the INDIAN CHIEF has already been highly praised for the ease with which it is handled.

Besides embodying the highly desirable features of the SCOUT in increased proportions, the INDIAN CHIEF incorporates several notable refinements. The cylinders of its Powerplus Motor have been provided with additional cooling flanges. The mud-guards are the new INDIAN Crowned type. The generator is driven by a spur gear, enclosed with the timing gear train, and is compactly housed at the forward end of the crankcase. A battery of increased capacity is provided, most conveniently located. The saddle is mounted on the new INDIAN spring seat-post. A new type Splitdorf Magneto embodying several decided advantages is standard equipment.

BATTERY CASE

MAGNETO AND GENERATOR

Further operating complications occurring during the critical year of 1922 were worsening troubles with labor. The local machinists' union had been demanding pay raises that the company was currently unable to meet. Some of the machining operations were contracted for on a piece work basis, and not a few of the workers were found to be on the job for only two or three days a week, but were collecting a full week's pay.

Another problem was that of pilfering and outright thievery of materials, some of which were ultimately resold to the company by unscrupulous individuals on the outside, who were apparently in league with the plant personnel involved. Matters came to a head with the loss of a large number of nickel bars from the Plating Department. Weschler immediately engaged the services of the Pinkerton Detective Agency, who placed operatives inside the plant. Two employees, Marvin Forbes and Nathan Greilech, were arrested and charged with the crime. Union representatives then threatened to call a strike if the alleged thieves were prosecuted and, after some negotiations, the matter was settled by offering the production workers a raise in hourly pay which was slightly over the prevailing scale.

It was during this period that some of the younger executives on Indian's staff became interested in a project allied with the general decline of the manufacturing activities in the New England area.

The northeastern states had been the leading industrial and manufacturing center of the country since early colonial times. Due to the expansion of industry necessitated by the war effort, there was much dispersion of manufacturing to other parts of the country. The burgeoning automobile industry became centered in Michigan, after Henry Ford founded his great factory complex in Dearborn in 1903. After 1920, the industrial leadership of the New England states declined. Part of the reason was the general dependence upon steam power and the consequent need for coal. Since the earliest days this had been imported from the vast coal fields of Pennsylvania and West Virginia and was sold, delivered, for $5.00 or $6.00 a ton. In subsequent years, John L. Lewis's United Mine Workers Union had gained sufficient strength to demand better working conditions and increased pay scales, until the price of coal delivered to the New England area rose to $20.00 a ton.

The rise in fuel costs worked a hardship on many of the small textile mills, shoe factories, and small manufacturing concerns, particularly as postwar inflation had substantially increased operating costs to the point where many of them had difficulty in competing with larger operations.

Many of the younger Indian executives were members of Springfield's Publicity Club, which was comparable to the modern Junior Chamber of Commerce. The outlook and attitudes of these young men was quite at variance with those of the Springfield Trade Club, which was made up largely of older men steeped in the innate conservatism of the typical New England yankee.

In considering the problem, some of the members, including Dick Richards, advocated the use of electricity to replace coal for running the factories. This had become a practical reality since 1920, when Charles P. Steinmetz had invented a system whereby electric power could be transmitted for long distances through high tension lines, without a drop in voltage.

The club next drafted a proposal for the formation of a public utility district within the New England area, with a view to soliciting memberships through the sale of bonds to finance the venture. The same procedure was later employed to establish the federally-sponsored Rural Electrification program and the Tennessee Valley Authority a decade later. To stimulate interest in the project, it was decided that various club members should interview various industrialists, to ascertain if any support for the proposal might be forthcoming.

Frank Weschler was informed of the scheme and he immediately gave it his wholehearted support. He went so far as to give Richards some time off from his regular publicity duties, to make calls at various factories and interview the owners.

As promising as the proposal seemed, the ultraconservative New England factory owners rejected it almost to a man, stating that it was at variance with accepted practises and that they saw no need to replace their traditional steam power plants with electricity.

Their shortsightedness ultimately doomed their industry to failure, however, and by 1930 most of the more progressive manufacturers had moved their operations to other parts of the country, leaving an economic vacuum in the northeastern states.

A lighter side to Richards' duties in the Publicity Department was the teaching of Miss Frances Loeb to ride a Scout. This young lady, whose home was in Boston, became interested in learning to ride a Scout, and as the daughter of one of the bankers who had a hand in Indian's financial reorganization in 1913, found a ready access to the factory and its personnel. As a very short and stout young woman, with short legs, she persuaded Theron L. Loose to design and build a special low frame for her machine, which afforded a very low saddle position. She became an expert rider and for several years thereafter entered numerous endurance and trial events in the New England area, reports of her exploits appearing in various trade and club magazines of the period.

1922 was a year of further attrition in the domestic motorcycle industry. Reading-Standard, Iver Johnson, Schickel, and a couple of other obscure makes, all of whom had experienced very limited production in the postwar years, suspended production. Apart from the big three, Cleveland remained in the now miniscule, lightweight, utility type, along with the newly introduced Neracar, designed and promoted by A.C. Neracher. This last was a rather curious car-like two-wheeler, with central pivot front axle steering and extremely wide mudguards. A very reliable and stable machine that offered good weather protection, its designer soon withdrew it from public sale and took his operation to England where it continued in production for some years thereafter.

The motorcycle market dropped to the point where less than 25,000 units were being produced annually by the entire industry. In spite of this bleak outlook, Norman Shidle published an optimistic article in *Automotive Industries* on August 10th, entitled 'The Motorcycle Turns a Corner'. In it he suggested that with scientific

**Below:** *A small ultra light single seater biplane built by C. Turner and C. Fasig during the early 1920s. It was powered by a 61 cu in V twin Powerplus engine with direct propeller drive.*

**Bottom:** *The Snyder 'Baby Bomber,' a small biplane with a 21 foot wingspan and a weight of 315lb designed by O.H. Snyder, an aeronautical engineer employed by the US Army. Its Powerplus engine drove the propeller through a 2:1 chain drive reduction gear. Top speed was 62mph.* **(US Army Air Force)**

THE GREAT DECLINE 1914-1923

market analysis and controlled methods of production, the general picture for the industry was improving. He was no doubt inspired by the fact that both Dick Richards, at Indian, and Hap Scherer, at Harley-Davidson, were pursuing their own studies in these matters for the benefit of their individual companies. Scherer, however, resigned shortly afterwards, when his company suspended production of its Sport Twin, and concentrated efforts on two models of their heavyweight V-twins.

As a paradox to the declining domestic market, the export demand for American big twins remained strong; so much in fact, that 50% or more of total production went to overseas markets. Indian's position was particularly strong, with over 3,000 machines each year being sent to Australia alone. For several years during this period, Indian showed the largest registration of any make in South Africa.

The American export market was so strong, in fact, that one make, the Emblem, a soundly designed V-twin manufactured in small numbers by W.G. Shrack in Angola, New York, ceased domestic sales entirely. Their entire production was sent to Europe, where they were particularly popular in Holland, Belgium and in the Scandinavian countries, until production ceased in 1925.

While motorcycle competition declined generally due to lack of factory support from all manufacturers except Indian, hill climb events became more popular. Features such as at Rochester, New York, York, Pennsylvania and San Juan Capistrano, California, were regularly scheduled. As time went on, the meets became more and more of the 'stunt' type, as slopes of 45 degrees or more were selected, being often unclimbable by even specialized machines powered with racing engines fueled with blended mixtures. The outstanding star of the 1920's was Orrin 'Orrie' Steele, who rode professionally for Indian. His hell-for-leather style was seldom imitated by others, as it required singular courage to perform. Steele would start his engine, rev it to full throttle and drop the clutch, at the same time throwing himself well forward over the handlebars. Hill climb machines carried kill buttons on the throttle grip, being held open by a small peg jammed into place against a small spring. The peg was tied to the rider's wrist with a piece of cord. If the rider had to come off his machine, or bail out for a backwards somersault, the peg would come free and stop the engine. This not only made matters safer for the rider but prevented the riderless machine from charging into the spectators. During the mid-1920's and early 1930's, most of the Fox or Movietone newsreels that were a part of every motion picture show featured a thirty to sixty-second shot of some daredevil motorcycle hill climb.

A sad occurrence in the 1922 competition season was the death of Albert 'Shrimp' Burns, on the very fast back-stretch of the Toledo, Ohio, dirt track on August 13th. He was riding the same old number 50 factory 61 that had taken Charley 'Fearless' Balke to his death at the Hawthorne, Chicago, a few weeks before. Paul Bower, a promising young Indian rider lost his life, again at Toledo, when he lost control of his 61 and crashed through a fence.

Another financial disaster for the company in 1922 was its ill-starred participation in an attempt on the part of a syndicate of midwestern investors to revive the once famous Flying Merkel motorcycle. This well-designed V-twin machine from the board of the talented Joseph Merkel suspended production in 1916, partly through the lack of continuing availability of German ball bearings used in its famous 'ball bearing' engine, as well as lack of competent factory management and quality control.

The new backers proposed that Indian extend its existing contract with Brown and Sharpe for engine castings, to include small quantities of those designed for Merkel, which could then be shipped to the latter factory for finishing. In addition to a slightly updated Flying Merkel twin, it was planned to add a new design in the form of a motor wheel, which could be installed in place of the usual rear wheel in a bicycle, thus opening up what was hoped would be an additional penetration of the utility market. Weschler, after some hesitation, agreed to enter into this transaction, hoping thereby to enhance needed gross income for the company.

The castings for the motor wheels were ordered first, and during the summer about 200 of these unfinished units were shipped to the State Street Factory.

In the meantime, the proposed financing of the new Merkel group was suddenly withdrawn and Indian was left with the castings on its hands. In order to save something from this debacle, Indian production workers machined the castings and completed the units, which were then fitted to Indian's standard roadster bicycles. These units ran after a fashion but woefully short of power, and, after a few were sold to dealers, the whole project was regretfully written off with considerable financial loss.

In spite of 1922's troubles, the Advertising Department issued a special advertising brochure to celebrate Indian's twenty-first year. It was a large, multi-colored fold-out showing pictures of the various models of machines produced since 1901.

Another advertising promotion that had its inception during the 1920's was the annual Indian Day, scheduled on or near the 22nd of each February. Franchised dealers were urged to participate by cleaning up their shops, and advertise an open house day in their local press outlets. Extra catalogs and novelty favors were supplied at cost by the factory, and the dealers were expected to supply free refreshments such as doughnuts, coffee or soft drinks for the entertainment of old customers or prospective new buyers. Visitors were asked to fill out name and address cards, which were then sent to the factory for inclusion on catalog mailing lists.

A postwar program to promote employee goodwill and fellowship was the annual company picnic, which was held in July or August, usually at some secluded site along the Connecticut River. Employees attending were urged to wear dress up attire, and in some years Weschler ruled that all men present must wear white knickers and white shirts with neckties.

At certain times stag picnics were held for the male employees and these featured nude swimming. Sometimes new staff members were initiated into the Order of the Black Cloud, which included being dunked in the water and then being coated with thick wheel grease from a large pressure gun. At other times, athletic contests, such as baseball games, volley ball, or tug-o-war competitions between members of the Office and Production Departments, were featured.

1922 was a financial disaster for the company. With gross sales of $3,007,450.00, the total expenses for the year were $4,370,710.00, leaving a loss of $1,273,238.00. While some of this loss was due to problems with labor, and the Merkel fiasco, much of it was due to the expenses of carrying an inordinately high and costly inventory of raw materials that had been purchased at inflated postwar costs at the instigation of Edward Buffam.

At a Board of Directors meeting in November, some of the members were reported to be in favor of selling the company to the highest bidder. Weschler, together with certain of the loyal staff members and other executives, fought against this move, rightly claiming that a part of the loss covered the usual quarterly dividends of 1¾%

*Sales and Office Personnel, 1922. This photo was taken during the 1922 Annual Sales Conference at the front entrance of the Indian factory office. Only about half of the personnel involved are shown. Many of the absentees were 'sleeping-it-off' in their rooms at the old Highland Hotel. There had been a big party the night before! Front row (standing) Left to right: Bill Prentice, Kipp, T.C. Butler, Glen Grandall, Cleo Pineau, Bob Haley, L.D.Richards, Second row: Art Anderson, Ray E. Garner, Frank J. Weschler, O.P.T. Daenitz, Bill McCann, Back group (in order as they appear) Left to right: J.B. McNaughton, Frank Long, Ed. Carritt, Oby O'Brian, Bill Carey, Ed. Buffam, Fred Hunt, Bill Freeman, Erle 'Red' Armstrong, George Sherman.*

paid to the preferred shareholders represented by Board members.

Weschler was able to show the Board a new set of projected sales and expense figures for the coming 1923 season, based on Richards' market analysis studies, that could at least enable the company to hold its own financially, pending the initiation of improved management techniques. The poor rating and consequent drop in value of Indian's common stock was an alarming factor, but nothing could be done at that time to reinstill public confidence.

After several stormy sessions, President Skinner ultimately authorized Weschler to proceed as necessary, with full authority to implement such measures in all Departments to effect stabilization of Indian's precarious position.

Weschler immediately set about this herculean task with his usual dedicated enthusiasm. Edward Buffam was allowed to retire. James MacNaughton was retained as head of the Sales Department but with an admonition that his authority did not extend to production matters.

The production force was reduced to conform to the industry's now admitted declining sales, and production lines were reorganized accordingly. One of the problems was the containing of the vast size of the State Street factory in relation to the reduced production schedules, as this was now projected for a yearly output of roughly one-fourth of its peak year in 1913 of over 30,000 units.

The 1922 three-model line of Scout, Chief and Standard was carried on for 1923 with few changes in detail.

The now venerable Standard was given a new pair of valanced mudguards with flat steel stays, which replaced the rod type that were fitted since the Hedstrom days. The spring frame was strengthened by the addition of some extra gussets and electric lighting was fitted as standard.

The Scout was continued with only a few improvements in the lubrication system, and was still a good seller, both at home and overseas.

*A ten foot long model of the State Street Factory that was used for sales and exhibition purposes in the early 1920s. The smoke stack of the power plant is placed in the center rather than in its proper place at the right.* (Leslie D. Richards)

The Scout continued to establish an amazing number of endurance and dependability records in the hands of private owners. Its durability was such that a factory slogan 'You can't wear out an Indian Scout' was a feature for several ensuing years in advertising literature.

A private owner, Paul Remaley of Portland, Oregon, set out on July 10th from Blaine, Washington, on the Canadian border, in an attempt to break the Three Flag record currently held by Wells Bennett, who rode a 61 cubic inch Excelsior. Remaley made the trip to Mexico in 43 hours and 21 minutes, lowering Bennett's time by 2 hours, 48 minutes.

Not satisfied with this, he set out on August 15th to better the Transcontinental Record, also held currently by Wells Bennett, who had recently made the mark on an 80 cubic inch Henderson Four in five days, 17 hours and 10 minutes. Remaley made a trouble-free run for a new record that was 18 hours under Bennett's mark. The factory had actually discouraged Remaley in what they considered a futile attempt against the record of a larger capacity machine, and gave him no official support.

Competition activities in motorcycling were still curtailed by the lack of factory support from both Excelsior and Harley-Davidson. While Indian still officially supported racing, it had but a meager budget for such activities. Charles Gustafson, Jr. managed what competition was possible with limited finances. A big event won by Indian was the 300 mile National, held that year at a new dirt oval at Wichita, Kansas, when M.K. 'Curley' Fredericks gunned his 61 around a very fast track for a new record of 2.27.48.

*Executive and Managerial Personnel at the annual Company Picnic in 1922. I regret the large number of blanks. These were mostly outsiders such as bankers and suppliers who had been invited to the party by courtesy. Many of them I never knew or met. This party was always a day of games and fun and hilarity. The collars and ties and clean white shirts were soon discarded. A tug-of-war between factory and office ensued, also swimming-in-the-raw (therefore no ladies). A new employee was initiated into the Black-Cloud-Degree. Stripped naked he was dunked in the lake, hauled out, masked and then smothered head to foot with carbon black from pressure guns. This was the year that Multog got his. Front row, seated: 1, Al Hicks, Chicago; 2, Bill Freeman, Chicago; 3, ?; 4, ?; 5, Harry Glenn, Atlanta; 6, Bill Carey, Parts; 7, ?; 8, ?; 9, Cleo Pineau, Canada; 10, Glenn Crandall, Chicago; 11, Bob Haley, Orders; 12, Stan Bouton, Service; 13, ?; 14, ?; 2nd row, kneeling: 1, Bill McCann, Export; 2, ?; 3, ?; 4, F.J. Weschler, V. P.; 5, ?; 6, J. B. McNaughton, Sales; 7, L. D. Richards, statistics; 8, ?; 9, Clarence Multog, Chicago; 10, ?; 11, ?; 12, ?; 13, Erle Armstrong, Racing; 14, ?; Back row, standing: 1, ?; 2, Parmley Hanford, Secretary; 3, W. H. Parsons, Mc. Ill.; 4, Ted Stack, Publicity; 5, Art Anderson, Sales; 6, Fred Hunt, NY State; 7, ?; 8, J. W. Leahy, Accounting; 9, J. T. Cronin, Credit; 10, Earl Robbins, Service; 11, T. L. Loose, Factory Supt.; 12, ?; 13, ?; 14, ?; 15, ?; 16, Bill Prentice, Sales; 17, ?; 18, ?; 19, ?; 20, ?; 21, Obie Obrian, Sales; 22, ?; 23, Chas. Gustafson, Testing; 24, ?; 25, Frank Long, Politician (Leslie D. Richards)*

Much of the competition was now in the hands of private enthusiasts, many of whom had been allowed to purchase factory racers for their own use. The factory endeavoured to keep a limited supply of parts on hand for these competitors. Many of the regional dealers who had been factory-designated racing managers maintained local racing machines from their own supply of parts and were paid for these, plus their shop time, by the factory. Weschler continued to send out gratuities to winners of outstanding events, or in areas where the advertising value of Indian wins was deemed important for advertising purposes.

1923 marked the last year that Indian was represented in the TT races. Freddy Dixon, who had enthusiastically carried Indian's colors at Brooklands, had entered a special 500cc side valve factory special in 1922, but was forced to retire with engine trouble in the last lap, behind the winner, Alec Bennett. He entered the same machine in 1923, and managed third place, one minute behind the second place winner, G.M. Black, who was riding a Norton.

Dixon's machine is still in existence and is owned by an Indian enthusiast in England, who is a member of the Vintage Motor Cycle Club. An identical machine, and thought to be the only other replica surviving, was once owned by Ted Hodgdon, who rescued it from a factory storage room after World War II. It now resides in the United States, where it is on view in a museum. A previously forgotten third replica was unearthed in another

Right: *1923 TT entrant
Freddie Dixon on his 500cc
side valve factory racer.*
(The Archives of the Hendee
Manufacturing Company)

Below: *One of three racing
machines built by the
Experimental Department
for the 1923 Island races.
This one, from the Russell
Harmon collection, is fitted
with a 500cc ohv engine.*
(Ronald Mugar)

part of the factory by Ed Kretz, during the 1930's and was recently acquired by Russ Harmon, of Fullerton.

In spite of the efforts of Norman Shidle, Dick Richards, and Hap Scherer to point out the necessity for the production of lightweight machines for a potential utility market, none of the members of the big three listed such models. Through Richards' marketing studies and the concurring conclusions of Tommy Butler, Weschler was by this time well convinced of the validity of the industry's need of promoting models of broader appeal.

However, the company's finances were in too precarious a condition to risk the costs of developing new models and the popularity of the Scout as a middleweight machine was in itself a sign that it was penetrating a wider area of the market.

A potentially serious competitor to the Scout in the Australasian and Southeast Asian export field was the sudden appearance of an exact replica, manufactured by some obscure manufacturer of household appliances in Osaka, Japan. While its production was obviously an

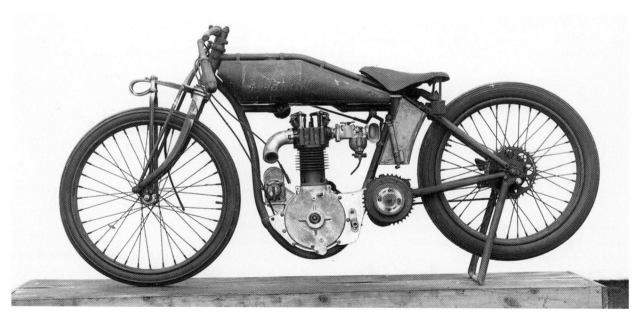

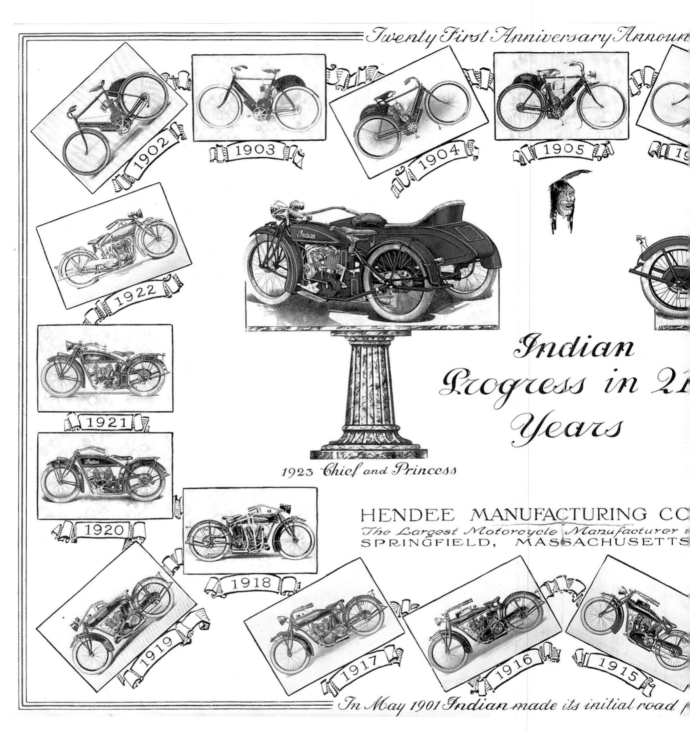

*Indian*
*Progress in 21 Years*

*1923 Chief and Princess*

HENDEE MANUFACTURING CO
*The Largest Motorcycle Manufacturer...*
SPRINGFIELD, MASSACHUSETTS

*In May 1901 Indian made its initial road...*

**Special advertising brochure commemorating Indian's 21st anniversary showing examples of some machines produced.**

infringement on all of the basic patents covering Scout design registered by Indian, the absence of any international agreements in those days regarding original patent rights rendered legal action impossible.

One of these Japanese machines was shipped to the factory in 1923, and upon close examination proved to be

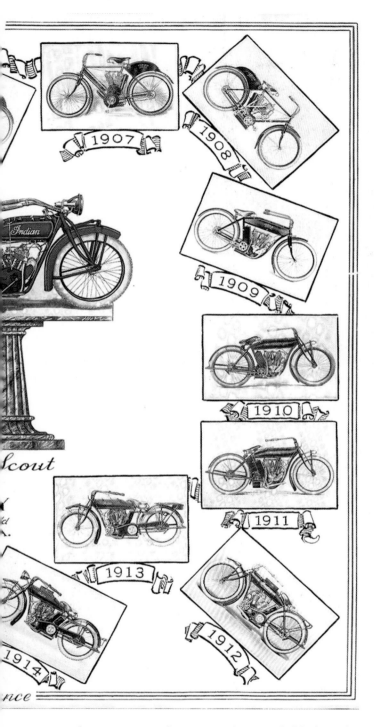

Another replica of the Scout appeared in Germany in 1923, where the machine was a very popular seller. It was named the Mabeco, and was built by a Scout enthusiast named Max Bernhard, in a small factory located at 22 Brensdauer Allee, in Berlin. Bernhard manufactured a limited number of machines until 1926, which were frank copies of the Scout, except that twin headlights and a double set of rear mudguard stays were fitted. His operations were taken over in 1927 by his shop foreman, Reinhold Kleiber, who moved the shop to 36 Prinzlauer Allee, and assembled a limited number of machines copied from the 1927 45 cubic inch Scout. He also built an overhead valve edition of the Scout, intended for racing.

A 37 cubic inch Mabeco engine was fitted to an ultra-light airplane in Germany by H. Klemperer in 1924, as there was much interest in this type of machine due to restrictions imposed on Germany by the Treaty of Versailles against the manufacture of heavily-powered machines. The machine was reported as having performed successfully.

Dick Richards resigned from the company in the Fall of 1923, being ultimately discouraged with the future of the motorcycle market in the United States, together with the fact that in spite of his extensive marketing studies, the company was disregarding his advice concerning the utility market. Weschler regretfully accepted his resignation and presented him with a new Chief sidecar outfit as a parting gift, in recognition of his dedicated service. Richards still treasures the company invoice marked Paid in Full, signed by Weschler. He journeyed to Colorado, where he established a parcel delivery and messenger service in Denver, utilizing Scout machines with commercial box bodies.

In the Fall of 1923, the company's Advertising Department proudly announced that at the end of the year's production, 250,000 Indians had been produced since its founding in 1901.

The year was also a triumph for Weschler, for, in spite of a modest production of 7,036 units, sales income totalled $2,687,797.00, with a net profit of $207,737.00. This latter figure, while moderate, was a healthy sign of efficient management after the staggering losses of the year before. After payment of the usual 7% dividends on the $1,000,000.00 of preferred stock, there was an earned $1.38 a share on the 100,000 shares of outstanding common stock with $100.00 par value. In his overhauling of Indian production schedules and procedures he had achieved economies in material purchases and, in further retrenchment, had reduced the production force to about 750 men.

Indian's position in the export market during this time was particularly strong, and, almost strange to relate, fully

such an exact copy that it was indistinguishable from the 1921 originals. Some knowledgeable executives of the production staff privately remarked that in some ways it was better finished! It was noted that even original-type gold leaf transfers showing US Patent numbers were affixed to the steering head lug!

50% of its production was still being sold overseas. Large quantities of machines, mostly Scouts, went to Australia and New Zealand. Indians were also popular in South America. At the Brazilian International Centennial Exposition, Indian was the only make to receive a gold medal for general mechanical excellence.

Indian's sporting successes overseas were no less impressive. Freddy Dixon won the Belgian Grand Prix on a 500cc side valve racing single. The Championship of Italy in both the 1,000 and 750cc classes was won on Chief and Scout models. The 1923 Argentine Tourist Trophy race was won by Antonio Gerli, riding a Super Chief.

The Board of Directors was much elated with the dramatic upturn in the fortunes of the company. With a burst of optimism, they decided to reorganize the company, seek new capital for expansion, and, most especially, increase production of the Scout, as orders had lately been running ahead of production. During the recent financial and production problems, Indian had lost its leadership in sales to Harley-Davidson, whose market had now expanded somewhat at Indian's expense. There was scarcely any visible evidence of more Harleys on the road, however, as most of their increased production had gone to their export markets.

At the November meeting of the Board the company was formally reorganized as the Indian Motocycle Company, the new name replacing that of the Hendee Manufacturing Company under which it had operated since 1901, when organized by Hendee and Hedstrom.

There has been continuing speculation throughout the years concerning the reason for dropping the 'r' from the word 'motorcycle' in the company name. According to company records of the Board's action, this was done simply to avoid any possible legal actions arising from patent suits, which had been a continuing problem within both the motorcycle and automobile industries since the earliest days of organized manufacture.

In the reorganization of Indian, the company became public, its stock now going up on the big board on Wall Street. An additional 100,000 shares were created with a provisional sales value of $25.00 per share.

It was rumoured around the company, but never actually substantiated, that Pierre S. du Pont, President of the giant du Pont de Nemours Corporation, had underwritten the initial public shares offering. It may well have been the case, the du Ponts had been diversifying their industrial holdings ever since Pierre S. had wrested control of General Motors Corporation from its original founder, William Crapo Durant, in 1915.

As a further change in company management, Frank Weschler was elected President. While he was in no way in financial control of the company, he had lately acquired some of the preferred shares through an arrangement with the Board of Directors through the efforts of President Skinner, said to be in the approximate amount of $100,000.00. This not only gave him a share in the profits, but important voting rights on the Board as well.

It was also reported that Weschler had informed the Board a year or so earlier that he felt it necessary for him to obtain titular control of the company, if he were to continue on in his capacity as General Manager which gave him ultimate authority over all matters affecting control of the actions of the managerial and executive staff.

This promotion was well received both from within and without the company, as Weschler was popular with most of the employees and dealers, who were all well aware that he was now solely responsible for Indian's survival through the difficult postwar period. His able management of production matters through the 1922 crisis had been a conclusive demonstration of his dedication to Indian and of his capabilities of guiding its future.

A final footnote to the close of 1923 was the ultimate withdrawal of the American motorcycling manufacturers from the international governing body of the sport, the Federation Internationaliste Motorcycliste. Billy Wells, who had held a seat on Indian's Board of Directors for some years, had been acting as a liaison representative between the American manufacturers and that body. In Indian's 1923 reorganization, he was not renominated to the Board, and for some reason the American Motorcycle Association did not see fit to appoint anyone else to continue in this post. As Indian was the only American manufacturer who had, up to that time, ever officially supported international racing, it appears that the others of the big three did not see fit to continue this representation. At any rate, motorcycle historians have generally agreed that this event marked the beginning of America's traditional isolation from international motorcycle sport.

While Indian's economic fortunes showed promise during the close of 1923, under Frank Weschler's capable management, both its future prospects of greatly enhanced production and sales were definitely limited, as were those of the other manufacturers who still survived on the domestic scene. The cheap, mass-produced, American light car, together with unlimited quantities of low cost fuel and lubricants, coupled with a general growing prospect of increasing economic prosperity, was now relegating the motorcycle to minority status in the transportation field.

**Above left:** *During its salad days the Indian company featured the best in machine tooling. This 1923 photograph shows a battery of Eberhardt milling machines fabricating chain sprockets. Note the overhead belt drives.* (Leslie D. Richards)

**Right:** *Al Herbert of New Zealand who for some years held the 500cc grass track record in Australasia. His 1912 racer is fitted with a 1924 ohv valve factory special.*

# The Personal Motor

## only $185

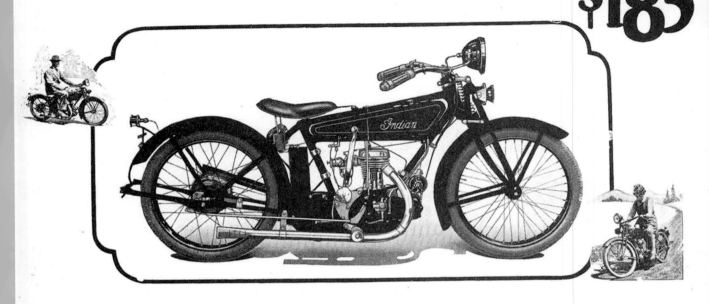

## PRICE, $185

COMPLETE ELECTRICAL EQUIPMENT, $30 EXTRA

F. O. B. Springfield, Mass.

### Model "L" Specifications

**MOTOR:** Single cylinder, vertical air-cooled, "L" Type, removable head, with wide copper and asbestos gasket (motor car type), Bore 2¾, stroke 3 37-64, piston displacement 21.25 cu. in. Valves: Indian side by side poppet, right hand side. Valve mechanism enclosed and efficiently lubricated. Diameter of valve 1⅝". Lift 9-32. Piston: Cast iron, two rings at top ⅛". Piston pin ⅝". Connecting rod: Lower end roller bearings.

**CARBURETOR:** Schebler H-¾" with 1" air valve, clamp type.

**IGNITION:** Splitdorf high tension. Spark plug, metric.

**LUBRICATION:** Automatic, motor driven, adjustable feed oil pump and auxiliary hand pump.

**STARTER:** Gear and sector type, mounted on transmission case, proper mesh of gears always retained. Adjustable spring tension on sector.

**CLUTCH:** Dry disc, adjustable to desired tension. Positive and smooth engagement. Friction fabric acts against steel plates. Control by hand lever conveniently located on left handle bar.

**TRANSMISSION:** Three speed, progressive sliding type, direct drive on high. Gear shift by direct acting lever. Quick, easy and positive. Main shaft carried on Timken roller bearings.

**HANDLE BARS:** De Luxe integral with stem. Affords comfortable riding position and positive control.

**CONTROLS:** Indian "Twist-of-the-Wrist" throttle, left grip; spark, right grip. Wire cables enclosed in handle bar. Cable casings covered with leather.

**DRIVE:** By roller chains, ⅝" pitch, ¼" wide. Both chains independent and adjustable. Efficient chain guards. Motor sprocket 15-tooth, clutch 38-tooth, countershaft 19-tooth, rear wheel 43-tooth. Gear ratios—5.733 to 1 on high; 10.32 to 1 on intermediate; 18.576 to 1 on low.

**FRAME:** Keystone type, two sections, constructed of heavy gauge tubing reinforced. Exceptionally low saddle position.

**SPRING FORK:** Indian truss type, spiral spring suspension.

**BRAKE:** Internal, powerful and positive, operated by foot lever conveniently located above foot rest on right side. Friction fabric 1-inch wide, brake drum 5½-inch diameter, integral with rear hub.

**WHEELS:** 26-inch diameter with CC type rims, black finish.

**TIRES:** Firestone clincher, non-skid tread, 26 x 2¼" approx.; 650 x 65 m. m.

**WHEEL BASE:** 54 inch.

**STAND:** Indian hinged type with spring latch.

**TANK:** One unit having separate fuel and oil compartments. Gasoline capacity 2 gals. approximately. Oil capacity 2 qts.

**SADDLE:** Indian special suspension. Large, comfortable saddle top, low riding position, 29-inches from ground.

**FOOT RESTS:** Quick, adjustable, rubber covered.

**MUD GUARDS:** Large, one piece steel construction.

**ELECTRIC SYSTEM:** Electric current for head light, tail light and horn, furnished through Splitdorf generator, and Wico 6-volt, 12-ampere hour battery acting entirely independent of ignition. Head and tail lamps controlled with switch.

**FINISH:** Indian Red.

**WEIGHT:** 235 pounds.

# Easiest to Handle!

## You'll like it right from the start

# Chapter 4

# PROSPERITY AND GOOD FEELING

The year of 1924 arrived in an era of widespread prosperity. The immediate post-war economic upheavals had been alleviated, and business, as well as the stock market, was booming. President Coolidge, a dour yankee who had succinctly stated that what was good for business was good for the country, allowed the nation to drift toward a laissez faire attitude concerning individual and corporate financial activities, and calmly took a long nap every afternoon.

The radio was enhancing communication, Hollywood was spreading sophistication, and the unpopular Prohibition law was stimulating the consumption of illicit alcoholic beverages. Bootleggers and organized crime were reaping a golden harvest, and the Roaring Twenties were well underway.

Purchasing power was reaching an all-time high, with luxury goods, and particularly automobiles, in increasing demand, more than eleven million motor vehicles now being on the road. Motorcycle production and registrations continued to decline, with about 150,000 registrations listed throughout the forty-eight states. In short, the future looked bright everywhere except for the domestic motorcycle industry.

Harley-Davidson, now the acknowledged sales leader, had projected a production of 12,000 machines for the year, from a still amortized factory complex that had been optimistically built to turn out 35,000 units four years before.

Frank Weschler, still somewhat shaken after the recent near failure of Indian, viewed the contemporary scene with no little caution, and planned for the production of 8,000 units. His projections were based largely on Dick

Richards' recent reports on marketing trends, together with his own realistic appraisal of Indian's chances on the domestic and export markets. In spite of the declining interest in motorcycling, he optimistically planned a factory-supported competition program, in the established tradition that had been bravely carried on since the company's earliest days.

Further sobering events portending the industry's decline were the death throes of the Ace Motorcycle Company and the now sharply decreased production of Excelsior twins and Henderson Fours.

The already limited sales of lightweight utility machines were reduced when A.C. Neracher moved his Neracar manufacturing activities to England. Cleveland, the last holdout in this uninspired lightweight market, announced its intention to abandon its two stroke for an excursion into the four cylinder luxury field, a rather doubtful decision in view of current trends.

Another growing threat to the motorcycle was the mass-produced cheap car. This factor has been largely blamed for the drop in sales of the two-wheelers in earlier times, but actually did not become serious until about 1924. By this time, mass production efficiencies in the automobile industry had reached a point where the ubiquitous Model T Ford could be sold for as little as $285.00 at the factory gate, and for an additional $25.00 could be fitted with a self starter. The Star automobile, launched optimistically in 1922 by the ebullient Billy Durant, who aspired to offer competition to Ford with a somewhat less

**Opposite:** *Reprint of factory literature announcing the new Indian Prince for 1925.*

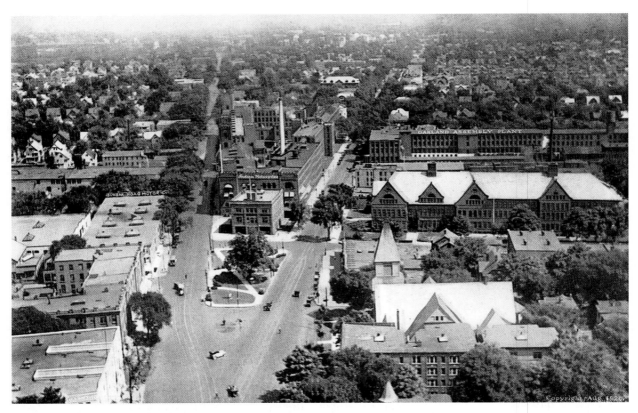

*An aerial view of the Indian factory complex in the 1920s. State Street (left) and Wilbraham Road merge in the foreground, with Winchester Park and the municipal fire station in the apex.*

ungainly vehicle, was selling well for only slightly more.

Either of these makes could now be purchased for about the same price as a classic heavyweight V-twin motorcycle. Both were substantially cheaper than a sidecar outfit and offered more passenger carrying capacity, and weather protection.

As a result of these trends, interest in motorcycling was limited mostly to die-hard enthusiasts, riders, and dealers. Manufacturers withdrew into their own circumscribed sphere of activity. As a general public trend to ignore motorcycles, their owners now appeared to comprise hell-for-leather, mechanicartisan or cowboy types, the odd iconoclastic business or professional man, thrill-seeking undergraduate, occasional feminine rider, or eccentric commuter.

This isolationist situation was further abetted by the general lack of motorcycle advertising in media other than trade publications, leading to further inbreeding of the industry.

The now dwindling trade press did nothing to alleviate this situation and confined its coverage mostly to the printing of exaggerated sales statistics, dealer activities, club news, and regional or national sporting events. Road tests of new models, or critical evaluations of current engineering or design trends, were conspicuous by their absence, as was any definite editorial policy.

In contrast to otherwise drab publications, there were several journalists reporting motorcycle activities who were able to bring color to motorcycling events of the day.

E.B. Holton was an Inspector of Weights and Measures for the State of New Jersey. An enthusiastic Indian rider, he habitually used a sidecar outfit in connection with his position, the nature of which was such that he enjoyed much free time to pursue his interest in both motorcycling and journalism. He had been one of the founders of the New Jersey Motorcycle Club, one of the largest of its kind on the Eastern seaboard, was its early day competition manager, and also edited its bulletin. He later wrote news articles for the leading publications, and promoted a number of time trials and endurance runs after the close of the war. Each Spring, he visited the Indian factory to collect a new sidecar outfit, as he recorded prodigious mileages both in connection with his work and through his attendance at various motorcycling functions.

Another widely known journalist and Indian enthusiast was L.E. 'Red' Parrish. He was employed by the Goodrich Tire Company as a pathfinder, to check tourist routes and to measure travel distances which were included in the famous Goodrich strip maps, presented to motorists at service stations and retail tire shops as an advertising promotion. He also researched and accumulated historical data on various cities and towns, which were used in the hundreds of billboards the company erected at strategic locations around the country, for the benefit of travelling motorists. Like Holton, he covered thousands of miles each year, criss-crossed the country innumerable times and also purchased a new outfit from Indian at the beginning of each season.

J.L. Beardsley was another journalist who wrote vivid reports of sporting events and biographical articles on leading professional riders of the day, which were also widely published in the trade press. Rewrites and

condensations of these articles have been featured in various contemporary motorcycle magazines in recent years and have done much to recreate the thrills of the vintage days of the sport.

With his new position of enhanced authority as President of the company, Frank Weschler immediately set about organizing production and sales activities as well as outlining the duties of the personnel involved to implement them.

He reached an early agreement with MacNaughton regarding his final authority over company policy, and the latter, apparently wishing to keep his position as Sales Manager, agreed to these dictates.

Now that the recent crisis of 1922–23 had been overcome, Colonel Hubbell resigned to enjoy his interrupted

**Right:** *A 1924 factory bill climber first ridden by Howard Mitzell in the East, and later by Al Lauer in the West. It is fitted with one of 25 engines hand-built by the Experimental Department with overhead valves. These 45cu in engines developed over 60hp on alcohol fuel.* **(Charles Vernon-Ronald Mugar)**

**Below:** *A dirt track racing machine, once owned by the factory, fitted with the 60 hp ohv special engine.* **(Charles Vernon-Ronald Mugar)**

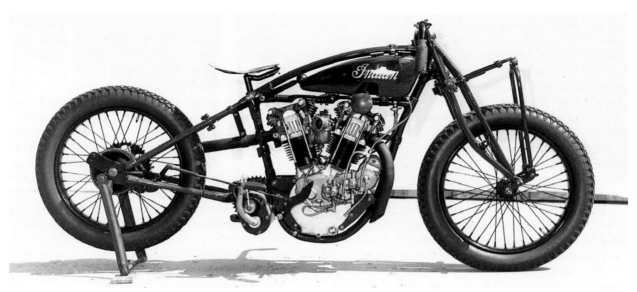

retirement, and Charles Franklin resumed full responsibility as Chief Engineer and Designer, which included overseeing certain aspects of production presided over by Theron L. Loose, who continued his duties as Plant Superintendent.

The position of Publicity Manager, lately vacated by Dick Richards, was filled by Rene D. Peppin, a newcomer who had formerly been a newspaper man.

Frank Waters had recently resigned from the company as Advertising Manager, and his position was filled by T.A. 'Ted' Slack, who had formerly worked in the Advertising Department of the Firestone Tire Company.

Dealers and riders everywhere were generally well pleased with Weschler's elevation to the office of company President. His dedication to Indian and his enthusiasm for motorcycling in general were a byword in the industry, and his managerial abilities had been well tested in his heroic efforts which resulted in saving the company during its recent crises.

Weschler repaid this trust by immediately instituting an active policy of keeping in close contact with the needs of the dealers, both in facilitating prompt shipments of new machines and spare parts to dealers and factory branches alike. Special attention to providing adequate customer service was stressed, and in addition, a strong advertising program was launched by which dealers could keep in touch with old customers and prospective new ones.

To facilitate dealer servicing of customers' machines, with a view to reducing shop time and consequent overheads, the factory instituted the distribution of a series of leaflets entitled 'Service Shots' which contained hints and tips on machine adjustments, particularly in regard to new models as they appeared. They also gave advice on special considerations in servicing police and commercially used machines for these specialized uses. Much of the content was gathered from Erle Armstrong's notes, used in the factory service school courses. Dealers were issued binders in which to preserve these sheets for future reference, and surviving copies are highly prized today by antique enthusiasts in overhauling and tuning old machines.

Rather than spending the large sums required for space in general magazine media, the company management decided to concentrate on providing dealer aids for local use, such as large pictures and posters for display in showrooms. The advertising value of Indian's racing victories was exploited by printing large posters shortly after each event. These were sometimes in the form of giant telegrams, which were intended as window displays, and were mailed to dealers as soon as possible, to keep the information timely.

The dealers were also urged to keep card files containing the names and addresses of shop callers, and the factory would follow these up with current sales catalogs.

Aid and advice was also given concerning the use of conditional sales contracts for installment purchases of new or used machines, as this was still a somewhat undeveloped sales practice, even in 1924.

As the once large group of ancillary motorcycle accessory manufacturers had gradually retreated from the field following the decline of motorcycle sales generally, the surviving manufacturers were now obliged to enter this field to service their own customers. These ancillaries included such extras as rear luggage racks, front wheel stands, leg shields, passenger pillion saddles, spot lights, speedometers and similar items.

Speedometers and sirens were fitted as standard to law enforcement units, although the former fitting was still an optional extra on standard machines fully a decade after they were standard fixtures on automobiles.

Items of clothing were also offered for dealer stocking, such as riding coats and breeches, boots, helmets, caps, goggles, sweaters with the Indian script prominently displayed, and weatherproof rainsuits for those stalwarts who regularly rode in the rain or snow. Apparently the general clothing industry had yet to take the motorcyclist market seriously.

These goods were obtained in quantity by the company, through various wholesale suppliers to the trade or directly from their manufacturers, and were sold to the dealers, at a small mark-up, the theory being that they were a definite sales aid to the retail level.

The two model ranges offered for 1925 consisted of the Scout and Chief, with the bulk of the production concentrated on the Scout. Sales of the Scout had been phenomenal for the times, and a number of new dealers were added to the company roster from enthusiasts who envisioned a new sales opportunity. Some former dealers, who had deserted the company during the difficult years, renegotiated their franchises, and by Spring Indian counted about 1,300 such outlets in the United States alone.

As the initial design of both models seemed adequate in both performance and dependability, they were continued with very minor changes for the ensuing season. The only exception was the addition of a Big Chief model of 74 cubic inches, otherwise identical to the original 61 inch model except for cylinder dimensions, and which was added to the line at the suggestion of many dealers who wanted the utmost in speed and power.

The Standard was at long last dropped from the line, although it had enjoyed a loyal following from all corners of the globe since its first introduction in 1916. Now outmoded, the management decided that its modernization would be superfluous in view of the fact that the Chief had been planned to take its place.

While the Standard was basically a very sound machine, a few of its inherent weaknesses had never been entirely eliminated. The rear suspension system had been somewhat strengthened in the models produced between 1917 and 1920 by the addition of extra gussets in the spring brackets, although it still required frequent attention in keeping the bolts tight. The kick-start mechanism was another source of weakness, as the bracket that supported the crank was bolted to a long stud attached through the rear engine plate. This was prone to loosening and required frequent adjustment to keep the ratchet in proper relationship to the standing pinion. The most serious fault was in the primary drive train, as under fierce acceleration the bolts securing the upper part of the gearbox housing would loosen, allowing the latter to twist, causing misalignment of the primary chain. This problem became more apparent with the fitting of the more powerful 74 cubic inch engine that was optional after 1920.

Generally speaking, however, the Standard had been a very satisfactory machine. It was powerful, reliable, and easy to maintain. Nearly 100,000 units were produced during its model life, including the War Department contracts, and it saw yeoman service all over the world.

The author is the owner of an authentically restored 1918 Standard, fitted with a 1920 74 cubic inch engine. With a top speed of nearly 90mph, the machine will cruise effortlessly at 55–60mph. While the center of balance is quite high by modern standards, the handling and steering are excellent, a legacy from its background of race breeding.

Many of these models were still in use for two decades after production ceased, and numbers of sidecar outfits were seen in England up to the time of World War II. The author recalls two examples that were maintained as utility machines and were in daily use in 1939.

It was the Standard Powerplus engine that did much to establish Indian's reputation for ruggedness and longevity, and as a simple and uncomplicated design it inspired later designs by other makers.

In the early 1920's, interest in private flying had been stimulated by the accelerated design progress resulting from the widespread use of aircraft during the recent war. Private manufacture of civilian aircraft was somewhat curtailed, however, as vast numbers of Army surplus training planes selling at giveaway prices were immediately available. These models were expensive to maintain, which led to some speculation on the part of aeronautical engineers concerning the future of ultra-

light 'flivver planes,' or 'Motorcycles of the Air.' In the absence of small aircraft powerplants, most of them were powered with motorcycle engines.

Several experimental models were built and flown, some using a converted 61 inch Powerplus engine. In order to allow the use of a large, slow-turning propeller, a two-to-one reduction gearing was made up from chain sprockets and shafts utilizing motorcycle parts. O.H. Snyder built and tested two examples of his 'Baby Bomber' biplane using a Powerplus engine, and offered building plans for sale at $12.00 a set. It is reported that half a dozen had been built by private owners by 1925.

A smaller, single bay biplane, was built in 1924 by two young engineers, C. Turner and C. Fastig. It was also designed for use with the 61 cubic inch Powerplus engine, which in this case was fitted with direct drive, as the machine was much lighter than Snyder's design. It was reported to have flown well. A year or two later an enthusiast named Epps designed an ultralight monoplane which specified a converted Powerplus or Chief engine for power. Weighing less than 500lbs with pilot and fuel, it performed well with a directly driven propellor.

One unresolved problem in fitting V-twin motorcycle engines to ultralight aircraft was that of engine vibration, due to the characteristic unequal firing sequence. While this factor could be neutralized by the dampening effect of a heavy motorcycle frame, the situation was quite different in an ultralight airframe, and structural failures were often experienced. Four cylinder motorcycle power plants later became more popular, due to their smoother running characteristics.

Competition during the 1924 season was somewhat curtailed, due to the lack of factory support from Excelsior and Harley-Davidson, who did not field any professional riders. Weschler decided that Indian should still maintain its place in the sporting field, in spite of a reduced budget for its support. Charles Gustafson, Jr. was team manager, following the resignation of Charles Spencer, and old timers have reported that he did an excellent job with limited funds.

Charles Franklin superintended the rebuilding of about a dozen of the eight-valve racing engines left over from the 1921–1922 season. With improved carburetion and altered cam and valve action, these engines developed increased power.

The racing engines were bench-tested in a small brick building lined inside with heavy boiler plate, which was in the factory courtyard. The testers made their observations through shielded inspection windows, to avoid fatalities if a crankcase or cylinder disintegrated during full throttle running. An engine especially designed for Orrie Steele's famous hill climb machine was said to have developed over 70hp at 9,000rpm, burning blended fuels.

The biggest race meet that year was a three-day event held at Toledo, Ohio, on June 24, 25 and 26. Indian entered a strong team consisting of Johnny Seymour, Paul Anderson and Paul Bower. Harley-Davidson's team leaders were Jim Davis and Ralph Hepburn, the latter making his last appearance in motorcycle competition. The main events were scheduled for 30.50 cubic inch singles instead of the more usual 61's. Davis and Hepburn had both purchased factory built machines from Harley that they had raced the previous seasons, and hired former racing mechanics to tune them.

The 10-mile event was a blanket run for most of the distance, with Davis nosing out Johnny Seymour by a wheel length, to win. He also narrowly won the 25-mile event, establishing a new record in the 30.50 class. His time was 2 minutes, 10 and ⅕ seconds.

Tragedy marked this meeting when promising young Paul Bower was fatally injured when he went through the infield fence, after he skidded in the north turn.

The Indian factory had about 15 board track machines out on loan to the more promising riders and these were maintained either by factory mechanics or by local racing managers, at various points around the country.

1926 saw the last of the more spectacular races on the board tracks of the country. Joe Petrali, on a special 45

cubic inch Excelsior, broke three national records on July 2nd, during the qualifying time trials on July 9th for the Championship races at Altoona, Pa. His mile time was 33.44 seconds for a speed of 107mph. The five mile run was made at a time of 2.57.7. The ten miler was yet another record time of 5.57.5 for a speed of 101 mph.

But it was Jim Davis, now an Indian professional, who stole the show, with a record lap of the mile and a quarter oval in 39⅘ seconds, for a speed of 113mph.

At the big meet on July 9th, Joe Petrali won the 20-mile feature race on his Super X Excelsior. Indian's M.K. 'Curley' Fredericks thundered around the saucer for a then all-time board track record of 114mph.

Joe Petrali, who won the National Championship for Harley-Davidson in 1925, was a former Indian rider. As a young boy he had already become an enthusiastic motor-cyclist and owned a number of well-used pioneer machines, beginning with a belt drive Flanders. He later purchased a second-hand Indian Standard from Jud Carriker, in Santa Ana, during 1920. As an expert rider who was known to be utterly fearless in competition, he was for several years Harley's star professional. In later years, Petrali was employed by Howard Hughes engineering organization and accompanied Hughes on the one and only flight Hughes ever made in the famous five-minute flight over Long Beach harbor in his huge wooden flying boat.

During the Spring of 1926, Charles Franklin perfected a racing version of the side valve Powerplus type twins, with special high compression cylinder heads, high lift cams, and twin carburetors, one for each cylinder. Four of these engines were built by the racing department,

*A 1925 Velocette Model K with 21 cu in obc engine. This machine is an identical model to one purchased through the Indian Factory by Charles B. Franklin for evaluation during prototype work on the Prince. (Jeff Clew)*

two being of 61 cubic inch displacement and two of 45 inches.

On August 21st at the Rockingham mile and a quarter oval at Salem, New Hampshire, Fredericks had already won two 25-mile races on one of the new 61 inch machines. Jim Davis had won the 20-mile National on a 45 inch model. At the half time of the race, Fredericks, with a terrific burst of speed, turned one flaming lap at 120.3mph for an all-time record that was never beaten on any board course.

It is significant to note that while most of Indian's and its competitors' racing records had, since 1911, been won on four and eight overhead valve specials, the ultimate marks were made on specially developed side valve machines. These results have remained as a lasting tribute to Franklin's engineering genius in the field of engine design.

General interest in board track racing declined from that time on, the two surviving courses being Rockingham and Altoona, which featured their last meetings during the 1928 season. The extreme danger to the riders and the deterioration of the tracks have both been mentioned as the reasons for board track racing demise. There was also less general interest due to the fact that during the latter years of the sport Indian was the only factory that supported it or fielded teams or machines.

During the early Spring, Indian's management decided to again enter the lightweight market. These plans were at once at variance with the policies already in force by the other big three factories, who were now manufacturing only big twins or, in the case of Excelsior, fours.

Surviving employees of the Engineering and Design department advanced a number of reasons for this decision. The continuing popularity of the Scout gave rise to the thought that a smaller and cheaper machine along Scout lines might have a similar appeal. Then there was the rumour throughout the trade that Cleveland was about to drop its two-stroke lightweight, in order to concentrate on a small four-cylinder machine recently developed for them by L.E. Fowler. There also may well have been the admonition of Richards lurking in the backs of their minds, concerning the necessity to offer machines more suited to novices and younger riders, who might be interested in a small type of motorcycle.

Another reason that has been cited for this new undertaking was the fact that the English motorcycle industry, whose products were now enjoying a soaring popularity both at home and abroad, was offering a vast range of light and medium weight machines, and that Indian might do well to attempt to compete in this market. There was also the fact that Indian's name still carried much magic on the English scene.

*A 21 cu in ohc racing engine built by Indian's Experimental Department. This example is Number 4 of 12 made during 1925, and is owned by Russell Harmon. The Velocette parentage is clearly apparent.* (Ronald Mugar)

At any rate, Charles Franklin had been keeping in close touch with overseas developments, and had purchased several examples of some of the leading makes for evaluation at Springfield. He was particularly impressed with the newly-developed model K Velocette which was fitted with a 21 cubic inch overhead camshaft engine. This design represented the most advanced type of single cylinder motorcycle engine, as the use of bevel gear drive from the crankshaft to the valve gear was most efficient, obviated the clatter of the more usual push rods, and gave an extraordinary amount of power. After some experimentation, however, it was decided to finalize the design on the traditional Indian side valve type, as the overhead camshaft engine with its bevel gear drive was very costly to manufacture.

The result was a lightweight single cylinder machine which was named the Prince, and which was laid out along contemporary English lines. The solid frame was of the diamond pattern, the lower angles of which were formed by the engine plates. This type of frame came to be known as the 'Keystone' type in the United States. The front forks were of the English girder type, with a pair of tubes on either side forming a truss which was supported by a single barrel compression spring.

The single cylinder 21 cubic inch engine carried a single chain primary drive to a light pattern foot-operated clutch and three-speed hand change gearbox that was based on Hedstrom's 1915 design. The fuel tank was a somewhat ungainly wedge shaped affair that was clipped between the tank rails, and carried an oil reservoir for the total loss lubrication system of the engine.

The prototype machines were reported to have handled well, were easy to start, and had sufficient power to give a top speed of well over 50mph and to provide adequate hill climbing ability. After these tests were completed, the management gave the production staff orders to prepare for Prince manufacture in the Fall for the 1925 sales season.

One of the major production problems at that time was that the great factory was operating at about 25% capacity, being about one quarter of what it had enjoyed in the peak year of 1913. In planning for 1925, it was decided to revamp the assembly lines and the grouping of certain machine tools in order to facilitate the new production quotas. This left much empty space in the building and some of this was leased or rented at times to outside individuals for other uses.

One of the best remembered of these outside tenants was a man named Edward Parker. who had developed and patented a process for rust-proofing metal parts, utilizing a sulfur dioxide compound combined with the material. The process was known as 'Parkerizing,' the work being done in a part of the basement that faced State Street. Certain of the Indian parts were treated with this compound, including the bell cranks and rods supporting the forks.

The subject of the Indian Company diversifying its manufacture to include other products had been raised by certain of the Board of Directors and other company personnel as a means of utilizing now available factory facilities not required for motorcycle production. This matter had been brought up on several occasions since 1921, when the realistic state of the motorcycle market had become painfully apparent. President Weschler, in his characteristic loyalty to Indian, had stoutly maintained that the function of the company was to produce only motorcycles. There was, however, the indisputable fact that the company was carrying extra expense in the maintenance and upkeep of unused space, not the least of which was the real estate tax levy against it.

At this juncture, Tommy Butler, who was now back at Springfield with the Sales Department since the recent closing of the Chicago factory branch, came forward with an idea of diversification into the field of small industrial engines.

Butler proposed that detuned and derated Scout and Prince engines could be adapted quite easily for this use, provided they were cooled by a simple fan arrangement

with shrouding of the cylinders. Butler further argued that the production of such engines could be initiated without disrupting motorcycle production, and would penetrate a growing market which could materially increase Indian's production volume for added profits.

As Weschler was still averse to any diversification, and Butler could find no support for the project among the Board of Directors, he decided to resign. He came to the west coast and shortly thereafter became Sales Manager for the pioneer Indian sales agency in Los Angeles operated by C. Will Risdon. At this writing he lives in retirement on his country estate outside of Boise. As an outspoken man, not given to withholding his honest opinions, he was often considered the gadfly of the Indian company and his name has not been mentioned for many years in connection with Indian history. As a talented man who contributed much to the company's well being during his tenure of employment, however, his efforts should not be forgotten.

Another former member of Indian's Sales Department who resigned from the company, but who stayed with the industry was Ray Day. With a background in practical engineering and mechanics, he pioneered the use of aluminum alloy pistons in both cars and motorcycles. Day formed his own company, and manufactured his product under the trade name of 'Day-Lite.'

Other engineering and design projects inaugurated by Franklin, other than development work on the Prince, included the fitting of Ricardo-type detachable cylinder heads to the Prince, as well as the Chief and Scout.

The one-piece cylinders with the head integral with the barrel had been used on all side valve Indian engines since the introduction of the first Powerplus model. While this arrangement had been refined in subsequent editions, it still had the disadvantage of being subject to some distortion and consequent risk of valve warpage, if overheated during prolonged hard running. The new arrangement, together with slightly larger cooling fins and altered combustion chamber shape, was reported as producing 20% more power, as well as making top overhauls and valve grinding much simpler.

Under President Weschler's capable management, Indian's financial picture brightened markedly during 1924. The production force had been reduced to 750 men due to the general drop in motorcycle production, but plant efficiency had been enhanced by the reorganization of assembly methods.

This undertaking was nominally under the direction of Theron L. Loose, but most of it was superintended by Erle Armstrong, still at his prime occupation of overseeing quality control of the product and enhancing assembly line efficiency. Armstrong possessed the authority to shut down the assembly lines at any time, to rectify any faults that might occur.

For the Company year ending August 31st, gross income from sales totaled $3,940,00.00, with a net income of $88,012.00, after paying the usual 7% annual dividend on the preferred shares. While this was substantially less than the $207,738.00 profit reported the year previously, most company indebtedness had been retired through Weschler's efforts, and the company faced the coming sales year with a clean slate.

The sales year of 1925 was opened with a strong advertising campaign in the trade press, with much emphasis on the Prince. The Indian dealers viewed the new lightweight with the usual mixed emotions, as the majority still favored heavyweight machines, even though most of them were pleased with the public reaction to the lighter Scout. Some of the dealers who had leanings toward favoring utility sales did very well with it, and large numbers of sales were made to ride-to-work utility riders, Western Union messenger boys, novice riders, and not a few intrepid feminine newcomers to motorcycling.

Billy Wells showed great interest in the Prince's sales possibilities in Great Britain, where motorcycle sales were increasing and where there was valuable prestige with the Indian name. While some dealers and riders were disappointed that it was not designed as the now popular overhead valve type, its acceptable top speed and acceleration, as well as its rugged design and ease of maintenance, made it a strong competitor within the current large number of British makes.

Wells was reported to have sold several hundred machines in the British Isles within the first few months of the year. Substantial numbers of European orders were filled through Stokvis and Sonen, in Rotterdam.

American V-twins also continued to be popular sellers in Great Britain, really volume sales being limited only by their necessarily high prices. In fact, it has been the expressed opinion of several motorcycle historians that the late George Brough's introduction of his famous luxury machines was originally inspired by the wide acceptance in England of the Yankee invaders. Even his early models were designed along American lines, and his forks were a frank copy of the Harley-Davidson type.

The new improved Chief, in both 61 and 74 cubic inch models (the latter now known as the Big Chief) was well received by heavyweight enthusiasts, and was becoming increasingly popular with law enforcement bodies.

The municipal Sales Department was now headed by W. Stanley Bouton, following the resignation of Frank Long, and his duties included liaison work between local dealers, the factory and appropriate law enforcement purchasing or procurement agencies. With the now almost static state of general motorcycle sales, this side of the business became more critical than ever to the surviving manufacturers, not only financially but from the standpoint of name brand prestige.

The general public, then as now, was usually quite unaware that municipal or law enforcement sales of any given make of motorcycle, or other type of vehicle, were

*Leslie D. Richard's Sales Manager, O.B. Senter, demonstrates a 1925 Prince to an elderly gentleman and a young schoolboy at the former's Denver, Colorado salesroom. Both subsequently purchased Princes. (Leslie D. Richards)*

# The Personal Motor

Here's the 1926 INDIAN PRINCE with the streamline beauty of the INDIAN SCOUT. It is still two hundred pounds lighter than the average motorcycle. You can learn to ride it in five minutes.

## Specifications

MODELS: INDIAN PRINCE, Model L.
INDIAN PRINCE, Electrically Equipped, Model LE.

MOTOR: Single cylinder, vertical air-cooled, "L" Type, removable head, with wide copper and asbestos gasket (motor car type). Bore 2¾", stroke 3 37-64", piston displacement 21.25 cu. in. Valves: INDIAN side by side poppet, right hand side. Valve mechanism enclosed and efficiently lubricated. Diameter of valve 1⅝". Lift 9-32". Piston: Cast iron, two rings at top ⅛". Piston pin ⅝". Connecting rod: Lower end roller bearings.

CARBURETOR: Schebler plain tube, clamp type.

IGNITION: Splitdorf high tension magneto. Spark plug, metric.

LUBRICATION: Automatic, motor driven, adjustable feed oil pump and auxiliary hand pump.

STARTER: Gear and sector type, mounted on transmission case, proper mesh of gears always retained. Adjustable spring tension on sector.

CLUTCH: Dry disc., adjustable to desired tension. Positive and smooth engagement. Friction fabric acts against steel plates. Control by hand lever conveniently located on left handle bar.

TRANSMISSION: Three speed, progressive sliding type, direct drive on high. Gear shift by direct acting lever. Quick, easy and positive. Main shaft carried on Timken roller bearings.

HANDLE BARS: Top integral with stem. Comfortable riding position and positive control.

CONTROLS: INDIAN "Twist-of-the-Wrist" throttle, left grip; spark, right grip. Wire cables enclosed in handle bar. Cable casings covered with leather.

DRIVE: By roller chains, ⅝" pitch, ¼" wide. Both chains independent and adjustable. Efficient chain guards.

### NEW FEATURES for 1926

Streamlines now conform in beauty with SCOUT and CHIEF models.

Additional comfort with INDIAN-Mesinger bucket saddle, lower saddle position and longer handle-bars.

Seventeen improvements include the following: New keystone frame in two sections and heavy gauge tubing with reinforced joints affords secure anchorage for motor. Vanadium steel tubing at stress points.

Tank capacity increased one-half.

Special INDIAN Schebler carburetor makes easier starting.

Battery box with both side and top removable gives easy access.

Generator placed higher with longer quiet running chain.

Rear chain guard extended in curve over sprocket.

Increased clearance between fork crown and mud-guard.

Motor sprocket 15-tooth, clutch 38-tooth, countershaft 18-tooth, rear wheel 43-tooth.
Gear ratios—6.05 to 1 on high; 10.89 to 1 on intermediate; 19.61 to 1 on low.

FRAME: Keystone type, two sections, constructed of heavy gauge tubing reinforced. Exceptionally low saddle position. Vanadium tubing at stress points.

SPRING FORK: INDIAN truss type, spiral spring suspension.

BRAKE: Internal, powerful and positive, operated by foot lever conveniently located above foot rest on right side. Friction fabric one inch wide; brake drum 5¼ inch diameter.

WHEELS: 26-inch diameter, wire, 36 spokes, front and rear 26" x 3"C C rims, black finish.

TIRES: Firestone clincher, non-skid tread. 650 x 65 m.m.; 26" x 2¾" approx. 26" x 3.30" Balloons optional at slight extra charge.

WHEEL BASE: 54 inch.

STAND: INDIAN hinged type with spring latch.

TANK: One unit having separate fuel and oil compartments.
Gasoline capacity 2¾ gallons.
Oil capacity 3 quarts.

SADDLE: INDIAN-Mesinger, Bucket Seat. Large, comfortable saddle top, low riding position, 28 inches from ground.

FOOT RESTS: Quick adjustable, rubber covered.

MUD GUARDS: Large, one piece steel construction.

ELECTRIC SYSTEM: Electric current for head light, tail light, and horn, furnished through Splitdorf generator, and Wico 6-volt, 12-ampere hour battery acting entirely independent of ignition. Head and tail lamps controlled with single switch.

FINISH: INDIAN Red.

WEIGHT: 265 pounds.

not based on the excellence of the product but rather on a diverse number of monetary and political circumstances. While the choice of make or type of machine was generally influenced by the opinions of the law officers or employees who rode them, the final decision was largely dependent on the penury of a tight-fisted purchasing agent, or the expediency and/or corruption of whatever elected politicians or tenured civil servants were involved.

The variety of predicaments involved in these transactions could be infinite. In some towns and cities the business might be rotated between two or three competing makes, each being expected to trade for his competitor's used machines at often ruinously low prices. In other situations, the make of one particularly favored dealer might be bought continuously, which often involved sub rosa kickbacks to the officials involved in the purchase. In many areas, machines were purchased competitively on the basis of the best discount off the established list price. Often, the business was transacted at an actual loss to both dealer and factory, who made substantial concessions to keep their own make in the picture.

The immediate advantage to the local dealer was, of course, the service and maintenance business that logically accompanied the sale. Flat rates for various services were established, which were supposed to afford a legitimate profit to the dealer, including the sale of engine lubricating oil and grease. While on the surface this servicing would appear to be a continuing source of steady income for the dealer, in practise this was usually not as lucrative as projected. Police officers operating the machines were often in the habit of demanding riding gloves, goggles, articles of clothing such as scarves or jackets, or even service or repair work for their personal machines, in rare cases. The dealer was then expected to bill these items to the official owners under the guise of service work, or to present them as outright gifts.

While local sales were nominally in the hands of franchised dealers, the factory Municipal Service Department was generally called in to expedite the larger orders. A part of the transaction was usually the trading in of used machines, which were condemned when they reached the 40,000-mile mark. These were available in large numbers, at various times, from large police departments such as New York City or from the East Bay region of California, which included Oakland, Berkeley and Alameda. As the average dealer often did not wish to tie up large amounts of capital in many used machines, the surplus was distributed through the factory to other dealers. Sometimes the condemned machines were sold at public auction and such sales were an outlet for many fours, as many riders desiring them could not afford the high original price.

Large numbers of Indians were sold for law enforcement use in the north eastern, eastern, and south eastern states as the factory in Springfield was closer to these areas than their competitors, with consequent lower freight rates. After 1926, some machines were delivered by trucks.

Indian's export business in the British Isles was dealt a crippling blow in the Spring of 1925 when the Chancellor of the Exchequer levied a 33% import tax against all foreign motorcycles. This drove the retail prices so high that the importation of American machines ceased almost overnight. Billy Wells valiantly stayed in business for a few months, but with no relief in sight he regretfully ceased operations after sixteen profitable and eventful years.

As there were numerous older Indian machines in use as well as many postwar examples, including a number of Princes, the factory maintained a small spare parts outlet in London for some years. The actual repair and maintenance of Indians was then carried on in a number of small specialist shops operated by enthusiasts, a few of whom were still active until the beginning of World War II.

Indian continued to enjoy substantial popularity in Australasia, however, as import levies were as yet not unfavorable. A Scout won the West Australia Reliability Trial against a large field of heavier machines. George Lambert also won the 1,000cc class of the flying mile championship in New Zealand on a 61 cubic inch Chief.

In 1925, Indian topped all comers in Australian competition, winning the solo and sidecar championships, the Victoria Junior TT race, the Australia Heavyweight Championship, the Tasmanian Sidecar Championship, as well as the Adelaide to Melbourne Solo Record.

Late in the season, Paul Anderson set a new record on an eight-valve special at Sellicks Beach, South Australia, recording 125mph.

The Excelsior Company scooped the entire industry with the introduction of a 45 cubic inch version of their 50° V-twin. They had formerly offered a two-model range in the post war years, consisting of a 61 inch twin, together with the perennially popular Henderson four, which had been continued with only detail changes since redesigned by Arthur Lemon in 1919. Lemon had also redesigned the 61 inch twin in 1921, along Indian Scout lines, with helical gear primary drive and unit construction of the engine and gearbox. When the 45 inch model proved to be a good seller, the 61 inch model was made available only on special order.

Not to be outdone, President Weschler directed Franklin to design an engine of similar capacity as an optional fitting to the still popular 37 inch Scout. This was first offered to the public the following Fall, for the 1927 season.

Indian again was active in competition during the 1925 season, with an augmented racing budget now that the company was happily in a sound financial condition.

The very fast dirt track at Harley-Davidson's home city, Milwaukee, was the scene of a portion of the National Championship races in 1925. Harleys won the first round of races when, on August 9th, Eddie Brinck won the 10-mile event in the 30.50 class over Jim Davis and Joe Petrali, all of whom rode Harleys. Davis also won the 5-mile event, with Johnny Seymour on an Indian coming in second, and Harley-mounted Joe Petrali coming in third.

1925 also marked the first year of 21 cubic inch racing, instigated by Harley-Davidson who, in that year, introduced their soon-to-be-famous 'Peashooter' line of 21 inch side valve and overhead valve engines. Harley riders, competing on the only make available, were, of course, the winners of all three places in the meet held on August 9th. Eddie Brinck, the Dayton, Ohio speedster, won the 5-mile event for a time of 4.20. He also captured the 10-mile over Jim Davis and Johnny Vance in 8:45⅓.

The most memorable victories of the year, however, were claimed by Indian at the famous mile oval at the New York State Fairgrounds at Syracuse. On September 19th, which the sports writers called 'Johnny Seymour Day', this fearless Indian enthusiast set four world's records and won three National Championships, in a burst of sensational riding on his 30.50 special, which was specially built for him that Spring. This race meet attracted a crowd of over 100,000 fans, as auto racing events had been scheduled to run alternately.

Seymour first set a new track record in the qualifying trials, for a flying start one lap of 44.30 seconds. He then went on in the 5-mile National, to defeat Harley aces Joe Petrali, Jim Davis, and M.K. 'Curley' Fredericks, with a new record of 3.43.78.

Ten days later in Michigan, he demolished three more records, winning the 10-mile National in 7.30.40, the 15-mile National in 11.19.6, and the 25-mile National in 19.15.5.

Seymour was a popular champion, as he was a born showman as well as being a courageous rider. His contemporaries universally described him as being utterly without fear. He is said to have survived his racing days and is reported to be still living in the Chicago area at this writing.

All in all, 1925 was a very successful year for Indian. Its competition records had been impressive and sales both at home and abroad had held firm, in spite of the virtual loss of the British market. Best of all, Indian's financial situation had improved to the point where a net profit of $201,000 was recorded for the fiscal year ending August 31st. Sales for the year were over $500,000.00, more than those of the previous year, and actual cash on hand was more than double liabilities. Best of all, a dividend of $1.45 per share was paid to the owners of 100,000 shares of no par common stock, which did much to bolster public confidence.

The three model Indian range was continued for 1926, with detail improvements to all models.

The Prince's frame was slightly altered to allow for the fitting of a between-the-rails fuel and oil tank, with the same contours as that of the Scout, except that it was of somewhat narrower cross section and gave the machine a much more symmetrical appearance.

The intake porting, on both the Chief and Scout, was altered for slightly more efficient carburetion, these models having been fitted with Ricardo-type detachable heads the previous season. Both machines were now fitted with low pressure balloon type tires of 3.85 inch cross section as standard, which gave a softer ride, although some speed enthusiasts claimed that these provided less accurate steering. This type of tire was also offered on the Prince, as an optional extra at a slightly higher price.

Sidecars were, of course, included in the line, with optional commercial bodies, along with the American La France chemical firefighting unit.

A surprise model offered at midseason was an overhead valve version of the Prince. This was thought to have been introduced to counter the threat of the overhead valve Harley 21 cubic inch 'Peashooter' model, which had been announced the preceding Fall.

The new machine was available in Standard Indian red or in all-white, at no extra charge. The cycle parts were identical with the side valve model, except that a hand-controlled clutch was fitted, activated by a lever on the right handlebar grip as in current English practise. This machine was not shown in the regular catalogs, and from all available information only a couple of hundred were built. The engine was used as the basis for a special road racing machine that was built in small numbers for the European market a couple of seasons later.

Along with the detail mechanical improvements offered from time to time, Franklin adhered to an engineering policy that he had instituted during the days of the Powerplus designs, namely, of making new innovations capable of being fitted to previous models. This not only simplified the maintenance and production of the spare parts stock, but was instrumental in keeping older machines on the road. This is probably the principal reason so many old Indians survived through the years.

Indians continued to enjoy healthy sales both at home and abroad. At the annual company picnic held that Summer, President Weschler was happy to announce to both staff executives and production workers that the once depleted treasury now contained a surplus of over $800,000.00.

In 1926, a young motorcycle enthusiast and a recent graduate of Boston's Northeastern University, named Theodore A. (Ted) Hodgdon, joined Indian's Advertising Department as a copy writer. He was later to serve this Department in various capacities, ultimately becoming Advertising Manager.

It was during this Summer that Weschler, with the unanimous concurrence of the Board of Directors, opened negotiations with Michigan Motors Company of Detroit, the new owners of the remaining assets of the now defunct Ace Company. Weschler had reasoned that with the now sound financial condition the company enjoyed, it could well afford the acquisition of the Ace machine. With the single cylinder Prince, the light twin Scout and the heavyweight Chief, the addition of a four would give Indian a complete coverage of the motorcycle market.

The Ace machine had had a rather tenuous history, which is described in the following chapter. The ultimate owners of the manufacturing rights had hoped to resume its production, but inadequate financing and improper management had brought proceedings to a halt after only a few machines had been assembled in the Spring of 1926.

The stockholders of Michigan Motors had hoped to at least recoup their original investment in the sale of the machine, but were in no position to drive a hard bargain. Motorcycle financing in general was in more or less poor repute in Detroit, as the details of the Ace misadventure were well known there. Max Sladkin, the original financial backer of Ace in 1919, had already lost a fortune. His nephew, Adolph Eidelson, told the author that Sladkin would have faced bankruptcy at Ace's demise had he not had the foresight to commingle his remaining assets with those of his wife's father, who was a wealthy man. He died in 1935 at the age of 55, as the result of a heart attack.

Weschler's negotiations with Michigan Motors dragged on until the Fall, the latter group attempting to hold out for more money than Indian was willing to offer. It has been reported that the sale of Ace's assets did not take place until a few days before the opening of the National Motorcycle Show, held at the end of January, 1927.

Indian's sporting program opened in 1926 with the

*The limited production ohv model Prince of 1926, with hand controlled clutch and foot pegs in the contemporary English and Continental style.* (Theodore Hodgdon)

establishing of two speed records at Daytona Beach, Florida, early in January. Ace speedman Johnny Seymour, together with Charles Gustafson, Jr., and two mechanics, arrived at the sand course just after New Years Day, along with a 61 cubic inch eight-valve twin and a 30.50 single.

The average of a two way run with the twin gave Johnny a new world's record of 132mph. On the afternoon of the same day, he racked up a 17½ second mile on the 30.50 for a new mark of 115mph. These records stood for nearly ten years.

Orrie Steele retained his hill climbing crown at the National meet at Rochester, New York, when on August 15th he topped the 450 foot 45° Egypt hill in 14 seconds, on his potent 70hp factory special.

In January 1925, Dick Richards had been visited by Arthur Anderson and Bob Haley from the factory, who had persuaded him to take a franchise in that area. Floyd Clymer, who had once been a Harley-Davidson dealer, had taken the Indian franchise for the Denver area in 1919. Since developing his later famous Clymer spotlight for automobiles in 1925, however, he had been neglecting his motorcycle business and sales had fallen off alarmingly. The factory Sales Department had been desirous of reviving the dealership under another owner, and as Richards' loyalty to Indian was well known

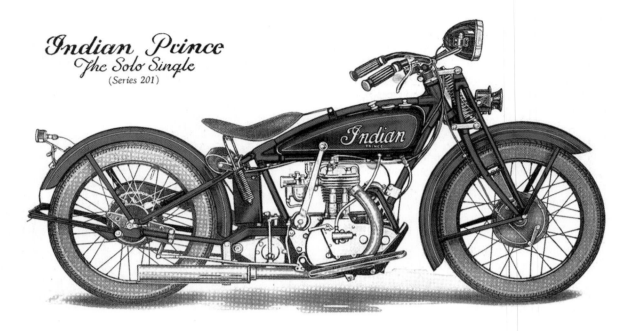

*Indian Prince*
*The Solo Single*
(Series 201)

**The Prince in final form, with balloon tires and heavier front forks.**

in Springfield, it was logical that the factory should extend this offer to him.

Richards had been importuning the factory to give special emphasis to his former commercial use of sidecar outfits in their advertising campaigns, but up until that time little had been accomplished in this regard.

At any rate, Richards did very well with his Indian dealership from the start, and sold a large number of Prince models, both to private as well as commercial users. He also entered his own Prince machine in local sporting and reliability runs, and effectively demonstrated the capabilities of the model.

Always a keen student of motorcycle marketing, Richards was well aware of the potential of single cylinder lightweights, and wrote an article about the matter which he submitted to *Motorcycling and Bicycling Illustrated*; this article entitled 'Let the Siren Yowl' was published in the March 31st, 1926 issue.

Richard's article stirred up no little interest within the trade, as, while his opinions represented a minority of the dealers' thinking in the matter of lightweight machines, there were many dealers and riders who had agreed with him. Walter Davidson, then President of Harley-Davidson, was sufficiently moved to write Richards a personal letter in reply.

In the late Fall, at the conclusion of the year's production, President Weschler authorized the Advertising Department to announce that the factory had recently produced the 275,000th Indian since the Company's founding. This figure, most probably accurate from Indian production figures presently available, indicates an average yearly production of 8,000 units, together with the announced 250,000 machines produced up to 1923.

This was somewhat at variance with a press release to the trade journals earlier in the Spring, with the statement that: "17,500 machines to be produced this year, with a present backlog of 1,200 orders." This was the last time the Indian company ever announced production figures to the public so far as is known.

1926 was another successful year from the financial standpoint. For the twelve months ending August 31st, the company showed a net profit of $211,993.00, after paying preferred dividends. $1.59 a share was paid on the outstanding 100,000 shares of no par common stock.

The company opened the 1927 sales year with the proud announcement that the Indian range now included a complete line of machines from a lightweight utility through to the luxury four cylinder Indian Ace. Included were two versions of the continuingly popular Scout, one with the original but improved 37 cubic inch model, and a more powerful 45 cubic inch model, which competed with the recently introduced 45 cubic inch Excelsior.

The 45 greatly enhanced the Scout's popularity, as it offered enhanced power and speed with but a minimal increase in weight, and, as in the case of its parent model, offered superb handling, steering and road holding within the limitations of its solid frame.

The larger engine greatly enhanced the sporting proclivities of the Scout, and the AMA established a new

*The immortal Jim Davis at Rockingham, New Hampshire in 1926. The machine is one of the last series of factory built racers, with Scout fuel and oil tanks, modified Scout-type frame, but retaining the Powerplus style front forks with scrolled spring. The 61 cu in engine is a side valve Powerplus Special with twin carburetors. (Theodore A. Hodgdon)*

45 inch category, to cover its competition activities now that the similar Excelsior had its counterpart.

Sometime during this period a now-forgotten practical mechanic invented the 'stroker' Scout, which innovation was to play a significant role in the popularity of the current and later Scout models for the next three decades.

The theory behind 'stroking' was to increase the piston displacement and swept volume of the cylinder, and consequently increase the power and speed capabilities of the Scout.

This modification was undertaken by first entirely dismantling the engine and substituting a pair of Chief flywheels for the originals, along with the heavier Chief crankpin. As the latter wheels were too large in diameter to fit the smaller Scout engine cases, their outer edges were milled down about a quarter of an inch. Because the connecting rod eyes were at a greater distance from the crank than the originals, the resultant longer throw substantially increased the stroke. In consequence, the displacement of the engine was now 57 cubic inches. In order to keep the piston in proper relationship to the top of the cylinder, special shorter-than-standard 'stroker' pistons were fitted, readily available from accessory manufacturers. These short-skirted pistons quite naturally were subjected to greater wear by virtue of their small bearing surface inside the cylinder, resulting in a rocking action. A set of them would last about 10,000 miles, even under hard use. Replacement at stated intervals was scarcely a problem, as the simple side valve engine could be readily overhauled in a minimum of working time.

The result of this modification was that the already high performance Scout could produce really startling

*The actual machine on which M.K. (Curley) Fredericks established an all-time board track record of 120.2 mph at Rockingham on August 21st, 1926. A single carburetor Powerplus engine is now fitted in place of the original. (Russell Harmon-Ronald Mugar)*

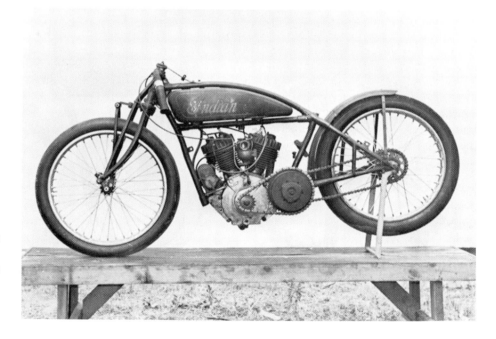

*Indian's racing star Johnny Seymour who established two new speed records at Daytona Beach, Florida in the spring of 1926. The single cylinder 30.50 cu in record of 115 mph and the 61 cu in twin cylinder record of 132 mph were made by changing engines in the same machine. These marks stood for nearly ten years.* **(Archives of the Indian Motorcycle Co)**

*The actual machine, now fitted with a 30.50 cu in engine, used by Johnny Seymour in 1926. It is now a part of the Russell Harmon collection.* **(Ronald Mugar)**

power, speed and acceleration. If, during the conversion, the internals were given a high polish, and if the exhaust and manifold passages were reamed out to provide enhanced gas flow, the Scout could then easily outperform the standard Chief, the only advantage of the latter then being its higher torque capabilities on long mountain gradients or pulling power for sidecar work. In consequence, the 'Stroker' Scout was often entered in 74 cubic inch competition events, particularly in hill climbing, where it usually gave a very good account of itself.

The matter of stroking posed many problems for referees and scrutineers overseeing sporting or club events, as there was invariably the odd competitor who attempted to enter a modified machine clandestinely as a standard 45 incher.

The most visible change in the 1927 Scout and Chief was the fitting of larger mudguards. The narrow ribbed type of the Scout, which had been fitted to the original models, was replaced by a wider D-section type, as were those of the Chief, whose original mudguards were similar to those of the last Standard models. This change enhanced the appearance of both machines, and complemented the fitting of the larger diameter balloon type tires.

1927 was a year of continuing prosperity. The most pressing of the huge national debt incurred by the war had by now been retired, and a business-orientated Republican Congress had by this time abolished the war time excess profits tax, corporation taxes, and surcharges on individual income taxes. With the resultant stimulation to general business and manufacturing activities,

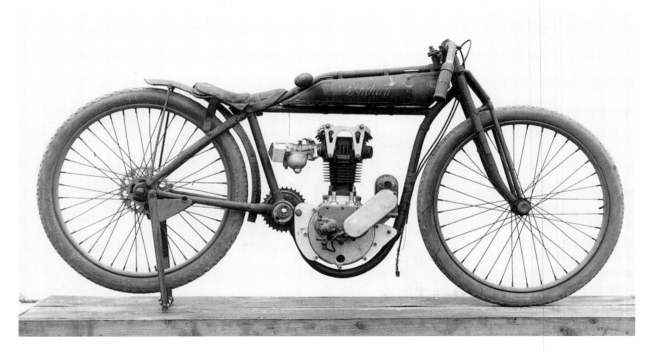

fostered by an ever-growing population, economic growth was now at an all-time high.

While general interest in motorcycling during this period was still minimal and was confined to a relatively small number of enthusiasts, it was regarded nostalgically as the golden age of American motorcycle club life. There were still enough manufacturers in the game to offer prospective purchasers some comparative choices of machine, and most clubs welcomed any sociable rider, whatever his brand of machine.

Many of the more energetic dealers helped to promote this healthy state of affairs by sponsoring picnics or meetings, featuring mild competitions for standard machines, which took the form of field meets and gymkhanas. L.D. Richards sponsored a well-attended meeting for all riders in the Denver area. B.A. Swenson, the one-time 'Terrible Swede' of the old bicycle days, sponsored a yearly fish fry at Providence, Rhode Island, where for many years his Indian agency sold the largest number of machines. Hap Alzina also sponsored many such meets, as did Hap Jones and Ed Kretz in later years.

Motorcycle sales had recently been steady, at least within the framework of the limited domestic market, although production was now below 25,000 units per year for the whole industry. This decrease was said to be due to the fact that much of the export market had been lost as the result of foreign tariff increases, although Australasia and South Africa continued to favour Indians as the most popular imported make.

In view of the healthy surplus of available capital in Indian's treasury, due mostly to the heroic efforts of President Weschler, a majority of the Board of Directors proposed that a holding company be formed independ-

ently of the Indian Motorcycle Company, for the purpose of trading in the shares of outside manufacturing concerns. The Board reasoned that as the production of motorcycles had more or less become static, there was no valid reason to expand manufacturing capacity or to invest any more surplus capital in additional plant facilities.

President Weschler was adamantly against this proposal. He argued that replacement of certain of the now well-worn tooling was in order and this could be accomplished with a part of the surplus funds now on

# Master of the Road

INDIAN BIG CHIEF meets the demand for the last word in speed, power, and stamina. New refinements have improved its comfort and ease of control, as well as added to its heavy duty characteristics.

## Specifications

MODELS: INDIAN BIG CHIEF, 74 cu. in. Model HEP.
INDIAN CHIEF, 61 cu. in. Model HE.

BRAKE: INDIAN extra heavy, two piece, external contracting. Has a range of action and braking surface greatly in excess of every ordinary requirement so as to positively and quickly take care of any emergency. Diameter 6¾", width 1⅜".

CARBURETOR: INDIAN Schebler Automatic, model H-1¼", compensating type. Has variable air and fuel adjustments, gives dependable power and remarkable flexibility in operation.

CLUTCH: Multiple disc. Alternate steel and raybestos discs, operating in oil.

CONTROL: Throttle, left grip; spark, right grip; by INDIAN "Twist-of-the-Wrist," with wire cables enclosed in handle bars. Exposed cable covered with leather. Brake pedal on right side, clutch pedal on left side. Valve lift compression release by push rod on right side of tank.

DRIVE: Primary drive, helical gears, insuring constant adjustment, connecting motor and transmission, completely enclosed, running in oil bath.
Final drive: ⅝ x ⅜ roller chain.
Gear ratio: Solo—4.85-1; sidecar 5.36-1. For HEP 74.
Gear ratio: Solo—5.09-1; sidecar 5.66-1. For HE 61.

ELECTRIC SYSTEM: Electric current for head light, tail light, and horn, furnished through Splitdorf generator and Wico 6-volt, 20 ampere hour battery, acting entirely independent of ignition. Head and tail lamps controlled with single switch. Ammeter combined in casing with switch mounted within easy view and reach of the rider on frame top tube.

FINISH: INDIAN Red with gold striping.

FOOT BOARDS: Folding type with rubber mats.

FORK: INDIAN triple stem type. Leaf spring suspension.

FRAME: INDIAN double tube type, reinforced, constructed with vanadium tubing throughout. Construction insures extremely low saddle position.

GUARDS: Pressed steel, one piece construction, rear guard hinged.

HANDLE BARS: Heavy service type integral with head bracket. Triple connection to fork.

IGNITION: Splitdorf high tension Magneto; frame is of die cast aluminum.

LUBRICATION: Automatic, adjustable pressure feed and auxiliary hand-pump.

MOTOR: BIG CHIEF 74: 2 cylinder 42 degree "V" type, air cooled 3¼" bore, 4 7-16" stroke 73.625 cubic inches piston displacement.
CHIEF 61: 3⅛" bore, 3 31-32" stroke, 60.88 cu. in. piston displacement.

Cylinder: L-Head.

VALVES: Poppet, right hand side, valve mechanism enclosed and efficiently lubricated.
Piston: Cast iron, three (3) rings, pin ⅝" diameter.
Connecting Rod: Selected drop forged steel, specially heat treated.
Bearings: Crank and main bearings roller.

MUFFLER: INDIAN Tubular type.

STAND: INDIAN hinge type with spring latch.

SADDLE: INDIAN - Mesinger stretched leather bucket type with suspension springs.

STANDARD EQUIPMENT: Combination dim and full electric head lamp, tail lamp, ammeter and switch, motor driven horn and push button, tool box and tool kit.

STARTER: INDIAN gear and sector type. Sector acting on ratchet pinion mounted on mainshaft of transmission.

TANK: One piece, forming fuel and oil compartments. Gasoline capacity 3⅜ gallons. Oil capacity, 3 quarts.

TIRES: Goodyear or Firestone Balloon 27 x 3.85, Nominal, for 26" x 3" Rims.

TRANSMISSION: Mounted in unit with motor. Three forward speeds, progressive type. direct acting shift lever insures convenient gear shifting.

WEIGHT: 425 pounds, sidecar, 198 pounds.

WHEELS: 27" diameter, wire, 40 spokes, front and rear 26" x 3" C C steel rims, knockout axles.

WHEEL BASE: 60½".

Actual Piston Displacement bore and stroke represent the only difference in the detailed specifications between BIG CHIEF 74 and CHIEF 61 models.

### NEW FEATURES
### for 1926

New form handlebars—wider and longer, graceful curve downward at grip ends—gives natural wrist resting position.

Improved INDIAN-Mesinger bucket type suspension saddle. Saddle position lowest ever. Adjustable to rider's weight.

Tilted footboards moved forward and raised to give an even better riding position and greater road clearance.

INDIAN improved outside brake, having two brake shoes and 20½ square inches of friction surface—smooth in operation—positive in action.

Foot starter improved. Gives greater leverage. Insures ease in starting motor.

Removable cap on cam case cover permits ready removal of generator without disturbing other parts.

Larger tool steel keys rigidly lock flywheel and pinion on shafts—making permanent assembly and alignment.

Transmission gear shift lever redesigned to insure easy operation.

*Left: The Leader-of-the-Line in the mid-1920s, the 61 cu in Chief and 74 cu in Big Chief. The 1925 models featured oversize balloon tires and Ricardo-type cylinder heads.*

hand. He also advocated the needed strengthening of Indian's outstanding shares of no par common stock, in order to bolster public confidence in company activities. He further suggested that the Board might do well to purchase all or part of the outstanding common shares, and convert them to the preferred type, which would at once enhance the Board's present holdings in the company.

Weschler was overruled, and the Board then laid plans to invest the surplus in speculative holdings outside the company. And so it was on August 27th that President Weschler regretfully tendered his resignation to the Directors and abruptly severed all connection with the company to which he had given his unswerving loyalty for nearly all of his adult life.

There was no little consternation among the executive office staff and many of the production workers at the new turn of events. It was well known throughout the company, as well as the trade, that Indian's survival through the past difficult years had been due solely to Weschler's almost singlehanded heroic efforts. In virtual command of company operations since 1916, there appeared to be no other executive from within the ranks who could fill his place.

Some of Weschler's close associates reported in later years that his state of health had markedly deteriorated. It is possible that he felt privately that a new course of financial direction of the company could lead to further economic crises, and that he now did not wish to undergo any more anguish connected with the threat of possible future financial troubles in a new situation of which he did not approve.

He was almost immediately offered the position of President of the Baldwin Chain Company of nearby Westfield, which, among other products, manufactured motorcycle chains. He kept in close touch with Indian affairs, however, and in close contact with most of his old company associates. His name was sometimes mentioned in Indian's subsequent advertising literature, such as the special issue of the *Indian News* published in 1931 to commemorate the company's 30th anniversary.

Weschler's health failed in later years, and he passed away in the Spring of 1935, at the comparatively young age of 56. A veritable giant in a now-troubled industry, he was probably in his time the most popular and respected man within it, and his passing was mourned by associates and competitors alike. It was often said that whenever Indian's better days were discussed, while it was Hendee

and Hedstrom's remarkable talents that made Indian's initial success, it was the genius of Franklin and the dedication of Weschler that made possible the company's survival in an infinitely more critical period.

The days of Weschler's Presidency have been described by many contemporary Indian enthusiasts both within and without the factory organization as one of the most congenial periods since the Golden Decade before World War I. Not only was the company stable financially, but within the now diminished domestic motorcycle industry there was a general era of good feeling. The three leading manufacturers were all on a reasonably stable financial footing, sales were steady, and while rivalry was keen, the bitterness and vindictive type of competition that occurred in later years had not yet appeared.

While enthusiasts were now existing in lesser numbers, many were not only using their machines as utility mounts, but were enjoying the avocation of touring, as the nation's roads were now generally in a more passable condition. Articles on touring activities featuring trips made by individual riders, or suggested routes for others to follow, now appeared in increasing numbers in the trade press.

*Theodore A. Hodgdon.*

# Chapter 5

# INDIAN FOUR

The story of the Indian four cylinder motorcycles and their ultimate development is complex and deserves a separate chapter in itself. Its history not only deals with the original designer and several of his collaborators, but also ultimately involves other makes of machines which include the Henderson, Ace, and latterly, the Cleveland.

There had been much active interest in multicylinder and four cylinder motorcycle engines since the earliest days of the industry, as the pioneer designers and builders experienced many technical problems in balancing the first rough-running singles. Prototypes of four cylinder machines had been built in England as early as 1897 by Colonel H.C.L. Holden. Alexander Binks had also undertaken a similar project five years later, and proposed to offer prospective buyers the option of an engine with the cylinders in line, or set across the frame. The first commercially successful design, however, did not appear until 1904, when a young Belgian engineer named Paul Kelecom developed such a machine for the great Belgian National Arms Factory, the Fabrique Nationale D'Arms de Guerre, popularly known as FN. The first four cylinder FN machine featured a small in-line engine of about 19 cubic inch displacement, with atmospheric inlet valves and mechanically-operated exhaust valves. It embodied such advanced engineering refinements as a semi-automatic lubrication system, and magneto ignition, with a really efficient timing mechanism which replaced the troublesome, fragile timer and coil battery ignition of that era. The machine was fitted with a shaft drive, although no clutch was fitted to the early models. A prototype machine was subjected to a six weeks trip through Europe in the winter of 1904 by a

works tester, M. Ormond, and performed perfectly under rather severe weather and road conditons.

The design naturally made quite an impression on American motorcycle designers and engineers. It inspired one Percy Pierce, son of George N. Pierce, the manufacturer of the then prestigious Great Arrow (later Pierce Arrow) automobile, to design a four cylinder machine along FN lines. The elder Pierce provided an entire factory building in Buffalo, New York, for its manufacture, which was undertaken in the Spring of 1909. The machine was a successful performer and was built to very high standards of quality, but its high selling price of $400.00 prevented widespread sales and the motorcycle division of the company finally suspended production in 1913 after about 3,000 machines had been built, when the venture did not prove profitable.

Another young engineer who had also been experimenting with various types of small engines since the turn of the century and was greatly influenced by the FN, was William G. Henderson. He was born in Glasgow, Scotland, in 1875, and his brother, Thomas, who later assisted him in his work, was born two years later. The Henderson family, who were remotely related to Alexander Winton, pioneer bicycle and later automobile manufacturer, emigrated to the United States in 1878 and settled in Rochester, New York. After young William's school days were over, he worked in various automotive and engineering projects until 1909, when he commenced exper-

*Opposite: **A rider's eye view of a 1941 Four, showing the instrument panel and control layout. This machine is fitted with the optional right-hand throttle control. (George Hays)***

imenting with four cylinder motorcycle engines. He envisaged an improved version of the FN designed especially for American conditions, but arranged for economy of manufacture. With the help of his brother, Tom, he assembled his first prototype in the Spring of 1910. This machine had a substantial cradle type lower frame to support the engine, which was connected by a single heavy down tube to the steering head, and was fitted with leading link type spring forks. The 28 inch wheels were shod with 2½ inch section tires. The wheelbase was 65 inches, as Henderson intended that two riders would be accommodated in tandem, with the passenger mounted in front of the driver, on a saddle clipped to the top of the tank rail. As the driver's saddle was placed well aft, a pair of very long handlebars were required. The long fuel tank was of circular section, with rounded ends. The open space between the front of the engine and the down tube carried a single, wide aluminum footboard, to accommodate the passenger's feet.

The engine design was original with Henderson, and featured a number of engineering innovations. While the basic design of the in-line four cylinder four-stroke engine had been already well established in the automotive field, the arrangement of the valves was still a matter of controversy. The atmospheric inlet valves fitted to the FN and the T head type of the Pierce, which had separate camshafts on either side of the cylinder base, had distinct disadvantages. The former were prone to sticking due to carbon formation, and the latter allowed for much cylinder head distortion if overheated during hard running. After some experimentation, Henderson settled on the overhead inlet, side-exhaust system, which later became known as the F-head configuration, latterly seen in the Willys jeep engines built in World War II. The inlet valves were placed in the top of the cylinder head and were activated by an overhead rocker, connected to the camshaft by a push rod. The side exhaust valves were connected to the same camshaft. Henderson reasoned that the incoming combustion mixture would cool the exhaust valves and would allow for a more efficiently disposed combustion chamber, the shape of which was like a wedge, and later became known as the squish type. Magneto ignition was fitted, and a drip type oiling system took care of lubrication. The initial engines displaced about 58 cubic inches.

While admitting the efficiency and cleanliness of shaft drive, this was ruled out on the basis of high production costs. The first machines were single geared and fitted with a belt drive, the countershaft sprocket running off a bevel gear behind the flywheel. An Eclipse-type clutch was fitted to the engine sprocket, a proprietary fitting used in many contemporary single cylinder makes. After a few of these machines were assembled, a chain drive was substituted for the belt, enclosed in a dustproof case. A car-type clutch was then added to the flywheel, the single gear being retained. The engine was started by means of a hand crank on the right-hand side.

The machine performed well, starting easily, the engine being very flexible and capable of outstanding acceleration. It was handsomely finished in black, with much gold pin striping on the mudguards, and red panels on either end of the fuel tank.

Henderson managed to raise sufficient capital to lease and equip a small factory on the outskirts of Detroit, Michigan. He advertised his new model in the trade press, announcing that 1,000 units would be offered for the 1912 season. The venture was helped by the fact that the four cylinder motorcycle offered by both FN and Pierce had already been well received, and the Henderson selling price of $325.00 was well below that of both of these forerunning makes. All of the 1912 production was sold before the year was out.

Much advertising value was gained by the fact that one Carl. S. Clancy made a round-the-world trip on a Henderson during the initial Summer of production, starting and finished at New York City and covering over 18,000 miles. This exploit was given much publicity in the newspapers, as well as the trade press.

The 1913 models were improved by strengthening the frame and forks, lowering the riding position and installing a larger saddle, fitting a more attractively streamlined fuel tank, and adding a more effective rear wheel brake. Production increased to 2,300 units, all of which sold readily.

In 1914 a two-speed gear in the rear hub was fitted, and the engine displacement was increased to 61 cubic inches, but the original drip oiling system was still retained.

In 1915 the wheelbase was shortened to 58 inches, making for better handling on rough roads. This change made for a more symmetrical machine, and sales interest greatly increased. In January, a young automotive engineer named Arthur J. Lemon joined the design staff.

No marked changes were made in 1916, but in 1917 the old drip oiling system was replaced by crankcase lubrication, the oil being carried in a sump and delivered to the cylinder walls by the lower ends of the cranks, as was then popular in most automobiles. A three-speed gearbox was also fitted, as an integral part of the engine case, together with a larger and much stronger clutch. The Henderson was now really coming into its own, with many new dealerships added to the roster and a substantial export market was built up.

To emphasize Henderson's prowess and dependability, a well known competition rider named Alan Bedell was engaged to attempt to better the current transconti-

VOL. II, No. 1.    Published by the EXCELSIOR MOTOR MFG. & SUPPLY CO., Chicago, Ill.    January, 1923.
For Its Dealers Throughout the World.

## EVOLUTION OF THE HENDERSON DE LUXE MODEL

Here's the first Henderson. Note the belt drive, the extra long wheelbase and other striking features. It doesn't look much like the trim and graceful 1923 De Luxe Model.

IN the early '90's, nearly everybody rode a bicycle. During these same years, inventors in different parts of the world were developing the gasoline engine so that the eventual combination of the two was a perfectly natural step. For several years though, motorcycles remained little more than motorized bicycles—bicycles with engines hitched on. The bicycle riders of those days were grateful for the relief from the hard work and tedium of pedaling, so the early motorcycle riders were not very critical, and a little help with the pedals on bad hills was willingly given.

Naturally, the power-plants of these earliest motorcycles were of the simplest possible type of one-cylinder engines. With the passing of time, these little motors became more and more dependable and finally development reached the stage where they would run and keep running day after day. But in the history of the world, man has never been permanently satisfied with anything which still offered room for improvement. Refinements in single cylinder motor construction continued over a period of several years, and the final result was a big, husky, one-lung, slow-speed power-plant which was strong, durable, reasonably dependable and economical. The long intervals between the husky power strokes were responsible for perceptible jerks with every shot, which even the belt drives could not entirely dissipate. Compensating devices of various kinds, slip sprockets and clutches gradually came into use to eliminate the roughness of single-cylinder power, but all of these involved slipping or sliding somewhere in the transmission, which in smoothing out the violence, also dissipated some of the power.

As time passed, the different motorcycle factories attacked the problem of increasing the enjoyment of motorcycling by developing machines which would not have the jerkiness of the singles. Logically they decided that the one hefty power stroke which jarred rider and machine, could best be overcome by adding another cylinder, in other words employing two smaller power impulses with an interval between instead of the one big shot. There was one serious obstacle in the way of adding cylinders, viz: the small space available in the motorcycle frame for carrying the power-plant. This necessitated a very efficient and compact engine,

so the "V" twin was the solution for its contour naturally conformed to the conventional motorcycle diamond frame.

In spite of its unequal firing interval and imperfect balance, the "V" twin was immeasurably better than the old single, and its compactness and ease of mounting, led to general adoption. The early "V" twins were fast, powerful and efficient, but as a rule, they were noisy and did not want to throttle down for slow running in traffic. By this time, it became evident that the real solution of the problem was a

The 1918 Henderson

The world's finest—the Henderson De Luxe Model

four cylinder motor which would give *four evenly spaced, evenly balanced power impulses* instead of the two hefty irregularly spaced shots of the twin. Furthermore, the four cylinder type was naturally adapted for unit automobile type construction, and could be mounted in a loop cradle frame close to the ground, giving a very low center of gravity.

The old Pierce Company brought out the first four-cylinder American motorcycle in 1909. Considering the early date, it was a good job. It had some features which were in advance of the times and several of these even bordered on the freakish. The frame was made of large tubing which also served for the

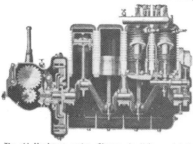

The old Henderson engine—Observe the light crankshaft, splash oiling system, overhead intake valves and other features which naturally limited its performance.

Note the many advanced features of the De Luxe Motor which have made it the finest motorcycle engine in the world.

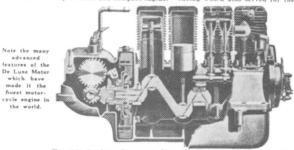

The 1923 De Luxe Powerplant—Note the heavier crankshaft, the pressure-feed oiling system, the compact side-by-side valves and sturdiness of all parts.

*1923 Excelsior factory literature describing the development of their own De Luxe Four designed by Arthur Lemon. As the Ace motorcycle had already been in production for three seasons and was based on the original Henderson design, Excelsior's advertising writer took special pains to downgrade this design.*

nental record established by Cannonball Baker in 1914, on an Indian twin. Bedell left Los Angeles in the late Spring, and after incredible hardships over the trackless deserts of the southwest, and the bottomless mud of the midwest, reached New York City after seven days and

sixteen hours, breaking Baker's record by nearly four days for the 3,296 miles.

The Three Flag record from Canada to Mexico was also held by Cannonball Baker, by virtue of his 81 hour run made in 1915, on an Indian. Roy Artley, another competition rider of note, was engaged for the 1,667 mile run by Henderson. Starting at Blaine, British Columbia, on July 22nd, he made the hazardous run to Tijuana, Mexico, in 72 hours, 25 minutes, shaving nine hours off Baker's previous record.

In spite of encouraging sales and growing popularity, not all was well at the modest Detroit plant. Henderson suffered the common fate of many of the motorcycle manufacturers of those days, in possessing but limited operating capital. He was constantly forced to borrow money on short term notes from various banks, to meet material costs and often overdue payrolls. In the meantime, Ignatz Schwinn, the one-time German immigrant bicycle frame brazer who had ultimately become the proprietor of the great Arnold Schwinn and Company bicycle factory in Chicago, had his eye on the fledgling Henderson Company for some time. In addition to his mass production of bicycles, he also manufactured Excelsior motorcycles, a sound, if undistinguished, line of single and twin cylinder machines whose patent and manufacturing rights he had secured from the original developers in 1907. He reasoned that the addition of a high performance four-cylinder motorcycle could extend his coverage of the market then dominated by the giant Indian Company and their growing rival, Harley-Davidson. In November, 1917, he made Henderson such a lucrative purchase offer for the manufacturing rights to his machine (reputedly in the six figure category), that Henderson decided he could not refuse. As a part of the transaction, both the Henderson brothers and Arthur

Lemon were to join the Excelsior Company, and supervise the manufacture of the Henderson.

By February, 1918, all of the dies, tooling, finished and semi-finished parts and other equipment had been moved to the large Cortland Street plant in Chicago, where the production capacity of the four was greatly increased.

Schwinn purchased a large amount of advertising space in the trade press to announce his new acquisition. The only change made in the machine was the imposition of a large red X on the Henderson tank transfer.

The sales of the Henderson boomed during that Spring and Summer, due to the increased production facilities. Schwinn decided that a change in its design was in order, to bring the Henderson more in line with his own ideas of what a luxury four cylinder motorcycle should be. He reasoned that a simpler and more economically made engine could be designed, along with increasing the motorcycle's overall dimensions, to make it a more impressive vehicle. William Henderson resisted this suggestion, pointing out that his machine was already a very capable performer and had further undergone several seasons of refinement. Schwinn was adamant, so

*Maldwyn Jones, one time racing star and now an engineer for the Schebler Carburetor Company, poses on a 1923 Ace with Arthur O. Lemon (center) and Everett M. De Long. (Ace Motorcycle Company)*

the Henderson brothers resigned from Excelsior in December, 1918. Arthur Lemon elected to remain, and was immediately placed in charge of the Engineering and Design Department. He was responsible for the new 80 cubic inch side valve design placed in a larger frame that superseded Henderson's original design, and later redesigned the twin cylinder Excelsior machines.

During the subsequent recriminations, Schwinn threatened to sue the Hendersons for breach of contract, and the Hendersons returned to their old home in Detroit to await developments. In the meantime, William set about designing an entirely new four cylinder machine, based on his accumulated experience.

When it became apparent that legal action from Schwinn was not immediately forthcoming. William Henderson looked about for financial backing to launch a new company. At this point brother Thomas decided that he had had enough of the hectic motorcycle business and elected to enter a general export business in New York. William ultimately found a backer in the person of Max Sladkin, who had for some years been associated in financing bicycle factories. A suitable factory building was located in Philadelphia, which was also outside the legal jurisdiction of the state of Illinois. Production facilities were set up to manufacture the new machine, which was to be named the Ace. Its engine was of the same general design as the successful 1917 Henderson, except that the cylinder displacement was increased to 75 cubic inches, to give more power and speed. In order to avoid any possible future legal difficulties with Schwinn, no parts of the Ace would fit any of the previous Henderson designs, even the magneto being of opposite rotation. It was a rakishly handsome machine, with a low saddle position, and was painted a deep blue outlined with gold pin striping. It had yellow wheels.

An intensive sales campaign was launched in the Fall of 1919, with much advertising space in the trade and general press. The initial deliveries to dealers were scheduled for January, 1920. As Henderson and his designs were already well known to the industry, an instant market was available, and at an initial selling price of $375.00 the Ace was a very attractive proposition.

During the time he was associated with Schwinn, Henderson's name had also been prominently featured as the designer, and he had been a member of the industry ever since his epoch-making machine in 1911. Many dealers immediately sought franchises which also prompted the planning of an ambitious export program. A production figure of 4,000 machines for the first year was promised, but due to limited financing and plant facilities, less than half of this number were made the first year, and there were many unfilled orders.

Sales were promising at the opening of 1921, but the company underwent a serious financial crisis that Spring. Due to the large volume of initial orders, most of the available funds had been spent for raw materials and such component parts as lighting sets, wheels, tires, and saddles. Funds were soon exhausted. In order to prevent a suspension of production which would have been fatal to the company's future at this critical time, Sladkin managed to hurriedly raise about $500,000 from Philadelphia bankers, which enabled Ace not only to maintain production, but also to enlarge the plant facilities somewhat.

With the selling price now reduced to $1325.00 to stimulate sales, 1922 was a banner year. Sales increased, both at home and abroad, and many competition records were attacked to enhance public interest. Cannonball Baker was engaged to attempt to beat the 1917 transcontinental record set by Alan Bedell, on a Henderson. Starting from Los Angeles in May, he suffered a fall and damaged his machine when only a short distance out from that city. He started again in September, and this time was successful in beating the old record by 17 hours, a remarkable achievement under very poor road conditions.

A number of local endurance runs were also entered that year, with victories in the Pittsburgh and Syracuse events. The modest selling price attracted the attention of law enforcement bodies, and numerous sales were made to police departments.

On December 19th, 1922 another tragedy struck the Ace organization. William Henderson, in company with other riders, was testing a new 1923 Ace on the streets of Philadelphia when he was struck down by an automobile, while riding out from a filling station. He suffered multiple skull fractures and concussion and died without regaining consciousness.

This sad event could have well been the death knell of Ace, as all design and production operations were under his personal supervision. A dramatic reprieve from this impending disaster was the immediate offer of Arthur Lemon to resign from Excelsior and step into the breach as Chief Designer and Production Superintendent. His offer was accepted immediately, and Lemon moved to Philadelphia within the week.

Much was made of Lemon's defection to Ace in the trade press, to the chagrin of Schwinn. The latter had already sent another noted endurance rider, Wells Bennett, across the continent on a new De Luxe Henderson to seek a new record. After incredible hardships and several falls, he was able to clip a little over seven hours from the Ace record, made by Cannonball Baker.

With the help of Henderson's former associates in the Engineering Department, Lemon continued to refine and improve the Ace engine. An improved version, with the displacement now raised to 77 cubic inches, was fitted to a hill climbing machine which won a classic contest held annually at Rochester, New York, in 1923, with the noted 'TNT' Terpenning as the rider. This engine was then known as the Rochester engine, and was fitted to subsequent standard machines in slightly detuned form. Aces were entered in every major endurance run of the 1923 season, with signal successes.

*The 1927 Indian Ace as shown here was actually a 1924 Ace with Indian red paint finish and tank transfer.*

In 1923 the Engineering Department was augmented by the addition of a young four cylinder motorcycle enthusiast named Everett O. De Long. His name had first become known to the industry in 1920, when he had designed, in collaboration with Cannonball Baker, a 90° V-four engine that in prototype form had been mounted in an Indian Powerplus frame.

In the late Fall of 1923, Lemon designed further improvements for the new Ace motor. Manifold breathing was improved, the compression ratio was increased, lightweight pistons were offered as an optional extra, and larger

## SPECIFICATIONS

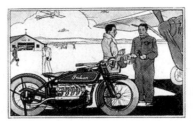

**BRAKES:** INDIAN ACE type. Two separate drums on rear hub. Heavy $\frac{7}{8}$″ linings, with ample means of adjustment. Total braking surface 29 square inches.

**CARBURETOR:** Ace Schebler, especially designed to meet the requirements of Ace four cylinder motor.

**CLUTCH:** Multiple steel disc type, built into flywheel running in oil bath. No adjustment required.

**CONTROLS:** Throttle, right grip. Spark, left grip. Service brake pedal on right side, emergency brake pedal operated by heel on left side. Clutch foot pedal on left side, with auxiliary hand lever on left side of tank. Gear shift also on left side of tank.

**DRIVE:** Helical bevel gears from motor to transmission, in constant adjustment, running in oil bath. Final drive $\frac{5}{8}$″ x $\frac{3}{8}$″ heavy roller chain. Gear ratios: Solo, 4.12 to 1; Sidecar, 4.71 to 1.

**ELECTRIC SYSTEM:** Electric current for head-light, tail-light and horn furnished by Splitdorf generator and Wico 6-volt battery acting entirely independently of ignition. Ammeter mounted on top frame tube in easy view of rider. Motor driven horn.

**FINISH:** INDIAN Red with gold striping.

**FOOTBOARDS:** Folding type with rubber mats.

**FORK:** INDIAN ACE type double with straight sides. Coil springs completely enclosed.

**FRAME:** INDIAN ACE type cradle suspension. Side braces strengthen rear fork.

**GUARDS:** Pressed steel, crowned, with drop sides on front guard.

**HANDLEBARS:** Wide, heavy service type with triple connection to fork. Sport bars, heavily nickeled — optional.

**IGNITION:** Splitdorf high tension magneto.

**LUBRICATION:** High pressure force feed system distributes oil to all bearings under pressure proportionate to riding speed and needs of motor. Oil pressure gauge on right side of motor in plain view of rider. All oil contained in motor base, with oil measuring gauge easily accessible on left side of crankcase.

**MOTOR:** INDIAN ACE 4 cylinder, air-cooled, $2\frac{3}{4}$″ bore, $3\frac{1}{4}$″ stroke, 77.21 cu. in. piston displacement. Cylinders F head type, with inlet over exhaust. Pistons of "Bohnite" aluminum alloy. Three rings, with lower groove bored for oil return. Valves, side by side poppet type, $1\frac{1}{2}$″ diameter, with $\frac{1}{4}$″ lift, all inlet valve mechanism enclosed in airtight bonnets. Connecting rods: selected drop forged steel specially heat treated. Split at big end for bearing adjustment. Bearings: bronze, babbit lined, on connecting rods, crankshaft and countershaft, adjustable to take up wear.

**MUFFLER:** Aluminum muffler and exhaust manifold in one unit. Nickel-plated tail pipe.

**SADDLE:** INDIAN ACE bucket style, with full $4\frac{1}{2}$″ of up and down travel on double coil springs.

**STAND:** INDIAN ACE hinged type with spring latch.

**STARTER:** Step starter with folding foot pedal.

**TANK:** One unit, forming gasoline tank and tool box. Capacity $3\frac{3}{4}$ gallons. Incorporates strainer, sediment trap and reserve cock.

**TIRES:** Goodyear or Firestone Balloons optional, size 25″ x 3.85.

**TRANSMISSION:** Mounted in unit with motor. Three forward speeds, progressive type, notched gear shift lever quadrant.

**WEIGHT:** 395 pounds.

**WHEELS:** 25″ diameter, wire, 40 spokes front and rear 24″ x 3″ or 18″ CC steel rims, knockout axles.

**WHEEL BASE:** 59 inches.

main bearings were fitted to cope with increased power. The intensive competition program was continued, with many well publicized successes, and sales boomed.

In November of 1923 another financial crisis struck the company. It appeared that the $325.00 selling price, while attracting many buyers, was insufficient to cover production and selling costs, and Ace was now almost hopelessly in the red. Some additional financing was desperately arranged, and a change in top management was made at the request of the shareholders. New personnel included Clarence Miller as President, and Frank Snook as Sales Manager. The company continued its almost frantic competition program, and poured more funds into advertising.

In order to attract further public attention, it was decided to launch an attack on the world's straightaway speed record. A specially-built lightweight four cylinder engine was fitted into a racing frame, at a reported cost of $8,000.00. In December, 1923, a section of paved highway on the outskirts of Philadelphia was closed, with the co-operation of local law enforcement officials, and Red Wolverton, a noted speed rider of the day, managed an amazing 129mph run through an electrically timed trap. An ultralight racing sidecar, with a platform-type body, was then attached to the machine, and with Everett De Long as passenger stretched out in a prone position, a new record of 106mph was established for three wheelers. Much publicity was naturally forthcoming from these exploits, and the Ace management offered a $10,000.00 cash wager to any other make of motorcycle that could better these records. The actual racing machine was triumphantly exhibited at the 1924 National Motorcycle Show held in Chicago, during the following January.

Ace production continued until the late Spring of 1924, with the retail price now raised to $375.00. The company's financial position was still extremely precarious. Arthur Lemon was ordered to cut the work force down to a skeleton crew. Funds continued to dwindle, however, and the company ultimately suspended production on November 30th, 1924.

A little known facet of Ace history is that during their 1923 financial crisis some of the castings for Ace engines were obtained through the Indian Company, then known as the Hendee Manufacturing Company. It will be recalled that in 1917, the Indian Company closed their own foundry and thereafter obtained all their engine castings from Brown and Sharpe of Providence, Rhode Island, as it was found more economical to purchase them from a specialized firm rather than make their own on the premises. L.D. Richards recalls seeing numerous Ace engine castings in a separate department in the State Street Plant. The late George Nethercutt of Dayton, Ohio,

*Engine and frame details of a 1929 Indian Four. From late 1928 through 1931, the Four, aside from the cradle type frame, was made up from 101 Scout cycle parts.* **(George Hays)**

recalled that as a young apprentice machinist in the Indian factory during this period, he was called upon to surface about 300 raw castings of Ace engines. It would appear from this evidence that Ace made some sort of an arrangement with Indian to obtain these castings, along with their own orders from Providence.

The assets of the company next passed through two different organizations. The first group moved all the dies, tooling, and a supply of partially finished machines and spare parts to Blossburg, a small agricultural village in northern Pennsylvania and commenced operation in an old tanning factory, hoping thus to operate with greatly reduced overheads. Ace enthusiasts of the day recall seeing a somewhat limited assembly line set up between the long rows of huge wooden tanning vats. About three hundred machines were assembled, most of which were said to have been sold to law enforcement bodies before a lack of capital brought a shut down in the Spring of 1925. In the Summer of 1926, what was left of Ace was moved back to Detroit, backed by some limited fresh capital, which was to form the Michigan Motors Corporation. This effort also failed, after a couple of hundred machines had been produced.

Everett De Long left the Ace Company during its initial demise but was shortly afterward retained by the Harley-Davidson Motor Company to lay out a tentative design for a four cylinder machine, as the Harley-Davidson organization was then considering entering the four cylinder field. De Long made a wooden mockup of a proposed prototype, but the company dropped the project after considering the high production costs due to the variation of four manufacture from their twin production schedule. De Long was subsequently hired by the Cleveland Motorcycle Company of Cleveland, Ohio to work on a new four cylinder design for them, to replace a rather archaic T-headed model previously designed by L. E. Fowler. The result of these efforts was a high performance four based on the original Ace configuration, that was in very limited production from 1927 through 1929, at which time the company became insolvent.

At this juncture, the Indian Motocycle Company opened negotiations with the Michigan Motors Corporation, with a view to purchasing the Ace manufacturing rights and adding this to the Indian line of single and twin cylinder machines. Under the capable management of Frank J. Weschler, Indian's fortunes had greatly improved and there was a substantial surplus in the treasury. After prolonged negotiations, the sale was consummated in December of 1926. The price was never officially divulged, but it was rumored that the transaction involved both cash and a quantity of common shares of Indian stock in the amount of $175,000.00, a considerable loss to Michigan Motors shareholders.

An Ace machine from the last run of Michigan Motors production was hastily added to Indian's elaborate display at the annual Motorcycle Show, held at New York's Madison Square Garden from January 31st to February 5th, 1927. This example was painted a light green, with dark green double pin striping outlining the fuel tank and mudguards. The wheels were black and were fitted with the then new low pressure (27 inch x 3.85 inch) balloon type tires that were becoming popular in both cars and motorcycles. Arthur Lemon, who had been engaged by Indian to head the Design and Production Department of Ace, was on hand to answer questions and to assure the many Ace enthusiasts that their favorite mount would at long last be available once more. Hundreds of orders were booked, from both riders and dealers.

In March, carloads of Ace dies, tooling, semi-finished machines and parts began arriving at Springfield from Detroit, and production lines were set up with the hope that the first machines would be ready for distribution by June. The only marked changes in the first machines, as produced by Indian, were that the machines were painted Indian red and had black wheels. The familiar Indian script was fixed to the tank sides, with the word

*The 1932–34 Indian Four with the heavier frame and forks, wheelbase lengthened to 60 inches, and streamlined two piece fuel tanks.*

Above: An early Indian, *possibly 1903, with engine no. 268 owned by Dave Hansen.* (Garry Stuart)

Right: *1906 Camel back.* (Garry Stuart)

Below: *1909 Indian Twin restored by Dewey Bonkrud.* (Chuck Vernon)

Above: *1912 Indian 8-valve racer restored and ridden by Chuck Vernon on a rally in Joshua Tree.* (Chuck Vernon)

Left: *The Hedstrom Indian Single Cylinder engine, 1913 version. Restored by Chuck Vernon.* (Chuck Vernon)

Below: *1914 8-valve racer, owned by Stephen Wright.* (Garry Stuart)

Above: *Max Bubeck 1915 Indian.* (Garry Stuart)

Right: *Model 0 1917.* (Garry Stuart)

Below right: *"Harry Sucher Special" 1917 Indian Big Valve Racer. Restored by Chuck Vernon with many parts contributed by Harry Sucher.* (Chuck Vernon)

Above: *Harry Sucher with "Harry Sucher Special".* (Chuck Vernon)

Left: *1925 Indian Prince.* (Garry Stuart)

Below: *1926 Indian Scout with special factory OHV conversion. Restored by Chuck Vernon.* (Chuck Vernon)

**Top:** *1930's Indian Sport Scout.* (Marc Gallin)

**Above:** *1937 4 'upside-down' engine with over-head exhaust, side-valve intake and updraft carburation.* (Garry Stuart)

**Right:** *1938 Indian Sport Scout with owner John Eagles.* (Chuck Vernon)

THE IRON REDSKIN

Above: *1939 Indian 4.* (Garry Stuart)

Left: *1939 Indian 4, Max Bubeck. Max won the Jackpine Enduro riding this cycle.* (Garry Stuart)

Below: *1930's Dispatch-Tow. Apparatus attached to the front fork was used to clamp onto an auto bumper and tow the cycle.* (Garry Stuart)

Above: *1940's Indian Scout.* (Marc Gallin)

Right: *1942 Indian 841. These had hand clutch, foot shift 4-speed transmission and shaft drive. Only 1000 were made and never saw action.* (Garry Stuart)

Below right: *1947 Rainbow Chief owned and built by Gary Stark between the ages of four and sixteen. This cycle recently attended the 2009 Scotland International Indian Rally, ridden by Gary.* (Garry Stuart)

Above: *1949 Scout. This was the first year for the vertical-twin 440cc engine.* (Garry Stuart)

Left: *1952/53 Chief.* (Garry Stuart)

Below: *1950's Warrior Police Special with vertical-twin 500cc engine.* (Garry Stuart)

Above: The *1952 Big Frame Warrior prototype never reached production.* (Garry Stuart)

Right: *Century Chief tank detail.* (Garry Stuart)

Below: *Century Chief. This is a running prototype built by Wayne Baughman in his attempt to resurrect the Indian name. The attempt failed.* (Garry Stuart)

Above and left: *The Chief model (on left shown being ridden by Roland Brown) built by the Gilroy Indian Company in Northern California. The company produced Indians from 1999 through 2003 before facing bankruptcy.*
(Roland Brown, left photo by Brian J.Nelson)

Below left: *1946 Indian Chief.*
(Roland Brown, photo by Oli Tennent)

Below: *Roland Brown riding Bob Stark's Indian Chief "Big Red". This has been owned by Bob since 1951 and ridden 240,000 miles.* (Roland Brown, photo by Oli Tennent)

Above: *Bob Stark's 1941 Indian Four with telo forks, hand clutch and foot shift.*
(Roland Brown, photo by Oli Tennent)

Right: *Original Indian literature.*
(Garry Stuart)

Below: *Model 741 owned and restored by Bob Stark, and previously owned by movie actor Steve McQueen.*
(Roland Brown, photo by Oli Tennent)

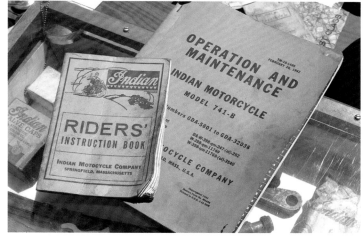

**Above:** *1948 Indian Chief with Tim Graber, President of Southern California Antique Motorcycle Club.* (Marc Gallin)

**Left:** *Indian Scout 45" racer model 648, one of 50 special racers built in 1948. This one, owned and restored by Bob Nichols, is still raced currently in vintage races.* (Marc Gallin)

**Below left:** *Max Bubeck's 1950 Indian Warrior with which he won many enduro races.* (Marc Gallin)

Above: *Bob Stark's Indian shop.*
(Marc Gallin)

Right: *1930's Indian Scout with Gerry Unis.*
(Marc Gallin)

Left: *1947 modified Indian Chief and "Hobo"*
*John at Borrego Springs annual club meet.*
(Marc Gallin)

Top left: *Sport Scout racer (Ed Kretz).* (Garry Stuart)

Middle left: 1956 *Indian Woodsman built by Royal Enfield under contract with the original Indian Company from 1955 to 1959.* (Garry Stuart)

Left: *Indian Velo 500 built by Floyd Clymer in the 1960s.* (Garry Stuart)

Above: *UK Wall of Death using Indian 101 Scout, favoured for its excellent handling.* (Garry Stuart)

Below: *Chuck Vernon with his Crocker 36-61-1X. Restored by Chuck Vernon. Note the Hemi heads.* (Chuck Vernon)

After the 2003 Gilroy bankruptcy, a new Indian Motorcycle company was formed and has been producing new Indians from 2009.

Top: *2010 Chief Vintage in Indian Red and Ivory Cream.* (Indian Motorcycle)

Above: *2009 Chief Deluxe in Thunder Black with tan leather and fringe.* (Indian Motorcycle)

Left: *Harry Sucher with trophy. Many thanks to Harry for his many years of dedication and being the author of* The Iron Redskin. (Marc Gallin)

*The 1935 Indian Four, still fitted with the Ace type engine, but with the gracefully-contoured mudguards designed by Briggs Weaver. (George Hays)*

ACE in small block letters beneath. After about one hundred machines had been produced, subsequent models were fitted with smaller diameter 25 inch x 3.85 inch balloon tires, the arc of the mudguards being slightly reduced to follow their smaller contour.

The Indian advertising brochures published at the end of August 1927, announcing the 1928 Indian line, stated that it would henceforth have a high pressure oiling system, an innovation developed by Arthur Lemon to enhance high speed engine reliability. The catalogs further described the Indian Ace as the Collegiate Four, and featured the low, flat, sports type chrome-plated handlebars as fitted to the last sporting Aces. The model remained essentially Ace-like until August, 1928, when the new catalogs announced that the new Indian Four would subsequently be produced.

In order more closely to integrate the four into the Indian line, and to facilitate more economical production, all essential components except the engine now followed contemporary Indian design. The cycle parts, including upper and lower tank rails, fuel tank contours, seat and chain stays, wheels, mudguards, and fork were those of the 101 Model Scout, which had just been brought into production earlier that Spring. The only variation was the fitting of an additional leaf to the fork spring, to cope with the added weight of the heavier engine.

These features brought the new four into line with the other Indian models, and it was designated the Model 401. The change, however, brought certain vibration problems not encountered in the original Ace design. An iron brace was fitted from the lower tank rail to the top of the cylinder head in an attempt to correct this fault. When this did not entirely cure the problem, the Ace type single down tube was changed to the twin down tube, as used in the parent 101 Scout machines, the arrangement being essentially a modified 101 Scout frame. According to a list of factory engine numbers, about 800 401 models were built before this change was made. Old time factory employees, however, state that only about 350 model 401 single down tube machines were actually built before the double down tube change was made. About two dozen authentic 401's still exist in the hands of antique enthusiasts.

The 402 model was announced in June, 1929. Its main distinguishing feature, other than the new frame, was the fitting of a new five bearing crankshaft as an improvement over the original three bearing Ace type, along with some 14 other advertised improvements by Arthur Lemon, for enhanced performance and reliability.

The ultimate result of these initial changes was a rather small compact machine of lithe and graceful appearance, as seen in the already popular 101 Scout. The exposed position of the crankcase precluded its use as an off-the-road machine, and the company wisely advocated its use as an easily started, high performance luxury touring mount, that was equally well suited to the needs of law enforcement. Its high selling price of $445.00, which was necessitated by the high cost of manufacturing its engine, quite naturally limited sales, as

*The 1936–37 'upside-down' four, with overhead exhaust and side intake valves. The photo shows the 1937 model designated as the Sport Four which featured a special intake manifold with twin carburetors.*
**(Theodore A. Hodgdon)**

the cost was then about that of a standard Ford or Chevrolet touring car.

The next radical change in design came in 1932, with a heavier frame and forks, a two-piece saddle type tank that replaced the earlier between-the-rails Scout type, and new, heavier mudguards. By this time the world-wide depression had made itself felt, and the factory management decided to economize on all production. The famous 101 Scout was discontinued, the standard Scout then taking its place, and all Indian machines then listed, which included the Four and Chief, shared the same cycle parts. There were minor changes in the Four engine, which are listed in the Appendix.

The Four was continued with very minor changes through the depression years of 1933–1934, but without the supervision of Arthur Lemon, who resigned to enter the wholesale bicycle business in Kalamazoo, Michigan. Sales of the Four were very limited, even though its retail price was reduced to $395.00 and Lemon feared that both the model and his job faced oblivion.

After very limited sales in 1934, probably about 200 machines, the new Indian chief designer, G. Briggs Weaver, made a change in the contours of the mudguards for 1935, somewhat following contemporary automotive practise. These gave the Four more streamlined and modern appearance, but otherwise it closely followed the previous year's 403 series.

In 1936, the Four was designated as the 436 model, and a rather radical change was made in the arrangement of the upper cylinders. The intake valves were shifted to

the side, with the exhaust valves placed in the top, necessitating a whole new manifolding arrangement. The idea behind these changes was a hoped-for increase in speed and power. While the 401 through 403 series Fours had possessed adequate performance for the road conditions existing in the late 1920s and early 1930s, the continuing improvements in road conditions generally, and the development of high speed expressways, had come to offer more taxing conditions for the earlier models' high speed capabilities. While the changes in the 436 models did bring about some increase in speed and power, the new type valve gear required frequent adjustment and, in some cases, proved unreliable. In order to recover the cost of the redesign and new tooling, the 436 was continued for the following year as the model 437, (also called the Sport Four,) in spite of some buyer resistance to the ungainly appearance of the new manifolding arrangement. The only marked change was the option of the fitting of two carburetors, which offered some additional speed and power without a marked improvement in reliability. In all, about 1600 of these models were produced during their two seasons of production.

A wise decision was the designing of an entirely new engine for the 1938 season, which was designated as the Model 438. Its cylinders were cast in pairs, with greatly increased cooling fin area and a new high efficiency manifold. All tappets and rocker gear were enclosed in demountable covers and were more positively lubricated. The same 77 cubic inch cylinder dimensions of the old Rochester Ace engine were retained, but the power increase was such that the new machine could attain

speeds of up to 100mph, yet throttle down to a walking pace in high gear. An attractive aluminum instrument nacelle and switch receptacle was fitted, and with its sweeping mudguards and a wide range of option color choices, the new model was undoubtedly the most handsome model of the Four yet produced. Many new buyers were attracted, including orders from law enforcement bodies.

For 1940 a plunger-sprung rear frame was offered, along with fully valanced mudguards similar to contemporary automotive practise. Not all enthusiasts approved of these, as they were considered to cause some instability at high speeds in strong side winds. But many agreed that they offered superb weather protection to the touring rider.

The 1941 models were similar, except for minor changes in chrome trim and a chrome-plated headlight shell that was fitted to some models. 4.50 inch x 18 inch tires were offered as standard, but 5.00 inch x 16 inch types were offered as an optional extra and gave a much softer ride. A few similar machines were built until March of 1942, mostly to fulfill law enforcement contracts, as all civilian sales were halted except those certified by the War Production Board after the Japanese attack on Pearl Harbor in December, 1941.

A serious drawback to the other than limited sales of Fours during the late 1930's and early 1940's was its necessarily high selling price, due to excessive production costs. The retail price rose from $695.00 in 1938 to $1095.00 in 1941–1942. This last was somewhat more than the cost of an eight-cylinder Buick sedan.

The Four was not reintroduced after World War II, as production costs due to the resultant inflation would have been astronomical. Then, too, the then President of the company, Ralph B. Rogers, was, as shall be seen, more interested in the marketing of lightweight machines. In response to the many inquiries from enthusiasts, an official statement was issued stating that continuing Four production would result in further financial losses for the company.

In spite of the accolades that have been accorded the Four by many enthusiasts, it was far from being a perfect motorcycle. The older Indian Aces and early 400 series models, while easy to start, smooth running, and possessing fantastic acceleration for their time, were prone to overheat if driven for prolonged periods at speeds over 50mph. There were design weaknesses in both the clutch and gearbox, each of which compounded the problems of the other. The primitive car-type sliding gear set was prone to much wear, especially if carelessly shifted, and the slider gear often required early replacement. The single plate clutch was subject to dragging, especially under cold weather conditions, or if starting up after prolonged rest. It often required much application of the kick starter to free the plate, and usually starting off was accompanied by much gear clashing. The fault

*The 1940 Indian Four fitted with full valanced mudguards and rear springing, but still fitted with 4.50 inch x 18 inch tires.* **(Theodore A, Hodgdon)**

was not corrected in the later models, and a solution was not found until 1965, when Dr. Earl Chalfant, a Four enthusiast from Pennsylvania, invented a pressure plate with Neoprene inserts that finally corrected the trouble. Most well restored Fours today are fitted with this device. Repairs to the engine are consequently expensive, as the unit construction of the engine and gearbox, in the absence of an access door for the gears, makes mandatory the removal of the engine from the frame to effect even minor adjustments to the clutch.

The improved engine design of the 438 models, which were fitted from 1938 through the last models built in 1942, offered coil and battery ignition as standard in order to reduce production costs, although a magneto was available as an optional extra at a $50.00 increase in cost. This system, built by Delco, was reliable, but there was a fire hazard from the fact that the fuel tap in the forward half of the gas tank was positioned over the distributor. A leaking tap could cause a conflagration if raw gasoline found its way into the distributor points. Some enthusiasts have rectified this fault by placing a sheet iron plate over the top of the distributor. Another method is to reverse the shaft so that the distributor is behind the generator, well away from the forward end of the tank.

While the later Fours are capable of maintaining modern freeway cruising speeds, some machines have been modified for enhanced performance by boring out the cylinders and fitting standard Sport Scout pistons. Due to the heavy cylinder walls, there is sufficient material to make this modification with safety. With the resultant 90 cubic inch cylinder displacement, there is a

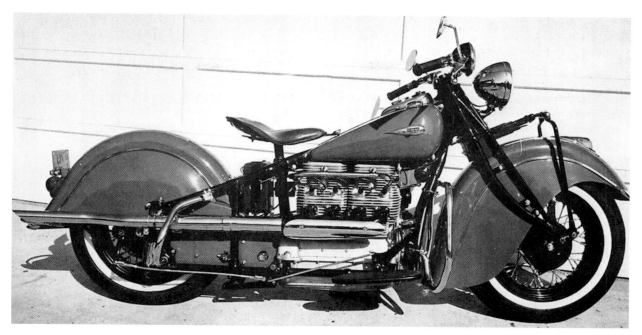

The 1940–41 Four with 5.00 inch x 16 inch tires and chrome plated headlight. (Theodore A. Hodgdon)

definite increase in power and speed, and the main bearings appear substantial enough to carry the extra load imposed.

The Fours in all models were essentially road machines, as none of them ever handled too well in the dirt or under rough going. The exposed crankcase was always vulnerable to damage, under the best of conditions.

The four cylinder Indians were produced only in limited numbers during their fifteen years of life. Born on the eve of a world wide depression, their sales were limited to those fortunate few who could afford the high initial cost. A computerized tabulation of the series of engine numbers indicates that a total of about 12,000 were produced. Knowledgeable factory employees, however, have stated that only about 9,400 machines were actually produced, the discrepancy due to lack of numbering continuity. Of this number, it may appear surprising that nearly half of all the Fours ever produced still survive. The reasons are simple. As a high-priced and highly prized luxury machine, they were not generally secured in their old age by impecunious boy racers, and many were carefully treasured by enthusiasts long after they were worn out. Some were secured by private owners as condemned from law enforcement use, as a large part of the Four production was originally sold for this purpose, and thus escaped the usual second-hand markets.

Nearly one thousand of the various models are owned by members of the very active Indian Four Cylinder Club, Inc. whose perennial President, John Wickham, is active

in his retirement years fabricating new parts for Fours. Large numbers are also owned by members of the Antique Motorcycle Club of America, and the Classic and Antique Motorcycle Club, as well as other similar organizations overseas. Numerous enthusiasts are actively engaged in making new parts, such as gear sets, clutch assemblies, trim details, battery and tool boxes, chainguards and other small items. Robert Paulette of Midway, Kentucky, presently has a large stock of Four parts, and undertakes overhauling, as does Charles Myles of Sloansville, New York, and Kenneth Young of Long Beach, California. Aside from all these encouraging activities, it is heartening to note that with each passing year a few more old models come to light in unlikely places.

A recent modification to the Indian Four crankshaft oiling system has been suggested to enhance the lubrication of the rear main bearings. The procedure is to drill oil passages from the number two and four bearings to the adjacent connecting rods. This will allow the oil to pass from the number one main bearing through the crankshaft to the other main bearings. This change is described as helping to prevent the chronic overheating of the rear cylinder during prolonged high speed running, especially in hot weather.

If the machine is to be ridden long distances, rather than being relegated to just being a show machine, the fitting of a small oil cooler below the front of the crankcase is also suggested.

# Chapter 6

# THE YEARS OF CHAOS 1927–1931

The new board of directors, which took control of the Indian Motorcycle Company in the Fall of 1927, named a newcomer as its President, Louis J. Bauer, an industrialist who had formerly been associated with Bauer Brothers Machinery Company of Dayton, Ohio. Bauer's manufacturing activities in that city had met with no little success, and he was able, together with two other new associates on the Board, to purchase sufficient shares of the preferred stock to give this combination majority control. With him came his son, Jack, a recent graduate of the University of Wisconsin with a degree in automotive engineering, who was appointed to a position in the Engineering Department.

Both Bauer and his son had more than a passing interest in motorcycle manufacture, but both they and the other majority shareholders on the Board were also interested in diversifying the company activities into other products.

At the same time, announcements were sent out from the Publicity Department to all dealers, assuring them that the basic company policies as formerly pursued by President Weschler would continue unchanged. Included in these releases were tributes to Weschler's long dedication to the company and accolades to his managerial abilities. The fact that he had actually resigned was glossed over, his sudden departure being termed a 'retirement'.

Motorcycle manufacture was continued as originally scheduled for the 1928 season, and included the Prince, 37 inch and 45 inch Scouts, 74 inch Chief and Four. The 61 inch Chief was discontinued soon afterward, as most buyers now preferred the more powerful 74 inch model.

At the same time, a separate holding corporation called the Indian Motocycle Acceptance Company was formed. Surplus treasury funds were then transferred to this company, apparently for the purpose of speculating in the shares of other companies.

In an article appearing in the *New York Times* on January 28th, 1928, it was announced that the company realized a net profit of $64,575.00 during the last quarter of 1927, after expenses, depreciation and federal taxes, including a gain of $103,543.00 on the sale of capital stock of the Wire Wheel Corporation of America, which funds were transferred to the Indian Motocycle Company from the Indian Acceptance Company. After the usual payment of 7% dividends on the preferred stock, earnings of 47 cents a share were paid to the owners of the outstanding no par common stock.

In this year, the traditional company fiscal business year was changed to conform to the calendar year. Sales of motorcycles during this period amounted to $1,124,204.00, together with an operating loss of $30,459.00. As 6,027 machines were produced, it may be assumed that an excess of Indian Motocycle Company funds had been transferred to the Indian Acceptance Company for speculative purposes.

Motorcycle sales generally continued to be firm within the current production schedules set by the big three factories, with the Indian Scout the most widely sold model, regardless of make.

In view of the Scout's continuing popularity, the management decided that a slight modernization of its

**Opposite:** *A rider's eye view of a 101 Scout.* (George Hays)

overall design was now in order. Up to this time the only visual modification from its original 1920 form had been the fitting of the wider and more fully valanced D-section mudguards in the Fall of 1926, although there had been several technical improvements in the engine-gearbox unit which have been mentioned. Charles Franklin repaired to his drawing board and the result was the Scout which was to make him immortal in the world of motorcycling.

The frame was lowered at the seat post, which afforded a saddle height of only 25 inches. This innovation, while generally new to American riders, had been popular in both England and on the continent, and often lowered the silhouette in some designs to the point where all parts of the machine, except the steering head, were on a level with the top of the wheels.

The wheelbase was lengthened to 57½ inches and while the original fork and suspension were retained, the rake and trail were altered slightly in the light of recent experience with factory racing machines. The lowered frame necessitated a somewhat shorter fuel tank of smaller capacity, which was redesigned in a more bulbous but streamlined form. It proved most attractive and was still of the one-piece between-the-tank-rails pattern.

The original Scout engine in both original 37 inch and later 45 inch, had for its forward mounts a pair of cast iron

*Newly elected Indian President Louis E. Bauer and executive staff at the annual company picnic held in the summer of 1927. Bauer is eighth from the left, in the third row. His son Jack is in the center of the top row.*
**(Theodore A. Hodgdon)**

**Right:** *Advertising announcement of the 45 cu in Scout as printed in trade and hobby magazines. Aside from the larger engine, this model was practically identical to the standard 37 cu in model.*

angle brackets that were bolted on either side to lugs, in the forward ends of the cradle frame. Under severe usage these were sometimes prone to fracture. To obviate this weakness, the new Scout now had the mountings cast integrally with the crankcases, which were formed as an elongation of the latter and were through-bolted to the frame lugs by means of a single, heavy stud.

Another very useful feature was the fitting of a front wheel brake. While such had been fitted as standard for several seasons to most English and continental machines, the idea appeared to be slow in occurring to American designers. Stopping power in most domestic designs was mediocre at best, as the standard externally contracting band type brake lost much of its efficiency in wet weather. A double-shoe arrangement with an internally expanding band inside the drum was fitted to the last Hedstrom Indians and was a definite improvement, but this was not seen on the later postwar Franklin models. At any rate, the internal expanding front wheel brake on the 101 was a great improvement and was also fitted to the Four and Chief.

The new Scout was a lithe, compact, and highly functional machine, seemingly poised for flight even when standing at rest, and it attracted widespread attention immediately. The new model, now designated as the 101, superseded the previous Scout design in March, when it was placed in production.

# Now!

## New *Indian* Scout 45

Now for the fun! Now for the thrills! Now for the big "kick" of outdoor sport at its best! Here it is—the new Scout 45—inviting you out to a real world of adventure!

The Scout 45 has a super-powerful motor, snappy acceleration, large oversize brake, classy sport handle bars. Holds boundless power for the veteran rider, easy handling features for the novice. Takes you anywhere—any time—and brings you back safely. Ride the 45 a mile —and see what a champion sport solo it really is!

**DEALERS:** A few territories still open for agency of Indian Motocycles. Wonderful opportunity for ambitious, energetic men. Write today for particulars. Address:

## *Indian* Motocycle Co.

### Dept. I.N. Springfield, Mass.

*The Police Special and Sports Solo*

**Easy to Own a Scout "45"**

Call on your nearest Indian dealer and find how easily you can own a Scout 45 under our generous pay-as-you-ride plan. Or mail coupon below for the complete interesting story of this popular model.

*Ride the 45 a mile!*

Indian Motocycle Co., Dept. I.N. Springfield, Mass.

Send me FREE descriptive circular on the new Indian Scout 45. This places me under no obligation.

Name----------------------------

Address-------------------------

City----------------------State--------------

Age 12 to 16 ☐    16 to 20 ☐    over 20 ☐

*Check nearest age to help us suggest the model for your requirements.*

L. E. Bauer and his son Jack, give the Indian Ace and the "45" a tryout.

IT is bound to be of interest and a source of real satisfaction to *Indian Riders* to know that L. E. Bauer, Chairman of our Executive Committee, and a member of the Board of Directors, is a real motorcycle fan. Not a mechanical change of any importance on any *Indian Model* is approved by "L. E." until he gives it a personal road test. While the final approval of every important change is a serious duty, the expressions prove that it is a real pleasure.

The accompanying illustration shows "L. E." on the first *Indian Produced Ace* and his son Jack on the Scout "45." Jack, a graduate of University of Wisconsin, is now a member of *Indian's* engineering staff.

The new machine created an initial sensation. With the refined Scout engine now developing more than 20hp, it gave the 370lb machine snappy acceleration and a top speed of about 75mph. The happily chosen kick-start ratio made starting fairly easy, and, coupled with its compact size and moderate weight, it was attractive to the novice as well as feminine riders. The 50mpg fuel economy and ability to haul a light passenger or commercial box sidecar also appealed to utility riders.

Overall performance aside, the most sterling quality inherent in the 101 was its outstanding handling capabilities and its stability. On smooth roads it could be ridden hands-off at any speed, the steering being accomplished by slight body movements of the rider. A favorite trick of Scout enthusiasts was to demonstrate its self-steering qualities by performing hands-off U-turns on a city street of average width. Another stunt, which demonstrated the machine's stability was its ability to be turned sharply within a short radius, at a steep angle of heel. A daring boy racer would often cut sharp figure 8's, preferably on a paved street, where the after end of the footboards could drag and cause sparks to fly.

This same near-perfect balance made the 101 the standard vehicle for carnival 'wall-of-death' riders, and old, stripped-down Scouts may still be seen performing in travelling circuses or amusement parks.

These attributes, credited to Franklin's genius as a designer, together with Indian's long racing heritage, made the 101 a suitable competition mount, as, when stripped of its standard mudguards, lighting set, tool box and other non-essentials, it weighed just over 300lbs, enhancing its handling qualities. This delighted a whole generation of aspiring boy racers and budding competition stars.

As a young man the author vividly recalls turning a 46 second mile on a county fairground horse track on such a machine, with a somewhat modified and carefully tuned engine. In spite of a rough surface, the machine's inherent handling qualities made it controllable for the 100mph speeds on the straights and the 70mph required through the turns to make this time.

Once a few demonstration machines had been shown by dealers, orders literally poured in, and a night shift was added to the production force, bringing the daily Scout production to 75 machines.

Knowledgeable motorcyclists and automotive historians have since been in almost universal agreement that the 101 was probably the best all around machine of its time. Fast enough to overhaul the average family car, it was widely employed in law enforcement. Its small size and moderate weight made it an attraction to novice riders, yet its high performance pleased many experienced riders of heavyweight twins, large numbers of whom became Scout enthusiasts. Many of these riders then enhanced performance by 'stroking' the engine as soon as it was broken in. Many Scouts were used in various commercial activities, such as by messengers who rode solo, or with light commercial sidecars.

In addition to the 45 cubic inch model, a 37 inch version was offered in identical form, except for cylinder dimensions. As most riders preferred the higher speed and power of the larger model, the latter version sold in but limited numbers to those who sought economy in utility work. It was carried in the catalogs through the 1930 season, when it was discontinued.

In spite of its sterling qualities, the 101 possessed a few less desirable features. The iron pistons fitted to the initial production models were prone to seize with prolonged high speed running, a fault corrected with the fitting of optional light alloy Lynite-type pistons on later models. The low cradle frame with limited ground clearance precluded extensive off-the-road use. Some riders requiring colonial travel overcame this difficulty by fitting 19 inch wheel rims. With its rigid frame and somewhat heavy fork action that offered only about 1½ inches of travel, the Scout rode very hard on roughish roads, obviating anything but moderate cruising speeds.

The fitting of the front wheel brake was fortuitous, as the exposed band on the rear wheel became totally useless, when even slightly damp. This situation was not improved until the last models produced in 1931 were fitted with an internal expanding mechanism that was more effectively protected from the elements.

The Scout's minor faults, however, were accepted as a matter of course by the riders of those days who could readily appreciate its generally outstanding qualities.

Franklin added further laurels to his name with the 101. Its continuing popularity through the next decade did much to enhance Indian's reputation for soundness of design. Even in a time of declining interest in motorcycling in the United States, the Scout attracted many new converts to the sport, and a number of new dealers, both new to the game and deserters from other makes, sought franchises on the strength of the Scout's reputation.

The American V-twin motorcycle design again proved its general durability in a once well-publicized but now long forgotten road test in the Soviet Union, during the Summer of 1928. In the Spring of that year, M. Vorochilof,

Commissar for War, released a news story stating that the historically poor Russian roads were now in such a state that if the country were invaded by some hostile foreign power, it would be impossible to move either men or material by motor transport to hold a line of defense. To dramatize this situation, the War Department scheduled a 3,000 mile test run, using various motor vehicles, including automobiles, trucks and motorcycles. The route was laid out from Moscow to Tiflis and included the primitive military road over the rugged Caucasus Mountains.

The motorcycle contingent included six American machines, representing Indian, Harley-Davidson and Excelsior, together with twelve other machines manufactured in England, France, Germany and Austria. It was reported that only the American big twins survived the arduous journey, all the others succumbing to various mechanical troubles along the way.

This event marked the first time since the institution of the Communist regime that foreign visitors and newspaper reporters were tendered an official welcome to the Soviet Union.

*Prototype model of the proposed Indian Light Car built in 1928. Powered with a 74 cu in Chief Indian engine-gearbox unit, the drive to the rear axle was by means of a long chain to a differential unit. Excessive vibration problems eventually ended the project.* **(Theodore A. Hodgdon)**

In the Spring of 1928 Ted Hodgdon was promoted to the post of Assistant Advertising Manager. A part of his duty was to edit a new company publication called *Indian News*, which supplanted *Wigwam News*.

With the resignation of T.S. 'Ted' Slack as Advertising Manager soon afterward, Hodgdon was promoted to fill this position. Sometime later his staff was augmented by the addition of Emmett Moore, a young journalist who was later to become a writer of articles on historic motorcycling subjects for the trade press. Following World War II he was associated with the US branch of BSA Incorporated. He also joined Hodgdon in the formation of the Antique Motorcycle Club, in 1954.

The Board of Directors continued their stock speculation activities through the Indian Acceptance Company. The actual number of securities or the names of all the various companies involved are unknown today as records are not available.

During this period, experimental work included the construction of a small automobile, under the direction of Jack Bauer. The first prototype was about the size of the contemporary English Austin Seven, which was then enjoying wide sales both in Great Britain and in overseas markets. Bauer's auto was powered with a standard Chief 74 inch engine-gearbox unit that drove the rear wheels via a long chain that activated a differential type axle. Arthur Lemon was a passenger in this machine as it was

driven in chassis form to a body builder in Connecticut for the fitting of a light roadster body. He reported that the car was subject to excessive vibration.

The vehicle continued to evidence vibration problems, even after the fitting of the body, and after further tests with unsatisfactory results, the project was abandoned. Young Bauer then designed another small car, again along Austin Seven lines, but with automotive rather than motorcycle components. These cars were powered with small four cylinder water-cooled Continental engines, similar to those which were used by Billy Durant in his Star cars. A total of five prototypes were built with varying coach work, which were reported to be of attractive styling. After spending about $50,000, the light automobile project was abandoned. One of these cars is said to survive in the hands of an antique automotive enthusiast in Springfield, but no photographs of this or the other models appear to be available.

The actual reason for discontinuing work on this project was never officially divulged, but it is obvious that the company would have had difficulties in penetrating the highly competitive automobile industry. It was later reported by some former employees that the rumor that a new company was planning to market an Americanized version of the Austin Seven had somewhat dampened the management's ardor, especially since an already well-proved chassis was to be the basis of the new project.

This rumor proved to be correct, as such a company was officially launched in the Spring of 1929, with an assembly plant at Butler, Pennsylvania. This machine proved reliable and very economical to operate, but its performance was somewhat restricted by the heavy American style coach work. The venture collapsed in 1934, after about 40,000 units had been sold. A reorganized company later built a few restyled versions until 1939, when the Bantam again disappeared from the picture. American motorists never took to the baby car, whose selling price was indefensibly nearly that of the starker versions of the overwhelmingly popular Chevrolets, Fords, Stars and Durants which offered far greater comfort, performance and durability. Extreme economy of operation was never much of a selling point with earlier American motorists what with the then seemingly inexhaustible quantities of low cost oil at ten cents a quart and gasoline at fifteen cents a gallon.

Due to the preoccupation of the management with the light car project, only 5,077 motorcycles were produced in 1928, the majority of which were the ever-popular 101 Scout. As a result of the costs expended on the light cars and the diversion of capital to the Indian Acceptance Company, a net operating loss of $419,029.00 was reported for the year.

The company's excursions into the light car experiments, and the diversion of company funds, became a great source of anguish to many of Indian's dealers and owners, when the news inevitably leaked out. While the motorcycle market was generally static, the diminished production of Scouts was extremely unfortunate as large numbers of orders for them actually went unfilled.

The sales program for 1929 saw the continued production of the Scout, Chief, and Four with but details changed only from the previous year, the most notable being the fitting of a front wheel brake to the Chief. The Prince was discontinued, mainly due to lack of dealer emphasis as most of them were now concentrating on sales of the Scout.

Another significant reason for the Prince's demise, however, was the declining market for American machines in the export field, which came about through a rather complex set of changes in the international trading picture, and which was to have a further depressing effect on the already troubled domestic motorcycle industry.

The United States had emerged from the war virtually unscathed, aside from some 50,000 casualties, which were minimal when compared to the losses in manpower suffered by the European and English combatants. The vast postwar economic growth enjoyed by the United States had resulted in the retirement of the bulk of the war debts by 1926, and a year or so later the country was enjoying unprecedented prosperity. Wage earners, professional and business men, together with a myriad of companies and corporations, were all enjoying healthy incomes. The only exception were those engaged in agriculture.

Due to an overproduction of foodstuffs, receipts for various crops remained low, but at the same moment the farmers' costs for machinery, fertilizer, and general consumer goods were constantly rising, due to the pressures of a growing inflation. The price of farm products was kept low due to the lack of protective tariffs, and many foodstuffs were concurrently being imported to compete with domestic products.

There was much pressure in Congress after 1926, especially from the midwest farm bloc, to institute high protective tariffs for the benefit of agriculture. This resulted in the drafting of the McNary-Haugen farm bill, so named for its congressional sponsors, which, among other things, called for increased tariffs against foreign products, graduated price supports for domestically-produced agricultural products, together with projected government purchase of surplus foodstuffs for resale on foreign markets.

A politically expedient bill that had aroused much popular support, it easily passed both Houses of Congress in the Fall of 1926, but was vetoed by President Coolidge, who was adamantly opposed to any government interference or participation in private business. The bill was again presented to him in 1927, and again in 1928, with the same result. But in 1929, newly elected President Herbert Hoover signed the bill into law, amid much general rejoicing.

The immediate result was the retaliation on the part of many foreign governments by the erection of high tariff barriers against American manufactured goods, especially motor vehicles. This state of affairs particularly affected the Indian company in the Australasian markets, where Indians had long been popular sellers and from which had come vast quantities of beef and crop foodstuffs. The export of Indians ceased almost overnight with the new 25% import duty, together with a sharp increase in shipping costs. Indian's best remaining overseas markets were now South America and South Africa, which as yet had no significant vehicular manufacture.

Another significant motorcycling event during this period was the reorganization of the American Motorcycle Association. Up to this time the AMA had been operating more or less as an autonomous riders' organization, free of trade influence. With the general decline in national motorcycle registrations to about 150,000 machines, a majority of whose owners were not interested in supporting competition, its strength had become seriously eroded. In order to stave off its impending collapse, the remaining big three manufacturers and certain of the trade and accessory suppliers acting as an unofficial committee through their own previously instituted M & ATA, acted to support the AMA financially on a pro-rata basis. A small permanent office was established in Columbus, Ohio, manned by a small staff headed by E.C. Smith as executive secretary. Smith remained in this position from 1928 until his retirement in 1954, when he was succeeded by Lin Kuchler.

Aside from the need of motorcyclists and motorcycling generally for an official spokesman, it was highly necessary that rules for various competition events be enforced. With the current weak position of the AMA, there were already many unsanctioned or 'outlaw' events being held, to the detriment of the sport.

During the early Spring of 1929, President Bauer launched another diversification from motorcycle manufacture, with the announcement that the company would now enter the automobile accessory field with a patent shock absorber.

The conventionally evolved automobile designs of the late 1920's employed almost universally some type of elliptical leaf springing in their suspension systems which was based on those previously used on horse-drawn

*Left: **The standard 37 cu in Scout fitted with a commercial sidecar. This 1927 model machine was almost identical to the early Scout models except for the newly introduced fully valanced mudguards.** (Leslie D. Richards)*

*Right: **Denver Indian dealer Leslie D. Richards' 1927 Indian Chief commercial outfit, used as a shop service vehicle.** (Leslie D. Richards)*

spring wagons. While these devices provided adequate suspension and spring action on smooth roads, they were prone to much pitching and excessive rebound action in rough going, with discomfort to the passengers, and hard steering, along with frequent breakages of spring leaves.

As most manufacturers had yet to fit shock absorbers or other dampening devices to production-type cars, several manufacturers such as Gabriel, Houdaille, and Gruss marketed various types of snubbing devices as accessories. One of these was also manufactured by the Hartford Shock Absorber Company of Hartford, Connecticut. It consisted of a small two-piece clamshaped cast iron clamp that was bolted around the outer surface of the spring, about midway between the crown and shackle, and for which they held the original patent. Its action was to inhibit excessive travel of the spring during compression and expansion. This small company was said to have been one of the several firms acquired by President Bauer through his financial manipulations involving the Indian Acceptance Company.

A production line was set up in the State Street factory to fabricate the new shock absorber, together with a separate Advertising Department to handle the merchandising. This was headed by an advertising specialist from New Jersey, a genial 240lb giant of a man named F.H. Dickieson, who was assisted by about twenty new staff

members. An advertising campaign was launched, with full page announcements in several automotive trade and accessory publications, extolling the virtues of the new product that was offered at an introductory price of $15.00 per set of four. The idea behind this promotion was that automobile dealers, repair garages and auto accessory stores would handle the retail sales and installation, which normally took only a few minutes to effect.

The announcement of the new product antagonized many of the dealers to whom it was made plain by the factory that it was not to be included in present or future franchise agreements involving the sale of Indian machines. Many dealers as well as owners were also perturbed by the fact that inevitably motorcycle production and distribution would be curtailed by the shock absorber program, as it had been during the previous year as the result of the light car program.

The regular Advertising Department made heroic efforts to reassure the dealers that supplies of machines and spare parts would be shipped on schedule, as well as attempting to placate those who had become the most critical of the new project. In order to make it appear as a closely related company product, a large number of Scout delivery combinations were used to deliver supplies of shock absorbers to the more adjacent outlets.

In order to stimulate volume sales to dealers, the devices were shipped on consignment, in which, after a

stated period, the unsold items could be returned to the factory, payment only being due on those actually sold. The problem was, however, that the shock absorbers proved unsatisfactory, even after frequent readjustments by the dealers installing them, and the whole project ended in a fiasco. Their dampening action was ineffectual. The exact cost of this project was never publically revealed, and no official records survive. Knowledgeable former employees have stated, however, that in their opinion the company lost well over $250,000.00 in the ill-starred venture.

As Dickieson and his crew of advertising experts departed for greener pastures, President Bauer immediately proposed to launch the company into the household appliance field with a refrigerator activated by natural gas.

During the height of Dickieson's sales campaign, James B. MacNaughton suddenly resigned as Sales Promotion Manager. It has been reported that he never offered any concrete reason for this action, but former company employees have stated that he was visibly antagonized by the hiring of Dickieson to fulfill a special role in company affairs. He next assumed a similar posi-

*Leslie D. Richards poses with four of the eight Western Union messenger boys who purchased Princes for delivery duties during 1928. (Leslie D. Richards)*

tion with the Stuart Laundry Machinery Company, which occupied a small factory a few doors away from the Indian plant. He resigned from this concern a couple of years later to form his own advertising company. In failing health, he passed away in March 1933, from complications following a respiratory ailment. While there was no question of his loyalty to the Indian company through the years of his tenure, he appears to have been a controversial figure among his fellow employees, as many conflicting opinions concerning his attitude and personal habits have been voiced by those who knew him.

His position was immediately filled by James A. (Jim) Wright, a young man who had previously been the sales manager for a small machine tool company. Wright expressed immediate enthusiasm for Indian's cause, and, being possessed of a pleasing personality and an engaging manner, he at once became very popular with company associates and dealers alike. His dedication to motorcycling activities in general soon won him the presidency of the M & ATA, a post he held for eleven consecutive terms until 1942, and he performed yeoman service for the industry in general during the difficult years.

While the factory was buzzing with rumors about the venture into the household appliance field, only a few of the top executives in the Advertising Department were actually aware of the details of the proposal. At any

At left: "Hap" Alzina takes a ride with "Big Chief" Bauer and "Doug" McGregor of the Engineering Department; right, Sales Manager McNaughton wishes "Hap" the best of luck as the latter hops off on a tour with an Indian 4.

rate, one of Bauer's assistants brought about a dozen photographs of a very plain looking white refrigerator into the advertising office and requested that some sales promotion brochures be developed concerning it. The staff members were told that it was run by natural gas, similar to the then familiar 'Serval' type unit, except that the appliance in question was supposed to be an improvement.

A small quantity of advertising brochures were made up, featuring the Indian trademark, and relating the refrigerator to the world-wide acceptance of Indian products. These were subsequently forwarded to President Bauer's office. Nothing more was ever heard of the project.

Coincidentally there were other rumors of the planned production of gas cooking stoves and air conditioning units, but they proved entirely false. Several old time Indian executives have since stated that they believe these sub rosa activities were a part of a secret campaign on the part of Bauer and others in the top management to boost the sales of Indian common stock, which was now being traded on the New York Stock Exchange and which was enjoying a rather poor reputation following the recent shock absorber debacle. It was also rumored several of the top company executives were buying and selling Indian stock under specific orders from within the Board of Directors, and were prospering handsomely.

*Excerpt from the January 1928 issue of* **Indian News.** *These early Fours were 401 models with the single front frame tube.*

While all these digressions from motorcycle manufacture were taking place, the servicing of dealers with both new machines and parts was seriously disrupted. Complaints began coming in concerning new machines received with parts missing, such as clutch plates, brakes parts, cylinder head gaskets, etc. The Order Department seemed also to be neglecting its duties, as many orders for spare parts went unfilled, or, if filled at all, were hopelessly jumbled. It was reported that many of the Department heads had been commandeered into service in the Shock Absorber Department, leaving less experienced or indifferent hands in charge of motorcycle production and servicing.

Many of the dealers who had personal friendships within the company management traded on these relationships to get preferential aid in correcting their difficulties. While such intercessions often achieved desired results, they often led to much hard feeling among other dealers who did not enjoy such factory contacts. Not a few surrendered their franchises in disgust and these included some who had lately joined the roster to cash in on the Scout popularity. A few subsequently changed their allegiance to Excelsior or Harley-Davidson.

The complexity of inter-dealer relationships, both between competitive makes and those franchised from the same manufacturer, has been a source of wonderment to automotive historians researching the swashbuckling days of motorcycling. Due to the minority position of the motorcycle in the transportation market, competition was very keen, and the dealer was usually a rugged individualist who would employ any expedient methods for his own survival.

The situation in Denver involving Dick Richards and Floyd Clymer is a case in point, and is mentioned because their conflict was well known among old-time motorcyclists and the facts are well authenticated.

It will be recalled that the Indian factory persuaded Richards to accept the franchise for the Denver area after Clymer, a one-time Harley-Davidson dealer there, had neglected Indian sales during the heyday of his famous through-the-windshield automobile spotlight. The local Harley-Davidson dealer, since Clymer dropped that franchise in 1918, was Walter Whiting, who, through his generally ethical dealing and pleasant personality, had built up a thriving business. Richards and Whiting, though competitors, were on a friendly basis, and worked co-operatively to build up the image of motorcycling in the Denver area.

In the Spring of 1929, Clymer apparently felt the urge to re-enter the motorcycle business. As he had been deposed by the Indian company, he sought ways to regain the Harley-Davidson franchise. The details of his machinations are today unknown, but the Harley-Davidson factory abruptly took away Whiting's franchise and awarded it to one H.D. Cooper, a former employee in Clymer's spotlight operation. The reasons behind this are, of course, unknown, but unsubstantiated rumors had it that Clymer paid the Harley-Davidson Company a substantial sum of money to effect the switch.

These unethical dealings would, of course, not be countenanced today, but there are instances still recalled where many of the motorcycle manufacturers of the day were not loathe to portion out franchises to the highest bidder, refusing to recognize prior contract agreements.

At this juncture, the deposed Whiting transferred his allegiance to Richards and his former sales manager, O.B. Senter, joined the latter's Indian sales force. Senter was later reputed to have amassed a tidy fortune in Florida real estate speculation.

The formidable competition from the Clymer-Cooper combine, coupled with the deteriorating relationship with the factory now plaguing all Indian dealers, forced

Richards into bankruptcy. He then for a time worked as an aircraft engine mechanic. In later years he prospered in the oil drilling tool business and at this writing is retired and living in Houston, Texas.

In addition to his motorcycle dealership and spotlight business, Clymer also established an inventor's marketing service with a small office and mailing address in Chicago. According to the company letterhead it was managed by one V.G. Martin. Through advertisements placed in mechanics and hobby magazines, an offer was made to obtain manufacturing and marketing outlets for new inventions, contingent on the prepayment of a substantial fee.

A relatively large number of individuals responded and it was later ascertained that Clymer collected about $250,000.00 in this manner. When it became apparent that no actual results were forthcoming, a number of disappointed inventors complained to the postal authorities. The investigators traced the ownership of the agency to Clymer in Denver, while undercover men posing as inventors mailed in a number of applications, along with their remittances, to the Chicago address.

After sufficient evidence of fraud was accumulated to sustain a case, Federal attorneys filed a class action suit in the Denver Federal District Court, charging Clymer and Martin with mail fraud on May 6th, 1929.

The subsequent trial was attended by a large number of complainants together with several motorcycle people, including Richards, Whiting, Senter and a number of Indian and Harley-Davidson dealers from adjacent areas. During the course of the proceedings, it was discovered that 'V.G. Martin' was, in fact, Vera Gladys Martin, a very attractive young woman.

The jury found a verdict of guilty on all counts against Clymer, but Miss Martin was found not guilty for lack of evidence. The judge offered Clymer a suspended sentence, and five years probation, if he would agree to make restitution to the defrauded inventors and not appeal the case. Clymer refused these terms and filed an appeal. He was subsequently turned down in the appellate court and was given a three- to five-year sentence in a Federal penitentiary on March 26th, 1930.

Records of the US Department of Justice show that he was received at Leavenworth Penitentiary in Kansas on March 29th. He was made a trusty for his good behavior and the warden actually allowed him to leave the prison on several occasions, to compete in motorcycle races in adjoining towns, as attested to by several old-time riders who lived in the area. He was released on July 21st, 1931, on an indeterminate probation.

In spite of continuing production troubles at the factory, a fair number of 101 Scouts were sold during the

1929 season. The far western states, and most particularly California, enjoyed a mild boom in motorcycle sales, due to the more or less all-year riding weather. In fact, many diehard enthusiasts moved to California for just this reason. Many of the new dealer franchises awarded in the wake of the Scout enthusiasm were established in that state, and many noted western competition riders such as Fred Ludlow, Bo Lissman, Miny Waln, 'Putt' Mossman, who later became a carnival stunt rider, Dewey Bonkrud, Al Thuett, Sam Parriott, P.A. Bigsby and others too numerous to mention became Scout fans. The Freed Cycle Company had two active dealerships, one in San Francisco and one in Los Angeles, and Hap Alzina in Oakland, as Indian distributor, was also a successful Indian promoter.

In 1929, the Harley-Davidson Company offered their first 45 cubic inch WL model twin, its side valve configuration being said to have been inspired by the success of the Scout. A rugged and reliable machine, it never equalled the performance of the Scout, nor was it capable of being stroked or as highly tuned as the latter. Then, it also never seemed to achieve quite the lithe styling of its competitor.

The performance of both these models was well tested during these years at the many informal race meets held on the dry bed of Lake Muroc, where a circular five-mile course was laid out. Fred Ludlow recalls running a 105mph mile here in the summer of 1929, on a Scout with standard cylinder dimensions, running on ethyl gasoline. The machine was stock in all respects except that it was stripped to reduce its overall weight and was carefully tuned.

While the 101 Scout continued to attract individual sporting devotees and club members, public interest in motorcycling as a spectator sport waned with the passing of the board tracks, the last example at Rockingham having been dismantled the year before. Their replacement was now flat track racing, which was said to have originated in New Zealand during the winter of 1927–1928. This was quickly taken up in nearby Australia, and spread to Great Britain and the United States during the following year.

While this type of racing did not have the gladiatorial appeal of the great ovals with their thundering, thin-tired, open-ported racers hurtling around at 100mph speeds, it was infinitely more attractive to people of more restrained sensibilities as the competition speeds attained were considerably lower, and the risks of injury to the riders negligible.

The flat tracks subsequently proved to be much easier and far less costly to build and maintain, as they could be laid out on any handy large lot or country field in a matter of a couple of days with a small road scraper, a matter of some importance in the coming economic depression.

Meanwhile, back at the factory, President Bauer and his associates on the Board of Directors viewed the financial shambles they had created, and decided to call it a day. Bauer tendered his resignation on June 7th, 1929, at a meeting of the Board held in New York City, but the news of this was not reported until two weeks later in Springfield.

In an article released to the trade press on July 7th, it was announced that a new group of men controlling the Indian Company had elected J. Russell Waite of Charleston, South Carolina, as President, but Bauer remained on the Board.

Waite was a member of a wealthy and socially prominent Charleston family who enjoyed extensive political connections in that city. He had once been Commissioner of the port, a political appointment tendered to him by President Warren G. Harding. A graduate engineer and a man of culture and refinement, he appeared for his day to be a rather unlikely type to express more than a passing interest in motorcycles.

In his opening statements for the benefit of the trade press, Waite announced that the company would henceforth direct most of its efforts toward motorcycle production and that such past diversification into shock absorbers, radiators, refrigerators and midget cars would no longer be considered.

Waite further assured the dealers that he was indeed a genuine Indian enthusiast and as such would do his utmost to promote efficient production of motorcycles as well as to build and maintain a close relationship with the dealer organization. This was indeed good news to the many dealers who had experienced difficulty in even attempting to communicate with his predecessor.

Jim Wright announced that no sweeping changes would be made in traditional company policy regarding motorcycle manufacture, and echoed Waite's pronouncement that dealer relations would be materially strengthened under the new management.

What was not immediately announced was the fact that the majority stockholders on the new Board of Directors represented Charles A. Levine, a financier and aviation enthusiast, who had both financially supported and accompanied Clarence Chamberlain on his transatlantic flight from Roosevelt Field on Long Island to Eisleben, Germany, in June 1927. As future events unfolded, it became evident that Levine planned to utilize a part of Indian's factory facilities for aircraft manufacture.

Aviation enthusiasts may recall that Lindbergh's transatlantic flight in May 1927, and subsequent crossings

Complete Leather Goods Equipment for the Indian Rider

Indian Handlebar Muffs

Indian Leather Jacket showing reverse side

Indian Leather Jacket, made of genuine horsehide

Snappy Indian Togs    Jacket-Breeches-Puttees

Indian Leather Helmet

Indian Riding Belt

Indian Gauntlet Gloves lined with mohair

Indian Puttees

Indian Driving Gloves with corded palms

You'll have to see these Indian Leather Garments to fully appreciate them. Each is exclusively Indian and of the famous Indian outstanding quality.   See your local Indian Dealer for further information.

Insist on Genuine Indian Leather Goods

**Left:** *Excerpt from the December 1928 issue of* **Indian News,** *showing specially made motorcyclist's clothing offered through dealer outlets.*

**Right:** *A special hand-built overhead valve Indian road racing machine produced in limited numbers for overseas markets in 1928. This model won numerous races in Germany that year.* **(Theodore A. Hodgdon)**

by Chamberlain, Byrd, and others, stimulated a sudden interest both in private flying and in the possibilities of commercial aviation in the United States. Previous to that time in the days following the war, interest in the matter had languished to the point where there was practically no domestic airplane industry.

The reasons for this state of affairs were varied. While the war had given an artificial impetus to airplane design progress, service airplanes were built with planned obsolescence and were heavily powered for short sustained performance, with little regard for economy of operation or servicing. With lurid newspaper reports dealing with the exploits of wartime 'aces', the 'Knight-of-the-Air' concept could not readily be translated to the individual possibilities of the man in the street.

Then, too, large quantities of surplus wartime training planes, usually of the cumbersome Curtiss Jenny or Lincoln Standard types, were readily available at bargain prices, which effectively strangled the acceptance of more costly, if more suitable, airplanes for civilian use.

Aviation for most people in the postwar decade was generally limited to the observation of the antics of stunt flyers at county fairs, which had the same general effect on popular interest in flying that motorcycle racing had previously had on the general public interest in motorcycles.

Lindbergh's exploit at least was a dramatic public demonstration of the future possibilities of civilian aviation and the nation became flight conscious almost overnight.

A large number of hard core flying enthusiasts with an interest in aircraft manufacture sought ways to enter this field. Most of them being lightly financed began at once to seek existing production facilities to convert to this use. Within the year over a hundred aircraft concerns came into being, most of them being in the midwest, but plant facilities anywhere suited to this use were at a premium. Levine no doubt viewed the great Indian factory complex as many others had done; a giant manufacturing facility now only in partial employment and readily adaptable to almost any type of manufacturing.

The new President and Board of Directors next addressed themselves to the more pressing problems facing the nearly bankrupt Indian Company. The treasury was depleted, leaving no working capital. Employee morale was at a very low ebb, and dealer relationships had deteriorated to the point that growing numbers were momentarily threatening to give up their franchises. Motorcycle production was carried forward, but to assure a constant cash flow to sustain operational obligations, all finished machines, spare parts and accessories were forwarded on a collect-on-delivery basis.

The inauguration of this policy at once brought a storm of protest from many of the surviving dealers. Many of them were operating on limited capital at best and the prospect of having to pay for goods as delivered seriously hampered their operation. Some of the larger dealers such as Al Crocker in Kansas City or the Freed Cycle Company in San Francisco opened charge accounts for small dealers in adjacent areas, as it was usual for agents in the larger cities to carry a substantial parts inventory.

In spite of these stringent measures, Indian's reserve and operating capital shrank to the point where, at the end of August, there were no funds left to meet the payrolls. There now appeared the dire possibility of having to suspend production. No short term capital was readily available, as the Springfield banks were somewhat loathe to extend any more credit considering Indian's history of boom or bust operation.

At this juncture Hap Alzina, who had kept in close touch with the company's financial problems, made his name forever immortal among loyal Indian enthusiasts by raising sufficient funds through short term loans from banks in the San Francisco area to meet the emergency. As matters turned out, Hap made no fewer than four transcontinental train trips that Summer, carrying $10,000.00 to $12,000.00 each time. Payrolls and the more pressing needs for materials and accessories were met, and, coupled with a steady flow of orders for Scouts, production haltingly got under way again.

In the Fall, a continuing three model range of Scout, Chief and Four was announced, all being substantially as produced the preceding season, except for detail improvements. The most notable change was the fitting of cast aluminum fuel tank halves to the Chief. These were replaced by the former conventional pressed steel type, however, in midseason, as the new type proved more costly due to the number of porous castings that came from the foundry.

During the Fall, rumors about the factory had it that the company was soon to undertake the production of aircraft engines and complete airplanes. Instead, the announcement was made that outboard engines for small boats were to be put into production.

This decision was no doubt due to the fact that boating in all forms had become increasingly popular in the United States during the prosperous 1920's. While the sport of yachting had become the vogue shortly after the Civil War, it was mostly confined to large sailing or steam powered vessels, whose purchase and operating costs limited them to only the very rich. With the development of the gasoline marine engine in the early years of the twentieth century, small launches with this power came into fairly popular use, but the cost of the engines and fittings was still rather high due to limited production.

It was Ole Evinrude's invention of the small outboard type marine engine shortly before World War I, and its subsequent refinement in the early 1920's, that brought power boating within the reach of the average citizen. It may well be said that the outboard engine related to power boating as did the early day motorcycle to the automobile.

Several manufacturing concerns came into being which were later to become prominent in the industry. These included the original Evinrude Company together with Elto, Johnson, Caille, Lockwood-Ash and a number of smaller concerns.

The outboard engine manufacturers had organized the Outboard Motor Association in the mid-1920's, in order to standardize engine sizes for the inevitable competition activities that were becoming popular

among owners. Cylinder displacement was based on the international litre formula, with A, B, C, D, and a 60 cubic inch F class, the smaller designation being below 10 cubic inches.

The engine which the Indian Company had secured was a horizontally-opposed water cooled two-cycle twin cylinder type, the then standard type of design used by most of the manufacturers, and was of the Class B designation, being of 19 cubic inch displacement rated at 15 horsepower. It had been developed by the Hartford Engine Company of Hartford, Connecticut. This concern had been formerly known as the Hartford Marine Engine Company, and had manufactured a line of small, heavy duty, two-cycle inboard engines, such as had been popular in the early days of the industry since 1909. This company had suspended marine engine production in 1922, and had diversified its activities along other lines, but was reorganized in 1926 to re-enter the marine field with an outboard engine. It has been said that this company was one of those acquired by the Indian Company by former President Bauer during his stock acquisition activities in the Fall of 1928, but no records are available today to substantiate this allegation.

Two of these engines were tested by members of the engineering staff late that Summer, on the nearby Connecticut River. While they started easily and ran smoothly, their power development appeared to be deficient when compared to engines in the same class as made by other manufacturers, and Charles Franklin set about conducting experiments with various changes in the port timing in an attempt to correct this fault.

In September, the production schedule for the 1930 sales year was established, and President Waite and the Levine-controlled Board of Directors set about to implement the inauguration of airplane manufacture that had been planned the previous June. This intention appeared somewhat inauspicious in the face of reports that for the first six months of the year the company had already sustained a net loss of $378,201.00. The original plans of the Levine group were to move the manufacturing facilities to Springfield. They had been established previously as the Columbia Aircraft Company by Levine himself, in a small rented plant near Long Island City, New York.

Levine, as an industrialist with an interest in expanding his activities, had apparently had the desire to enter the field of aircraft manufacture for some time. In the light of subsequent events, it is certain that he financed his transatlantic flight with the experienced Chamberlain as pilot as a means of gaining publicity for future activities in the field of aviation; in fact, he named his company after his famous airplane.

During these negotiations, Clarence Chamberlain himself was much in evidence, making occasional visits to the Indian factory and was dutifully photographed on a new Scout in front of the main entrance by Ted Hodgdon, as well as appearing in group pictures with Levine and Indian executives. There is no evidence, however, that he was ever himself financially involved in the proposed Indian merger, or that he ever had any official connection with it. Most probably he was merely lending his considerable public prominence as a transatlantic aviator, to give publicity to Levine's proposed venture.

The airplane design first planned for production at the New York plant was a frank copy of the transatlantic model which was originally built by the Bellanca Aircraft Company, from a prototype designed by the gifted designer, Guiseppi Bellanca. This airplane, a large, high wing, single-engine type with notable characteristics of stability, ease of handling, and load carrying, was a much-sought-after machine for long distance flights during this period. It is said that Lindbergh would have purchased one for his solo dash over the Atlantic, had its price not been too high for his limited funds.

The new machine, which was to be marketed as the 'Tridar', was supposed to enhance the usefulness of the original parent Bellanca, in that it was to have a large detachable float under the central portion of the fuselage, between the landing wheels, similar to that of the contemporary Loening amphibian biplane, allowing it to alight and take off from either land or water. For further utility it was planned that the float could be detached easily by unbolting its connections through the bottom of the fuselage, allowing the plane to be flown clear on its wheels.

While the idea had some practical aspects, experienced pilots faulted its design, as it was not provided with wing tip floats, attachments highly necessary for landing or taking off in rough water.

The actual acquisition of Columbia Aircraft by the Indian Motocycle Company was planned to take place through the latter's purchase of the outstanding shares of Columbia stock, which Levine valued at $250,000.00. A firm of industrial appraisers from New York were engaged to invesigate Columbia's assets, but ventured the opinion that these were worth only $50,000.00.

In the meantime, Columbia applied to the Aeronautical Branch of the Department of Commerce (now known as the Federal Aviation Authority), for certification, but for the design weakness mentioned, they were turned down. Levine had not informed Indian of this fact, and the government's witholding of a certificate of airworthiness was only discovered during the appraisal proceedings. President Waite thereupon urged the Board of Directors to immediately cease negotiations with Columbia, as the aircraft could obviously not be built if a flight certificate was not forthcoming.

Some of the directors backing Levine urged that more time be allowed Columbia to correct the Tridar's design deficiencies, but in the meantime the infamous Black Friday occurred, when the New York Stock Exchange experienced the surge of panic selling which was to presage the Great Depression. This news no doubt dampened Waite's already waning enthusiasm for the project, and he suggested that Indian concentrate its activities on motorcycles and the development of the outboard motor, examples now improved by Franklin undergoing further testing.

The upshot of the matter was that Levine's backers expressed their intention to sell their holdings in Indian now that the airplane project was a dead issue, at least for the present. Facing an uncertain future with the company, and not being in a position to ascertain just what new interests might be in line to acquire majority control of the stock, President Waite tendered to the Board his resignation as President on November 18th, although he wished to retain his seat on the Board.

The new group of majority stockholders who next took control of Indian were known as the 'Newark Group', and included as a partial listing, Arthur C. Dickinson of Philadelphia, William Irwin Tracy of New York, Henry C. Dodge of Newark, New Jersey, and Norman T. Bolles.

Bolles was elected President by this group, and was said to have had extensive experience in industrial management, according to publicity releases in the financial and trade press. It was further stated that he had been educated as an engineer, and was a naval officer during the war. What was not revealed until later, however, was that his main talents appeared to be in the field of stock and security manipulation.

No further press releases to either the trade or financial journals were made during the rest of the month, except that it was rumored that motorcycle production for the past year had dropped to a mere 4,635 units due, no doubt, to Indian's management preoccupation in other fields as noted.

On December 18th, President Bolles announced that an increase of the no par common stock of Indian Motocycle Company from 100,000 to 200,000 shares had taken place. It was reported that the meeting, held in Springfield, had enjoyed the largest attendance yet seen and that President Bolles' recommendations were unanimously approved.

Bolles further reported that the new stock issue would be underwritten by a new group of investors interested in the future of the Indian Company, although their names were not divulged. The additional shares were to be listed on the New York Stock Exchange, and the Board of Directors voted to amend the charter of the company to provide for the increased stock issue.

In Bolles' statements to the Board regarding the urgency of greater financing, he had mentioned that recent policies of the company had allowed for payment of accounts due through the medium of trade acceptances and notes. This policy was said to have been too vague in regard to the time of actually meeting these obligations, and that the company balance suffered as a result.

Bolles further noted that with the three changes of management within the past sixteen months and through various deviations from normal manufacture and sales policies, the company had lost well over

*Ernest Skelton (right) poses with the author and the latter's 'as found' 1929 Chief. This machine was actually produced in the Fall of 1928, and differed from the previous models in having the newly-introduced front wheel brake.* **(George Hays)**

$1,250,000.00. He stated that while certain assets of the company had been liquidated (no doubt surplus Indian Acceptance Company speculative stock shares), the plant and motorcycle manufacturing facilities remained intact and were free of obligation. Bolles went on to state that the new outboard motor was undergoing final testing, and that this line would be introduced to complement Indian's line of motorcycle products.

Another item of historical interest in 1929 was the marriage of Carl Oscar Hedstrom's daughter, Helen, to David A. Carlson. David Carlson had been employed for a time at Indian's San Francisco branch after 1915, and had been a co-worker with Hap Alzina. After an injury sustained in a motorcycle accident, he returned to the east coast and completed his education as an attorney. At this writing he still conducts a law practise in Portland, Connecticut.

On January 2nd, 1930, a release to the trade press stated that the Indian outboard motor, which was to be known as the 'Arrow', underwent successful tests in Springfield, on the Connecticut River, in the presence of several company officials. Those noted as present included Roy G. Lane, Sales Research Director, Theron L.

Loose, Factory Superintendent, Theodore A. Hodgdon, Advertising Manager, and James Wright, General Sales Manager.

A subsequent article mentioned that R.E. Davis, a boatbuilder of St. Petersburg, Florida, had tested one of the prototype engines in that city and had planned to receive an initial order of 100 units from the factory.

In the meantime, a number of press releases to both the trade and financial journals were issued under the direction of President Bolles, indicating that the Indian Company had surmounted its recent financial difficulties through the sales of additional shares of stock, together with an account of how this was accomplished.

Rumors now began to circulate along Wall Street that Indian's erstwhile burgeoning stock issues were being highly watered, as well as being subjected to an intense 'bull pool' campaign, reminiscent of the events attendant on Hedstrom's resignation in 1913. A news item in the February 20th issue of *The New York Times*, further substantiating this contention, announced that the Indian Motocycle Company had just authorized the issue of another 50,000 shares of no par common stock.

Hard on the heels of this release, the March 22nd issue of the *Times* carried another article, repeating the above announcement of the new stock issue and further stating that the company had now acquired the sole United States manufacturing rights for certain inventions of Louis H. Coatalen, Managing Director and Chief Engineer of Sunbeam Motors, Limited, of Wolverhampton, England. Coatalen's chief claim to fame up to this time had been his design of the well-known Sunbeam Arab aircraft engine, which had been built in large quantities to power the famous two-seated Bristol Fighter, widely employed by the Royal Air Force in the late war. He was said to have collected over one million pounds in royalties from the British Government for this design.

Coatalen had also recently designed Kaye Don's 'Silver Bullet' racing car, which was presently being tested at Daytona Beach, Florida, for an attempt to break the unlimited land speed record of 231mph for cars, set by Sir Henry Seagrave the previous year. It was stated that both Coatalen and his wife were presently in Florida, supervising the preparation of the new machine.

In regard to Coatalen's numerous inventions, it was not stated which of them was proposed to be manufactured by the Indian company, but the inference was that it was intended to manufacture an updated version of the famous 'Arab' engine for application to light aircraft currently being manufactured in the United States.

It was suspected by a number of knowledgeable investors that the alleged dealings with Coatalen were undertaken to give favorable publicity to the company's

doings in order to stimulate sales of the latest issue of common stock, all in the best 'bull pool' tradition, and in no way were related to any bona fide plan to actually undertake aircraft engine manufacture.

President Bolles and his associates' activities relating to their stock manipulation schemes quite naturally aroused the ire of numerous investors who had recently purchased shares, finding to their dismay that the actual market value of their holdings was considerably less than they had paid for them through brokerage houses designated as agents for the company.

There were reports of several intended lawsuits against the company by recent investors, which, in those swashbuckling days of 'caveat emptor' stock trading would have little prospect of securing redress for the investors who were admittedly dealing in highly speculative ventures.

One such lawsuit is on record as actually having been filed, however, when on April 5th, 1930, one Isadore Unger filed an action in the Springfield Superior Court,

*The 1929 Chief as restored by Ernest Skelton, showing the typic Indian front suspension.* (George Hays)

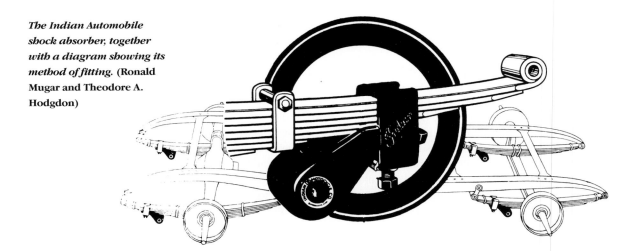

petitioning it to appoint a receiver for the Indian Motocycle Company and charging President Bolles, Lawrence Wilder of Boston, Arthur G. Dixon of Paoli, Pennsylvania and several John Does, with mismanagement and malfeasance in the conduct of the affairs of the company.

In the plea filed by Unger's counsel, George A. Bacon, it was charged that the recent 50,000 shares of no par common stock were sold to the public at $17.00 per share, but that certain officers and directors of the company were able to purchase the same for $15.00 per share. He also asked that other shareholders join him in his petition.

During the following week the company counsel, under President Bolles' direction, filed an answer in Judge Dillon's court in which he charged that Unger was not, nor had ever been a shareholder in the company, that he had filed his action to harrass the management, and otherwise to cause the public to lose confidence in the future of the company which he declared had never looked better.

In the midst of these charges and countercharges, an article appeared in the April 23rd edition of the *New York Times* announcing that the Indian Motocycle Company had acquired a controlling interest in du Pont Motors, Inc. It was reported that E. Paul du Pont would continue as President of du Pont Motors in addition to his election to Indian's Board of Directors and Chairman of its Executive Committee. His brother Francis I. du Pont was also elected to serve on the Board. It was also noted that the du Pont Motor Company had authorized the sale of 250,000 shares of no par common stock.

That President Bolles and his own Board of Directors had been for some time attempting to divest themselves of their Indian Company holdings was no secret on Wall Street. While substantial blocks of shares had been sold following much artificial publicity generated by their continuing 'bull pool' operations, the trading prices of the stock had been falling steadily ever since the instigation of these activities in January of 1930. Just how favorable a deal du Pont had been able to make for a majority of Indian's stock was never made public, but rumor had it that Bolles, who was under continuing pressure for redress from disgruntled stockholders, was happy to vacate his own and his Board of Directors' holdings for some thirty cents on the dollar.

Bolles' manipulation of Indian stock ultimately came under the scrutiny of the Senate Banking and Currency Committee, then the only government body to attempt any sort of regulation of public stock sales. The late Fiorella La Guardia, then a congressman from the state of New York, and later the well-known Mayor of New York City, chaired this Committee during 1932. After congressional investigators had delved into numerous complaints, former President Bolles, a Wall Street broker named Harry Content, and Howard Hansell, an independent speculator who had handled the flotation of some 100,000 shares of Indian stock, were subpoenaed to appear before the Committee.

One of the principal witnesses was A. Newton Plummer, who was said to have paid several New York financial writers for giving 'bull pool' operators, who were his clients, publicity beneficial to their operations. Plummer was said to have been under indictment already, in New York, for dealing in forged securities.

The ultimate disposition of the matter was never made public. In later years La Guardia, upon being interviewed concerning the matter, refused to comment on the outcome of the hearing. It was alleged by some that some prominent members of the Democratic Central Committee for the state of New York were found to have been involved in the affair, and it was thought that La Guardia may have deemed it impolitic to pursue the matter further.

Space considerations preclude a detailed discussion of the intricacies of Bolles' manipulation of Indians' and other stock issues, during his brief tenure of office. Suffice to say they represent a classic example of a type of dealing that was unfortunately too often the rule during the frantic stock trading taking place during the high-flying days of Wall Street. The methods used by Bolles were such that in subsequent years numbers of graduate college students seeking masters or doctor of philosophy degrees in either economics or business administration, have used his activities as the subject matter for their theses!

Another surprising development was that scarcely had the news of the du Pont acquisition by Indian been made public when a news release in a Springfield newspaper dated April 26th stated that Isadore Unger had withdrawn his petition for receivership for the Indian Motocycle Company. His declaration stated in part: "since filing the bill, this stockholder on whose behalf the suit was filed, says he has made further inquiries into the facts and now wishes to withdraw. He believes it is to the best interests of the company to allow the present management more time in which to ascertain whether or not they can successfully manage the affairs of the company".

The Unger affair poses several interesting possibilities in this particular phase of Indian history. In his sworn statement answering Unger's petition, President Bolles stated that Unger was not and had never been an Indian stockholder, a fact that placed the burden of proof on Unger had the matter ever gone to trial. The fact that du Pont Motors obtained majority control of Indian's preferred stock tends to indicate that the filing of Unger's suit could have influenced President Bolles and his associates to find it expedient to divest themselves of their holdings as quickly as possible, especially if

*The author's 1930 101 Scout, as restored by Johnny Eagles. Most motorcycling engineers and historians agree that this model was one of the best all-around machines the industry ever produced.* **(Ronald Mugar)**

through their own knowledge of their manipulations of Indian's stock, they feared Unger's petition might soon bring other threatened criminal action against them. The sudden withdrawal by Unger of his petition within days after du Pont interests gained control of the company relieved him of the responsibility of actually substantiating that he was, in fact, an Indian stockholder. In the absence of any other corroborative evidence in the matter, the reader is left to draw his own conclusions regarding any alleged connections between Unger's actions and du Pont.

E. Paul du Pont was a member of the noted du Pont family of Wilmington, Delaware, whose vast industrial empire has had a greater impact upon the economic and industrial history of the United States than any other similar organization.

The du Pont family originated in France, and its lineage can be traced back to the fifteenth century. The appellation 'de Nemours' was added in the eighteenth century to designate the family's area of origin as the name du Pont was then as common in France as Smith or Jones are in the United States today.

The du Pont Company today, with its main offices in Wilmington, Delaware, controls more total wealth than the Rockefellers, Vanderbilts, Mellons or Astors, and is responsible for more than 1,200 products. Aside from gunpowder and explosives, these include paints, chemicals of all kinds, cellophane, rubber goods, and a myriad of plastic products, to name but a few.

The du Pont name was not new to the transportation field, as Pierre S. acting on the advice of his Treasurer, John J. Raskob, had purchased 26.6% of General Motors stock just after World War I, at a cost of $49,000,000.00. This combine had been put together by William C. Durant in 1908, and included Cadillac, Buick and Oldsmobile, as well as several truck manufacturers.

With such a background of great wealth, E. Paul could easily have grown up as a country club dilettante, but as a young schoolboy he evidenced a De Dion-like interest in things mechanical. He owned at various times countless examples of early cars, as well as one of Oscar Hedstrom's earlier single cylinder motorcycles.

In fact, young du Pont's interest in engineering crystalized in 1916 when he established a small manufacturing plant in Wilmington, Delaware to build a line of small marine engines which powered naval launches and other small auxiliary craft during World War I.

After these contracts were concluded in 1918, he launched a small automobile manufacturing plant in Moore, Pennsylvania in the Summer of that year, and exhibited a prototype at the National Automobile Show in Madison Square Garden in January of 1919.

His products were assembled from proprietary components, but were carefully made to a high standard of quality and were mostly two seated sports type vehicles. Of necessarily limited production, some 557 examples were made between 1920 and 1931, when the onset of the depression effectively killed off the market for such specialized high priced vehicles. The last dozen or so examples were assembled in the Spring of 1931 in the basement of the Indian factory, under the supervision of the former Moore plant's George Mason.

While E. Paul had a more than passing interest in motorcycles, the fact has been established that his initial reason for acquiring the Indian Motocycle Company was to utilize a part of its long unused facilities to manufacture aircraft engines. Both E. Paul and his brother, Archibald, had lately developed a passionate interest in flying since the Lindbergh flight to Paris, and both were among the first to obtain private pilots' licenses. These plans were not implemented, however, when the new management took over. The recent stock market debacle of the preceding year had yet to make itself felt economically, but experienced industrialists were now viewing the future with caution. Then, too, there was the fact that Indian's finances were in very poor shape, and considering the company's past ill fortune with diversification, it appeared unwise to launch any new venture.

Du Pont made only a few changes in Indian's now thin ranks of executive personnel, with Loren F. Hosley assuming the position of Plant Superintendent with the death of the veteran Theron L. Loose.

No changes were made in Indian's then current three model production schedule, except that as expected, du Pont paints were immediately substituted for the former industrial brands that had been long used. Du Pont ordered spray booths set up to finish all painted parts, which had formerly been treated via the dip-tank-through-conveyor method and often resulted in an imperfect finish.

The time-honored Indian red color had been subjected to minor changes through the years, and appeared to take on a darker hue in the late 1920's. The generally accepted paint formula employed by restorers is the du Pont Dulux 'Hiram Walker' shade, the same as used in the lettering of the signs advertising the popular whiskey of that name, but the acquiring or mixing of the correct old Indian red is still a matter of some controversy among some enthusiasts.

As the 'Arrow' outboard engine production was already scheduled, and as advertising manager Ted Hodgdon had already prepared an advertising campaign, it was decided to proceed with this project. Most of the technical problems involving power development had now been solved, and the engine was capable of driving a light planing-type hull at speeds up to 30mph at full throttle, although its performance was still not equal to that of its well established competitors. The retail price, established at $180.00, was well in line with what was then being asked for 15hp class B engines.

With some of the hard lessons of the recent shock absorber fiasco still fresh in mind, Indian's top management at once decided to include the outboard engine franchise as an option in all those presently held by the now diminished roster of dealers.

A mark-up of 25% from the wholesale cost was considered to offer a fair margin of dealer profit.

In spite of the company's high hopes, the Arrow project was a miserable failure, as privately predicted by the more experienced manufacturers within the industry who had been eyeing Indian's progress.

In the first instance, the more successful operators offered a comprehensive line of A through F class engines which could be fitted to a very wide variety of boats, giving them a larger market penetration for substantial volume sales necessary for success. Indian's single model offering was of a size too large for the average rowboat or skiff, yet too small for adequately powering the very popular 16 to 18-foot V-bottomed runabout types.

Then, too, most of Indian's dealers were not located adjacent to navigable waterways; the vast network of inland lakes and waterways now present was not in existence before the days of the Tennessee Valley Authority and similar projects in the Pacific Northwest, South and Colorado River areas. Most of the dealers were primarily motorcycling rather than boating enthusiasts in any case, and simply refused to exercise their option of handling the engines.

The factory had optimistically projected a production target of 5,000 units for the 1930 season. This was subsequently cut back to 4,000 in the late Spring. It is reliably estimated that only about 2,000 engines ever reached the dealers, however, and not all of these were actually sold to customers.

With the obviously poor response, President du Pont halted Arrow production in mid-August. The remaining engines on hand were shipped to a few waterside dealers who requested them, and the company rang down the curtain on the whole dismal affair. About half a dozen Arrows survive today in the hands of antique outboard engine collectors.

The amount of financial loss to the company is not known, as no records of the matter exist. Perhaps the most serious aspect of the matter was the interference in motorcycle production, most particularly of Scouts,

which were still being ordered by dealers as fast as produced. Motorcycle production for that year totalled only 3,790 machines. President du Pont could now only observe with alarm his first season of tenure with a total company loss of $744,678.00.

With a firm determination to concentrate on motorcycles, the company bravely announced its 1931 sales program. The three model range was to be continued with minor improvements, the most noticeable being the fitting of heavier gauge cadmium plated wheel spokes which were slightly polished, relieving somewhat the rather severe look of the former black painted wheels. The headlight brackets or 'horns' which had been used since the earliest days on both cars and motorcycles to support these one-time optional fittings, were replaced by a simple bracket cast into the forward end of the

*New England slant artists photographed at the factory in 1930.* **(Indian Motocycle Co)**

*Kenny Schofield of Los Angeles with his specially tuned 1930 101 Scout that officially clocked 107 mph on the Muroc Lake Course.* (Sam Pierce)

handlebar, which had the effect of slightly lowering the headlight. The cast aluminum fuel and oil tank halves fitted to some 1930 Chief models was dropped entirely in

*The 101 Scout in its more familiar Western guise: A 'California Bobber' owned and restored by Dewey Bonkrud.* (Ronald Mugar)

favor of the pressed steel type. A most definite improvement was the first offering of a really comprehensive selection of paint colors in either solid or varying combinations – du Pont Dulux, of course.

The most critical problems facing the company at the end of 1930 were the falling away of sales incidental to the general decline in business, following the stock market collapse, the insecure condition of Indian's finances, and the diminished dealer representation suffered since President Bauer's regime.

Sales Promotion Manager Jim Wright tirelessly visited dealers in various areas of the country, bolstering the courage of those who wavered in their loyalty and urging likely enthusiasts here and there to take up franchises surrendered by others. Charles Franklin, as usual, spent as much of his time as possible working on prototype designs, including overhead valve and overhead camshaft engines, but the stringencies of the times prevented any serious thought on the part of management in deviating from the current model range.

After 1930, President du Pont took more of a personal interest in motorcycling. He kept a sumptuous apartment in Springfield, but quite naturally spent much of his time at his luxurious mansion near Wilmington. Here he kept a stable of the current Indian models and all of his four sons soon learned to ride them.

He was also in the habit of presenting machines, mostly Scouts and Fours for their easy starting characteristics, to various young du Pont nephews and cousins, and soon the Brandywine Valley was alive with the purr or bark of Indian motorcycles.

Many of these youngsters brought down maledictions from their elders for some of their less than polite tactics of riding over lawns and gardens of some of the palatial estates in that most exclusive area of Delaware. One of the worst of their offenses was to stop in front of Christ Church on a Sunday morning and gun their engines to disturb the services as many of them did not like the rather stern vicar then in charge. The crowning blow came when a number of them tore up a part of the lush lawn at Granogue, the ancestral estate of Eleuthere Irenee. A hastily passed ordinance by the village council subsequently barred motorcycle riding in certain parts of the valley.

Du Pont's only daughter, Carol, now married, maintained a home in Springfield where she acted as her father's official company hostess. Many dealers, important visitors and racing men were entertained here during the ensuing decade.

It was some time during this period that a mysterious incident at the Indian factory occurred involving the assembly of a small, prototype aircraft engine, the details being recalled today only by a small handful of former employees.

The word was passed down to the various Departments that an outside individual had rented a portion of the toolroom to conduct certain experiments, the nature of which was to be kept secret, and that staff co-operation was to be mandatory.

Shortly thereafter, a pleasant, friendly man, cryptically known only as 'Mr. Hewett' arrived at the factory and sequestered himself in an isolated area of the toolroom. He showed great affability to those factory personnel with whom he came into casual contact, and showed a willingness to converse about a variety of subjects except the actual work in which he was engaged. It was at length surmised that he was connected with a wealthy family in some manner connected with the Mack truck concern.

At a later time, a member of the Advertising Department was informed that he was to take photographs of 'Hewett's' subject material, but that he was not to discuss this matter with anyone. Somehow a couple of these photographs soon came to light and 'Mr. Hewett's' hush-hush project was revealed to be a four cylinder horizontally opposed light aircraft engine!

The whole affair was subsequently forgotten until the following year when the soon-to-be-famous Piper Cub light airplane, later to be known as the Taylorcraft, appeared on the aeronautical scene. This useful little aircraft was a high wing monoplane and carried two passengers in tandem, which effectively narrowed its frontal area to enable it to be fitted with a small engine of moderate power. This took the form of a horizontally

opposed flat four, manufactured by the Continental Engine Company of Detroit, and was designated as the model A-40 developing 40 horsepower.

The significance of this attractive little airplane to those Indian personnel who had some knowledge of 'Mr. Hewett's' former activities was the fact that the Continental engine was almost an exact copy of the engine that had been built in the toolroom! No details of the official connection, if any, between the original prototype and the Continental engine were ever divulged. But the similarity was so marked that the relationship was unmistakable. Considering the misfortunes the Indian company had encountered with diversification, it is interesting to speculate what good luck it would have had had it been able in some manner to secure the manufacturing rights for the later popular A-40 engine.

In spite of worsening business conditions, Indian's Advertising Department under the direction of Ted Hodgdon, optimistically prepared a special edition of the *Indian News* denoting the company's thirtieth anniversary. Included were a brief account of Indian's past history, pictures of top company executives, an appreciation from former President Weschler, still President of the

*The prototype model of the later famous Continental A-40 airplane engine that was built mysteriously in the tool room of the State Street factory.* (Theodore A. Hodgdon)

Erle "Pop" Armstrong on the boards. In 1915 Erle won the 300 mile Tacoma, Wash. board track race with a speed of 79.83.

Ralph Hepburn, who first won fame riding the two wheelers, later became an outstanding automobile driver.

Two present day Indian dealers, Jud Carriker of Santa Ana and Charley Moist of Long Beach "pour in the soup" at one of the Beverly Hills board track meets.

The field dashes past in a blur of speed as one of the board track races gets underway at Altoona.

Jim Davis at the Beverly Hills track. He was one of the greatest competition riders of Class A days and is now active as an outstanding Motorcycle official.

Curly Fredericks, board track speed king ready for action with an overhead Indian single.

Start of the 25 Mile Championship event at Sheepshead Bay in October, 1919: The race jobs were towed to start and came around for a flying start. On the pole is Otto Walker, with Teddy Carroll and Ray Weishaar next, and Gene Walker on the outside.

nearby Baldwin Chain Company, and photographs of new models. A few copies of this booklet still exist and are treasured as a memento of the old Indian days by a small number of enthusiasts, including the author.

In the Spring of 1931, an event occurred which was to have vast repercussions on the entire American motorcycle industry.

Law enforcement sales, while a controversial and often troublesome aspect of the motorcycle industry, had lately been more fiercely competed for among the surviving big three manufacturers. Although profits in this area were usually meager, or even non-existent, the general decline of motorcycle sales had prompted attention to the advantage of adding to production volume.

A lush plum ripening in this field appeared with the news that the state of California was soon to call for bids for 150 police machines for use by the California Highway Patrol, which had recently been expanded by incorporating it into a centralized arm of the state law enforcement system.

Representatives of the big three manufacturers at once set about conferring with their factory's management on this matter, including Indian's recently appointed California distributor, Hap Alzina, who planned to submit a highly competitive bid for a fleet of Indian Chiefs. Harley-Davidson, of course, would enter the arena with its newly-introduced side valve 74 inch VL model.

The Excelsior company, however, decided to enter the fray by a more devious route, with its higher priced but growingly popular KJ and KL Henderson Fours, the latter a special high speed model.

The 80 inch side valve four was continued by Excelsior with detail modifications until 1928, but in later years its reliability came to suffer through progressive raises in compression ratio and more radical valve timing in the constant search for higher performance. In the early Spring of 1928, Arthur R. Constantine, a talented engineer who had been employed by Harley-Davidson since the war, was hired by Ignatz Schwinn to modernize and update the Henderson.

The result of Constantine's efforts was introduced for the 1929 season as the K model, and was an entirely new machine. Still adhering to the traditional Henderson cylinder displacement, it was an improved F head design that was a fitting tribute to William Henderson's original configuration. A large, heavy machine, with deeply valanced mudguards and a well-proportioned streamlined fuel tank, it not only looked impressive but had a performance and endurance capability that was now well ahead of the currently produced Indian Four which still carried a merely improved 1919 engine from Henderson's Ace.

Fours of any type were always favored by law enforcement riders due to their lack of vibration, acceleration capabilities and a more comfortable ride than either the currently produced Indian Chiefs or 74 model Harley-Davidsons.

In order to capitalize on this favoritism, and at the same time perhaps overcome the high cost penalty, the Excelsior management engaged John J. O'Conner to act as an agent for Excelsior in the negotiations with the California Highway Patrol.

O'Conner at this time was not officially connected with the motorcycle industry nor had he been since

**Left:** *Excerpt from factory literature showing significant racing activities during the 1920s.*

**Right:** *Typical Southern California motorcycle club gathering in a rural setting in 1930.* **(Sam Pierce)**

# The Joys of Outboarding

SUMMER is truly the time for INDIAN enjoyment and what is more delightful than sharing the pleasures of water travel with a jolly crowd of girls and fellows? America is full of pleasant inland waterways, which are being travelled more and more by INDIAN outboard-driven craft. Let your dealer show you the joys of Outboarding.

being discharged from the Indian Company by Frank Weschler in mid-1919. He was, however, the then Editor of the *Pacific Motorcyclist and Bicyclist* magazine, later to be known as *The Motorcyclist* and which was then owned and published by Arthur E. Welch in Los Angeles.

The details of O'Conner's machinations in the matter are not known, but a few weeks later it was suddenly announced that the state of California had purchased a fleet of 150 Hendersons, most of which were to be based in the various Highway Patrol districts in southern California.

As this action was completely at variance with the established practise of purchasing state vehicles through advertised competitive bidding, a violent protest was immediately lodged with state officials by Hap Alzina, on behalf of a number of outraged Indian dealers and several equally incensed Harley-Davidson dealers. No answers to their queries of state officials were forthcoming. Alzina then theorized that O'Conner had been engaged by Schwinn through his self-proclaimed pronouncements as a motorcycling expert and trade magazine editor, and also by virtue of the fact that he was acting as Secretary to the California Motor Officers Association. This latter body had been formed in 1926 and was first known as the City and County Motor Officers Association. It acted as the spokesman for motorcycle officers generally, largely in the matter of upgrading pay scales and promoting improved working conditions.

As an aside to O'Conner's role in this affair, he was shortly discharged from his secretarial post by the motor officers on the allegation that he had misappropriated about $30,000.00 from their benevolent fund! The story told by several old time police officers is that while there was sufficient evidence to convict him, official charges were never made as it was decided that the image of the association would suffer unduly. As an outcome of the affair, Welch fired O'Conner and replaced him with a capable young journalist named Howard B. Rose, who ably edited the magazine for several years afterward.

News of the controversy soon reached the ears of the then Governor of California, the free-wheeling James J. 'Sunny Jim' Rolph, newly-elected to office after several terms as mayor of San Francisco. A spokesman for the Highway Patrol, and later its Chief, E. Raymond Cato, issued a vigorous denial of any wrongdoing on the part of state officials.

While protocol in the matter had obviously been breached, Alzina and his Indian and Harley-Davidson cohorts could now find no legal redress and retired to lick their wounds.

On the heels of Henderson's triumph in California, the motorcycle industry was shaken by the news announced in July by Ignatz Schwinn that production of

**Left:** *Publicity article in the Spring edition of the 1930* **Indian News** *showing the ill-fated Indian Arrow outboard engine.*

**Right:** *Factory sponsored rider Burton Albrecht who, on July 21st, 1931, hung up a 36 second mile on the Ascot Speedway in Los Angeles. This record stood for nearly two decades.*

both Hendersons and Excelsiors was being terminated and that henceforth the company would concentrate on the manufacture of bicycles.

The result immediately placed Indian and Harley-Davidson in direct competition for the nation's law enforcement business. What with worsening economic conditions, police contracts suddenly gained in importance as a survival factor for the remaining manufacturers, who now girded themselves for the fray.

The two models competitively available for about the same price for such work were quite naturally the Indian Chief and the newly-introduced Harley side valve VL model, which superseded the venerable JD model which had been in continuous production with detail improvements from 1915 through 1929.

The Indian Four, which had been momentarily eclipsed by the K model Henderson, was still preferred by some departments for suburban patrol duties for its easy starting and smooth running, although it was less suited to high speed highway patrol work than the more rugged Chief. Several municipalities, such as New York City, Vancouver, British Columbia, Philadelphia and Oakland, California, to name the more prominent users, maintained large fleets of them.

In the Fall of that year, Harley-Davidson's President, Walter Davidson, decided to resolve his company's stake in the matter by instituting an alleged nationwide blitz campaign for sales in an attempt to corner the nation's law enforcement market. The exact details of this matter are not a matter of official record in Harley-Davidson history. In fact, there is no documentary evidence to support this story other than the author's interviews with veteran dealers and motorcycle owners who have given varying accounts of the matter.

It has been alleged that Walter Davidson offered any domestic law enforcement body one or any other number of VL 74 cubic inch twins for the price of $195.00, together with the trade in of any other make of machine in use, whether Harley, Indian, Excelsior or Henderson, without regard to mileage or condition. The offer was to be consummated through special factory agents who would handle all details direct from the factory, and without reference to any of their own dealers, who would forego their own sales commission in return for obtaining the maintenance and servicing of any machines sold.

These reportedly high-handed tactics antagonized many established Harley-Davidson dealers, who rightly averred that such infringed on their franchise contracts, and not a few of them gave up their dealerships outright, some even deserting Harley for Indian.

The unhappiness of the Harley-Davidson dealers was nothing as compared to the anguish generated in the Indian camp, which rightly viewed the episode as a cut-throat attempt to destroy all competition, as the $195.00 cash differential was only a few dollars more than the VL's manufacturing cost. Worse still, several hundred still

*Left: A 1930 Scout commercial sidecar outfit sold by Leslie D. Richards to a Denver, Colorado merchant.* **(Leslie D. Richards)**

*Above right: Of the 557 du Pont cars produced between 1920 and 1931, the last dozen were assembled in the basement of the State Street factory after E. Paul du Pont, their originator, took over control of Indian in 1930. This speedster model is thought to be one of these cars.* **(Old Cars Magazine)**

serviceable Indian machines taken in trade were summarily junked by the Harley factory.

Walter Davidson was reported to have terminated the offer after a few months, apparently appalled by the storm of rage that was forthcoming from all segments of the motorcycle industry. One Indian official, who must remain nameless, publicly stated that the heads of all of Harley-Davidson's founders should be cut off and impaled on the parapet of the Juneau Street factory, the same fate relegated to Cromwell, Pym and Ireton whose heads were affixed to London Bridge by the cavaliers following England's age of the Restoration.

This unfortunate occurrence has been cited by veteran motorcyclists as probably the most important single cause of the subsequent bitter and savage rivalry between the two factories that in the end proved most detrimental to motorcycling in general in the United States.

A signal contribution to technical motorcycle progress during this period was the introduction of the now familiar three-wheeled vehicle, which was called the Dispatch-Tow. The initial work on a prototype was said to have been inspired by a conversation between some of Indian's top officials and the management of the Springfield Packard car dealership, whose establishment

was then only a few doors away from the Indian factory. These men complained that much employee and service time was wasted in the necessity of having two men pick up and deliver customers' automobiles for repair or routine servicing, in an era when automobiles required more frequent lubrication and running adjustments than is the case today.

Charles Franklin repaired to the drawing board and within a few weeks a prototype was ready for testing. It consisted of a standard 101 Scout fitted with a low compression engine, with two rear wheels set on a differential type axle that were driven by the usual chain and a box body carried between them. A yoke type towing device was fitted to the front axle, its forward end fitted with a clamp for attachment to the car's rear bumper. When the vehicle was driven under its own power, the tow bar was swung upward and fixed in a vertical position parallel to the fork legs. The practical use of this handy three-wheeler was that one man could ride it to its destination, pick up the automobile, return to the shop, and deliver it back in the same manner.

Announcements describing the new machine were placed in a number of automotive trade journals, some of them featuring it in company with a luxurious Pierce Arrow sedan. Also offered for sale along with the vehicle was a smartly custom fitted chauffeur's uniform for the operator, at a price of $25.00. The Dispatch-Tow was well received by automobile dealers and nearly 400 of them were sold the first season. Harley-Davidson, taking the cue from Indian, offered their own version the following year, based on their 45 cubic inch WL twin.

Another event of 1931 which would have far-reaching effect on Indian's future fortunes was the hiring by the Indian Motocycle Sales Company of Kansas City of a one-time Kansas farm boy, Samuel West Cecil Pierce, as an apprentice mechanic. Sam, or 'Sammy' as he became known to his many friends, subsequently followed a somewhat uneven but always successful career as a motorcycle dealer, handling both Indian and foreign makes, as well as participating from time to time in the new and used car business. He also possessed a flair for automobile design, and as a freelance operator was responsible for the well-known Ford Ranchero model, a perennial seller ever since. During the early post World War II years, he established an Indian parts supply business from various locations in the San Gabriel and Monrovia areas adjacent to Los Angeles.

Sam's later dedication to the cause of preserving old Indians soon became legendary. With tireless enthusiasm and with a vociferously expressed but tongue-in-cheek hatred for Harley-Davidson, he subsequently criss-crossed the nation with a large truck collecting old Indian machines and parts, and was once said to have over 100 tons of them stockpiled in his San Gabriel establishment.

It is difficult to estimate just how many old machines Sam had been responsible for saving, but it has been stated on good authority that nearly every other Indian on the roads of the world today carries at least one essential part purchased from Sam. In addition to the sales of used or old stock new parts, Sam has also offered newly manufactured items such as gear sets, pistons, piston rings, oil pump internals and other highly necessary spares.

In later years Sam's organization has been augmented by his association with a younger enthusiast, Charles Mathre. Sam is less active in the business today, but still hunts out old Indians on occasion and rightly claims to have saved dozens of old machines and countless tons of old parts from the junk man.

**Below left:** *Transatlantic aviator Clarence Chamberlain dutifully poses on a 1930 Scout at the front door of the Indian Factory during the period when his one-time financial backer, Charles A. Levine, was negotiating for control of the Company.* (Theodore A. Hodgson)

**Right:** *Charles B. Franklin's 1931 prototype of the Indian Dispatch-Tow three-wheeler.* (Theodore A. Hodgdon)

One of Sam's many projects in keeping the memories of Indian's competition supremacy alive was in later years the sponsoring of the activities of a perennial Indian racing man, Bert Munro, the New Zealand grandfather who bought a new Scout in 1920 and has been modifying it for various forms of competition ever since.

Munro's final efforts resulted in the Scout's engine being rebuilt into an overhead valve 61 cubic inch special, and, with a lengthened wheelbase and a home made streamlined shell, it was entered in the annual speed trials held each Spring at the famous Bonneville salt course in Utah.

Munro, who did all of the conversion work himself, using the most primitive of methods, ultimately coaxed the outfit up to speeds around 196mph in the early 1960's. Sam aided the lightly financed New Zealander with travel expenses, shop facilities, and transportation to the race course. Munro has not been back now for some years, and his machine is still in storage in Sam's shop, awaiting his possible return.

Another motorcycling landmark of 1931, credited to Indian advertising executive Ted Hodgdon, was the popularization of TT type competition, whose format was based on the English style course. New York City's Crotona Motorcycle Club, under the guidance of Reggie Pink, pioneer importer of British machines in the Bronx since 1927, laid out such a course in a rural area near Somers, New York. Hodgdon attended the meet, and was duly impressed with the enjoyment of this form of competition that was possible by private entrants riding their own street machines. He wrote a report of the matter in a subsequent issue of the *Indian News*, and prevailed upon Jim Wright, then AMA President, to incorporate this type of event in the AMA rule book. This type of event, forerunner of Class C competition, greatly expanded interest in motorcycle sport for the interest of private owners, and for the general benefit of the industry in increased sales.

As the year progressed to late Summer, it was becoming painfully apparent that general economic conditions throughout the civilized world were deteriorating. What with 3,170 machines shipped during the current sales season, Indian's management decided that a retrenchment in its manufacturing and assembly program for 1932 was in order.

To economize on production and yet modernize somewhat Indian's overall design, which had remained basically unchanged for the past four seasons, a new frame which was somewhat larger and heavier was designed for fitting to both the Chief and the Four. To accommodate the latter engine, the bottom parts of the cradle were elongated somewhat and the proper lug mounts were used with that machine. New and somewhat larger two-piece fuel and oil tanks were fitted which could be common to both. All the remaining cycle parts, such as forks, handlebars, chainguards, mudguards, lighting sets, ignition systems, and all other fittings were common to both machines.

The famous 101 Scout model was discontinued, and to cater to a hoped-for continuing demand for a 45 cubic inch model, the Scout engine was also fitted to the above layout and cataloged as the Standard Scout. The whole program was now in essence confined to a line of three models that were similar in all respects except for the engines, with consequent substantial savings in overall production.

As expected, there were anguished recriminations from most of the die-hard 101 enthusiasts, as the Standard Scout being larger and about 80lbs heavier than its predecessor could never have the performance or handling qualities of its distinguished parent.

# Growth of the Indian Factory Since Early Days

THERE is perhaps no greater evidence of INDIAN's progress, than these photographs which were taken at various times during the last thirty years. They show clearly and impressively, the growth of the INDIAN Factory as the popularity of the INDIAN Motocycle has increased, making more manufacturing space a necessity to meet demands of sportsmen not only in America but in foreign lands as well.

The first building was originally occupied by a school called "The Industrial Institute", and all the additions were made from this structure, so that today, the old Industrial Institute building still remains as a cornerstone for the great plant that occupies two city blocks.

INDIAN men are proud of their plant and proud of its fine military record during the war. During 1917 and 1918 it was turned over to the United States Government, and over forty-one thousand olive-drab INDIAN Motocycles went forth from this plant to serve the colors—over sixty per cent. of all the motorcycles used during the war by our forces.

The photograph at the right does not actually show all of the building used during the years 1911 and 1912. Another building of considerable size was necessary until the large addition shown below was built.

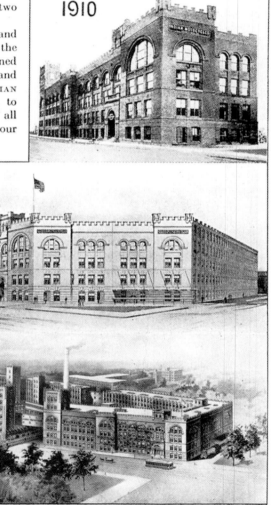

1905

1910

1912

1931

*NOTE:*
The ancient motorcycle, part of which is shown in the picture at left, is a 1902 INDIAN which now rests in the Smithsonian Institute at Washington

Loring F. Hosley
Vice-President
and
General Manager

E. Paul duPont
President

James A. Wright
Director of Sales and
Advertising

Thomas M. Darrah
Secretary and
Treasurer

Frederick W. Fisher
Factory
Superintendent

## INDIAN EXECUTIVES OF TODAY

*G*REAT men conceive ideas—spend years shaping them into successful industries—then pass the torch to other hands.

So it has been at Indian. The men who helped to found the Indian so many years ago have retired, and their tasks have been taken over by some of the men shown on this page.

These men—and every other man in the Indian Organization—even to the faraway corners of the globe—appreciate the mighty work done by the pioneers of earlier days. They have a keen realization of the responsibility which lies with every man at an Indian post today, and they are determined that as the years roll by—more Indians and finer Indians shall go forth from the Wigwam.

Theirs is the task of carrying on the great work begun by the founder of Indian—Thirty years ago.

Charles B. Franklin
Chief Engineer

Theodore A. Hodgdon
Assistant
Advertising Manager

W. Stanley Bouton
Assistant Sales
Manager

**Left:** *Excerpt from Indian's thirtieth anniversary advertising showing the growth of the Indian factory complex.*

**Above:** *Indian executive staff in 1931.*

# 1931 Guardians of Law and Order

The Pennsylvania State Highway Patrol, Indian mounted, maintains a continuous supervision of traffic throughout the 8,000 miles of state roads in the Keystone State. In addition, it is of invaluable service to community forces in keeping law and order.

Here are some of the boys who ride for the State of Massachusetts under Captain Charles T. Beaupre. Captain Beaupre's statistical figures show an amazingly low cost of operation and maintenance for a large fleet of Indian Scouts over many millions of miles.

Los Angeles, the largest city on the West Coast, and famed for its beauty and its fine climate, has this fleet of huskies mounted on Indian 74's, to help control traffic and keep law and order. This picture was taken a few months ago when they took delivery of a brand new fleet of Indians.

**Left:** *Indian machines as used in law enforcement duties.*

Another fault of the Standard Scout, as a consequence of a continuing search for economical manufacture, was that the combination of the Scout engine with the Chief primary helical gearing produced an annoying whine, particularly when run at fast speeds. Practical mechanics and owners applied various graphite lubricants, or even resorted to filing off the sharp edges of the pinions, but no one was ever able completely to cure the trouble.

The Standard Scout found its ultimate employment for use with suburban police patrols, as it was a smooth running and vibrationless machine, with its small capacity engine in a rather massive frame. Condemned examples were almost invariably 'stroked' by later civilian owners, as the performance in original form could only be described as mild. The model was in very limited production for several seasons, in its original form, and was ultimately discontinued after the 1937 season.

President du Pont could take comfort only in the fact that Indian's financial losses for 1931 were approximately one half those in 1930, but still a staggering total of $392,340.00.

Yet a characteristic happy note to climax the years of chaos was that in competition Indian riders won all of the National Championship races during 1928 and 1929. In 1931, Burton Albrecht turned a 36 second mile on a racing Scout at Oakland's Elmhurst speedway, a time that is seldom equalled even today. In the same year, Miny Waln established a 21 cubic inch record for the mile, that still stands.

As the Excelsior Motor Company terminated all of its competition activities at the close of the previous season, Gene Rhyne, their competition and hill climb star, transferred his activities to the Indian Company. During 1931 he garnered all the first places for the wigwam in the 45 cubic inch class.

During the Fall, Charles B. Franklin, who was now in a poor state of health, requested and received permission to take a leave of absence from his duties in the Engineering Department, in the hopes that a rest would improve his condition.

*Indian publicity announcement for 1932, with a photograph of President E. Paul du Pont and three of his sons, taken at his country estate at Wilmington, Delaware.*

## A MESSAGE FROM *Indian's* MOTORCYCLING PRESIDENT

IN THE year 1902—twenty-nine years ago—I rode my first Indian Motocycle. What a far cry it is from that old-timer to our present-day Indians with their easy starting and perfection of detail and a smooth power output that makes speeds of more than twice the 1902 speed an every-day occurrence.

All year long, the Engineers at the Indian Factory have been developing and testing the fifty or more new features that you will find on the 1932 Indians.

The new Indians possess more motorcycling value—with more possibilities for real sport and dependability than have ever before been offered to the motorcycling public.

Soon I intend to have a stable of the 1932 models in my own garage at home, where four of my sons, who all ride, can enjoy with me the many advantages to be found in these advanced motorcycle designs.

To Indian riders all over the world I extend best wishes for many happy miles of sport.  Sincerely,

INDIAN MOTOCYCLE COMPANY

*E. Paul du Pont,*

President

# THE GREAT DEPRESSION

# Chapter 7

The decision of Indian's management to effect a drastic retrenchment in production and operating procedures was well taken, as by mid-1932 the world-wide economic depression had reached catastrophic proportions in the United States. One third of the work force, variously estimated at 13 to 15 million people, was now unemployed. One third of the nation's railroads were in bankruptcy, 5,000 banks had failed, and in some rural areas, particularly in the south, more than one fourth of the real estate was under foreclosure. Countless small business enterprises were failing everywhere, and many people were actually going hungry. To meet this emergency, many cities and towns depleted their meager treasuries to establish soup kitchens to feed the needy, many of whom had already lost their homes. The average citizen in America, generally without knowledge of complex economic forces behind the catastrophy, almost immediately blamed President Herbert Hoover and the Republican Party then in power.

Motorcycle sales, in company with those of all other goods, fell alarmingly. To compound this problem, the government of Canada, where American machines and, most particularly, Indians, had long been popular, imposed a 20% import tax on all but British machines. This levy was instituted in sympathy with the dire economic plight of the mother country, after the latter had launched a 'Buy British' campaign which was extended to all Commonwealth countries. This new policy all but concluded further sales of American machines in Canada for the time being.

Factory production personnel was now drastically reduced, and the executive and clerical staffs were pared to the bone. As a further measure of economy, a four-day work week was instituted, with concomitant reduction in pay. Several of the executive staff subsequently resigned, including Ted Hodgdon who found a better paying position with a local paper products company.

During this period, production employees were paid on a piece work basis, which meant that their wages were scaled to the actual work turned out, without reference to time involved. This practise was by this time instituted by many diverse types of manufacturing firms who still survived the depression.

As a further means of economy, Indian's management found that many small components could be produced more economically by outside concerns specializing in various types of machine work. Many small shops and factories in the area adjacent to Springfield contracted to produce such parts, but not all were produced in the immediate local area. Crankpin and lower bearing assemblies, for instance, were supplied by Albert G. Crocker, a Los Angeles Indian dealer who also operated a small machine shop.

Road testing of machines, was now eliminated. Indian's assembly lines terminated at the top floor of the factory. Here, a test bed was set up, consisting of a pair of large fiber-covered rollers set in the floor and a fixed steel frame into which the finished machine was clamped. After fuel and lubricants were added, the machine was tested at various throttle settings for about half an hour. The engine was cooled during testing by a

**Opposite:** *Ed Kretz entering the south turn at the old Ascot Speedway in 1941.* (**Ed Kretz**)

large electric fan. The exhaust gases were carried outside the building by means of a hose, whose inner end had a fitting that clamped over the tail pipe. After all running adjustments were completed and the power output was judged satisfactory, the fluids were drained from the tanks and engine, and the machine was sent down an elevator to the crating department, and readied for shipping.

Two new lightweight twin cylinder models were introduced in 1932, their initial development coming about in a rather unusual manner. A group of Indian executives, including Loren Hosley, Jim Wright and Ted Hodgdon had attended a short track motorcycle race held in Yankee Stadium in New York City. On the return train trip to Springfield, Hodgdon, who had lately conceived an interest in lightweight machines, evolved an idea for such a model that could be built up economically from Indian components, the tooling jigs and dies and many parts being already on hand. He envisioned a lightweight V-twin utilizing the Prince design, the cycle parts being identical except for the engine.

He presented the idea to Hosley, who almost immediately agreed to the feasibility of the project and who built up a prototype during the following week.

The new model, which was to be cataloged as the 'Motoplane' was essentially a resurrected Prince, except that the tank rails were altered slightly to accommodate a more modern two-piece saddle-type fuel and oil tank in place of the former between-the-rails types of the 1920's. The engine was basically the time-tried 45 cubic inch 101 Scout type, but now fitted with dry sump oiling, which was a definite improvement over the older total loss system. In addition, new cylinder barrels were fitted, which carried deeper finning for enhanced cooling, together with enlarged breathing passages and a larger carburetor which added considerably to the original power output.

In order to utilize the Prince clutch and gearbox, the familiar unit construction of the engine and gearbox was eliminated, the crankcase of the engine being carried within two sets of plates bolted to the frame, the drive being now an outside double row chain covered by a sheet metal case.

For further economy of production, battery and coil ignition was fitted as standard.

The girder forks of the original Prince were now fitted with a steering damper and friction controls for the spindles, and the whole design closely followed contemporary English practise as to overall appearance and fittings. This was further enhanced by the optional fitting of foot pegs in place of the more usual footboards and a hand controlled clutch which was placed on the right handlebar, the front hand brake lever being on the opposite side.

Only one color finish was specified as standard, the machine being all black except for a Chinese red fuel and oil tank with the Indian script in gold lettering, outlined with a single gold stripe.

With its short wheelbase and low weight, the Motoplane was a fast and quick-handling machine possessed of vivid acceleration and fully justified Ted Hodgdon's hopes for a simple low-cost sports type machine that could be entered in various types of competition events by an owner-rider. While of rather stark appearance, it was a good buy at the modest selling price of $250.00.

*The Los Angeles 45 Club on a Steak Run to Ojai, California, August 1932. Founder and President Paul A. Bigsby on 101 Scout at left.*

A similar machine was built a short time later, fitted with a 30.50 cubic inch V-twin engine, which was basically a sleeved-down edition of the original 37 cubic inch Scout of 1920, but with improved finning, breathing capacity, and dry sump lubrication. Intended as an economical utility machine, and retailing at $225.00, it was a good value for the times, and even with its small engine showed surprisingly good performance. It was first cataloged as the 'Pony' Scout, but was later to be known as the 'Junior' Scout.

An engineering anachronism in both of these models was the original and continuing use of the old-style clincher rims for beaded-edge tires, which were still fitted up to the end of production of the Junior Scout in 1942. Old-time company employees have stated that this was due to the fact that a fairly large stock of Prince wheels were on hand in the Parts Department, when production of the Prince was discontinued at the end of 1928.

Another version of the story is that both the Budd and Kelsey-Hayes concerns, who supplied most of the wheel rims used by the trade, had a large stock of such on hand after 1934, when Harley-Davidson suspended production of its 21 cubic inch single which used this type of wheel rim. It was reported that Indian could not refuse a bargain offer to clear out this old stock.

Ted Hodgdon's last official act before resigning from the company was the production of advertising copy and sales literature for these machines. While holding various other sales positions with other concerns in later years, he always retained a keen interest in Indian affairs. During the ensuing years he was frequently engaged by the company to write publicity articles and road test reports, and during World War II he produced riders'

manuals covering the operation and servicing of military models. His role in the founding of the Antique Motorcycle Club has already been discussed and at this writing he is in retirement, generally recognized as America's leading motorcycle historian.

Indian enthusiasts, as well as others within the industry, were greatly saddened in October at the news of the passing of Charles B. Franklin at his home in Springfield. During his leave of absence his health had at first improved somewhat. His condition worsened by Fall, however, and he succumbed from complications of a respiratory ailment. His death was a great blow to Indian, as during his tenure he had been responsible for the finalization of all designs since 1916, including the Powerplus engine, the lightweight models 'O' and 'K', as well as the immortal Scout and Chief, and all of the various racing and hill climb machines. Passing on as he did at the relatively young age of 52, it is interesting to speculate upon what further advanced designs might have come from his board had he lived on.

Due to the economic stringencies of the times, and in the absence of any immediate plans for new models, his position was filled by Loren Hosley, who supervised the activities of the Engineering Department in addition to his regular duties as Plant Superintendent.

In spite of the depressed state of the motorcycle business, the company offered a wide range of accessories and riders' clothing to their dealers, in the hope that this could add to their sales volume. A substantial forged iron side stand which greatly facilitated parking a machine, which had been offered as an accessory since 1928, was now offered as a standard fitting. Rear package carriers and front wheel stands were now cataloged as standard

*Dewey Bonkrud's authentically restored 1932 Standard Scout. Like most of its kind, it has been stroked to 57cu in.*
**(Ronald Mugar)**

fittings on all export models. Short wave radio communication sets, which had been a standard fitting for law enforcement automobiles during the past two seasons, were now made available for police motorcycles. These were housed in a metal case, carried on brackets over the steering head.

Gross sales for 1932 reached a new low of $913,994.00, far below the $1,575,272.00 of the preceding year. Financial losses were $232,346.00, somewhat less than the $392,398.00 loss of 1931, but rather severe in spite of the most rigid economies that could be effected and still keep the factory in operation. Fewer than 3,000 machines were shipped during the year.

The year of 1933 opened with even more dismal prospects of continuing economic decline. President Franklin D. Roosevelt and a Democratic Congress had been swept into office by a landslide vote the preceding Fall and took office the following March with the hopeful slogan that 'all we have to fear is fear itself.'

The financial position of the Indian company was by this time most precarious and President du Pont at once sought ways to at least partially alleviate its difficulties.

On February 23rd, an article appeared in the *New York Times* announcing the reorganization of the Indian Motocycle Company, which was a masterpiece of financial legerdemain. To quote: "Stockholders of the Company have been called to consider on April 10th a reorganization. A new issue of 45,480 shares of non-cumulative 6% preferred stock would be created and 38,600 shares issued to the Indu Company (presumably a holding company created for Indian's benefit) in exchange for promissory notes of the Indian Company held, to the extent of $386,000.00. The remaining 6,880 shares would be issued to present holders of 7% preferred stock on a share-for-share basis together with a waiver of the accumulated $24.50 dividends as yet unpaid accrued on the older preferred stock. Common stock would be reduced from 500,000 shares to 150,000 shares and exchanged on a basis of one new for each 10 old shares.

"Holders of the new preferred stock would have a right to convert their shares at a rate of two shares of common to one each of preferred shares before January 1st, 1940. An additional 30,040 common shares would be set aside for sale to officers, directors and employees with directors' approval at $6.00 per share until January 1st, 1937 and $7.00 per share until January 1st, 1940, the new common and preferred stock to have equal voting rights."

Indian's stockholders appear to have been unmoved by these suggested shufflings of the company's paper assets, as seen by another article in the *Times* dated April 13th. To quote: "A plan to reorganize the Indian

Motocycle Company providing for a new issue of 45,480 shares of non-cumulative 6% preferred stock at $10.00 per share par value and a reduction of common stock from 500,000 to 150,000 shares submitted to a shareholders meeting in Springfield on Tuesday was rescheduled for lack of a quorum. No action was taken."

On April 26th there was a further delay: – "The meeting of the Indian Motocycle Company stockholders, previously adjourned from April 10th, was adjourned yesterday until May 15th, when the management's capital reorganization plan will be considered. More than 58% of the common and preferred shareholders have approved the plan, it was announced."

The plan was at long last ratified on May 21st, when it was reported that Indian's shareholders voted approval of the reorganization.

What with the nation's economy now at its lowest ebb, the general motorcycle picture had deteriorated rapidly along with every other form of endeavor. Registrations for the whole of the United States sank to 95,684 machines. Interest in club activities waned, as prospective participants simply had not the means to support them. The financial position of the AMA was greatly weakened as few members were now able or willing to pay the nominal $1.00 yearly membership dues. E.C. Smith operated his small office practically single handed, eking out his own and the organization's survival from small contributions from the few sustaining members of the M & ATA.

All of the motorcycle trade magazines became defunct except the *Western Motorcyclist and Bicyclist* which was by this time known as *The Motorcyclist*. Its paid circulation dwindled to a mere 15,000 copies, as few devotees appeared willing to pay the $1.00 per year subscription cost. In order to keep the last public forum of motorcycling alive, the AMA made the magazine its official publication, along with a small monthly contribution to help pay its expenses.

The country's motorcycle dealers were also greatly impoverished. Most of the larger dealerships in the principal cities survived by making drastic reductions in personnel, as well as taking on other lines of merchandise such as bicycles, lawn mowers, outboard motors, hardware items, and even household appliances. A few secured franchises for the lately introduced Austin Bantam light car.

Dealers in the smaller towns and villages were particularly hard hit, especially in the more rural areas. Many of these businesses quietly expired when their customers passed from the picture and there was no more repair work. Others stayed open by specializing as fix-it shops for bicycles, home appliance repair, saw filing and other marginal pursuits.

# ANNOUNCING
## *the NEW* *Indian*
# MOTOPLANE

**$250**
F. O. B.
SPRINGFIELD, MASS.

12 Color
Combinations
Optional

Real speed! Lightning acceleration! Power! Punch! The new Indian Motoplane is an amazing creation capable of performance never before achieved in the history of motorcycling! While not actually a racing motorcycle, it is designed and constructed solely for *sport* — for the red-blooded fellow who is satisfied with nothing short of the speediest, snappiest job on two wheels.

The Indian Motoplane's 45 cubic inch motor incorporates dry sump lubrication, high quick-acting cams, aluminum pistons of special lightweight design and many other features created to produce speed and performance.

Ride the Indian Motoplane – crack open the throttle – experience a new thrill – this new Indian will obey your every whim! Study the design and examine its details. You'll want to own the new Motoplane!

## "DRY SUMP" OILING A PROMINENT FEATURE

The Indian Motoplane is identical with the Indian Scout Pony with the exception of the motor. It is complete with ride control and steering damper, assuring complete comfort and safety at all speeds and road conditions.

The Motoplane motor has the new "dry sump" oiling system - so-called because the oil is not stored in the motor base, but in a separate tank. In this system, a double automatic pump is used - one section pumping the oil into the bearing surfaces of the motor and the other returning the surplus oil to the oil tank. The pump is so designed and adjusted to give ample lubrication for the most extreme high speed and power

requirements. At slow speeds, the excess oil is returned to the reservoir.

Thus, for the first time in the history of American motorcycling, exactly the proper amount of lubrication - no more, no less - is provided regardless of throttle opening or motor speed. "Dry sump" oiling, heretofore only found in airplane motors, eliminates all guess work and worry regarding motor lubrication. It also reduces oil consumption to an absolute minimum. Indian engineers' simple instructions are — "Fill your tank with the proper amount and grade of Indian oil - ride as you please for the next 1000 to 2000 miles - then change your oil."

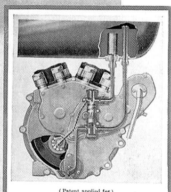

( Patent applied for )

Cross-section view of the 1933 Indian dry sump motor. Oil is drawn by the pump through a filter screen in the supply tank and fed in ample quantities to the connecting rod bearings. Here it is thrown by centrifugal force to the other revolving and reciprocating parts of the motor. All excess oil drains to the sump at the bottom of the crankcase, is drawn by the pump through a valve at the sump outlet and is returned to the oil tank for re-circulation.

*1932 Factory announcement describing the 45cu in Motoplane.*

On the surface, it might have appeared that the motorcycle, particularly the smaller types, would be attractive to certain segments of an economy-conscious public during these times, but such was not the case. Automobile production during the late 1920's and 1930

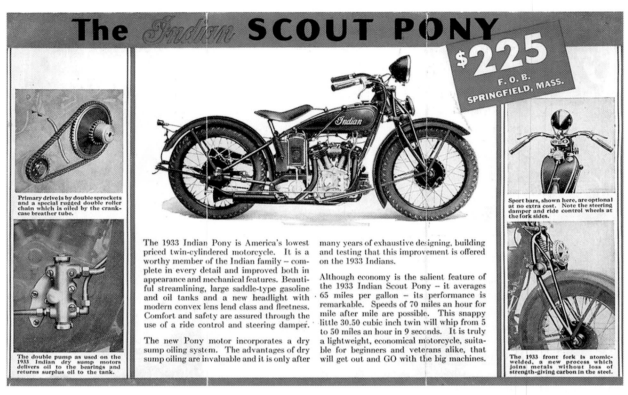

The 1933 Indian Pony is America's lowest priced twin-cylindered motorcycle. It is a worthy member of the Indian family — complete in every detail and improved both in appearance and mechanical features. Beautiful streamlining, large saddle-type gasoline and oil tanks and a new headlight with modern convex lens lend class and fleetness. Comfort and safety are assured through the use of a ride control and steering damper.

The new Pony motor incorporates a dry sump oiling system. The advantages of dry sump oiling are invaluable and it is only after many years of exhaustive designing, building and testing that this improvement is offered on the 1933 Indians.

Although economy is the salient feature of the 1933 Indian Scout Pony — it averages 65 miles per gallon — its performance is remarkable. Speeds of 70 miles an hour for mile after mile are possible. This snappy little 30.50 cubic inch twin will whip from 5 to 50 miles an hour in 9 seconds. It is truly a lightweight, economical motorcycle, suitable for beginners and veterans alike, that will get out and GO with the big machines.

*Primary drive is by double sprockets and a special rugged double roller chain which is oiled by the crankcase breather tube.*

*The double pump as used on the 1933 Indian dry sump motors delivers oil to the bearings and returns surplus oil to the tank.*

*Sport bars, shown here, are optional at no extra cost. Note the steering damper and ride control wheels at the fork sides.*

*The 1933 front fork is atomic-welded, a new process which joins metals without loss of strength-giving carbon in the steel.*

***1932 Factory announcement describing the 30.50cu in Pony Scout.***

had been particularly heavy and, due to the exigencies of the times, there was now a glut of serviceable used cars, available at giveaway prices. Stately classics such as the larger Packards, Pierce Arrows, or Cadillacs in almost pristine condition could be had for from $100.00 to $200.00, on account of their fuel thirst, with lesser makes selling at proportionately less. Model T Fords in good condition brought from $50.00 to $75.00, and a rough-appearing but running model could be bought for $15.00, this even with serviceable tires.

Under such conditions, sales of even very good used motorcycles were limited, and their used prices were necessarily higher, due to their scarcity. A good 101 Scout might cost from $75.00 to $100.00 and well worn and often stripped models brought at least $50.00.

In spite of the times, a few enthusiasts kept the flag flying, and there were also limited law enforcement sales. The Pony Scout, now reduced to $225.00, sold in small numbers, mostly to commuting riders who were basically enthusiasts. The Pony's chief competitor was Harley-Davidson's 21 cubic inch single. While a machine of lesser power and performance, its $195.00 retail price and fantastic fuel economy were attractive. The actual selling price of both was often shaded by hard-pressed dealers,

if a live prospect was in view, and the two factories, once adamant on holding the line in such matters, looked the other way.

The only racing competition was now either on mostly crude flat tracks or an occasional program at a county fairground horse track. Due to the weakened position of the AMA, most of these were unsanctioned events. Dirt stars of the time included Miny Waln, Burton Albrecht, Cordy and Jack Milne, Bo Lissman and Jack Parker, who went on to greater fame on English cinder tracks, along with Wilbur Lamoreaux and 'Sprouts' Elder. The latter obtained the position of patrolman on the California State Highway Patrol, and later was killed in an accident in the line of duty. Al Pechar, for several seasons a well-known Indian competition rider who had already made his mark in the States, later had a successful competition tour of Australia and New Zealand.

The Pony Scout and Motoplane were continued for 1933, along with the larger twins and fours of the previous year, which were essentially unchanged in design and detail finish.

While the Pony was eminently satisfactory, certain design deficiencies became apparent in the Motoplane with its more powerful engine. The light, two-piece frame was prone to flexing under fierce acceleration, sometimes to the extent of throwing the drive chain from its sprocket, a condition never before experienced with the more usual massive cradle type. The light pattern clutch and gearbox also gave trouble, even though the former had been fitted with stronger springs to cope with the increased power. Another weakness was that the gearbox sometimes twisted on its hanger under hard going, a similar fault encountered in the earlier Standard designs that had an identical configuration.

To obviate this fault, many Motoplane owners modified the frame so that old Standard gearboxes and clutches could be fitted, as many of these in complete units or in parts were still in good supply. Being of much heavier construction than the light pattern Prince type, this conversion eliminated the difficulty in most cases.

Due to Indian's low production for that year, only about 450 Motoplanes were produced. An interesting design, both from its performance and its depression-designed engineering for high performance at a rock-bottom price, its general appearance has often been criticized by Indian enthusiasts as not being quite up to the make's usual high standard of styling.

The Motoplane's most important legacy to Indian's posterity, however, was its improved cylinder design, which, in line with Indian's policy of engineering new improvements to fit both new as well as older models, would also fit the previous 101 Scouts. The fitting of these, with their enhanced breathing capabilities and larger carburetors, so improved the performance of the older 101's that they were continued in limited production as replacement parts until 1940. The author's 101, authentically restored to original condition by Johnny Eagles, is so fitted, and in otherwise stock form has exceptional acceleration and a top speed of well over 90mph.

Indian's production for 1933 was at its lowest ebb, and of 7,418 machines produced that year nationwide, its share was only 1,657. Gross sales amounted to $512,758.00, with a net loss of $76,340.00.

It was during this generally depressed economic period that the leaders in the industry sought ways and means to attempt to raise the now badly sagging morale of the dealers, encourage new converts to the sport, and to revitalize motorcycle competition, which was by this time very limited in both rider participation and general public interest.

The first problem to be surmounted was the now bitter warfare between the dealers and owners of the two surviving factories, partly stimulated, as was reported, by Walter Davidson's alleged blitz sales campaign for law enforcement business two years before. The situation had now worsened to the point that normal club proceedings had in some cases become impossible. Some clubs, already weakened by loss of members, had split into Harley and Indian camps and were now ineffectual, insofar as the AMA was concerned. Motorcycling's public image was further besmirched by club outings or casual race meets, ending in fights and brawls between the two opposing factions.

The next problem was to revive individual interest in competition on the part of owners, which had been catered to lately with the introduction of the Motoplane. Before this project could be taken very far, a new set of rules required promulgation within the governing body of the AMA.

*Reprint of 1934 Indian catalog showing accessories and the 24 color options offered in that year.*

# Here Are Some of *Indian's* Distinctive Accessories

Indian's new Corbin Brown Speedometer. Introducing for motorcycles the first indirect lighted Speedometer. Gone is the old style objectionable pillar lamp post replaced by this beautiful instrument with dial and hands illuminated by an indirect hidden glow. Self contained and completely protected from the weather.

The Indian Police Radio receiver is the last word in radio. After years of cooperative effort with a world leading Radio manufacturer, Indian presents this small, sturdy, compact, self contained and highly efficient short wave receiver. Mounted on the cross bar, easily installed or transferable, to any make or model. Reasonably priced. An outstanding Police accessory.

Whether for the efficient Police motorcycle officer or the sporting rider this attractive, inconspicuous but husky all steel safety guard is a very welcome and appreciated feature. As a protection to the rider or the machine itself the new Indian Safety guard is worth many times its very reasonable price.

The new Indian Jiffy stand, positive, quick acting. A slight movement of the foot—set springs the new sturdy jiffy stand. While holding the machine upright and safe when desired, a push, and the stand folds back out of sight and out of the way. A great labor and time saver yet strong, safe and durable.

Indian all-steel tubular welded luggage carrier, pleasing in appearance, strong and firmly attached. This accessory is worthy of attachment on police or private machine alike. The new convenient weather proofed "First Aid" container is clamped to the carrier which also provides for attaching a Pyrene Fire extinguisher, saddle bags, or Police flares.

| | | |
|---|---|---|
| 1 | Indian Red — Complete Machine | |
| 2 | Black — Complete Machine | |
| 3 | Dark Blue — Complete Machine | |
| 4 | Cream — Complete Machine | |
| 5 | Chinese Red — Complete Machine | |
| 6 | Light Blue — Complete Machine | |

| | |
|---|---|
| 7 | Indian Red Machine — Black Tank |
| 8 | Indian Red Machine — Dark Blue Tank |
| 9 | Indian Red Machine — Cream Tank |
| 10 | Indian Red Machine — Light Blue Tank |
| 11 | Black Machine — Indian Red Tank |
| 12 | Black Machine — Cream Tank |

TWENTY-FOUR BRILLIANT COLOR COMBINATIONS AT NO EXTRA COST

| | |
|---|---|
| 13 | Black Machine — Chinese Red Tank |
| 14 | Black Machine — Light Blue Tank |
| 15 | Dark Blue — Indian Red Tank |
| 16 | Dark Blue — Cream Tank |
| 17 | Dark Blue — Chinese Red Tank |
| 18 | Dark Blue — Light Blue Tank |

| | |
|---|---|
| 19 | Cream Machine — Indian Red Tank |
| 20 | Cream Machine — Light Blue Tank |
| 21 | Chinese Red Machine — Cream Tank |
| 22 | Chinese Red Machine — Light Blue Tank |
| 23 | Light Blue Machine — Indian Red Tank |
| 24 | Light Blue Machine — Chinese Red Tank |

As President of the M & ATA, which was still the main support of the AMA, Jim Wright was faced with bringing together the management of the now hostile factories and the less than cordial owners of the two makes.

In collaboration with E.C. Smith, a meeting was ultimately arranged between the top management of both factories and certain M & ATA members that Fall, in the Lexington Hotel, New York City. After some discussion, a new 45 cubic inch side valve competition class, designated as Class C, was established under which slightly modified stock machines were to be eligible for various types of amateur participation. The rules went so far as to specify that competing machines must be ridden to and from the contests, the hauling or towing of them being strictly forbidden. The rules for TT contests, as originally suggested by Ted Hodgdon in 1931, were also retained.

*Publicity photos of Putt Mossman, widely known carnival Stuntman of the 1930s who used Indian machines in his various acts.*

Professional or factory hired riders were relegated to Class A, although this class of rider was now no longer in existence due to curtailed factory budgets.

In order to provide close supervision of all phases of motorcycle sport by the AMA, the country was divided into a large number of districts, with an official referee appointed to govern and supervise all sanctioned meetings within his jurisdiction.

A somewhat obscure ruling at this time was the mandatory inclusion of 30.50 cubic inch (500cc) overhead valve engines for competition in the Class C category. This was to cause no little controversy a little later when a few English machines were being entered in this class of competition, especially as the maximum 7.5-1 compression ratios allowed under the rules somewhat penalized the performance of high efficiency singles.

Meanwhile, back at the factory, all operations were conducted with a minimum of staff and production workers, for the utmost in economy. Time and motion studies, along with material analyses, showed that specialized

# F.O.B. $300 and up
## (plus tax)

firms could turn out work at cheaper rates than could be effected at the factory itself. Accordingly, as much work as possible was farmed out.

A large part of the tooling was now standing idle. As a further measure of economy, President du Pont ordered much of this tooling to be sold at various times during the next two years. While a moderate amount of capital was realized in this manner, the result was ultimately to have a disastrous effect on Indian's future operations. Even more serious was the disposal of much equipment from the company tool room, which was to hamper the possibility of certain improvements in the existing model range at a future time.

The 1934 models were changed but little from the previous year, the most visible change now being that the rear portion of the front mudguards on the Chief, Four, and Scout closely following the arc of the wheel instead of forming a flare.

A change was also made in the engine unit of the Chief, where the helical gear drive was replaced by a four-row prestretched chain running over conventional sprockets and tensioned by a Weller-type slipper device, but enclosed in the same cast alloy case, retaining Indian's traditional engine-gear unit configuration. While the helical gears derived from the original Scout design were rugged and trouble free, they were prone to some noise after large mileages, and they were also expensive to cut and machine. Another definite improvement was the fitting of dry sump lubrication to both the Chief and Standard Scout, as seen in the Motoplane and Pony Scout of the previous season.

In the Spring of 1934, the general economic condition of the country was somewhat improved, along with a

## SPECIFICATIONS

BRAKES: Front wheel and rear wheel brakes, internal expanding type. Total brake area 25.5 square inches. Front brake hand operated, rear brake foot operated.
CLUTCH: Multiple disc, operating in oil.
CONTROLS: Twist type. Throttle, left grip; spark, right grip. Reversed controls optional.
DRIVE: Primary drive, 3 row chain, in oil bath. Adjustment does not affect rear chain. Final drive 5/8" x 3/8" roller chain. Gear ratio: Solo 4.81 to 1.
ELECTRIC SYSTEM: Auto-Lite generator, Willard 6 volt, 24 ampere hour battery, outside fill type. Lighted instrument panel.
FINISH: DuPont DuLux, Indian Red standard: a variety of other color combinations optional. Special colors at extra cost.
FORK: Indian truss type. Coil spring suspension. Forged side links. Fork and steering damper standard.
FRAME: Indian Keystone type. Low saddle position. Theft-proof lock standard.
IGNITION: Battery ignition standard. Splitdorf or Bosch magneto optional at extra cost.
LUBRICATION: Indian dry sump system. Surplus oil returned to tank. Alemite lubrication at necessary points.
MOTOR: Two-cylinder 42° "V" type air-cooled, bore 2⅝", stroke 3½", 45.44 cubic inches displacement. L head. T-slot, cam ground, Lynite pistons. All main bearings roller. Aluminum heads and special cylinders available at extra cost.
MUFFLER: Indian thru-valve muffler. Adjustable to city or country riding.
SADDLE: Compression spring type standard. Side spring type optional. Saddle position adjustable. Saddle top leather covered rubber cushion on bucket type base.
TANK: Two-piece, covering frame too tube. Petcocks on both halves. Capacity 3.7 gallons of gas. 2½ quarts of oil.
WHEEL BASE: 56½ inches.
WHEELS AND TIRES: Wire wheels—18" drop center rims. Tires 18" x 4.00". Goodyear or Firestone optional.
WEIGHT: 436 pounds.

*Reprint from 1935 Indian catalog showing photo and specifications of the new 45cu in Sport Scout.*

slight increase in Indian's sales, which ultimately totalled 2,809 units for the year. With these encouraging signs, President du Pont and his top management aides decided on the rather bold step of updating and improving Indian's range of machines which, up to this time, had more or less followed the same configuration since 1929. This new program was to inaugurate a range of models which would remain basically unchanged throughout the balance of the decade and the end of the so-called classic period of American motorcycling.

To aid in implementing this program, President du Pont hired G. Briggs Weaver as Chief Engineer, filling the position vacated by Franklin's death in 1932. Weaver had been employed previously as an engineer in two of du Pont's manufacturing operations: the marine engine project of World War I, and the subsequent manufacture of du Pont cars after 1919.

The Chief, Standard Scout, and Four were restyled, the most notable change being new mudguards, which were made very deep through the center with heavy valances, the ends of which terminated in a sweeping curve that was reminiscent of current automotive practise. For economy of production, the same pressings were used for all three machines. The mudguards of the Pony Scout, which was now cataloged as the Junior Scout, were made of heavier stock and carried a somewhat deeper valance, although they still followed the arc of the wheels. Due probably to the various difficulties mentioned, the Motoplane model was discontinued.

The fuel tanks of all models were made somewhat more bulbous for increased capacity, and were fitted with car-type bayonet filler caps that replaced the previous threaded pattern.

The Chief was now fitted with battery and coil ignition as standard, with a magneto as an optional alternative at $25.00 additional cost. This change was somewhat of an improvement, the Chief was by this time somewhat difficult to start, especially in cold climates. To broaden the power band of both the Chief and Standard Scout engines, a four-speed transmission was offered as an optional extra, for an added $15.00.

For the benefit of sidecar users, and most particularly for commercial work, an optional three-forward-speed and reverse gear transmission was also offered with these two models.

The surprise of the year, however, was an entirely new sports type machine, with a 45 cubic inch V-twin engine which was based on the previous Motoplane model, and also offered an alternative to the sluggish Standard Scout.

The Sport Scout, as it was to be called, was the result of the collaboration of Weaver, Hosley, Armstrong, and a newly hired member of the engineering staff named James (Jimmy) Hill. The latter was born in England but had come to the States with his parents while still a child. He was a trained engineer, an Indian enthusiast, as well as an able competition rider and had held various engineering positions in the Springfield area. While the ultimate Sport Scout design has been historically credited to Weaver, its final development was largely the work of Hill and some experienced associates on the engineering staff.

While labeled a Scout, the new machine was, in company with the Pony and Motoplane that preceded it, more properly descended from the Prince, as it was fitted with a two-piece bolted-up diamond frame and girder type forks. All its parts, however, were of new design that required new jigs and tooling as they were of much heavier pattern.

The fuel tank halves were identical to the three larger models, requiring only a differing lug arrangement for their attachment. The mudguards were also of the same pressings, except that the front one did not carry the deep valance which was formed in the other models by an extra strip of sheet metal.

The engine was inherited from the 101 and Motoplane, with identical cylinder dimensions, and was fitted with the latter's cylinder barrels, having the increased fin area and enhanced breathing capacity.

The primary drive train, clutch, and transmission gears were those of the Chief, making for economies in manufacture, although a three row chain was fitted in place of the four row Chief arrangement. Only the gear case was of slightly differing pattern, to allow it to be fitted to the engine plates that extended forward to support the engine crankcases.

Coil and battery ignition was fitted as standard, the system being identical to that of the Chief, with magneto ignition being offered as an optional alternative. Due to the forward position of the generator, the magneto was fitted on a bracket over the gearbox, and was driven by a sprocket that engaged the top of the chain over the clutch housing. While favored for competition work, there were later problems in maintaining the proper timing sequence, as this was prone to get out of adjustment as the chain tension changed with wear over high mileages.

The overall appearance of the Sport Scout was undeniably attractive, and as a compact machine of 56½ inch wheelbase, it was of close-coupled and cobby aspect, of a size similar to that of contemporary English roadsters.

The Sport Scout at once was subjected to critical scrutiny by the many hard-core 101 enthusiasts, who compared it to a design that by this time was literally immortal. The most controversial discussion settled around the matter of handling qualities, which, in the case of the 101 were now legendary. In fairness to the Sport Scout, comparison was difficult, as the English-type girder forks imparted entirely different steering characteristics than those of the now traditional Indian trailing link type, with the old style quarter elliptic leaf spring. At any rate, the Sport Scout's handling qualities ultimately proved themselves in competition.

Another point in question was the Sport Scout's diamond type frame. Built of heavy gauge tubing, it appeared to resist the torsional forces set up by the engine in heavy going, although the bolts holding the two sections together at the seat tube and under the gear case had to be tightened frequently for best results.

Many 101 fans argued that an updated version of Indian's traditional cradle frame would have been more satisfactory, but at the cost of a rather severe weight penalty. As designed, the Sport Scout weighed 440lbs. and a heavier frame would have undoubtedly added another 50lbs.

Many unreconstructed 101 enthusiasts fitted Sport Scout engine-gearbox units into 101 frames, at the cost of much frame modification. Sport Scout cylinders were also fitted by many on 101 engines, and gave a considerable increase in power due to their enhanced breathing and higher compression ratios. Many enthusiasts who wholeheartedly took to the new model, later overcame its rather high weight by 'stroking' the engine, as of yore, and with the resultant 57 cubic inches of displacement the Scout could, in many cases, outrun a Standard Chief, although the latter still had the advantage on long gradients and in sidecar service.

Whatever the controversies, the Sport Scout, which began reaching dealer's showrooms in September, proved to be a popular seller at $300.00 during the ensuing season. It was to uphold the latter days of Indian's sporting supremacy in the hands of such nationally known riders of the day as Woodsie and Frenchy Castonguay, Lester Hillbish, Jesse James, Ted Edwards, Stanley Wilinski, Johnny Speigelhoff, Jimmie Kelley, Al Chasteen, Ted Evans, Bill Tuman, Bobby Hill, Bobby Bear, Al Scoffone, Angelo Rossi, Jr. and last but not least, the immortal Ed Kretz, together with dozens of other owners of local reputation.

In addition to the five models noted for 1935, two sidecar and three commercial models were also offered.

The Dispatch-Tow, which had been discontinued in 1932 with the demise of its parent 101, was resurrected with the Sport Scout, which for this use was fitted with a low compression commercial type engine and lowered gear ratios. Two models were featured, one with a standard sized body and another with an optional oversized box of enhanced carrying capacity.

The sidecar range included a standard heavyweight model and a lighter weight sports type. Also offered was a commercial box body on the standard chassis but with heavier springs, capable of carrying 750lbs.

A new commercial model was the Package Car, a rickshaw-like three-wheeler consisting of a Chief with a commercial type engine forward, the rear portion consisting of a car-like channeled frame fitted with two wheels at the rear, driven by a chain which activated a differential rear axle. Sales of this unit were disappointing, but it was forced to compete with the newly-introduced roadster type pickup trucks, now offered by many automobile manufacturers, which could be sold at a lower price due to their high volume production. A small number of models were exported to foreign countries where fuel economy was paramount. The actual production figures are not available, but were thought to be fewer than 200 units, although the vehicle was available on special order through 1939.

In January of 1935, it was announced that special alloy cylinders and high compression heads were available to enhance the sporting performance of the Chief and Sport Scout. These were known as 'Y' type motors, the standard cast iron type being known as the 'B' version. A large variety of color combinations was also made available, giving buyers an almost custom selection of finishes.

Indian's 1935 offerings were certainly very ambitious, especially after the loss of $68,890.00 the previous year. The wide range of machines, together with the many options as to engine fittings and finishes, put the company well ahead of its competition, and Indian enthusiasts generally were quite elated. On the strength of this interest, a number of dormant dealers reactivated their franchises, and several new dealers joined Indian's roster.

By 1935 the American heavyweight V-twin motorcycle, as exemplified by the Indian Chief and the Harley-Davidson side valve model, had now reached its final form. Both were large machines of rather massive construction, weighing a little over 500 pounds and offering the ultimate in ruggedness and almost unfailing reliability. Choosing between them had now become strictly

*The author with a 1929 101 Scout fitted with a 1936 Sport Scout-engine and gearbox unit. This rare machine, originally built by James Cramer and later owned by Maury Biggs, illustrates a die-hard 101 fan's attempt to modernize his machine.*

Above: *Indian Vice President Loren F. Hosley congratulates Ed Kretz on his winning of the 1937 Daytona Beach Classic.* (The Archives of the Indian Motocycle Company)

Right: *Ed Kretz poses with his 1937 Daytona Winner's Trophy.* (The Archives of the Indian Motocycle Company)

a matter of personal preference. The Harley was said by some to have a slight advantage in top speed, but the Chief had the edge of acceleration. The Harley's clutch and gearbox were admittedly more rugged than those of the Indian. Indian's optional magneto ignition, not available on Harley, was popular with sporting riders, and the Delco distributor system on the battery-powered models was said to be easier to service and maintain than the field coil type used on Harley-Davidsons. Indian's main attraction, however, was its ease of handling and positive steering, and its race-bred trailing link front suspension gave safer control at high speeds than did the leading link type traditional with Harley. Then, too, Indian's attention to the development of the side valve engine made it the most powerful of its type in any given displacement.

While America was by tradition the ancestral home of the big twin, several makes were concurrently offered in Great Britain, together with a handful of obscure makes on the continent of Europe. Due to the smaller per capita income of English buyers, large capacity V-twins never achieved volume sales and were mostly employed with sidecars or in commercial applications; AJS, BSA, Royal

Enfield, James, Matchless, and Zenith marketed such models during the 1920's and into the 1930's. Most of these were of the utility type intended for family sidecar use. The high performance Brough Superiors and Vincent-HRD models were offered as luxury solo mounts, but due to their necessarily high retail price sold only in limited numbers.

The bread-and-butter English V-twins were greatly handicapped in competing with American V-twins in export markets, as their lighter weight construction and lack of power development rendered them less suited to colonial conditions. Their low engine power was primarily due to lack of technical development, as their engine sizes were beyond those specified for international competition.

The hand-controlled gear shift and foot-activated clutch control mechanism traditionally favored in America, but not often favored by English designers, had much to recommend it. The former offered positive control through a set of trouble-free linkage that was simple to adjust for slight wear. The large clutches required for large V-twin engines were more efficiently controlled by leg power, as it usually required 50 to 60 pounds of torque to activate them. The direct linkage via a foot pedal was most trouble-free in contrast to the English system of Bowden-type cables.

The American system was criticized by some journalists in the post-World War II motorcycling press and was adversely compared to the traditional English system. These writers apparently had not the technical background to analyze the varying control requirements of two diametrically opposed types of machines!

The 1935 competition season which it was hoped might inaugurate a revitalized interest in motorcycle sport, was opened early that year by the AMA competition committee, with a 200-mile National Championship road race held on February 24th, at Jacksonville, Florida, organized under the new Class C rules for stock machines.

To lend added color to the affair, a recent Indianapolis race winner, William 'Wild Bill' Cummins, was prevailed upon to act as starter. Harley-Davidson star Joe Petrali was referee, and Cannonball Baker acted as chief judge.

A strong field of sixty-eight riders lined up for the flag on the 1.6 mile course, which included varied straights and sharp unbanked curves. Veteran Indian rider, 'Red' House from Washington, D.C. was well in the early running, but dropped out with a blown tire. The meet was thereafter a seesaw contest between Harley-Davidson's Bill Carpenter, and Indian star, Rody Rodenberg, with an up-and-coming contender from the Harley-Davidson camp, Sam Arena, coming out from California for the contest. R.D. Johnson, on an Indian, made a strong bid in the later laps, but missed his pit stop and ran out of fuel near the finish. Carpenter and Rodenberg rode neck and neck toward the finish, the former running out of gas when nearly through the final

lap. William Bracey, an Indian-mounted amateur from Jacksonville was a surprise fourth. A well-noted third place was George Pepper, of Belleville, Ontario, who brought his 500 camshaft Norton in three seconds behind the winner. The event drew a record crowd of 10,000 spectators. Needless to say, the race was of signal satisfaction to Indian as an introduction of the new Sport Scout.

As an outgrowth of the various meetings held at the behest of M & ATA and AMA officials and sparked by Jim Wright, AMA Secretary E.C. Smith embarked on a journey around the country that January in an attempt to revitalize motorcycle club interest, encourage dealers of both makes, and to interest more individual riders in the sport. Smith's schedule and itinerary were published in advance in the *Motorcyclist* magazine so that dealers, clubs and individuals could meet with him to discuss the AMA program.

The unannounced purpose of the tour was, of course, to attempt to allay the now bitter rivalry between the two factories and the various dealers. Smith ultimately reached most of the larger cities and towns of the country during the year, travelling in a Harley-Davidson side-car outfit donated by that company. He was happy to report to concerned AMA and M & ATA officials in November that club growth and individual rider interest seemed to be improving.

As far as Indian was concerned, general business conditions and sales had improved markedly during 1935. General rider acceptance of the Sport Scout and Junior Scout had been promising, and it was hoped that substantial sales of the former model would indicate increased rider interest in Class C competition. 3,715 machines had been shipped on orders received and the company had shown a net profit of $18,765.00.

*Charles Vemon's authentically restored 1935 74cu in Chief.* (Ronald Mugar)

# Indian Sport Sidecar

America's most beautiful sport sidecar. The graceful streamlined all steel body and a seat position that is designed to give the utmost in comfort for long touring. Ample leg room is provided and the upholstering is soft DuPont high-grade leatherwove. The back of the seat hinges forward, giving access to a roomy compartment for luggage. The chassis is the same as used on the Indian standard sidecar, with its strong atomic welded chassis and perfection of springing.

# Indian Standard Sidecar

This roomy streamlined sidecar is built to give ultra-comfort and heavy duty service. Body constructed of heavy gauge auto body metal. Seat comfortably upholstered with DuPont high-grade leatherwove. The chassis is of seamless steel tubing, of a large diameter, atomic welded for strength and rigidity. Proper spring suspension assures riding comfort under all conditions. Front spring is full elliptic, while the rear of the body is mounted on a long semi-elliptic spring to avoid side sway.

*Reprint of factory catalog showing the two sidecar models offered during the 1930s.*

A sour note to the year's competition was the debacle at Keene, New Hampshire, where nine persons at a race meet were injured when contestants lost control of their machines and plunged into the crowd.

Interest in transcontinental speed contests had lagged during the preceding years, mainly because the improved roads had made such travel by individual riders more or less commonplace. Attempts on old records were still made, however, especially from Los Angeles to New York City, the distance now being reduced to 3,005 miles due to various road improvements made through the years. In 1934, Randolph Whiting, on an Indian Chief, set a new record of 5 days 3 hours. Later in the same year he lowered his own time to 4 days, 19 hours. That September Earl Robinson on a 45 inch Harley made a new record of 3 days, 6 hours. The next Spring Rody Rodenberg made a faster run on a Sport Scout with the phenomenal time of 2 days, 23 hours, taking only three hours off for rest during the entire trip.

The franchised Indian dealer, Leo Montigney, had closed his shop in Springfield during the depths of the depression, sales in the factory's home city being made by custom through a regular retail outlet as the factory had never made direct retail sales. This condition was later rectified by installing a regularly franchised dealer in the basement of the factory, who rented the premises and conducted business on his own account. The obvious advantage in purchasing a machine in Springfield was that no freight rate was added to the cost of the machine.

The first resident franchise was awarded to Fritz (Fritzie) Baer, a long time Indian enthusiast who was active in a local motorcycle club. His son, Bobby, later became an expert Indian competition rider. The operation was next conducted by Jules Horky, who remained until 1942, when he was drafted into the Army. He later acted as AMA Competition Chairman during the post war years.

Many motion picture actors took up motorcycling in the sporting climate of southern California. The various dealers in the area gave much publicity to the fact that such virile stars as Ward Bond, Clark Gable, Victor MacLaglen, Roy Rogers, Randolph Scott, John Payne and Robert Taylor were two-wheel devotees, as well as others of the motion picture colony. Ventriloquist Edgar Bergen purchased a Junior Scout from Floyd Clymer, and dutifully posed for publicity pictures with Charlie McCarthy perched on the tank top in front of him – appropriately attired in a small sized helmet and goggles.

Indian motorcycles were widely featured in various motion pictures, during the mid-and late 1930's. This was due mainly to the efforts of Floyd Clymer, who had become the Los Angeles distributor in 1934 after Al Crocker gave up the franchise to manufacture his short track specials. A tireless promoter, Clymer made various Indian models available on a loan basis to the leading studios, for the priceless advertising value of having the make viewed by millions of movie fans. An Indian Dispatch-Tow was ridden by Cary Grant and Irene Dunne in an escape scene in 'The Awful Truth.' The late Spencer Tracy played the role of a motorcycle policeman riding an

Indian Chief in 'Disorderly Conduct,' which also featured the child star, Dickie Moore. Another Dispatch-Tow was seen in an RKO release starring Ginger Rogers and Burgess Meredith. A 1922 Standard model was ridden both by the irrepressible Betty Hutton and her double in various stunts featured in 'The Perils of Pauline.' Stunt rider, Ed Kretz, donned grease paint to play the part of a motorcycle officer, appropriately mounted on an Indian, in 'She Couldn't Take It', featuring Ginger Rogers and George Raft.

20th Century Fox studio ultimately purchased two 1937 Chiefs for use in scenes involving motorcycle policemen. When their property was ultimately sold in 1973, these machines were unearthed in one of the vast warehouses, each with less than 2,000 miles on the odometers!

The Indian Company entered the 1936 sales season with no little optimism. While general business conditions were still far below normal, economists were noting encouraging upward trends. Rider acceptance of the very comprehensive range of machines offered the year before had been gratifying and these were continued with but minor improvements for the present year.

The Sport Scout was fitted with a larger capacity oil pump, and the heavily finned 'Y' type cylinders, offering enhanced cooling, were ordered in most cases by sporting riders, in preference to the standard type which were by this time sold mostly on the commercial models. The front mudguard of the Sport Scout was now the same as fitted to the other larger models, and the presence of the deeper valance enhanced its appearance.

The Junior Scout was reduced in price to $195.00. Production economies were effected by offering it only in one standard color, the traditional Indian red, and by eliminating the steering and fork dampers, which were referred to in company literature as 'ride controls.' The model was eminently suited for both utility and light sporting use, and the latter riders generally purchased the ride controls as an extra, as without them fork action was excessive and led to rapid wear of the spindles. The Sport Scout enjoyed almost phenomenal sales for the time, and was particularly favored by far Western riders, where climatic conditions favored all-season use.

The Junior Scout was less favored in this area, probably due to the vast distances of highways offering high speed travel that somewhat taxed its capabilities. It was fairly popular on the East coast and New England states,

*Reprint of factory literature showing the Dispatch-Tow Commercial model based on the Sport Scout.*

# The *Indian* DISPATCH-TOW

**Builds Up Good Will**

**Cuts Expense of One Man**

**Eliminates the Expense of an Automobile**

**Broadens Your Selling Radius**

**Increases Repair and Parts Business**

**Is an Effective Advertising Medium**

## The *Only* Means of Getting the Hurry-Up Job.. the *Cheapest* Means of Getting *Any* Job

THE TELEPHONE RINGS — FAST WORK IS NECESSARY

The DISPATCH-TOW Is on Its Way. Any One Can Drive It.

Slipping Through Traffic. Advertising Your Progressive Service All the Way.

In a Few Seconds the Heavily-Padded Clamps Are Attached.

In Comes the Job with the DISPATCH-TOW Riding Securely Behind.

Faster
More Economical
Better

Every garage owner—automobile dealer—tire dealer needs the service that an Indian Dispatch-Tow can give him. He owes it to his business to get in touch with the nearest Indian dealer and see this great business-getting unit demonstrated.
The Dispatch-Tow is a rugged, compact unit especially designed for the type of service. It is powered by a two-cylinder, 45-cubic-inch, air-cooled motor incorporating cam ground T-slot pistons and full roller mein and connecting rod bearings. Motor lubrication is by the Indian Dry Sump method, having continuous circulation and insuring maximum oil mileage.

The rear axle is of seamless tube construction. Differential is fully enclosed and of standard automotive type, having six bearings on the axle shafts. The chain drive operates a sprocket on the outside of differential housing—no chance for dust or dirt to enter the differential.
A big body, styled up to the minute, affords plenty of room for service tools and accessories. A rear tubular bumper is standard. Bodies available with either metal top or upholstered seat with hand rails, making accommodations for two extra service call men. Body leaf springs are controlled by double friction snubbers.

## The *Indian* DISPATCH-TOW.. *Builds Sales*

# *Indians* Speed---
## Again Startles Motorcycle World!

**Muroc Dry Lake**
CALIFORNIA
Sunday, April 6th
A. M. A. Sanction

Electrically timed 1 mile
run through ¼ mile trap.

**L. A. "45" CLUB**

**ANNUAL**

**SPEED TRIALS**

Over the table smooth bed of this famous Dry Lake, before a crowd of 3000 spectators, Indian riders on standard type side valve models not only won every class they entered in remarkable time, but an INDIAN SPORT SCOUT RIDDEN BY FRED LUDLOW WON THE FASTEST TIME OF THE DAY at the amazing speed of 128.57 m.p.h. The following results are positive proof of the tremendous speed obtainable in pocket valve Indian models.

### "45" INCH SIDE VALVE, FLAT HEAD MOTORS.

| | | |
|---|---|---|
| 1st—Fred Ludlow | '36 INDIAN Sport Scout | 128.57 m.p.h |
| 2nd—Carl Hurth | '36 INDIAN Sport Scout | 123.29 m.p.h. |
| 3rd—Kenny Schofield | '31 INDIAN Scout | 107.14 m.p.h. |
| 4th—Vaughn Dickerson | '36 INDIAN Sport Scout | 95.74 m.p.h. |
| 5th—Steve Packard | '30 INDIAN Scout | 94.17 m.p.h. |
| 6th—Glen Fulkerson | '36 INDIAN Sport Scout | 92.78 m.p.h. |
| 7th—Kunzman | '30 INDIAN Scout | 87.38 m.p.h. |
| 8th—Joe Koons | '29 INDIAN Scout | 87.38 m.p.h. |
| 9th—Alex White | '35 Harley-Davidson "45" | 86.54 m.p.h. |

NOTE:—The Indian Sport Scout owned by Carl Hurth made four trips through the speed trap at better than 120.00 m.p.h.

### "74" CUBIC INCH SIDE VALVE TWIN MODELS.

| | | |
|---|---|---|
| 1st—Al Chasteen | '35 INDIAN Chief | 125.00 m.p.h. |
| 2nd—Ed Kretz | '36 INDIAN Chief | 108.43 m.p.h. |
| 3rd—Harold Barnes | '35 INDIAN Chief | 107.40 m.p.h. |
| 4th—Frank Chase | '32 INDIAN Chief | 107.14 m.p.h. |
| 5th—Smith | Harley-Davidson "74" | 105.88 m.p.h. |
| 6th—H. McTevia | F-Head Harley-Davidson "74" | 98.90 m.p.h. |
| 7th—L. Hunt | '36 INDIAN Chief | 96.77 m.p.h. |
| 8th—Watson | Harley-Davidson "74" | 95.74 m.p.h. |
| 9th—E. Troutman | '36 INDIAN Chief | 93.75 m.p.h. |
| 10th—Horning | Harley-Davidson "74" | 93.75 m.p.h. |
| 11th—Earl Leary | '36 INDIAN Chief | 92.78 m.p.h. |
| 12th—West Hampton | Harley-Davidson "74" | 88.74 m.p.h. |
| 13th—C. C. Kesero | Harley-Davidson "74" | 88.24 m.p.h. |

### OVERHEAD VALVE MACHINES, ALL MODELS. (NO INDIAN OVERHEAD TIMED)

| | | |
|---|---|---|
| 1st—Hugo Sikora | '36 Crocker "61" O.H.V. | 126.76 m.p.h. |
| 2nd—Ed Hinkle | '35 Crocker 30:50 O.H.V. Single | 113.92 m.p.h. |
| 3rd—Glen Rathbun | '36 Harley-Davidson "61" O.H.V. | 111.11 m.p.h. |
| 4th—Nelson Rathbun | '36 Harley-Davidson "61" O.H.V. | 107.14 m.p.h. |
| 5th—Joe Walker | '36 Harley-Davidson "61" O.H.V. | 104.65 m.p.h. |
| 6th—Jack Gravell | '36 Harley-Davidson "61" O.H.V. | 102.27 m.p.h. |

*Reprint of factory literature showing speed records established on the old Muroc dry lake course in Southern California in 1936.*

however, as it offered satisfactory performance over the smaller distances involved and provided mild sporting performance at a small investment, where weather conditions limited the riding season.

Many dealers in this area offered prospective buyers a low cost package deal for factory delivery, which saved the shipping costs. A one-way bus or train ticket was provided to Springfield during a weekday, when fares were at the lowest cost. The new owner was given a tour of the factory, treated to lunch at the company commissary, and given a full tank of fuel with which to start the journey home.

The factory dealer publication *Service Shots* was expanded to include repair and tuning data on the Sport and Junior Scouts, and was now known as *Contact Points*. Particular attention was devoted to enhanced promotion of the Junior Scout, stressing the fact that the purchase of a small twin would ultimately lead the rider to trade it in on a more powerful model at a later time. Time payment sales contracts were advised in promoting new business, but caution was urged in selecting only those buyers who were steadily employed and possessed a good credit rating.

Harley-Davidson's answer to Indian's now formidable competition from a more diverse range of models was the introduction of a 61 cubic inch twin, with overhead valves. Harley's model range had shrunk to two machines, their traditional 74 cubic inch side valve and 45 cubic inch WL model, after dropping their 21 and 30.50 cubic inch singles in 1935. In addition to the new 61 they also offered an 80 cubic inch version of the side valve 74.

A notable improvement in these machines was the offering of a newly designed constant mesh transmission. Indian fans had long been looking for an improved gearbox configuration in their own machines, as the primitive sliding gear type featured in all Indian models was but a slight updating of the 1913 design of Hedstrom and Gustafson. This had worked well in earlier days, but with constant engine improvements through the years providing increased power, the slider dogs wore rapidly and required frequent replacement

under hard service. The Indian factory never offered any official defense in regard to their retention of this now obsolete fitting, but top management officials had been quoted as reporting privately that the money was simply not available during difficult times for experimentation and development of an improved system. The inherent weakness of Indian's transmission somewhat offset the signal advantages of its unit construction and Harley-Davidson always had the advantage of a much more rugged drive train.

The competition scene was marred, and the general image of motorcycling was damaged, at the 200-mile National Championship race held July 20th of that year at Swanzey, New Hampshire, when two people were killed and eight were severely injured.

Richard Ashbrook, a Harley-Davidson contestant of Washington, D.C., died when he failed to make a turn at 70mph and hit a tree. Spectator John P. MacMahon was killed a few minutes later when he, for some reason, walked across the course. Injured contestants in other crashes were Paul Bauer, Charles Leonard of Brooklyn, Delmar McDermott of New Bedford, Carl Capella and Clare Blake of New York, and John Hillbish, brother of Lester, of Reading, Pennsylvania.

Hanford Marshall, on a Sport Scout, won the event in 3 hours, 37 minutes for the $200.00. Dave Tancrede, Harley mounted and a 1934 winner, came in only 7 seconds behind Marshall, and Stanley Wilinski on a Sport Scout, was third.

The domestic motorcycle scene was enlivened in 1936 by the appearance of a new make of motorcycle launched in Los Angeles by Albert G. Crocker, one-time Indian employee and later a dealer and distributor in Kansas City and Los Angeles. While the new model's development was not a particularly well-kept secret within the trade,

*Glenn Orr's Chief in original condition that has clocked over 200,000 miles.* **(George Hays)**

the resultant product was something of a phenomenon. It is described in Appendix 1.

Following the encouraging rider acceptance of the Sport Scout during its initial season, sales increased during the ensuing year. The factory accordingly concentrated its main production efforts on this model. Sales of the Junior Scout were also gratifying, and the majority of all orders received were for either of the Scout models.

The Sport Scout was particularly attractive to sporting riders and club members, and numerous sporting groups throughout the country were often made up of owners of these machines. Fair numbers of feminine riders purchased Junior Scouts, mainly for their easy starting capabilities when fitted with the standard battery ignition, and not a few of these had graduated to a Sport Scout, after becoming familiar with motorcycling through riding the smaller model.

One of the advantages of the Sport Scout was its capability of being tuned to various degrees of performance. A 'stroker' machine could offer overall performance on a par with a Chief, without any sacrifice of ease of starting, smooth running, or flexibility of engine control.

With special attention to slightly altered cam action, port relieving, and internal polishing, the Sport Scout became a very formidable competition machine, adaptable to many types of road, track, or hill climb events. Much of the earlier experimentation in this regard was effected by Jimmy Hill and his engineering staff at the factory. Even as a stripped machine, the Sport Scout was still somewhat heavy, especially as compared with its earlier ancestor, the still popular 101. Some sporting enthusiasts substituted Junior Scout fuel and oil tanks to reduce top weight, a conversion easily effected by a slight alteration to the mounting lugs. In the same manner, Junior Scout forks were also substituted for the rather

heavy standard type, which also reduced weight without any adverse effect on handling and steering.

Space considerations preclude all but a brief summary of the literally hundreds of sporting victories won by Sport Scout riders, whether factory-sponsored semi-professionals, riders of distinction within their own immediate areas, or club members competing in local events.

The prowess of this machine is best described in connection with the life and times of the immortal Ed Kretz, who has been described by both contemporaries and motorcycle historians as perhaps the greatest all-around rider in both the classic and immediate post World War II era of American motorcycle sport.

Of Swiss-German extraction, Kretz was born in San Diego in 1911, the youngest of a family of 11 children. The family later moved north to Pomona, where the Depression found young Kretz eking out a living driving hay trucks from the Imperial Valley farms to Los Angeles.

Unlike many of the previously famous competition riders of the vintage era, Kretz was not known to have evidenced any interest in motorcycling until his early twenties. His first machine was a well-worn VL Harley-Davidson, which he purchased from Floyd Clymer's Los Angeles Indian agency for $125.00, trading in an old outboard motor for $40.00 as part of the transaction. A few days later he became interested in short track racing, having attended a meet held the previous weekend at the old White Sox Park. He then purchased a secondhand Rudge track machine from Clymer and after a little practise, began entering these contests.

The short tracks did not seem to suit Kretz' emerging hell-for-leather riding style, and his next public appearance was at a Targa Florio road type race, held on the old Ascot speedway. His mount was the old Harley, suitably stripped down for the occasion, presenting a rather

*The restored Indian Arrow racing machine, along with its streamlined shell, now on view at Harrah s Auto Museum, Reno, Nevada.* (Harrah's Auto Museum)

bizarre appearance among a field of professionally-mounted experts, one of whom was the noted Harley-Davidson rider, Byrd McKinney of Pasadena.

Kretz' pit crew consisted of a coterie of country boy friends, including Harry Sasaki, who later became a physician and who loaned him a rear wheel off his own street machine when Kretz blew out his own on an early lap. The course was around the five-eights mile banked track and over an adjacent hill. Kretz bored through the pack to win second place, this in spite of running nearly one lap with a flat tire at reduced speed and some time lost in the pits. His startling performance was duly noted by the experts present. Floyd Clymer, who had promoted the race, promptly contacted the Indian factory and made arrangements with the company to supply Kretz with a new machine for future competition.

Clymer next gave Kretz a job as a mechanic in his shop, at the then standard depression wages of $18.50 per week. During the following months Kretz gained valuable experience with a factory Scout at various TT races in the Los Angeles area. In 1935 he made another spectacular win at the Ascot 100-Miler, where he headed the field on the first lap.

Notwithstanding his auspicious start, his ride in this contest was marred by recurring mechanical troubles and pit crew inefficiencies that turned the day into a nightmare. For some unknown reason, the mechanics had wired the magneto leads to the sparkplugs through the seat springs of the saddle. As Kretz' weight compressed the springs periodically in his ride over the rough track, the engine kept alternately accelerating and dying. Kretz' progress was now quite naturally proceeding in spurts, until in desperation he rode into the pits. His crew at once diagnosed the trouble as a fouled sparkplug and installed a new one. Back on the track, it was the same off-again-on-again procedure. In all, Kretz made six

*A photograph of a typical small dealer-sponsored Southern California motorcycle club of the late 1930s.*

pit stops before someone located the trouble.

After a 45 minute loss of time in the pits, a lesser rider might well have called it a day, but once the Scout's engine regained power, Kretz rode like a veritable madman. He passed batches of riders as though they were standing still, averaging 2 seconds better than the fastest time trials of the previous day. During the remaining 43 laps he worked his way from 19th to 6th place. Observers recalling the race have stated that only the falling of the checkered flag prevented Kretz from ultimately overtaking the first placing riders.

In 1936 he entered the 200-mile National Championship race at Savannah, Georgia, where his spectacular tactics and the lowering by 10mph of the record set the year before won him national acclaim.

In 1937 the National 200-Miler was moved to Dayton Beach, where Kretz again repeated his 1936 victory.

On his return to the West coast, he entered most of the TT contests, his wins now approaching monotonous regularity.

His only limitation appeared to be the stamina of his engines, which were now supplied by the factory in batches of four to six in order to keep him in the running. While still employed by Floyd Clymer, all of his equipment was supplied through the Western States Indian distributor, Hap Alzina. He was, by this time, a full-fledged factory rider, being paid a $200.00 per month salary plus transportation and other expense money.

Now nicknamed the 'Iron Man,' Kretz went on during the ensuing post-war years to win 11 of the big National races. He led at Daytona on 14 different occasions, but won only twice, due to failure of his machines. He took the 100-miler at Langhorne four years running, won the New Hampshire twice, as well as the 200-miler at Savannah. He won the 100-mile National at Los Angeles' Carroll Speedway when 43 years of age, seemingly as tireless and alert as other competitors half his age. He was Pacific Coast Champion for 14 years.

Kretz successes have been attributed to his powerful physique; he stood but 5 feet 8 inches in height, but weighed in at a powerfully muscled 180 pounds. His skill, determination, and, above all, his lion-like courage, never faltered.

Although he appeared indestructible through 25 years of racing, he suffered two serious shoulder injuries, innumerable cracked ribs, together with frequent bruises, and burns too numerous to recount.

Kretz's courage and riding skill stood him in good stead during one of the last major races held before World War II; the 200-miler on the paved mile track at Oakland, California, in August, 1941, which featured one of the worst accidents to occur in American motorcycle racing history.

Kretz was proceeding at his usual blistering pace, well in the lead in the 38th mile, and had just lapped the field. Tommy Hayes, the Texas star rider, now in second place, saw Kretz approaching from behind and opened his throttle to its stop. Hayes next turned out to pass Ben Campanale in the north turn, but had entered it too fast. He hit a rough area at 100mph and was thrown from his machine and killed instantly.

Campanale, who was immediately behind, also went down, and Kretz just behind Campanale, was barely able to pass between the two machines. At this moment, Hayes' riderless machine, throttle still wide open, came charging into the gap. The three men following Kretz, John McCall, Jimmy Kelley and Sam Arena entered the pile up, McCall died instantly and Kelley was knocked unconscious. Arena, a highly skilled rider, laid his machine down at 100mph without serious injury, and was able to remount his machine and carry on with the race. The toll was two dead, with Campanale and Kelley in the hospital for nearly a year. Kretz kept his lead and was about seven miles ahead of the field in the 167th lap, when his front chain broke, just 32 miles from the finish.

*Ed Kretz coming out of the pits of the old Ascot Speedway in Los Angeles in 1938. Note the Junior Scout fuel tanks and front forks fitted to his racing Scout as a weight saving measure.* (Ed Kretz)

He was 44 years of age when the post World War II competition was resumed, but was able to win the 100-miler at Laconia. During this race he lost his rear chain, gave away 10 laps while in the pits, but regained first place through spectacular riding and finally came in first on the next to the last lap. In the same year, 1946, he gained three national wins; Daytona, Laconia, and Langhorne, a record never bested before or since.

Kretz and his wife, Irene, had two children, a girl named Donna and a son, Ed, Jr. In 1948 Ed Senior began coaching his son in the rudiments of racecraft, and in 1950 the two entered as a father-son team at Laconia. Ed, Jr. won the 50-mile Amateur event held on Saturday. On Sunday, Ed, Sr. entered the Expert event, and while well out in front in the 6th mile experienced ignition trouble. The fault proved to be in the magneto condenser, and after this was corrected in the pits, he spent the next 26 miles rocketing through the pack when, at the 38th mile, his front brake locked at well over 90mph and he was thrown to the pavement. Pulling himself into a ball, he managed to roll down the track and arise unaided to walk to the pits. His helmet was smashed and his jersey was burned from his back, and he was covered with bruises and abrasions. In spite of these injuries, he stood and watched the completion of the race, before being taken to a local emergency hospital. He continued to compete for a few more seasons after Indian's demise, favoring Triumph machines, as did Ed, Jr.

Kretz' personal appeal was heightened by his handsome, virile appearance and also by virtue of the fact that he was a born showman. His soft spoken, quiet manner was quite a contrast to his bull-like stance in the saddle, and he was highly favored by the many feminine fans who, in the later classic era, came to favor motorcycle racing as a spectator sport.

He became an Indian dealer in Monterey Park, a suburb of Los Angeles, in 1944, where, with his wide personal following and business acumen, he built up a lucrative and successful dealership.

One of his last official acts as an employee of Floyd Clymer was to supervise the uncrating and setting up of a group of 50 Chiefs that had been purchased by the California State Highway Patrol, for use in the Southern California area. The author's authentically restored Chief, presently returned to civilian specification, was originally one of these machines. Retrieved in 1957 from a desert automobile graveyard near Needles, California, it is both a treasured memento of Indian's later Classic days, and of the life and times of Ed Kretz, who was one of motorcycling's greats.

Norman Hartford, a one-time newspaperman who wrote much publicity for the motorcycle competition of

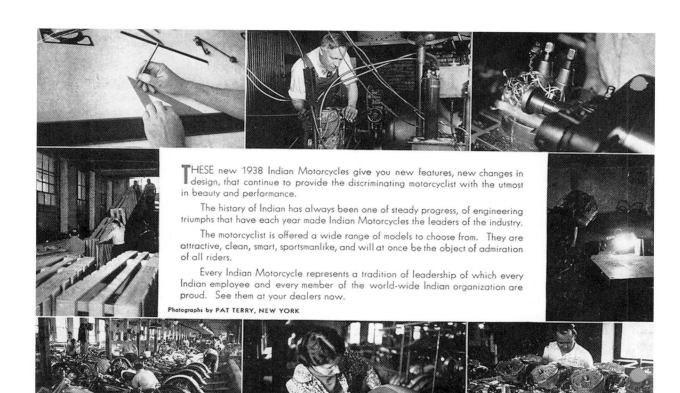

THESE new 1938 Indian Motorcycles give you new features, new changes in design, that continue to provide the discriminating motorcyclist with the utmost in beauty and performance.

The history of Indian has always been one of steady progress, of engineering triumphs that have each year made Indian Motorcycles the leaders of the industry.

The motorcyclist is offered a wide range of models to choose from. They are attractive, clean, smart, sportsmanlike, and will at once be the object of admiration of all riders.

Every Indian Motorcycle represents a tradition of leadership of which every Indian employee and every member of the world-wide Indian organization are proud. See them at your dealers now.

Photographs by PAT TERRY, NEW YORK

*Reprint of 1938 factory literature showing various operations in the State Street plant.* (**Photographs by Pat Terry, New York**)

the 1930's, has stated that Kretz was such a formidable contestant that many of his fans considered his victory at a race meet such a foregone conclusion that the main interest was centered on who would come in second!

Fred Ludlow, who himself achieved motorcycle racing immortality by winning five National Championships in one day, in 1921, has remarked that, in his opinion, given an indestructible machine, Kretz was unbeatable in any contest. Former stars such as Floyd Clymer and Jack and Cordy Milne, have all stated that no American rider in that century could match him on any speedway, TT course, or in a road race.

While Kretz caused Indian's Racing Department no little consternation in supplying him a continuing series of engines, his on-the-track testing of these was responsible for many technical improvements. For example, one fault discovered in the racing 45's was that oil surge in the crankcase was experienced on prolonged full throttle running. The factory then cast several sets of crankcases with a slightly enlarged inner diameter, which corrected the trouble. A small number of these were produced in post World War II days, and they were fitted to the factory racers entered at Daytona, in 1946 and 1947. The advertising value to Kretz' prowess was of incalculable value to Indian and his continuing victories

had much to do with the large sales volume enjoyed by the Sport Scout.

In his later years, Kretz secured the franchise for BMW and various oriental motorcycles in Monterey Park, which today is managed by Ed, Jr. He also became interested in sports car racing and was known as a record breaker with a small English Triumph. One of his personal cars in recent years has been an exotic 180mph Lamborghini.

His first wife, Irene, to whom he was married for 34 years, passed away in 1962. He later married the former Mary Titus of the noted Oklahoma oil family, with whom he now lives in his comfortable hilltop home in Monterey Park. Always willing to relive the old days, Kretz is happily a living legend of the golden age of motorcycle competition.

In mid-1936, the Sport Scout was fitted with an improved oil pump of enhanced capacity and better suited to prolonged high speed running. In spite of difficult times, Indian sales totaled $1,789,000.00 for the year, with an encouraging net profit after all expenses of

$111,589.00 that paid the stockholders $2.26 per common share. 5,028 machines had been sold, an increase of one-third over the previous year.

The present range of models was continued almost without change for 1937, except for the improved 'upside down' Sport Four as described previously. Company officials were encouraged by the fact that more inactive dealers were renewing their franchises, and a few newcomers entered the ranks with the promise of improving times.

Jim Wright paid special attention to maintaining and improving factory relationships with the dealers and tirelessly toured the country to promote this and the cause of Indian. Wright also spent much time and effort working with the M & ATA, and the AMA to improve the latter's organizational role in competition matters, and in the encouragement of club activities.

The house organ *Indian News* was expanded for increased coverage of club news as well as human interest stories, featuring individual riders. A series of articles described various technical advances in manufacture being carried on at the factory.

Indian received wide publicity in the Spring upon the official opening of the famous suspension bridge across San Francisco's Golden Gate Harbor entrance. Hap Jones, the young, energetic San Francisco dealer who had lately acquired his franchise, arranged with local officials to allow an Indian Chief to be designated as the first official vehicle to cross the span. Wire service News pictures featuring Hap and a pristine 1937 magneto-equipped Chief subsequently appeared in many of the nation's larger newspapers.

A significant event having to do with American motorcycle exports occurred in 1937. While the initial impact was concerned with Harley-Davidson, subsequent events were far reaching in their effect on the sale of domestic motorcycles overseas.

The Japanese and Far Eastern markets had been lucrative for American machines since the close of World War I. American machines had been particularly popular in Japan, where Indian enjoyed the bulk of this business up until the Bauer debacle of the late 1920's. In fact, Crown Prince (later Emperor) Hirohito as a young man owned an Indian Chief sidecar outfit as his personal vehicle for several seasons. As Indian's production declined, Harley-Davidson moved in, and under the capable management of their Far Eastern agent, Alfred Rich Child, enjoyed large sales.

Large numbers of 74 cubic inch twin sidecar outfits were purchased by the Japanese Army as well as by the nationalist forces of China, who were by the early 1930's locked in combat over the Japanese attempt to conquer Manchuria.

In 1930, Child decided that volume sales of Harleys could be increased by building an assembly plant in Japan, which would then place the make in a highly competitive position in regard to saving shipping costs from the States and in the use of low cost native labor.

Child secured a manufacturing license to produce the massively rugged 74 cubic inch side valve model and set up an assembly plant. The Japanese model was named the Rikua, and was virtually indistinguishable from its Milwaukee counterpart.

During the following year, the new militaristic government of Japan suddenly expropriated the factory and Child was forced to leave the country. This action, of course, ended any future Harley-Davidson sales, and terminated Indian's markets as well, as the Rikua could now be produced and sold at a 50% reduction in costs of any imported model.

A problem experienced by the Indian Company in 1937 was that the timing sequence of Chiefs fitted with battery ignition became prone to maladjustment, after limited use. The problem was first encountered in numbers of police machines just acquired in Ohio and Indiana. Erle Armstrong was dispatched to these areas to ascertain the trouble. It was found that the oil pump gears, which also activated the distributor rotor shaft, wore rapidly, leaving excessive backlash. The factory validated the new machine guarantee by fitting the ailing machines with magnetos. The Engineering Department at once developed an improved gear pump which corrected the fault.

After the mid-1930's there was some relief in the two-make monotony of the domestic motorcycle picture (Crocker's small annual production could scarcely be counted) when small numbers of foreign machines began to appear in limited numbers.

Reggie Pink had been the pioneer distributor of British machines in New York City since 1927 and appears to have been alone in this field in the United States until 1935, when Jack Frodsham opened a Velocette agency in Los Angeles. Johnson Motors in Pasadena secured an Ariel and Triumph franchise in 1937, and subsequently opened a small branch in San Francisco. It has also been reported that there were also one or two such agencies in Florida.

While these machines offered a lighter weight alternative to the domestically produced heavyweight machines, they never sold in any real numbers during an era when motorcycling in the United States was generally in the doldrums. Their advertising effort was strictly limited and few if any of their entrepreneurs appeared to have the means to promote sales on a more widespread scale. Their sales would no doubt have been better if dealers with established agencies could have been allowed to handle them. Such practises, however, were traditionally forbidden to all domestic franchise holders, and this edict was rigidly enforced.

Indian and Harley dealers were quick to point out that the imports were not as ruggedly built nor would they stand up to full throttle running, when compared to Yankee V-twins. This was generally true, except in the case of the International Norton models, which built up an enviable reputation with a representation of only about two dozen machines.

Due to the adverse factors mentioned, together with generally unfavorable economic conditions, only about 400 foreign machines were sold during the immediate prewar period in the United States.

In the Fall of 1937 a group of Indian enthusiasts made a now almost forgotten attempt on the world's motorcycle land speed record. It may be recalled that the dry lakes, called 'sinks', existing in the desert of Southern California, Nevada and Utah, the latter being the site of the famous salt flats which formed the bottom of prehistoric Lake Bonneville, were favorite places for high speed running. Lake Muroc was particularly favored as it was near Los Angeles, and for some years had been the

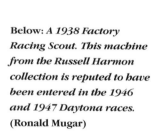

**Right:** *The author's 1938 Sport Scout as restored by Johnny Eagles.* (Ronald Mugar)

**Below:** *A 1938 Factory Racing Scout. This machine from the Russell Harmon collection is reputed to have been entered in the 1946 and 1947 Daytona races.* (Ronald Mugar)

scene of speed and record contests for both cars and motorcycles.

Some years earlier, Hap Alzina had secured one of the factory's 61 cubic inch eight valve engines, one of about a dozen built under Franklin's direction during 1924. This one had been overhauled and tuned at various times by Marvin 'Red' Fenwicke and Fred 'Pop' Schunk, Alzina's ace mechanics, and had been fitted to various frames for speed contests held on the lakes. The engine in question, it was alleged, was the same one used by Johnny Seymour for his record-breaking run in 1926, where he established an American mark of 132mph.

Alzina's and his crew's interest in such an attempt had been lately heightened by the fact that Harley-Davidson's speed star, Joe Petrali, had recently set a new record at Daytona Beach the preceding March. His specially built Harley had been an overhead valve 61 cubic inch twin with special cams, dual carburetors, and high 3–1 gearing. An interesting feature of this machine was that it had been partially streamlined with an enclosure around the rear wheel, a disced front wheel, and a streamlined fairing over the steering head to aid in lowering wind resistance.

Petrali's two-way average was 136.183mph and was remarkable in that it was ultimately made with all the fairings removed. In describing the event to the author during an interview in 1971, Petrali stated that during the initial tests the machine handled satisfactorily at speeds up to 110mph, but as the throttle was opened further the front wheel had an alarming tendency to aviate and make the machine unmanageable. The removal of the front wheel discs during subsequent trials did not correct the trouble, and Petrali's crew finally removed all the fairings. Harley's publicity department attempted to conceal the fact that the machine did not actually make its record runs as a streamliner, and no photographs of it in stripped form were released for publication. Much was made of the prowess of the machine in the trade press, however, together with the fact that Petrali had broken Johnny Seymour's previous record of ten years earlier.

The initial effort of Indian's proposed record attempt saw Fenwicke carefully rebuilding the old Indian engine, which entailed the fitting of many hand-built parts. He also engineered a set of his own special high lift valve cams, for which he was already justly famous in racing circles, and arranged the carburetion for the use of a special methanol fuel.

The frame, which was made as light as possible, was built up jointly by Fenwicke and another of Alzina's mechanics, Peter Anderson. It was an interesting combination of 101 Scout and Hedstrom era parts, some of which dated back to 1913! A set of 1920 standard forks were fitted, which carried the old style scroll-ended spring. A 101 fuel tank was fitted, together with an old style unsprung racing saddle.

The engine was set low in the frame and was supported by an extra heavy set of specially-made engine plates. A strengthened Powerplus gearbox and clutch were fitted, with a beefed-up hanger bracket to resist the torsional forces of the engine. While made up of many diverse standard and specially made parts, the machine was extraordinarily attractive as a lithe and functional vehicle.

Fred Ludlow, who was no stranger to record breaking since his phenomenal runs on a streamlined Henderson in 1924, and who had lately been active in various dry lake speed contests, elected to pilot the machine, which was to be christened the 'Arrow.'

It was the consensus of all concerned that some sort of streamlining should be fitted. As Petrali's problems with the Harley record breaker were by this time well known, it was decided to consult an aircraft designer named William (Bill) Myers, who was also an experienced motorcyclist, to study the aerodynamics of the problem. After due reflection he worked with an aircraft mechanic in building the shell, which was of streamlined form and fitted with a set of stabilizing fins to the tail. It was of aircraft-type construction, with light spruce framing and balsa wood ribs. The rear portion was made removable to admit the rider, and the whole was covered with aircraft linen with a dope finish. A pair of small retractable wheels fitted on either side just aft of the gearbox held the machine upright while at rest.

The interior of the shell was tailored to Ludlow's somewhat slight physique, and was such a close fit that his movements were quite restricted. Forward vision was provided by a small celluloid window set in the nose.

That Spring the machine was hauled in secret over the 400 mile distance from Alzina's shop in Oakland to Lake Muroc for initial testing. The outfit appeared to handle well at speeds up to 100mph, but during a somewhat faster run the engine threw a rod. The outfit was then taken back to Oakland, where Fenwicke rebuilt the engine. Due to the pressure of other work, and the onset of the hot desert summer, it was decided to shelve the project temporarily until the next season.

In the meantime, Fenwicke refined and tested the engine to the point where all internal parts were polished to a mirror-like finish. With the sparkplugs removed, the tension of one valve spring would turn the motor, transmission and the rear wheel.

When the machine was again ready, it was decided that the speed trials be moved to Bonneville. The salt bed would offer a safer course, and in Ludlow's opinion would also allow for high speeds. Then there was the disquieting rumor that Muroc would soon be closed to unlimited speed record attempts. This shortly afterwards came true, as the US Army took over this desert area to form Edwards Air Force base.

It was also decided to take along a Sport Scout and Chief that had been stripped and tuned to Class C competition rules, and to attempt to make new records in the 74 and 45 cubic inch classes as well. This move was inspired by the news that Indianapolis Indian dealer Roland (Rollie) Free had just taken two such models to Florida and had racked up speeds at Daytona Beach of 111mph for the Scout and 109 for the Chief. Ludlow was of the opinion that he could top these records on the faster salt course, and in addition he considered that both Fenwicke's and Schunk's abilities were superior to those available to Free.

The entourage arrived at Wendover, Utah, on September 22nd, 1938, and included all of the original crew, together with Chet Billings, then Editor of the *Motorcyclist*, who had been lately keeping in close touch with the proceedings.

The official AMA referee supervised the setting up of the course, with timing devices setting off a measured mile at the midpoint of the 13 mile course. It was decided to make the first run with the Sport Scout, and the crews turned out at 3 am on the morning of the 24th.

Ludlow made a two-way warm up run and the sparkplugs were changed. The timed two-way runs were then made, with an official average of 115.226mph, a new Class C record for 45 cubic inch machines.

The Chief was rolled out next, warmed up, and the first run to the north was made in 30.86 seconds. On the south run, the rear tire blew out, the torn tube bursting from the casing and striking Ludlow as he wrestled the machine to a stop, his long track experience standing him in good stead. As the rear wheel now needed changing and realignment, the machine was laid aside and preparations were made to run the Arrow the following morning.

At dawn on Sunday, September 25th, Ludlow was fastened into the shell, after Fenwicke had warmed up the engine, and made a preliminary run on the south course. At 5,000rpm, well below the engine's maximum, he noted a speed wobble at about 135mph. After some consultation, it was decided to cut away the two small stabilizing fins that had been fitted at the tail, as the turbulence set up at high speed was thought to be causing the difficulty.

Early the next morning, the Arrow was tried again, this time on the north course. The tachometer passed the 5,000rpm mark, and at a speed of what was later judged to be about 145mph, the machine went into a wobble, this time with such gyrations that the bars were torn from Ludlow's hands. At this point, Alzina ordered the Arrow runs scratched, and the Chief was readied for the course.

The 74 ran faultlessly on both runs with an official average of 29.65 seconds for a new class record of 120.747mph, made possible by Ludlow's superlative riding skill and the tuning skill of Fenwicke. The latter's cam modifications were offered in high performance production models of both machines during the following season, being appropriately cataloged as 'Bonneville' motors.

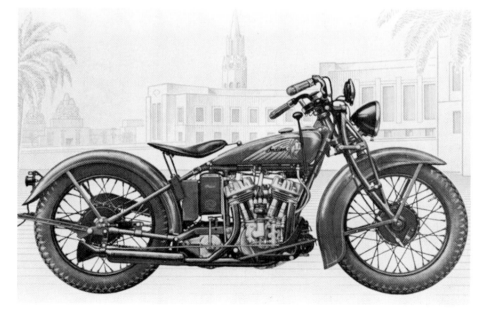

*The 30.50cu in Junior Scout in its final form as the 1940–1941 Model. The 1942 models were identical, except for the optional fitting of skirted fenders, similar to those fitted from 1940 onwards to the larger machines. Only a few Junior Scouts were built for the 1942 model year, as production reverted to War Department models in January 1942.*

The Arrow was never run again. Alzina considered that in its present form it was unsafe, and he stated that he did not intend to risk Ludlow's or any other rider's life in any more record attempts. It was taken back to Oakland where it languished forgotten in an out-of-the-way corner of Alzina's extensive premises for nearly thirty years. When Alzina retired in the mid-1960s and sold out his BSA dealership to BSA Inc. of New Jersey, the Arrow and a number of other old machines were ultimately removed to Auburn, California. Lauer subsequently presented the machine to Harrah's Auto Museum in Reno, Nevada, where it was recently restored to original condition, including its shell. It is now on view as another memento of Indian's historic racing past.

In reminiscing on the details of the ill-fated Arrow project, Ludlow told the author in 1974 that in his opinion the shell should have been made somewhat longer for better longitudinal stability. He also stated that the steering geometry of the Hedstrom-Franklin frame and fork arrangement, while well proved in board track

*The 1940 Sport Scout with skirted mudguards and strutted rear frame section. Open type mudguards were optional for this year only. Featuring new beauty and comfort – deep, full skirted fenders trimmed with chrome – "Air-tex" cushioned saddle with barrel type spring action – keystone racing frame – new fork head angle for greater control and safety at all speeds – plus the powerful 45 cubic inch engine – ever willing – ever capable of setting new high achievements for dependability and performance.*

racing at speeds of over 120mph, became critical when speeds beyond that figure were reached.

Ludlow's theories concerning the shape of the shell were vindicated in the post World War II years, when the late Noel Pope, the English racing star who posthumously holds the all-time speed record at Brooklands, made another attempt on the world speed record at Bonneville, sponsored by Teddy Comerford, the well-known London motorcycle agent.

Pope's machine was a 1939 61 cubic inch model SS 100 Brough Superior that was fitted with a shell very similar to that fitted to the Arrow. At about the same speed, the Brough went into a wobble and skidded for some distance on its side. Happily, Pope's injuries were minor.

In later years, the ultimate record was made with a machine of very elongated form, much like a torpedo, that was built very low to the ground, and scarcely resembled a conventional motorcycle. This suggests that a conventional motorcycle configuration has definite aerodynamic limits at speeds over 150mph.

Ludlow remained a member of Pasadena's traffic squad until 1955, when he retired at age 60. He presently lives in Pasadena, a much respected veteran of the vintage and classic days of the sport. Among his treasured mementos of his competition days is a handsome wrist watch, presented to him by the Indian Company for his Arrow achievement.

Sales of Indian machines remained strong during the balance of the 1937 season. The management decided that the designs of the larger machines could be

improved slightly for the following year, and Briggs Weaver responded by designing an attractive aluminum nacelle for the forward top of the fuel tanks, to house the ignition switch, ammeter, and speedometer head. The valance of the chainguards of the Sport Scout and Chief were deepened to enclose the chain run almost completely.

More spectacular was the augmentation of the pin striping on the tank sides, chainguards, and mudguards to form a rather intricate pattern that was most attractive, together with enhanced options as to color combinations. Many antique motorcycle enthusiasts consider the Indian designs of the late classic era as being the most well finished of this period, not only as to functionality of design, but as to color and detail finish.

The new engine design of this year's four cylinder model, as previously described, was of signal improvement, and was of such performance as to at long last offer an equal to the late lamented K model Hendersons. Numerous law enforcement orders were placed with dealers or through the factory's municipal service department as a result.

Production figures for this year were at an all time high, with 6,030 machines shipped for a net profit of $178,016.00 equal to $3.86 on each share of outstanding common stock.

No sooner had Indian's Fall announcements for the coming year been made than the country's economy took a sudden down turn. This was a great disappointment to business in general, as conditions had been improving slowly since the dark days of 1932 and 1933. Indian officials now viewed matters with no little alarm, as numbers of new dealerships had been added to the roster, which, along with some reinstated older franchises, had brought Indian's representation back almost to the thousand mark. Production estimates originally projected for 1938 were now hastily revised, and component part manufacture, still fabricated by piecework, was cut back by 33%.

While motorcycle sales suffered generally, Indian's market for the Junior Scout remained fairly strong. The Sport Scout was still selling well, particularly in the Southwest and Far West, where the climatic conditions allowed for almost year-round riding and where sporting riders abounded.

As the year progressed, income was enhanced by a gratifying number of law enforcement orders for Fours and Chiefs, and over 400 of these were shipped for this service alone.

The market still remained somewhat soft, however, and by the year's end only 3,650 machines in all models had been ordered. The financial statement showed a net loss of $11,767.00 which would have been much greater had not spring component production been held back.

1939 opened with greater promise with somewhat improving economic conditions, sparked to a large extent by the possibilities of an impending war in Europe. The 1938 line was carried forward without significant changes, except that on some of the larger models an upswept tail pipe was fitted to the exhaust line. This year

*Ed Kretz leads Ted Edwards (no 13) on another racing Scout, and Tom Hayes (no 18) Harley-Davidson during the 1940 race at Langhorne, Pennsylvania. (Ed Kretz)*

proved to be a profitable one for the company as 8,883 machines were ordered. Indian officials were jubilant over the fact that this topped Harley-Davidson's production of 8,312.

Indian received a welcome windfall in October, when Vice President Loren Hosley announced that Indian had just been awarded an order for 5,000 military type Chiefs with sidecars from the French Government, for use by their armed forces, which would amount to over $ 2,000,000.00. This affair appeared as somewhat of an anachronism to motorcycle historians, as France had been both the ancestral home of the automobile and of the first practical motorcycle engine as developed by De Dion and Bouton.

From the practical aspects, however, the situation was not unlikely, as Gallic individuality precluded the operation of any really large factories. Most of the French motorcycle production was distributed among several rather small factories manufacturing a variety of lightweight models, none having the capacity for large production, nor capable of manufacturing heavyweight machines suitable for the rigors of military use.

The French army order presented serious production problems for Indian, as plans had already been made to initiate production of the usual 1940 civilian models. Through lack of replacement of tooling facilities through the depression years, plant operation would be taxed to the utmost. It was ultimately decided to produce the army order in two increments, of 2,500 outfits each.

Meanwhile, somewhat drastic changes in Indian's overall design had been planned for the 1940 season. The Chief and Four were to be fitted with a plunger sprung rear frame, which was to offer a much softer ride. The mudguards of the larger models were designed along contemporary automotive lines, with deep valances that extended low enough so that stays were no longer fitted to support them, the valances being bolted to the frame in the rear and to the lower fork legs in front. The artistic pin striping was eliminated in favor of chrome beads running along the mudguards, and the Indian script on the tank sides was replaced by a small metal fitting that carried the name plate.

A structural weakness was later noted in some of the immediate pre-war Chief military and civilian models, where fractures in the upper frame joints and head lugs occurred after some use. To speed up production, some of the frames had been made up with welded rather than the more usual brazed joints. This fault was corrected in subsequent production, and a number of fractured frames were replaced by the factory.

A further detail change, which was optional, was the fitting of 16 inch x 5 inch wheels in place of the 18 inch x 4.50 inch size which had been standard for the past three seasons. While the fatter tires gave a softer ride, some enthusiasts claimed the steering was much less sensitive.

Although the spring frame gave a softer ride, particularly in the Four, certain handling problems were experienced in the Chief, as the resilient rear wheel action did not appear to mate well with the limited travel of the front forks. Experiments were conducted with a new type fork with hydraulic suspension, but due to the pressure of the war contract and resultant production problems, a new suspension did not appear until later, during the war years, and was initially fitted to the 841 shaft drive model.

In deference to the extra weight of the new mudguards, the previous open type was fitted as an option to the Sport Scout, as it was thought that sporting riders might take exception to a slight variation in handling qualities.

The new models were generally well received, especially the spring frame four, but some riders complained that the mudguard valances were sensitive to side winds, even though they offered superlative protection to the rider in wet weather or on muddy roads.

The Chiefs for the French Army contract were standard in most respects except that newly designed open type wide clearance mudguards were fitted, and the new spring frame was used. The first production models carried standard 18 inch wheels, but later were fitted with the 16 inch type.

Indian's now improved financial situation was reflected in an article appearing in the *New York Times* on October 26th, 1940. The Indian Motocycle Company year ended August 31st. Net profit was $703,082.00, equal to $5.77 each on 121,662 shares of common stock. Net profit in the preceding year for eight months was $65,705.00 or $1.18 each on 42,586 shares of common stock after preferred dividend requirements were met. E. Paul du Pont, President, said that sales of Indian motorcycles in the 12 months ending August 31st amounted to $4,968,164.00, the largest total since 1929. Production for 1940 totaled 10,923 units for both military and civilian models, and topped Harley-Davidson's output by 450 machines.

Production efforts were now directed toward the manufacture of both military and civilian machines, the details of the former activities being covered in the following chapter.

Civilian models produced during 1941 were almost identical to those of the preceding year, except for minor variations in chrome trim in some machines, and in the construction of the Mesinger saddle tops, which now had thicker interior padding. The four cylinder models now were fitted with 16 inch wheels as standard. The open type mudguard option for the Sport Scout was withdrawn, and these models were fitted with the same deeply valanced type already standard on the Chief and Four.

Few civilian machines were produced as 1942 models, and were mostly similar as before. The only marked change was the fitting of the Chief and Four plunger spring frame assemblies to the Sport Scout. The rear portion of the frame was modified to take these fittings, and was bolted to the central portion as previously described. Buyers also had the option of 16 inch wheels for this year's model.

The fitting of the valanced mudguards and spring frame to the Sport Scout somewhat penalized its performance, as the gross weight of the machine was now a little over 500lbs. Most owners resorted to stroking the engines for more power, to overcome this weight penalty. Due to growing military commitments, only approximately 450 of these models were produced before all civilian motorcycle production was terminated early in 1942.

By this time large numbers of Sport Scouts from past production were stroked. Several of the larger dealers, such as Eugene Shillingford of Pennsylvania, Edward Nichols in Chicago, Indian Motorcycle Sales of Kansas City, and Floyd Clymer in Los Angeles specialized in sales of stroker piston assemblies for this conversion.

The author's 1938–1939 Sport Scout, restored to authentic original specification by Johnny Eagles, was stroked on rebuilding. This conversion, along with slight internal modifications to the manifolds and careful attention to flywheel balance, has created a 100mph machine that will cruise tirelessly at 75mph on open freeways.

The American motorcycle scene presented several paradoxes during the immediate post-World War II era that is now considered the end of the so-called classic period of motorcycling.

The production of motorcycles in the United States was by this time mostly confined to the domestic market, as export sales had declined markedly during the past three or four seasons and was now almost entirely ended by the European war. In the process, the production and sales of both the major manufacturers had now equalized, Harley-Davidson having lost its commanding lead over Indian that it had enjoyed since the middle 1920's. With the present prospect of large military orders, both factories could now expect capacity production.

Motorcycling activities had become more or less stable during the late 1930's. Much of the bitter enmity and name-brand fanaticism suffered in earlier years had abated, and many clubs representing owners of all makes were functioning satisfactorily. What with this

happier state of affairs, many dealerships were enjoying gratifying prosperity.

At the same moment, motorcycling in America was almost totally isolated from other sporting activities. Local sporting or club events rarely received any publicity in local news media, and even the reports of the big National race meets received only a few lines on the back pages of newspapers. In many cases, only painful or fatal accidents involving motorcycles received more than passing attention from the press, apparently a holdover from the often bloody days of board track racing. Many motorcyclists actually appeared defensive concerning their personal involvement in the sport, and little conscious effort was seen to give favorable publicity to the motorcycle affairs in the general news media.

*George M. Hendee in 1940, three years before his death.*
**(The Archives of the Indian Motorcycle Company)**

The only trade publication which offered motorcyclists a voice was the *Motorcyclist* magazine, together with the house organs published for trade and rider benefit by the large factories. But their small circulation did not allow them to penetrate much farther than their chosen sphere of readers.

*The Sport Scout in its final form: the 1941–1942 model with full valanced mudguards, 16 inch wheels, and rear sprung frame. Due to the 500lb all-up weight of these models, most of them were stroked to 57 cu in by their owners.* **(Ronald Mugar)**

In spite of this now more or less stabilized state of affairs, the close of the 1930 decade saw the ultimate decline of motorcycling interest. During 1929, the three major factories then in existence produced 31,912 machines, and there were over 165,000 motorcycles registered throughout the United States. Total production dropped to a low of 3,266 units in 1933, and slowly climbed to an average of 13,000 to 18,000 machines per year in the late 1930's. By 1939, only 126,233 machines were registered. This numerical decline was also more notable for the fact that during this decade the population of the country increased by one third, and automo-

bile registrations more than tripled. The net result was that a motorcycle rider on the open highways and city streets became almost a novelty. Also, in the minds of many car owners, a motorcycle rider was synonymous with law enforcement, as in many areas the only machines to be seen were in this category.

As far as Indian was concerned, the late 1930's represented a pleasant afternoon before the coming twilight of the company's fortunes. The great Depression had been successfully, if vicariously, weathered, and the company had become financially stable. The roster of Indian's dealers now numbered slightly over a thousand – a far cry from the company's golden years, but gratifying under the present state of the industry. Many motorcycle journalists in recent years have, without apparently conducting adequate research into the true facts, made much of Indian's precarious financial condition during this decade. While it is true that serious financial losses were sustained in the 1929–1933 period, as a segment of a minority industry, the company made a remarkable recovery thereafter, and under very difficult conditions.

In the face of these tribulations, Indian's competition successes continued to uphold the glorious traditions of its great past, and the Sport Scout, as ridden by various well-known as well as unknown riders, is still remembered as a pre-eminent competition machine of the classic era.

In the American motorcycling scene as viewed over the past four decades, the life and times of both of the two ultimately surviving makes are intertwined, no matter which of them is under specific consideration. This fact has been demonstrated conclusively in this exposition of Indian history, as so many of its fortunes are related to its long time rival, Harley-Davidson.

An important point in question in this regard whenever historians review motorcycle facts, or when old time riders get together, has for many years been the matter of the relative production of the two factories. In spite of the long prominence of both makes, the true facts regarding them have long been a mystery.

Due to the decline in general motorcycling interest and consequent eroding of sales since the mid-1920 period, motorcycle manufacturers somewhat naturally developed a defensive attitude regarding their economic position in a country whose tradition was constant industrial growth. This state of affairs led to much secrecy regarding the actual internal affairs of each company, and, in consequence, actual production figures came to be a closely guarded secret by top management.

The source of actual production figures for all major industries has long been contained in the surveys of the United States Department of Commerce, and the domes-

tic motorcycle industry has generally been included. Examination of these figures, however, has indicated some discrepancies, and it is thought that in some cases the companies did not render wholly accurate reports when called upon to do so. In researching the matter further in order to at long last ascertain as accurately as possible true motorcycle production figures, the author has additionally consulted available factory records, often very fragmentary in nature, former employees of various companies within the industry, as well as confidants within the present industry who requested anonymity in return for their cooperation in providing information.

The results of this somewhat exhaustive survey are shown in the following table, and encompass the classic era through the depression years.

|  | Indian | Harley-Davidson |
|---|---|---|
| 1933 | 1657 | 5689 |
| 1934 | 2809 | 7897 |
| 1935 | 3715 | 10398 |
| 1936 | 5028 | 8879 |
| 1937 | 6030 | 11674 |
| 1938 | 3651 | 8158 |
| 1939 | 8883* | 8312 |
| 1940 | 10923 | 10461 |
| 1941 | 8720** | 15599** |
| 1942 | 20410** | 22867** |
| Total | 71,826 | 109,934 |

*Adjusted to full year, company fiscal year changed*
**Includes military as well as civilian models*

It will be noted from the above figures that Harley-Davidson production, as compared to Indian, was not on a two-to-one basis as has been frequently reported in later accounts of various incomplete aspects of Indian history.

Harley-Davidson's greater production during the early 1930's was a carryover of the advantage gained when Indian's production of motorcycles declined during the Bauer era. They also enjoyed substantial export sales during this period, which were mainly to the military governments of Japan and Nationalist China.

In short, the great Depression had now receded, not through the economic manipulations of a socialistically-oriented Government, but rather through the productive demands of a now expanding world conflict and the limitless need for war material. With production of all types of vehicles for the civilian market now severely curtailed, the American motorcycle industry readied itself to aid in the war effort.

# Chapter 8

# WORLD WAR II
# 1940–1945

Indian production during the opening months of 1940 was concentrated on military Chief and sidecar manufacture, to fulfill the French War Department contract. To facilitate this accelerated production, some three hundred additional machinists and assembly workers were taken on during January and February. In addition, experimental work on smaller types of military models was undertaken, as the United States War Department had recently requested that both Indian and Harley-Davidson submit prototypes for testing by procurement authorities.

The Engineering Department was somewhat handicapped in the projection of new models, as their facilities were already taxed to the utmost in the Chief production, as well as maintaining a normal supply of civilian models for dealers' orders. Most pressing was the problem of depleted and antiquated tooling facilities, the shop equipment having deteriorated during the depression days, without replacement. In the end, it was decided to make do with the tooling on hand. The initial military model, designated as the 640, was a rather successful permutation of Sport and Junior Scout parts, which could be assembled from standard components with jigs and other equipment on hand, much of which was hastily repaired by a night shift of mechanics familiar with this work.

The soon-to-be-famous 640 was fitted with what was basically a detuned 30.50 cubic inch Junior Scout engine, with a low compression ratio, mild valve timing and restricted breathing capabilities for ease of starting and longevity. These modifications naturally restricted performance, but vivid acceleration and high top speeds were not required for military duties. The engines were fitted with the standard in-unit enclosed primary chain drive and Chief gearbox and gears, which not only enhanced ruggedness but rationalized production.

The standard Sport Scout frame and forks were incorporated into the design for their well-proved characteristics, although still made as the bolted-up two-piece type. In order to increase the low ground clearance that had long been a standard feature of American V-twins, but not wholly desirable for possible operation over rough terrain, the forks had their legs extended about 1½ inches. The seat stays were also lengthened, which raised the rear of the machine to the point that nearly five inches of clearance were possible. Open type military mudguards of wide but shallow D-section were fitted, with generous wheel clearance to obviate all but the worst type of mud from clogging the wheels. The speedometer was mounted on the fork head, with a direct drive to the front wheel, to simplify servicing. A heavy duty carrier was attached to the top of the rear mudguard for the fitting of large capacity cowhide saddle bags, together with racks for extra fuel containers. A large air cleaner was fitted to the carburetor intake for use in dusty conditions, although it further inhibited the already restricted breathing capacity of the engine.

The 640 proved to be a rugged and durable machine, easily serviced, and capable of standing much abuse.

Opposite: *A large number of 340-B sidecars and 640-A military machines ready for shipment in a storage area of the State Street Factory, 1942.* (Theodore A. Hodgdon)

What with its small capacity engine and heavy top weight of 450lbs., its acceleration and top speed were less than a contemporary 100cc machine of today, but were adequate for average military use.

A somewhat more powerful model was developed shortly afterwards that was almost identical in other respects except for the fitting of the standard low compression commercial type Sport Scout engine. This machine was designated as the 741 model, and was much preferred for stateside use, as its better performance was more suited to American traffic conditions.

Both models were thoroughly tested under field conditions by War Department officials, and were accepted as satisfactory. An open-ended cost plus contract for a limited number of machines was placed, to allow the company to commence production.

The French Army order for Chiefs was completed late in March, and some 2,200 of the crated units were trucked to the port of New York. These were loaded on a freighter, the SS Hanseatic Star, a 6,000 ton vessel of Panamanian registry under charter to the Swedish Export Line. The ship sailed on April 12th cleared for Le Havre, but it never arrived and no trace of its ultimate fate was ever discovered. As the German U-boat campaign was then at its height, the ship was presumed to have been torpedoed and lost with all hands. This bad news was ultimately of much chagrin to the Indian Company, but it suffered no financial loss as the funds for payment had already been deposited in Indian's account in the Chase Manhattan Bank of New York.

What with the completion of the French order and the initial US War Department order, the company was hard pressed to supply the now suddenly growing demand for new machines from both civilian and law enforcement markets. As the general economic conditions improved due to government spending on the defense effort, many Indian enthusiasts were ordering new machines, no doubt partly stimulated by the thought that if war actually was declared on the Axis powers, they would not be available for public sale for some time. Law enforcement bodies throughout the country were expanding their activities to police the ever-growing numbers of defense plants that were springing up near various large cities. This necessitated the purchase of more police machines, purchasing agents no doubt motivated by the same reasons that were prompting civilian purchases. Enhanced production of Chiefs and Fours fitted with the newly-introduced skirted mudguards was undertaken to supply these orders.

Amid these accelerated activities, the managerial and production staffs were saddened by the sudden death, from a heart attack, of plant superintendent and Vice President, Loring F. Hosley. A genial and kindly man, who was popular for these attributes and well respected for his engineering and managerial abilities, his loss was a severe blow to the company during a very critical time. Close associates were of the opinion that overwork and the pressure of the defense effort were responsible for his untimely demise.

On March 12th, Dwight L. Moody, a veteran employee since 1917 who had risen from the ranks, was appointed General Manager to fill that now vacated post. He was subsequently honored with the title of Vice President and given a seat on the Board of Directors. An able and dedicated man, he carried on with the supervision of Indian's production, with the faithful assistance of Er1e Armstrong who oversaw the actual work on the assembly lines.

In deference to the superior efforts exerted by Indian's work force of 964 employees during the initial defense effort, President du Pont announced on March 21st that all salaried and hourly wage personnel would receive a 5% bonus for the past three months. He further announced that production was now at a record high of 75 units per day.

As a reflection of Indian's enhanced financial position, the Board of Directors on May 22nd voted a dividend of 30 cents a share on the outstanding 298 shares of $10.00 par preferred stock and 25 cents a share on the 121,409 outstanding share of common stock. It was also reported that money had been reserved to pay these to present holders of old preferred and common stocks, as soon as these were exchanged for new issues.

On October 26th it was announced that for the 1939–1940 year ending August 31st there was an accrued profit of $703,085.00 equal to $5.77 each on 121,622 shares of outstanding common stock. This was a ten-fold increase over profits of the preceding year. President du Pont later announced that sales during the past twelve months had totalled $4,968,164.00, the largest since 1929.

On December 6th, Edward D. Dunning, formerly Vice President in charge of engineering and production for the Kulair Corporation of Philadelphia, manufacturers of refrigeration equipment, was named Assistant General Manager to assist Dwight L. Moody.

At this juncture the War Department had become thoroughly convinced of the military value of the motorcycle after receiving reports of its utilization by both the German Panzer divisions in Europe and by the British in the North African campaigns. Accordingly, in January 1941, expanded open-ended contracts were awarded to both Indian and Harley-Davidson for as many military machines as they could produce.

Harley-Davidson was in a much better position to inaugurate large production than Indian, as its production had been somewhat greater during the preceding decade and its tooling facilities were in generally much better condition. While the cavernous Indian factory contained sufficient floor space for the production of 30,000 or more machines per year, the selling off of much of its tooling during the depression years, together with the oversight of not replacing remaining units when worked out, was now a very serious handicap to high volume production.

The problem of acquiring new machine tooling was a pressing problem facing all defense industry during this period, as production had seriously declined during the depression years when industrial and manufacturing activity was at a necessarily low ebb. The allocation of new machinery as it now became available created many complex problems for the War Production Board, which had been instituted to prevent bottlenecks in the production of war material. President du Pont and members of his staff were reported to have expended much time and effort to obtain desperately-needed tooling through this agency. They were ultimately able to obtain only a small portion of what was actually needed. Due to the heroic efforts of Moody, Dunning, Armstrong and others of the production staff, 10,976 machines came off the lines in 1941, the largest number since the Scout boom of 1920.

William S. Knudsen, President of General Motors, then on leave to serve as head of war production, and commissioned a Lieutenant General by President Roosevelt to give him broad authority, visited the Indian factory during a routine inspection of war production facilities in the Spring of 1942. He was said to have commented adversely on the generally run-down condition of the plant and its facilities, but noted that employee morale was high.

The country went on a full war-time footing after the Japanese attack on Pearl Harbor on Decembet 7th. Price controls were placed in effect to prevent inflation and profiteering, and civilian travel was closely restricted. Fuel and tire rationing curtailed private use of motor vehicles and the sale of new machines was restricted to essential users.

Motorcycle dealers were particularly affected, as the availability of new machines had been materially reduced since midsummer. Most dealers had planned to continue limited operation with repair work and with the sale of used machines. Many were then severely handicapped through the loss of key personnel through induction or enlistment in the services. Not a few agencies simply closed for the duration. A few of the larger establish-ments possessing machine equipment were able to obtain limited defense contracts for the output of minor items not related to motorcycling.

From the retail standpoint, business was now definitely a sellers' market. Used machines in good condition brought artificially high prices, Chiefs and Sport Scouts selling at $750.00 to $850.00. Used Fours often brought $1,000.00 or more.

Motorcycles came into much demand from utility riders due to fuel rationing. Many dealers ransacked their lots and storage yards for wrecked or wornout machines for rebuilding to meet this demand. Many derelict Scouts and Chiefs of all models reappeared, along with a few venerable Princes and nearly every defense plant had its contingent of these aged machines in the parking lot.

With the rapid expansion of the armed forces, many one-time dealers and mechanics were utilized as instructors to teach novices in appropriate services how to ride. Many competition stars, now in the service, such as Ed Kretz, were also active in the program.

Late in 1941 both Indian and Harley-Davidson each received orders from the British War Department for 5,000 military machines. While vast numbers of utilitarian Ariels, BSA's, Matchlesses, Nortons, Triumphs and lesser quantities of Velocettes were already in service, the authorities now feared for their future vehicle production since the recent destruction of the Triumph factory in Coventry by the Luftwaffe.

Most of Indian's share of this order consisted of the 30.50 cubic inch 640 models, as the British were interested in the utmost fuel economy. A few Chief sidecar outfits were also included, however.

At the war's end many were sold to civilians as surplus. As high tariffs precluded import of American V-twins, English enthusiasts welcomed these models, many of which were subsequently converted to civilian specification. They were in daily use in the decade following the war.

Competition and club activities had lagged at home during the 1941 season, as many riders and members were by this time in service. On January 11th, E.C. Smith, Executive Secretary of the American Motorcycle Association announced in a press release issued from the Columbus, Ohio headquarters that to save fuel and tires all official competition would be suspended for the duration of hostilities.

The last important races of the year were held at the Langhorne, Pennsylvania track on September 1st, 1941, when Tommy Hayes, on a Harley-Davidson, finished a half-mile ahead of Indian-mounted Ed Kretz, who experienced engine trouble.

Military production continued during 1942. This consisted of mostly 640 models for overseas service in Europe, with lesser numbers of 741's and Chiefs, a limited number of which were released to essential users or law enforcement bodies through the usual dealer channels.

Matt Keevers, a Springfield resident, joined the company during this period to head the advertising staff. With little formal attention to this Department required under war conditions, Keevers spent most of his time writing repair manuals covering the various military models. He remained with the company until its final reorganization in 1951.

On November 14th, President du Pont announced that the company had earned a $516,646.00 profit for the preceding year, after a $500,000 post-war reserve had been set aside. Net sales were put at $8,978,758 for a record total of 13,086 machines produced; truly a remarkable accomplishment considering the generally deplorable state of Indian's facilities.

1943 was an uneventful year, except for a small fire that broke out in the north wing of the factory. This was happily contained by an alert fire fighting crew. Sabotage was suspected, but never proved.

On August 10th, Sales Manager Jim Wright resigned from the company, close associates citing the fact that the wartime inactivity of his Department had left him somewhat bored with his position. His replacement was Harry A. Patton, who had formerly operated a company branch at 129 E. 129th St. in New York City.

Wright next took a position as Sales Manager for the Van Norman Machine Company, manufacturers of machine tooling widely used in automobile engine rebuilding. He then filled a similar position for the Hansen Screw Machine Company. While on a train trip in 1949 from Boston to Washington, D.C. he was found dead in his berth, the victim of an apparent heart attack. His passing was mourned by his many friends in industry. His dedication to Indian paralleled that of the late Frank Weschler, as he had been a leading force in the domestic motorcycle industry for fifteen years.

During the same month, Under Secretary of War, Robert P. Patterson announced that the Indian Motorcycle Company had been awarded the Army-Navy Production Award for achievement in production of war equipment, otherwise known as the 'E' for excellence award. Indian's production had been truly remarkable in the face of many difficulties, and was largely due to the dedication of all of the old and new managerial and production staff.

In an impressive ceremony held within the confines of the factory's vast courtyard, the award was presented to the company by Brigadier General Burton O. Lewis, Chief of the Boston Ordnance District. Robert L. 'Bob' Steele, of the staff of radio station WTIC, was master of ceremonies. After the Indian Motocycle Company color guard, under the command of Captain Phillip J. Burgess, had hoisted the Army-Navy 'E' burgee to the top of the flagstaff, there were acceptance speeches by Vice President Dwight L. Moody, and expressions of appreciation to the employees by President E. Paul du Pont. Lt. Commander William M. Saunders, USNR presented the 'E' pin to the employees, and John A. Bible, President of the Indian Employees Association, and a veteran of 31 years of service to the company, made the acceptance speech on their behalf.

Two other veteran employees also received special mention: Victor Beauchemin, whose 47 years of service went back to the earliest Hendee bicycle manufacture, and Margaret Ramsay, who had served for 26 years on the clerical staff.

Also honored were the names of 243 employees who were presently serving with various branches of the armed forces.

A very handsome program in booklet form was produced to celebrate the event, and copies of these, along with a reproduction of Under Secretary Patterson's letter of commendation, were made available to all who attended the ceremonies. Additional copies were sent to all franchised Indian dealers, and one of these mementos is in the author's extensive collection of Indian memorabilia.

A new experimental project during the late summer of 1943, instituted at the request of the War Department, was the developing of prototypes of a new military machine, designated as the Model 841. This took the form of a rather heavyweight machine with numbers of advanced features such as rear springing, shaft drive, four-speed transmission with foot shifting mechanism, newly designed hydraulically dampened girder type forks with central compression springs, and a 45 cubic inch side valve 90° V-twin engine that was set across the frame.

The new model was pleasing to ride, easy to handle and control, its somewhat limited top speed of 70mph due only to the necessarily detuned state of the engine as required for military service.

Plans were made to put the 841 into full production, but the War Department suddenly decided to concentrate on the now ubiquitous four-wheel drive Jeep as its field service vehicle, and ordered the project terminated after 1,056 models had been produced. The company retained most of these machines in storage, except for the odd dozen that had been sent to army proving grounds, and were later sold to the public as surplus at an established price of $500.00 FOB Springfield early in 1944.

While something of a curiosity, the 841 models were soon quickly purchased by Indian enthusiasts. Many were stripped of their military gear by their proud owners and their olive drab paint covered with Indian red. It is thought that about three hundred of these distinctive machines survive today, in the hands of various antique motorcycle collectors and Indian enthusiasts.

An interesting footnote to the story of the 841 is that nearly thirty years later the famous Italian Moto Guzzi concern brought out a model basically similar in all respects, but with a more powerful overhead valve engine. This model is currently favored by high speed touring buffs and is widely used by law enforcement bodies.

Another project instituted at the request of the War Department during this same period was preliminary prototype studies on an ultralight motorcycle, specifically designed to be utilized by paratroopers. The theory was that these machines could be contained in protective canisters with quick release doors, the whole being designed to offer instant mobility to paratroopers dropped behind enemy lines. Before much work had taken place on the project in the Engineering Department, however, the War Department suddenly shelved the matter and ordered termination of prototype work.

Early in 1944 Chief Engineer Briggs Weaver, together with three members of his staff, resigned to join the Torque Engineering Company of Plainville, New Jersey. It was rumored that this recently formed organization was experimenting with prototypes of lightweight European type motorcycles for possible introduction to the domestic market, when the war ended. As the war was currently at its height on both the European and Pacific fronts, and with the production of civilian goods of this type being curtailed by the War Production Board, this news received little more than passing notice. However, as shall be seen, the Torque Company was later to play a very significant role in Indian's postwar fortunes.

This company had been organized a couple of years previously by two young natives of Belgium, the brothers Jean and Paul Stokvis, who were nephews of one of the principal owners of R.S. Stokvis and Sonen, the prestigious Dutch export-import firm which had distributed Indian machines in Europe during the decade following the First World War.

Stokvis and Sonen's offices and port facilities had been totally destroyed during the leveling of Rotterdam by the Luftwaffe in 1940. The senior partners, however, were said to have had some prior knowledge of this event and were subsequently alleged to have transferred most of their liquid financial holdings to the safety of Swiss banks a few months earlier.

The Stokvis brothers in question had escaped to the United States just before Holland was overrun by the

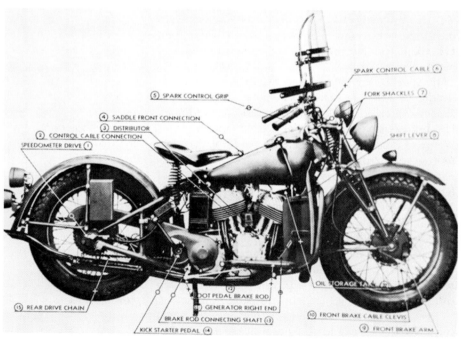

*The 45cu in Military Model. Originally designated as the 640-B Model, it was later known as the 741. The 30.50cu in model, similar except for the power plant, was designated as the 640-A model.* (Theodore A. Hodgdon)

Germans. It was an unsubstantiated rumor that their new venture had been capitalized by some $850,000 from the parent company's Swiss accounts. At any rate, with their previous experience in the world's motorcycle markets, it is certain that they correctly projected the future American interest in lightweight machines.

The Motorcycle and Allied Trades Association, which had been dormant for the past two years since the resignation of James A. Wright, held a meeting at the Lexington Hotel in New York City on January 20th, 1944. Arthur Davidson, Vice President and General Sales Manager of the Harley-Davidson Company, was elected President. Other officers elected were W.J. Greenop, Geneto Company, Vice President; Dwight L. Moody of Indian, Treasurer; and E.C. Smith, Columbus, Ohio, Executive Secretary.

It was unanimously agreed that the organization should make plans to stimulate postwar business, now that the war in Europe was winding down, and it was optimistically hoped that the expected postwar prosperity and the interest of returning service men in motorcycling could be capitalized on for the general expansion of the industry.

A sudden turn of events on February 16th, was the cancellation of all contracts for military motorcycles by the War Department. Plenty of military machines were on hand in Europe, and with Allied armies victorious everywhere, the thoughts of the high command were now turning to the Pacific theater of the war and the defeat of the Japanese. Military authorities were now agreed that while the motorcycle had served well in varied capacities in Europe, the jeep was better suited to the terrain of the jungle islands that would be traversed in the subjugation of the Japanese forces currently occupying them.

In March, the Indian company obtained new war contracts for the manufacture of shell casings and fuses for naval ordnance, with spare part production for military motorcycles being continued.

The net income for the 1942–43 period dropped to $248,033 due to the sudden inflationary cost of raw materials that occurred after the initial costing estimates had been determined for that production period.

In the early Spring of 1944, the Army announced that 4,600 military motorcycles, 1,900 of these being Indians, were now declared surplus and sold to the public. Regional procurement offices in Washington, D.C., New York, Boston, Chicago, Cincinnati, Fort Worth, Denver, Seattle, and San Francisco offered lists of the number and type of machines available in their respective areas.

In August it was announced that another 3,500 surplus machines would be made available through the same sources, about half of which were Indians. Most of these motorcycles were purchased by dealers who were eager to at long last obtain some machines to sell. The majority of them were sold to customers on order, before the machines were shipped from the army depots.

In September, the Indian company received an incredible piece of bad news in connection with its continuing manufacture and stockpiling of component parts. The War Department purchasing agents declined

to pay for these, claiming that the termination of military production voided prior commitments for machine orders. Indian's management had interpreted their contracts as covering these items in relation to the machines already produced. In their consternation, Indian officials contemplated filing a legal action against the Government, but their general counsel advised against this move as being too costly, time consuming, and altogether futile now that hostilities appeared to be nearing an end.

*The 340-B 74cu in Military Model. It was originally designed for the French Army in 1939, and was subsequently supplied to the US Army and other Allied Forces. It was also made available for domestic law enforcement and other essential uses in the US during the war years.* **(Theodore A. Hodgdon)**

The financial losses on this transaction amounted to $411,789, wiping out the $500,000 surplus set aside for post war development.

The vast parts stock, which represented the possible future assembly of nearly 12,000 machines, was disposed of at knock-down prices to dealers, salvage concerns, and individuals not directly concerned with the trade.

While this unfortunate occurrence greatly complicated Indian's now worsening financial troubles, it was a blessing in disguise for the future benefit of countless Indian enthusiasts. Many of the 640 components and all of those relating to the 741 and Chief models were adaptable to prewar models. It was obviously possible to build up new machines from a complete set of these parts. It is for this reason that so many Indians survive to this day. Even at this writing, small stocks of such parts are continually being unearthed in out-of-the-way places.

On March 30th, 1945, an article appeared in the *New York Times* announcing that President du Pont had been elected to a new post as Chairman of the Board of Indian's Directors. Rowland Burnstan, who held a Doctor of Philosophy degree in engineering and was President of the Lawrence Aeronautical Company of Linden, New Jersey was named Vice President and General Manager in place of Dwight L. Moody, who tendered his resignation. Also elected to the director-

*The 45cu in transverse 45 inch twin with shaft drive. Designated as Military Model 841, over 1,000 of these machines were built to special order for the US Army.* (Theodore A. Hodgdon)

ship was Walter A. Bowers, of Princeton, New Jersey, the Lawrence concern's General Counsel.

These sudden changes in management were brought about by Burnstan, who had obtained an option for the Lawrence Company to purchase the assets of the Indian Motocycle Company.

President du Pont's reasons for offering to sell the company were never made public. Close associates, however, have indicated that the now aging du Pont, who was in failing health, did not feel competent to continue his struggle with Indian's multitudinous problems. He was known to be pessimistic about the future of the domestic motorcycle industry in the changing times, as the whole affair had been, at best, a marginal operation during his first decade of Indian ownership.

The elevation of key Lawrence personnel to the Board of Directors was in no way a finalization of any formal purchase agreement, but was merely an option to purchase in order for them to work out ultimate details of the transaction while at the same time giving them time to assess their own tentative plans of future operation.

With only fragmentary company records available concerning this matter, much of what next transpired is open to conjecture, especially regarding Lawrence's plans for Indian's future. It is not known whether or not they seriously contemplated future motorcycle production, but at the same time it was obvious that the manufacture of aircraft engines, and possible complete aircraft as well, was being seriously considered.

Negotiations dragged on throughout the Summer, with no sign of any firm commitments from any of the principals. It was known that there was quite a bit of

haggling about the purchase price, as President du Pont was adamant concerning the value of the goodwill the company had built up through the years with its motorcycles. The Lawrence contingent pointed out the obvious rundown condition of the plant facilities and most especially the need for complete replacement of now decrepit tooling.

A recapitulation of Indian's war effort made in September showed that a total of 42,044 military machines of all types had been supplied to the US and allied armed forces. This included some 9,000 machines shipped to the Soviet Government under Lend Lease, but did not include the 1939 order from the French army. In addition, about 4,500 non-military machines were sold through regular dealer channels to domestic law enforcement bodies and essential users. In spite of this large production during the past four years, the company now showed a net loss of $617,890 from various causes mentioned. Lawrence Aeronautical in the end did not see fit to exercise its option to purchase Indian, no doubt due to the poor condition of its finances.

On October 25th, it was announced that one Ralph B. Rogers, a young multimillionaire industrialist, had acquired, for an undisclosed price, slightly more than a majority of the outstanding shares of the Indian Motocycle Company that had formerly been held under option by the Lawrence Aeronautical Company. It was also revealed that the Atlas Corporation of New York, a closed-end investment trust of New York City, specializing in industrial finance, had a substantial part in the transaction. As a result, the Rogers group now held slightly more than 30% of Indian's assets, with the Atlas Company holding 20%.

Rogers was noted as being the head of a group of companies that were producing air dehumidification and air conditioning equipment, diesel engines, power lawnmowers, electric generating sets, railway motor cars, and other equipment. Included in the Rogers' group were the Diesel Engine Sales Company, The Edwards Company, Hill Diesel Engine Company, and the Ideal Power Lawnmower Company. Rogers further announced that Indian's present manufacturing facilities would be augmented by new machinery and equipment and that all the facilities of his other organizations would be at Indian's disposal.

President du Pont formally turned the operation of Indian over to Rogers on November 1st, and returned to his family estate at Wilmington, Delaware. In failing health, he passed away on September 26th, 1950.

E. Paul du Pont's long period of control of the Indian company had been a subject of no little speculation by large numbers of dealers and owners. The controversy appeared to center around the sincerity of his interest in motorcycling and in Indian's affairs. It is a documented fact that he was an enthusiastic motorcycle rider during the pioneer period of the industry. It is also true that he was greatly taken with the sporting side of motoring in general, as witnessed by his decade of involvement in the manufacture of du Pont cars, which were essentially specialized sporting vehicles.

At the same moment it was well known that he had originally planned to utilize a substantial part of Indian's manufacturing facilities for the production of aircraft and aircraft engines, when he obtained control of the company in 1930, as well as to continue the limited production of du Pont cars. It was only the intervention of the decline in demand for these products brought on by the worsening depression that necessitated the shelving of these plans.

It is at least much to his credit that he continued motorcycle manufacture through the very difficult depression years, encouraged the engineering staff to develop improved models, and supported a vigorous competition program at a time when funds were very limited. Such dedication was scarcely the attitude of a wealthy dilettante playboy, the label attached to him by some of his critics.

William Crapo (Billy) Durant, who was as knowledgeable as anyone concerning the transportation field at that time, and who had had much to do with the du Pont family in the General Motors affair, summarized his opinions regarding the matter for the author in an interview late in 1946, shortly before his death.

From his own knowledge, Durant stated that du Pont had originally planned to combine the production cars, aircraft, and motorcycles in one facility. When the depression intervened, du Pont logically carried on with the already-established motorcycle production, no doubt in anticipation of better times to come.

It was also Durant's opinion that under du Pont's ownership, the Indian company would not have been allowed to fail, even in the depths of the worst of the depression, as his assets present in other non-related family-owned companies, such as the Ball Grain Powder Company, would have been sufficient to carry Indian operations, even if conducted with substantial losses. Added to this was du Pont's inherent pride in his past financial successes, so it is certain he always had a fondness for Indian and its consequent survival.

At any rate, the acquisition of the Indian company by the Rogers' interests at this time marked the beginning of the most controversial and least understood era in its turbulent history.

# Chapter 9

# THE ROGERS ERA
# 1945–1949

Ralph Burton Rogers was born November 30th 1909, in Boston, where his father was employed as a salesman in the wholesale woolen trade. Young Rogers received his early education at the famous Boston Latin School, where entrance was obtained only by competitive examination.

The family being in modest financial circumstances, young Rogers helped to pay his own expenses by selling newspapers on the streets of Boston before school, in the Horatio Alger tradition. As an enterprising lad, he did his street corner competitors one better by selling his papers on various street cars in the busier parts of the city, investing in the five cent fare for the opportunity of penetrating a larger and more captive market.

He graduated from the Boston Latin School in 1926 and secured employment as an office boy at the City Central Corporation during the day, but continued his education by studying law at Boston's Northeastern University at night. He was unable to complete his studies for formal graduation, but in later years received an honorary degree from that institution.

A couple of years later Barrett Andrews, President of City Central, left the company to found a chain of personal finance offices. Recognizing young Rogers' developing business talents and his aptitude for management, he invited him to join the new venture. Rogers accepted Andrews' offer, and by the time he was nineteen years old he was managing five of the company's branch offices in the New England area.

In 1934 Rogers concluded that he did not wish to make a career of the personal finance business, and began investigating other areas of endeavor. He found the field of industry infinitely more challenging and decided to investigate the future of industrial management and sales promotion. Possessed of a keen analytical mind, together with being a markedly handsome man with a pleasing personality and a persuasive manner, he was eminently suited for the role he proposed to undertake.

His initial excursion into industrial sales promotion was in association with the Cummins Engine Company of Columbus, Indiana, a pioneer manufacturer of lightweight, high speed diesel engines that were subsequently to find wide application in the trucking and industrial field.

These had been previously developed by one Clessie L. Cummins as a refined improvement of Dr. Rudolph Diesel's original heavy duty slow speed type stationary engines, and their resultant light weight made them applicable to a wider range of industrial and automotive purposes. Cummins' somewhat inept marketing and sales promotion methods, however, had not met with much success. Rogers offered to set up a marketing and sales outlet for Cummins engines, and when this was accepted by Cummins, Rogers was given an exclusive franchise to sell its products in the Eastern United States.

Under Rogers' skillful management, business boomed and the Cummins organization was shortly to enlarge its plant facilities to supply the increasing demand for its engines. Automotive historians credit Rogers with helping to lay the foundations of the now widespread use of high speed diesels in the world's vast trucking industry.

**Opposite: *President Rogers and a group of production workers pose with a 1947 Chief.* (Paramount Commercial Studios)**

Rogers' next move was to expand his diesel engine sales activities by forming a new organization, named the Cummins Diesel Export Company, for which he contracted to distribute their engines overseas.

His next acquisition was the Hill Diesel Engine Company which was purchased from Ransom E. Olds, a pioneer automobile manufacturer who had marketed the famous Oldsmobile cars in the early years of the industry. The transaction was financed partly by Rogers from internally generated profits from his other companies and through financing provided by Olds. The Hill Company was a pioneer manufacturer of stationary industrial and marine propulsion units. This acquisition gave Rogers a commanding position in the diesel engine field as with the two makes of engines he could now offer both heavy and light duty units for numerous applications.

Shortly following the Hill purchase, Rogers also acquired the Ideal Power Lawnmower Company, manfacturer of Lawn Boy lawnmowers, also from Olds and under much the same terms.

Later, before World War II, he purchased the Edwards Company, a firm based in North Carolina which manufactured motor railway cars.

Rogers' capable management expanded the activities and scope of all these companies and when the war broke out he was able to negotiate a large number of defense contracts for the manufacture of various items required for the war effort. The activities of the Edwards Company were augmented to include the manufacture of refrigeration and air dehumidification equipment, pumps, hydraulic devices and electric generating equipment, all of which were produced in large quantities.

With this expansion, the financial aspects of his nowgrowing industrial empire was materially strengthened and he was able to pay off all of his obligations incurred both upon the acquisition of the various companies and for all war contract expansion requirements. With the end of hostilities in the Summer of 1945, and at the relatively young age of 35, his personal holdings were now considerable.

At the war's end, the now prestigious Cummins organization, which had profited enormously from various defense contracts, contemplated further expansion for enhanced penetration of peacetime markets. Its management now suggested to Rogers that to continue with their original agreement, he should devote all of his activities solely to the management of the Cummins Diesel Engine Sales Company and the Cummins Diesel Export Company, on their behalf.

In his reminiscenses concerning these events, in an interview with the author in 1974, Rogers recalled that this ultimatum from Cummins left him three courses of

action. First, he could remain with Cummins and sell out his other holdings; second, he could sell his holdings with Cummins and convert his other companies to peacetime pursuits, or, third, he could retire and live off the proceeds of his now not inconsiderable fortune. He ultimately decided to pursue the second alternative, as he enjoyed the numerous challenges of the highly competitive industrial management and marketing field and also considered that he owed an obligation to the many loyal employees in his various companies, many of whom had been with him since the earliest days of his career. To this end he decided to concentrate his efforts in strengthening the Edwards Company, with particular attention toward the air conditioning field, which he rightly considered to be a growing area of a soon-to-expand market.

At this juncture, the top management of the Atlas Corporation of New York, a closed end investment trust specializing in industrial finance, who made a point of keeping themselves informed as to the status of various manufacturing firms, were well aware of the precarious situation of the Indian Motocycle Company, heightened by the stalemated negotiations with Lawrence Aeronautical concerning its purchase. They were also aware that by the war's end the Stokvis brothers and Briggs Weaver, with his engineering associates, had completed the prototype designs of the continental type lightweight motorcycles which they now hoped to manufacture at the Torque Engineering Company at Plainville, New Jersey. Their plans had crystallized into two projected models: a single cylinder type of 11 cubic inches, and a vertical twin of 22 cubic inches. Also projected, but not yet developed, was a four cylinder model of 44 cubic inches, all of these machines using multiples of the same cylinder castings for economy of manufacture. While the Torque Company was now ready to undertake manufacture of these machines, they were unable to do so as they had by this time exhausted their original capital. For some reason which has never been satisfactorily explained, the original R.S. Stokvis and Sonen concern in Holland now refused to finance them any further.

Atlas president Floyd Odium had at this time just returned from an extensive tour of England and Europe, where he had noted with interest the general popularity of lightweight motorcycles. In privately reviewing the domestic situation regarding the possibilities of a revitalized market for such machines in the United States, the idea occurred to him that a combination of the ailing Indian Company with the fledgling Torque concern, together with adequate financing, might well have interesting possibilities.

In the meantime, and quite coincidentally, the Stokvis brothers had contacted Rogers in regard to their own stalemated situation. Having learned of his proven successes in industrial management and sales promotion, they had hopes that he might incorporate their Torque operation into his existing group of companies, or else purchase their manufacturing facilities outright. Rogers gave the matter some consideration, and in due course consulted with Odium in the matter. It was then he learned of the former's already formulated conclusions concerning the domestic motorcycling picture and his enthusiasm for the potentialities of the lightweight motorcycle market.

The upshot of the matter was that Rogers purchased the Torque Engineering Company in the late Summer of 1945. During the course of finalizing the details of this transaction, Odium continued to keep him informed of the situation at Indian, particularly regarding the now apparent impasse with Lawrence Aeronautical.

With his characteristic enthusiasm Rogers, with some urging from Odium, decided to evaluate the current status of the Indian Motocycle Company. In recalling his initial impressions, he could only describe the situation as a disaster. The plant was run down, dirty, and in a sad state of disrepair. The production machinery was hopelessly worn out, and the tool room was depleted of almost all of its necessary equipment. The top management was now largely composed of veteran, elderly employees, who appeared to have been exhausted by the company's strenuous participation in the war effort. Added to this, the now apparent uncertainties regarding Indian's future, together with the now seemingly fruitless negotiations with Lawrence Aeronautical, were having a telling effect on employee morale which was now at a very low ebb.

Rogers next turned his attentions to the present state of Indian's dealer organization, which then numbered about a thousand franchises throughout the country. He found that most of the larger establishments in the principal cities were operated by somewhat progressive owners or managers, who conducted positive sales campaigns and kept their premises in reasonably clean condition. Many of the dealers in the smaller towns and villages, however, were seen to be conducting their business in a somewhat haphazard and indifferent manner, with no conscious effort to sell machines aggressively, and more often than not operating in premises that were downright filthy.

During the course of his investigations, Rogers learned to ride a motorcycle, and made the acquaintance of a large number of individual riders, so as to gain a broad outlook on the whole picture of motorcycling. One of his sources of information was John Farrell, a pioneer motorcyclist who gave Rogers the benefit of many years of observation. One of his conclusions was that with the traditional domestic emphasis on heavyweight motorcycles, the average rider was a young, athletic, and somewhat adventurous type of man, who owned a machine for only a few seasons. When he married and took on family obligations, both the economic pressures of his changed circumstances and the social stigma then commonly attached to motorcycling, caused him to give up the sport.

At this juncture, Rogers himself was independently forming the same conclusions regarding the American motorcycle picture that had been voiced by Dick Richards, Hap Scherer, Norman Shidle and Tommy Butler twenty-five years earlier. While the overall picture looked bleak, Rogers became convinced in his own mind that if individual dealers could be taught modern progressive methods of selling and marketing and if a somewhat more erudite class of dealer could be brought into the field, motorcycling could be made generally more popular – especially if a broader range of machines, including lightweights, were made available.

Rogers next conferred at length with Odium, and their ultimate conclusion was that if Indian were purchased and merged with Rogers' other companies, and if the lightweight Torque machines could be included in Indian's line of heavyweights, Indian's already existing dealer network could be utilized as sales outlets, provided sufficient financing could be raised to pull Indian out of the red. While admittedly Indian's manufacturing facilities and lack of tooling were a liability, it was considered that the presence of its established dealer organization would be advantageous enough to offset this handicap.

As Odium was already enthusiastic about the practicability of such a course of action, he readily agreed to loan Rogers $4,000,000 of Atlas funds to make the project a reality. Rogers then entered into negotiations with Lawrence Aeronautical to take over their option still held with Indian. The latter was apparently eager to find an alternative to their present dilemma, and a public announcement of the transaction was made and duly reported in the *New York Times* article quoted in the previous chapter. Rogers then formally took control of the Indian Motocycle Company on November 1st, 1945.

It might well be stated here that the immediate postwar era in the United States was a difficult one for most manufacturers, particularly those concerned with heavy goods. Most had converted their production to aid the war effort, and were now facing reconversion to peacetime pursuits under a new set of economic conditions. Machine tooling, a serious bottleneck in war production, was still in short supply. Costs everywhere were rising due to the inevitable inflationary factors brought on by the war, and many essential goods were still in short supply.

Coupled with these difficulties, material shortages were further aggravated by the inception of the so-called Marshall Plan for the rebuilding of war-ravaged Europe. This program, worked out jointly through the efforts of President Harry S. Truman and certain leaders in Congress, made available vast sums of money for loans to foreign countries to give them credits for the purchase of American goods and raw materials.

The most serious material shortage facing industry at this time was steel, as American producers had all but exhausted their available stocks during the war effort. This was of significance to prime users, such as those manufacturers engaged in the transportation industry, and resulted in serious dislocation in the production of automobiles, trucks and railway equipment, all vitally necessary to peacetime reconversion.

Rogers first act upon taking over Indian was to arrange for the purchase of the old Indian factory complex in East Springfield that had been built by Hendee and Hedstrom during 1911 and 1912, from the War Assets Administration. After being vacated by the Hauck Wheel Company in 1942, it had been taken over by the government to house an electronics plant. While it was somewhat antiquated, it was a single storey building with a very large floor area, easily adaptable to the setting up of modern assembly lines.

The old State Street factory was written off as hopeless and arrangements were made for its sale. The interior was dismantled and the worn out tooling was junked. When the news of its coming demise was made public, many old Indian enthusiasts came from miles around to view its remains, and large quantities of obsolete parts from the Hedstrom days were salvaged, along with a number of historic racing machines. Also brought to light were a large number of weird and wonderful machines from the Experimental Department that had never before seen the light of day. A portion of the building has lately been occupied by a discount department store. Rumor has it at this writing that the premises may soon be demolished.

Rogers recollects that his only regret at the dismantling of the building and the final removal of Indian's effects was the inevitable destruction of James Clegg's fine wood carvings, depicting various momentous events of Indian history.

Meanwhile, Briggs Weaver and his engineering staff were readying the final prototype designs for series production, and preparing to move their Plainville operation to Springfield, as soon as the new facilities were completed. It was decided to concentrate on two models, the single, designated as the model 149 (which was to be called the Arrow), and the 249 model vertical twin, which was to be marketed as the Scout. In their final translation, the cylinder capacity was enlarged from 11 to 13 cubic inches, that of the twin then being double that of the single, with 26 cubic inches.

The overall design followed contemporary English and continental lines, with overhead valve engines, four speed gearboxes, handlebar controlled clutches and foot pegs, instead of footboards, as was the traditional American layout. The cycle parts were the same for both models, with hydraulically dampened plunger type forks. Plunger type rear springing was standard on the twin, but was offered as an optional extra on the single, which had a solid rear frame in standard form.

The engineering staff's next project was to determine the new machine's manufacturing costs, a vital element in determining the ultimate retail prices. It was also incumbent on this department to lay out the tooling, jigs, and dies for setting up the assembly lines, but by this time post-war inflationary factors were such that Rogers was forced to revise his original estimates. Accordingly he sought additional financing in the amount of $1,500,000 from the Chemical Bank and Trust Company of New York, a firm with which he had previously obtained loans for the financing of the prewar operations.

During the course of these negotiations, Robert Scott, the Chairman of the Chemical Bank Loan Committee, now queried Rogers concerning the actual cost estimates for initial motorcycle production. At this point, Briggs Weaver presented Rogers with some tentative figures on the net manufacturing and gross retail prices of the new singles and twins. These estimates came out as $100.00 and $195.00 for the single and $140.00 and $295.00 respectively for the twin. In considering these retail prices, Rogers concluded from his own marketing surveys that at these retail prices the machines would attract a vast new segment of potential buyers who previously had not been able to purchase new motorcycles.

Rogers made it clear, however, both to Weaver and Scott, that he intended to have these figures checked by outside marketing and engineering analysts, as he wished to make doubly sure of their projected accuracy before making any final commitments on actual plant operation. He further stated that as a condition of obtaining financing from the Atlas Corporation for his previous manufacturing operations, he had formerly engaged certain engineering study firms in Cleveland and Detroit for costing and time and motion studies. Rogers had prudently followed the advice of such firms concerning these former diverse activities as his own forte was marketing and industrial management and not mechanics or engineering.

Scott concurred with this proposal, but stated that the Chemical Bank would prefer that Indian engage the accounting firm of Leidesdorf and Company which had an industrial engineering segment within its organization. After Scott had been assured by Samuel L. Leidesdorf that his firm was competent to undertake this kind of analysis, the survey was initiated and Rogers advised that these studies would require about six months to complete. In retrospect Rogers now recalls that this single event was to have a most disastrous effect on the future of the Indian Motocycle Company.

As there was now to be a six month delay before production could be started on the Torque models, it was decided to engage in limited manufacture of Chief machines. This would supply the pent up demand from enthusiasts for new machines, provide the dealers with needed goods to sell, and also reassure all concerned that the company was at long last initiating a positive postwar program of motorcycle manufacture.

In the Spring of 1946, the new Chiefs began coming off the assembly lines using prewar jigs and tooling salvaged from the State Street factory, which had been adapted for use with the new tooling which had recently been arriving at the East Springfield plant. These models were essentially the same as produced in 1940, except that the new hydraulically dampened girder forks that had been developed for the 841 shaft drive War Department models

were fitted in place of the time honored leaf spring girder type. This change resulted in better steering and handling and appeared to overcome the problems encountered in this regard in the immediate prewar models.

Rogers now decided to make good use of this time by undertaking an extensive sales campaign for the benefit of the Indian dealers throughout the country. This was to not only acquaint them with his future plans for the company, but was also intended as an educational effort to help strengthen their sales and marketing techniques, which, as has been seen, had never been well applied to the country's long-dormant motorcycle industry.

Rogers' enthusiasm, his evident sincerity, together with his persuasive personality, rightly convinced many dealers that their future survival now depended upon updating their sales operations, and in general his suggestions were well received. A certain segment of them, however, apparently steeped in die-hard conservativism, did not take kindly to the idea of Madison Avenue sales techniques invading the motorcycle business. It was also true that many of the more rough-hewn and rustic types among them found it difficult to relate to the suave and sophisticated Rogers, who personified a new age and time with which they were completely unfamiliar.

Rogers also encountered a deep-seated demand on the part of many dealers, and not a few riders, for a revival of an updated Sport Scout which had been a popular

*James Hill (left) Sam Pierce, and Ed Kretz in the pits during the 1946 Laconia Races. The machine is a 1940 factory racer.* **(Indian Motocycle Company)**

seller before the war and which had been responsible for Indian's competition prestige for many years. Rogers attempted to assure these enthusiasts that he planned to produce both an updated Scout and Chief as soon as the Torque program was well under way.

Rogers' efforts were timely in that many old established dealers were now becoming alarmed at the almost dramatic appearance of British and continental machines on the heretofore static domestic market. They were forced to realize, if somewhat grudgingly, that a new era in motorcycling might well be close at hand.

This fact was well supported by the new interest in motorcycling created by these imports. The new models were generally of good quality, light in weight, and easier to manhandle in confined spaces than the traditional 450–550lb. American big twins. Their hand-controlled clutches and foot-operated gearboxes were also an attraction to novice riders. The sales of these machines were stimulated by the fact that due to the now booming postwar prosperity, money was more plentiful, coupled with the fact that after the austerity of the war years, recreational activities of all kinds were assuming great importance.

In spite of a growing market in foreign machines, all was not lovely in the garden. The first British machines, which made up the bulk of the initial imports, were mostly 350cc Ariels, Triumphs and Matchlesses, which were basically War Department models hastily converted to civilian finish and trim. These machines quite naturally did not have the formidable top speed or acceleration of the larger American machines, nor could they stand prolonged high speed running. Larger capacity machines, mostly of 500cc displacement were substituted as soon as their manufacturing facilities became available, but, they were not rugged enough to stand up to the abuse that American riders were accustomed to handing their traditional Yankee twins. The light pattern clutches and gearboxes also gave much trouble, as American riders, familiar only with the almost indestructible domestic types, abused them shamelessly.

Another initial problem was the weakness of many aspects of their distribution and retailing. A relatively large number of franchises were secured, many of them by people with no previous experience either with motorcycles or retail trade and predictably many of these failed.

Due to many production problems caused by lack of raw materials, that beset the factories at various times, supplies of machines and spare parts were often erratic. Some distributors were forced to cannibalize new machines from their stocks to satisfy their retailers' demands for parts. To further complicate the problem,

there was, then as now, a serious shortage of competent motorcycle mechanics.

Rogers, who by this time was thoroughly conversant with contemporary motorcycle sales and marketing problems, was quick to point out his solutions to these difficulties in his continuing visits to various Indian dealers.

Motorcycle competition got underway in earnest in 1946, after the five year hiatus enforced by the war years. The Five Star race meet at the Wisconsin State Fair saw a number of veteran Sport Scout riders again carrying the flag for Indian. The Five Mile Amateur Heat was a one-two-three win for the Redskins, with Bobby Baer, Bo Lissman and Chet de Paoli taking the three top places. The Five Mile Expert Heat was another Indian triumph, with Kenny Ingle, Fred Belliveau and Woodsie Castonguay sweeping the field. In the Fifteen Mile Expert Heat, Art Hafer, after a poor start, nosed out the reigning Harley-Davidson star, Jimmy Chann, nearly lapping the field at the finish.

At the Midwest Championships held at Milwaukee on September 2nd, Hafer also won the Five Mile Experts Heat from Harley-Davidson's Leo Anthony, with a time of 4.03. He mounted up an hour later to beat Chet Dyckgraaf on his formidable 500cc International Norton. On September 8th at London, Ohio, Indians nearly swept the field at a race meet sponsored by the Springfield Roamers Motorcycle Club, winning 22 out of 27 places. Johnny Spiegelhoff and Kenny Ingle made spectacular wins in the Expert heats.

At East Brainerd, Tennessee, on September 15th, rising Indian star Ted Edwards thrilled a crowd of 7,000 spectators by winning several spectacular heats at one of the first of a series of flat track races to be held in the South.

Indian was well represented by its veteran slant artists at the National Class A Hill Climbs, held that year at Mount Garfield, near Muskegon, Michigan. C.W. Hemmis, the Harley-Davidson expert, bested Indian's Jimmy Raupach in the 45 cubic inch event, topping the 360 foot slope in 7.91 seconds. Howard Mitzell and Clem Murdaugh took first and second places in the 74 cubic inch event, with times of 9.20 and 9.24 respectively. In the Class C climbs held the following week, Indian rider Brownie Betar placed second to C.W. Hemmis in the 45 cubic inch category.

During the Summer of 1946 motorcycling enthusiasts generally were perturbed at the suddenly growing numbers of iconoclastic antisocial types of riders, with bizarre and disreputable dress and eccentric behavior who began appearing at formally sanctioned AMA organized club events and race meets. Groups of these individuals often insulted and abused regular participants, frequently resulting in brawls and physical combat. An occurrence which focused the attention of the national press on this aspect of motorcycling was the affair at Hollister, California, a small agricultural community in the central part of the state, where organized club groups often met. A large group of these outlaws took over a scheduled meeting and terrorized the town for three days. It took a force of nearly five hundred Sheriffs deputies, Highway patrolmen and reserve law enforcement officers recruited from nearby areas to quell the disturbance.

This episode was later used as the basis for a motion picture starring Marlon Brando, Lee Marvin, and Mary Murphy called *The Wild One*, whose release brought forth strong protest from organized AMA clubs. In the late 1960's another series of similar productions, known in the movie trade as 'bikers', carried on the outlaw theme, and did much to harm the image of motorcycling in general.

In spite of the difficulties attendant to setting up the new production lines in the new factory, some 2,800 Chiefs were assembled. These were sold almost as fast as produced to eager Indian enthusiasts and nearly all of them were sold against advance orders. At year's end it was also noted that an amazing total of 9,064 imported machines had been sold, 8,596 of these being from Great Britain.

In the meantime, the reports of Leidesdorf's engineering analysts were in hand, and their costing estimates tallied almost exactly with Briggs Weaver's original figures. The factory then entered into a production schedule based on these estimates. An optimistic target of 20,000 machines was laid out for the first year. Rogers was now of the opinion that if all went well, this production could be increased by increments of 10,000 units for the following three years.

Production facilities were set up by the Fall of 1946, and on October 17th an article appeared in the *New York Times* describing the new machines, along with glowing predictions as to their sales as geared to an expanding market for lightweight machines. In the meantime, it had been announced that the Indian Company had now organized an extensive motorcycle accessory department, where the needs of every rider from a tie clasp to a windshield could be supplied.

Rogers' managerial staff was now expanded and his brother, Arthur, who was a graduate attorney, moved to Springfield to aid in setting up the new organization. Rogers liked to refer to the new models as 'gentlemen's motorcycles,' in the hope that an enlarged segment of the public could be brought into the sport.

In addition to the now accelerated activities of Indian's own Advertising Department, headed by Matt Keevers,

Rogers hired the firm of Lawrence Fertig and Company, which was a well established New York advertising agency and which handled the accounts of many large companies throughout the United States. The decision to hire them was made after the proposals of several other large firms had been considered. One Phillip Luken was one of the partners assigned to the Indian account, and from all reports did a very excellent job of covering the campaign. Large advertisements were placed in several of the country's leading magazines, on a scale that had never before been seen on behalf of any motorcycle manufacturer. Motion picture stars such as Alan Ladd and Jane Russell were retained to endorse the new machines. The popular sportscaster, Bill Stern, was induced to sign his name to a ghost-written booklet entitled *How to Ride a Motorcycle*. A reigning tennis star, Bobby Riggs, also went on record as favoring a general acceptance of the sport. Riggs went on to learn to ride a motorcycle in 1974, as the result of a wager with the motorcycle daredevil, Evel Knievel.

Lukens did his job well as an acknowledged expert in his field. He later went on to purchase the advertising

*Ed Kretz on a 1947 Indian Chief at a Field Meet at Puente, California.* (Acme Pictures)

company and is presently retired and living in Palm Beach, Florida.

Small batches of both models of the initial production run of the new machines were shipped throughout the country to various dealers. Rogers again undertook an extensive tour throughout the country, calling on established dealers to demonstrate the new models, contacting potential new dealers, and promoting sales of the extensive line of accessories now available through Indian.

The Torque models proved to be very stable machines, easy to ride and control, started readily, ran smoothly, produced an acceptable power output, and otherwise performed faultlessly. Ted Hodgdon rightly praised the new machines' sterling qualities in a published road test report, but privately commented that the overall dimensions and riding position were more suited to European riders, who were of rather smaller stature than the average American. This apparently was a design legacy from the Torque's European heritage. The author, who is a rider of some experience, rode both examples of the contemporary models as well as lately restored examples, and concurs in this opinion.

The handsome appearance of the machines, with their high quality paint finish and generous chrome plating, was also an added attraction, but in spite of this and the machine's good overall performance, a number of dealers questioned the fitting of the somewhat odd sized cylinders. The cubic displacement of the twin, at 26 inches, would quite naturally be somewhat less powerful than the competitive Triumph and BSA twins, with the more conventional 30.50 cubic inch displacement.

As production got underway at the East Springfield plant, it soon became painfully apparent that the Leidesdorf costing estimates were pathetically wide of the mark as production costs had actually doubled. This necessitated an immediate rise in advertised retail prices, to the consternation of many dealers who had envisaged mass sales based on the original figures.

In addition, the increased production costs were suddenly putting Indian in a precarious financial position, with new financing a must for the raising of additional capital. Rogers' first move was to merge the assets of the Hill Diesel Engine Company, with the Indian Motocycle Company. In an article appearing in the *New York Times* on January 30th, 1947, it was reported that the stockholders of Hill Diesel voted at a special meeting held the day before to merge and transfer all property and assets of that concern to the Indian Company. The shareholders voted to exchange their stock on a basis of three shares of Hill for one share of Indian Common. That this action was effected so quickly reflected the fact that Rogers was, in fact, the majority stockholder of Hill.

While this transfusion of added funds materially strengthened Indian's financial position for the moment, costs of Indian's manufacturing activities continued to climb, as it was during this time that inflationary costs everywhere were soaring.

A bright note in an otherwise discouraging picture was the news on February 23rd that Johnny Spiegelhoff, mounted on a prewar factory racing Sport Scout, had won the 200-mile National Championship at Daytona Beach, Florida, crossing the finishing line well ahead of a large field of newly-developed WR Harley-Davidson competition machines, together with a large group of especially prepared British machines which were now making a strong bid for racing superiority.

On April 1st, it was reported that L.J. Kinder, a plant superintendent of the Edwards Company of Sanford, North Carolina, had been appointed as Plant Superintendent at Indian, incidental to a reorganization of factory production personnel.

Costs continued to mount, however, and several small increases in retail prices were placed in effect during the ensuing three months.

In the middle of July, it became apparent that Indian was in serious need of additional capital and on July 31st the following article appeared in the *New York Times*.

"Final steps in the reorganization of the Indian Motocycle Company were approved at a special meeting of the stockholders in Springfield, according to Ralph B. Rogers, President. Shareholders voted favorably upon the plan to merge the Ralph B. Rogers Companies, Inc. into Indian. Stockholders of the Rogers' companies have already approved the plan which becomes effective immediately. The Rogers' Companies, which make air conditioning equipment and conduct other manufacturing, export and sales operations, own 33% of Indian stock. Manufacture and distribution of motorcycles will remain the primary function of Indian as the surviving Corporation. Loans with two banks were arranged for $1,500,000 on a term basis and following this consolidation of net assets of Indian, on a pro-forma basis, reflecting March dividends, will increase to over $4,600,000 as compared with approximately $1,600,000 prior to the merger, Mr. Rogers stated. This $1,600,000 included $700,000 provided by the Atlas Corporation for the purchase of common shares as a part of the plan for reorganization, he said. Upon completion of the plan, the capitalization of Indian will consist of 225,000 shares of no par Preferred stock of which 210,298 shares will be outstanding and 1,250,000 shares of no par common stock of which 793,126 shares will be outstanding with 75,000 shares reserved for optional purchase by the management."

The names of the two banks referred to but not named in the article were Rogers' personal bank, the Chemical Bank of New York, and the Midland Marine Bank, also of that city.

A short time later an additional loan was also secured from the Union Trust Bank of Springfield, which had often been a participant in Indian's recurring financial troubles between 1918 and the tenure of E. Paul du Pont beginning in 1930.

As full production was by this time well under way, the new machines began reaching the dealers in larger quantities, but another crisis arose. While the models found universal favor for their good handling and ease of control, they appeared unable to stand up to prolonged high speed running. In many cases the main bearing disintegrated after a few miles of cruising at wide throttle openings, and frequently the valve rocker mechanism would come apart. A further set of problems was encountered with the specially built Edison magnetos, which misfired badly at high speeds and often burned out completely. There were also many reported failures with the shift mechanism in the transmissions.

It is only fair to state, however, that beginning or utility riders, and more sedate touring types, generally found the machines dependable for these uses. This type of owner was much in the minority, as, up to this time, the 'gentleman rider,' as envisaged by Rogers, had not yet emerged on the domestic scene in any substantial numbers. In fact, most of the buyers of the new models were dyed-in-the-wool Indian enthusiasts who expected the machines to live up to the make's long-established reputation for ruggedness and who flogged them unmercifully in spite of some admonishing from responsible dealers who were more aware of their basic limitations as to high speed capabilities.

There was much consternation at the factory when continuing reports of mechanical failures came pouring in. Associates of Service Manager Walter Brown recall him standing sadly in a large area of the factory, surrounded by whole squads of wrecked engines sent in by dealers who were now demanding some validation of factory warranties.

This unfortunate occurrence sparked a growing chorus of demand from many dealers and riders for an immediate resumption of production of the prewar Sport Scout. The Western dealers were particularly

*President Rogers, with sons Robert and John, pose with a prototype single cylinder 149 Torque Model Indian at the 1947 Laconia race meet.* (Theodore A. Hodgdon)

adamant in the matter, as this machine had been a very popular seller in that area. Hap Alzina, who was still the factory distributor for the Western states, called a meeting of the dealers in his area, including such prominent Indian pioneers as Guy Urquhardt of San Diego, Jud Carriker of Santa Ana, Glenn MacGill of Stockton, Sam Pierce of Monrovia, and Hap Jones of San Francisco, as well as some other prominent Western dealers such as Ray Garner of Portland, Oregon. This group selected Ed Kretz, who owned a dealership in Monterey Park, to visit the factory, test the ailing Torque machines, and otherwise advise Indian's top management as to what course to pursue in the matter.

Rogers' answer to this campaign was that as he was obviously fully engaged in contending with the Torque model's troubles, coupled with his continuing financial problems, it was impossible for the Indian organization to presently engage in the production of any new models or in the updating of any previously produced machines.

Dealer pressure concerning the Scout matter continued, however, from all parts of the country. After another Western delegation of dealers, headed by Sam Pierce, actually journeyed to Springfield and invaded a Company Board of Directors meeting with their demands, security guards were engaged to surround the plant to keep out all unauthorized visitors.

In the meantime, hurried conferences were held among members of the engineering staff that lasted far into the night, as Briggs Weaver, and his associates attempted to assess the reasons underlying the Torque model's many mechanical problems. Arthur Constantine, the brilliant engineer who designed the famous K model Hendersons, was retained as a consultant. It became at once painfully apparent that while the Torque machines were basically sound in concept, insufficient time had been spent in testing prototype models under hard service conditions before finalizing them for series production.

With his usual forthrightness, Rogers ordered the Engineering Department to take proper steps to deal with the problem. Confidential letters were dispatched to the dealers, promising attempts to rectify the problems, and suggesting that in due time kits of improved component parts were to be dispatched to repair defective machines.

The notes owing both Atlas and the Chemical, Midland Marine, and Union Trust banks were not yet due, but Rogers now thought it best to confer with the officials of these institutions, appraising them on Indian's current problems and acquainting them with his proposed solutions. Floyd Odium of Atlas gave Rogers his vote of confidence, but the loan officers of the banks were quite perturbed. George Doty, Chairman of the Board of Directors of the Union Trust Bank, who was already prejudiced against Indian's chances of survival, went so far as, to express his lack of confidence in Rogers, to invoke a fine print clause in his bank's contract by impounding the company payroll funds held in their deposit. As the Company at this time had well over one thousand employees, Doty's precipitate action could well have been a fatal blow to the company. Rogers, however, was able to quickly raise sufficient capital from his own private funds to cover this loss, and a crisis was averted. The Union Trust Bank shortly afterwards called their loan, and Rogers was able to pay them off, to the relief of all concerned.

To aid in buying more time to aid in Indian's hoped-for recovery, Rogers journeyed to England to investigate the possibilities of obtaining for the company the import rights for certain makes of British machines. It was certain that production of the Torque models would be delayed while means of eliminating their present mechanical difficulties could be found. The consequent lack of new machines to sell would, of course, seriously handicap dealer operations. What with the growing influx of foreign machines, Indian's dealers would then be in a more competitive position in offering English products, coupled with the fact that inflation had now driven the necessary retail selling price of the Torque machines up until they were now on a par with competitive imports.

In this regard, Rogers made contact with one John Brockhouse, Managing Director of Brockhouse, Limited, an engineering firm in Southport, Lancashire. From once very modest beginnings, this concern had prospered during the war from defense contracts. A minor item of their production had been the Welbike, a small folding scooter powered with a 98cc Villiers engine-gearbox unit that had been widely used by paratroopers in the invasion of Europe. It was later marketed after the war in civilian guise as the Corgi, and had been purchased by utility riders during the general shortage of transportation following the cessation of hostilities.

Brockhouse was receptive to Roger's proposal to set up an import-export business, as he had been considering entering this field himself. Rogers' further proposed that Brockhouse join in Indian's manufacturing endeavor, as an infusing of added capital would strengthen Indian's now critical financial position, together with offering Brockhouse a base in the United States for export activities.

After some further negotiations, Brockhouse agreed to Rogers' offer, and made arrangements to invest $1,500,000 in Indian. This was finally effected after some difficulty, as Britain's Attlee government was, during this period, very adverse to permitting large sums of hard currency to be taken out of the country.

As a condition of his investment, Brockhouse insisted that he be allowed to install his own man as a member of Indian's production staff, ostensibly to act as his on-the-scene agent. For this post he hired one Frederick B. Stote, a graduate engineer who had formerly been associated with a small engineering firm in the Midlands. Rogers recollects that he foresaw possible future trouble in this arrangement, but Brockhouse was adamant, and in the end Stote duly arrived in Springfield, on the theory that his duties were to assist in Indian's efforts to improve the Torque model.

Meanwhile, limited production of Chief models was continued, to meet the demand from enthusiasts for the traditional heavyweight twins. This was undertaken not without some difficulty, as much of the production staff's energies were otherwise taken up with attempting to solve the difficulties with the Torque models. About 3,500 Chiefs came off the assembly lines for the 1948 season, most of which were on advance orders, although there was some resistance to the now increased selling price of $1,295.00 brought about by a continuing rise in production costs.

It was during this period that a prototype Chief was fitted with the well-known Vincent-HRD 61 cubic inch V-twin engine and gearbox unit, in an effort to produce a modernized version of this now ancient design. Rogers was well aware of the necessity of updating both the Chief and Sport Scout models, especially since the factory had been subjected to much continuing pressure from prewar riders as well as dealers, a large number of whom

appeared to be willing to accept nothing less. As has been related, the difficulties of tooling up for the Torque models, together with increasing costs, had temporarily side tracked plans for V-twin modernization.

A complete Chief chassis, less engine and gearbox unit, was shipped to Philip Vincent at the Stevenage factory in Hertfordshire, where the engine transplant was to take place. In describing the event in later years, Vincent was to note that the low profile of his original Rapide engine was capable of being fitted into the somewhat limited space under the Chief's fuel tank, because of the latter's somewhat low profile due to its unique overhead valve gear. Vincent was of the opinion that a slight lowering of the high 3.5 top gear ratio of his original Rapide design, together with raising the compression ratio from 6:8 to 7:5 or 8:1, would give the heavier Chief the acceleration and speed of the parent model. During the course of these experiments, an American style hand gear shift mechanism and foot clutch control were adapted to the Rapide unit.

After extensive road testing to iron out minor difficulties with the carburetion and control mechanism, the model was ultimately returned to Springfield. The engineering staff subjected the machine to further tests, and were highly pleased with its stellar performance, both on the road and with its generally good handling characteristics.

A subsequent suggestion from Indian engineering staff was that Vincent might well consider the production of an Americanized Rapide with large section tires, more deeply valanced mudguards, cow horn type handlebars, and other characteristic Yankee innovations which might well be a more economically produced version of an Indian-

*One of the first single cylinder 149 models with spring frame, produced in 1949.*
**(George Hays)**

Vincent. But the ultimate development of such machines came to nothing, however, as the subsequent agreement with Brockhouse for the importation of British machines to augment the Indian line included the Vincent marque and rendered such a combination superfluous.

The original Indian-Vincent remained at the factory for several months, and its occasional appearance in the Springfield vicinity gave rise to much speculation concerning the possibilities of a fabulous new Chief model. Unfortunately for posterity this interesting prototype was ultimately dismantled.

In the midst of the engineering staff's efforts to improve the design of the Torque models, Briggs Weaver resigned. His position was filled by Arthur Constantine, who was given the title of Vice President along with that of Chief Engineer.

It was next decided to concentrate developmental efforts on the vertical twin models. It later appeared that initial improvements of this model came to nothing, as at the annual Laconia races some fifty twins were entered by both factory and private riders but all dropped out before the finish with magneto failures. Old time Indian enthusiasts gained no little satisfaction from the news that of all the prewar Sport Scouts entered, more than a dozen finished the course.

Enthusiasm for the Sport Scout was further enhanced when Floyd Emde, riding a prewar racing model, duplicated Johnny Spiegelhoff's win at Daytona of the previous year by again capturing the coveted first place in the 200-miler, besting a strong field of WR Harley-Davidsons and a growing field of foreign contestants.

During this period it was decided to improve the standard Chief model, but due to lack of finances its updating was limited to minor modifications. The engine was stroked to 80 cubic inches, which, while not adding much to its 95mph top speed, greatly increased its torque and pulling power at low speeds. This was of great benefit for sidecar work, or for long distance two-up touring with a heavy load of luggage. To smooth out the power impulses of the now more potent engine, a shock absorber was fitted to the engine sprocket. A four-speed gearbox was fitted as standard. Its ratios were unfortunately selected, however, as first and second were so close as to be almost indistinguishable. With the added engine torque in hand from the increased cylinder displacement, a high top gear could now well serve as an overdrive for high speed cruising. A well designed hydraulically dampened fork was fitted, with carefully developed geometry which provided a machine that steered and handled well and had greatly improved riding comfort. Now designated as the 'Blackhawk' Chief, this final edition of a long-standard model was the ultimate development of Charles

Franklin's original 1912 design. Its numerous modifications were worked out by James Hill, with the assistance of Walter Brown.

Due to the failure of the original Torque design to stand up to more severe uses after detail modifications, the Engineering Department decided to bring out a new design. The new engine, still of vertical twin configuration, now displaced a more conventional 500cc and gave promise of more reliable performance. It was provisionally designated as the 'Warrior' and was designed to fit into the previous 249 model Scout frame.

As inflationary problems were still affecting production, Indian's capital was again becoming depleted. To stave off another financial disaster, Rogers sold both the Edwards Company and the Ideal Manufacturing Company to raise additional funds.

In the midst of these problems it now came to Rogers' attention that Stote had been sending adverse reports to Brockhouse concerning Rogers' handling of Indian's diverse engineering and marketing problems, as well as promoting dissention among factory personnel. A short time afterwards, Stote was seen to be expanding his criticisms of Rogers' management to the executives of the Atlas Corporation, as well as the concerned banks.

The crowning blow to Indian's hopes for survival came in September, 1949, when the British government devalued the pound from $4.05 to $2.80. The practical effect of this was to lower the retail prices of British machines nearly 20%. As the new 'Warrior' models were by necessity to be priced at about $850.00, Indian was no longer in a competitive position in the lightweight market.

The upshot of the matter was that a special meeting was called in New York by Indian's creditors to discuss Indian's future, Rogers being summoned from the Chicago area where he had been conferring with dealers. Frederick Stote was on hand to accuse Rogers of mismanagement, citing the technical failure of the early Torque models and the subsequent loss of dealer and public confidence.

Rogers defended his position, pointing out the accrued benefits to the dealers from his vigorous sales education campaign, his continuing close liaison with the company's financial backers, and the recent development of the improved 'Warrior' and Chief models with which he was certain Indian could now successfully penetrate the growing motorcycle market and show a profit. He further added that given a little more time he was certain that Indian could be pulled out of the red. During the somewhat prolonged discussion that ensued, the representatives of Atlas supported Rogers, with the Chemical and Marine Midland banks siding with Stote.

At this point, Rogers submitted his resignation as President of the Indian Motocycle Company. He felt that he could no longer abide the machinations of Stote, who was now unmasked as John Brockhouse's agent in what appeared to be a long calculated attempt to gain control of the company. He was also now unsure of the banks that held Indian's notes continuing confidence in his management, which would be a serious hindrance to any future attempts to solve Indian's mounting financial troubles. There was also the fact that after pouring what was later reported to be $4,500,000 of his own funds into Indian, his personal capital was now seriously depleted.

Another heretofore unreported fact contrary to much contemporary and later popular opinion was, according to both Rogers' own statements and supporting documentary evidence, that the Indian Motocycle Company was never in a state of bankruptcy during this or any subsequent period.

Another rumor, widely circulated at that time, was that large numbers of private investors lost substantial sums of money through consequent devaluation of Indian's holdings. This is also untrue and documentary evidence supports Rogers' present recollection that during his period of ownership neither he nor the Atlas Company ever went to the public to sell any form of stock or other debt instruments. All the financing was therefore provided through private sources, which were later augmented by conventional bank loans.

These facts therefore prove that the only financial losses incurred by Indian up to this point were sustained by Rogers himself.

The financiers' final decision was to separate the Indian Motocycle Company into two separate entities. The Indian Sales Corporation, with Stote as its President, and financed by the aforementioned banks, was now to distribute the British AJS, Douglas, Royal Enfield, Excelsior, Matchless, Norton and Vincent-HRD motorcycles in the United States, along with Phillips bicycles and Reliant delivery vehicles.

The manufacture of Indian motorcycles was to be taken over by Atlas, who assigned the management of its operations to one of their subsidiaries, the Titeflex Corporation, manufacturer of aircraft tubing, shielded ignition harness and other aircraft components.

When this news became public, there was much anguish among many loyal Indian dealers and owners, who felt that even if motorcycle manufacture continued, it might now well be of diminished quantity and perhaps would be carried on by less sympathetic owners.

The final dismemberment of the Indian company was also a sad blow to Rogers, whose previous record of accomplishment in the field of industrial management had been one of outstanding success, as well as a source of chagrin to those who had backed him financially.

As the captain of a sinking ship, Rogers quite naturally was forced to publicly shoulder much of the blame for the debacle. It is a serious indictment of the contemporary motorcycle press and the quality of its journalism that Rogers' position in the matter was both unkindly and inaccurately reported. No one apparently tried to make the effort to report the true facts of the matter at a time when the principals involved were readily available for interview and public records existed that could have revealed the true story at the time.

This gave rise to many ugly rumors that Rogers himself had sunk the company in connivance with Brockhouse, together with the fact that he had diverted vast sums of company money to his own use, all of which were, of course, without foundation. In the continuing absence of any public defense, Rogers was subjected to additional blame by many loyal Indian dealers and riders, who could not visualize the motorcycling world without their beloved machines.

An admitted weakness of Rogers' position was his own

*Ed Kretz puts a 249 spring frame twin cylinder model through its paces on the outskirts of Lincoln Park, California, in 1950. (Indian Motocycle Company)*

limited knowledge of engineering and mechanics. But on the other side of the coin few industrialists possess expertise in all fields of manufacturing endeavor. Historically most successful production ventures have depended upon a team approach. The high road of automotive and motorcycle history is littered with the wreckage of promising designs created by gifted engineers who had not the abilities to successfully promote and market them.

In the matter of motorcycle marketing, it is certain that Rogers was well ahead of his time. As representing a stagnated and inbred industry, the majority of motorcy-

cle dealers generally were more concerned with actual survival than expansion, and their business background was such that the recently emerging modern science of merchandising was simply unknown to them.

Most of Rogers' more vociferous critics overlooked the matter of his tireless efforts during his four year period of Indian control, to encourage dealers to update their selling methods, clean up their premises, and otherwise make the sport attractive to the general public. As it turned out, Rogers has happily survived at this writing, to observe with some satisfaction the vindication of his once-visionary concepts of motorcycle marketing by the oriental manufacturers who, with the aid of Madison Avenue selling techniques, have expanded the domestic motorcycle market to the point that over 7,000,000 machines are in use in the United States today, with their numbers still growing substantially. Many of Rogers' acquaintances in the manufacturing field, and others familiar with his activities, including the author, still believe that, given a little more time, Rogers could have made it with Indian. Such is the fascination of afterthought!

The reason for Briggs Weaver's failure to design a totally satisfactory engine has also been a matter of some speculation. While he was an experienced naval architect and marine engineer, his background for producing a sound motorcycle engine has been open to question. The marine engines he designed for E. Paul du Pont in 1914 were heavy duty, low speed, water cooled types, and, while well suited to their purpose, were logically vastly different from the conventional lightweight, high speed, air-cooled types traditionally fitted to motorcycles.

Then, too, his work with the later du Pont cars was remotely involved with assembly, production, and exterior styling rather than basic engineering, as these were made up mostly from proprietary components and were fitted with the already well proved Herschel-Spilman and Continental engines.

While as Chief Engineer of Indian after 1934, he was technically responsible for the design of the Sport Scout. This model, however, was largely based on the previous work of Franklin, and while its actual styling was done by Weaver, most of the development work was credited to James Hill and other members of the engineering staff, who were long familiar with its generic origins.

It is also alleged that Edward Turner, the noted designer of the Ariel Square Four and the famous Triumph vertical twin once commented adversely on certain aspects of the Torque engine design. The story goes that while Turner was in New York attending a sales meeting of Triumph's US dealers, one of Weaver's junior engineers brought a set of the Torque blueprints to Turner for his personal evaluation. The latter is reported to have expressed approval of the overall design but stated that in his opinion the machine could never make it with its present light pattern main bearings.

Following his resignation from Indian, Rogers retired from business activity for a short time, subsequently moving to Dallas, Texas.

Soon afterwards he joined with a group of prior business acquaintances to form an investment company, the object of which was to participate in the now rapidly growing economic potentials of Texas. Their first acquisition was the Texas Light Aggregate Company, a producer of building materials. Rogers shortly took over the management of this organization, which was expanded to form a new and larger company, which became Texas Industries, Incorporated. Under his capable leadership, this has now expanded into an industrial empire which includes the largest cement plant in the Southwest, and a holding company which owns industrial properties and office buildings in the Dallas area!

In his reminiscences of the past years Rogers looks back without bitterness to his one-time association with the Indian company and states that he regards the episode as a part of his varied experience in industrial management. He recalls one sour note, however, in his parting with John Brockhouse when the company was dissolved. Of the 18,000-odd Torque models produced, a few of the staff members retain various models for individual testing and for their own private use. Rogers himself rode a twin model as his personal mount. On leaving the company he asked Brockhouse if he could take this company owned machine with him as a souvenir of his days with Indian, but Brockhouse refused his request.

While Rogers is today a well-known figure in international as well as national industrial circles, with the swift passage of time few people living today recall him as the one-time President of the Indian Motocycle Company.

*Max Bubeck, winner of Southern California's 1950 Cactus Derby, with his 500cc Indian Warrior.*

# Chapter 10

# SWAN SONG

With the dismemberment of the Indian Motocycle Company into separate sales and manufacturing entities, the Indian Sales Corporation was now owned ostensibly by Brockhouse Limited, but was, of course, still heavily financed by the Chemical and Midland Marine Banks of New York. The manufacturing of motorcycles was now under the control of Atlas' Titeflex Corporation. A part of the dies and tooling required for the limited manufacture of Blackhawk Chief and 500cc Warrior vertical twins was removed from the East Springfield factory, but much of the equipment from the Torque operation was sold.

Historical events sometimes move in a full circle, and so it was with the final Indian production, as the operation was now moved back to Springfield and into the Myrick building on Worthington Street, a few doors away from the old Ford building where Carl Oscar Hedstrom had first assembled the original production motorcycles fifty years before. Both of these buildings have been subsequently demolished to make way for a new highway.

Titeflex placed one Henry Vernon as General Manager of the Indian Division, with James Badger heading its Sales and Advertising Department. The actual production was managed by a few veteran Indian employees, with James Hill in charge of engineering and the ever faithful Erle Armstrong overseeing assembly. Purists among students of Indian history have long argued as to whether it was Vernon or Ralph Rogers who served as Indian's last President. As Indian's final operations were undertaken as a division of Titeflex, it appears more logical to assume that it was indeed Rogers who filled that office, as he was in his tenure not only titular head of the company, but was in complete control of its financial operations as well.

A little known historical vignette of Indian's last days of production was that Floyd Odium, of Atlas, offered Rogers the managership of Titeflex's Indian Division once the new production lines had been set up. In spite of the upheavals in the parent Indian company, he still had faith in Rogers' ability in managerial and promotional capacities, and hoped to obtain his services in launching the new operation. Rogers recalls that Odium's offer was somewhat attractive to him, especially as it now offered an opportunity for vindication of his interrupted motorcycle sales and marketing theories. He somewhat regretfully declined the offer, however, as he had already committed himself to joining an investment organization in Texas.

Titeflex's initial manufacture of Indian motorcycles was launched somewhat cautiously, as it was by this time well known that public confidence in Indian affairs had been badly shaken by events of the recent past. It was, therefore, decided to concentrate on Chief production, which, as a traditional model long favored by loyal enthusiasts, showed the best prospects of enjoying continuing sales.

Titeflex also planned a limited production of a new Torque type model which was now known as the 'Warrior' and was fitted with an improved 500cc version

*Opposite: 1952/3 Indian Chief, one of the last motorcycles manufactured before the Indian division of Titeflex was closed down in August 1953. (Garry Stuart)*

of the former 26 cubic inch type. This was fitted in a high clearance short wheelbase frame, in the guise of which would today be called a 'street scrambler'.

The initial sales and marketing program was now hampered by the fact that the majority of Indian dealers had dropped their franchises. Some had left the motorcycle field for other pursuits; others had taken dealerships for British machines. A substantial number of California and other western dealers had already secured BSA franchises, largely at the instigation of Hap Alzina, who had at long last given up on Indian and was now the western distributor of this marque. Others secured Ariel and Triumph agencies, as both these makes, now under the ownership of the Sangster organization, were very popular with American riders. Their western distribution was still in the hands of William E. (Bill) Johnson, who had pioneered their importation in 1937.

A few loyal Indian dealers still stayed with the ship, however, even though handling other makes. The Blackhawks were sold mostly to long time heavyweight enthusiasts on special order, as their necessarily high selling price had now risen to $1,495.00 due to increasing production costs.

The early 1950's saw a continuing interest in motorcycling, with substantial sales of foreign machines, mostly British, and continuing loyalty to limited numbers of Indian Chiefs and growing numbers of Harley-Davidsons, the latter company now greatly expanding its production.

The sales of motorcycles was now aided by the fact that dealers generally could handle more than one make of machine. This situation had not existed in prewar days, due to the restrictions that had been placed on them by the two surviving American factories, but in greater degree by Harley-Davidson. It was reported the latter not only refused to permit their franchise holders to sell any other make of two-wheeler, but also forbade them to sell any accessories not obtained through Harley-Davidson channels. These restrictions had at long last been removed in 1949 through a class action suit brought against this company by a group of dealers.

General interest in motorcycling was further enhanced during this time by the emergence of a new publication from the Peterson Publishing Company of Los Angeles named Cycle. This organization had been started shortly after the close of World War II to produce a number of magazines dealing with sport cars, which had lately become popular in the United States, as well as for hot rod and other custom vehicle enthusiasts.

This new magazine offered a welcome addition to the motorcycling scene as it attempted to offer a more objective view of the sport and actually featured mildly critical road tests of new and popular machines such as had not formerly appeared in domestic publications. This publication was shortly afterwards purchased by Floyd Clymer, who attempted to further its objective policies, both in feature articles and editorials.

Titeflex's Indian division continued the manufacture of Chiefs through the 1953 sales season. A few Warrior models were produced in 1951 and 1952 and proved to be generally satisfactory machines, but the Warrior's unfortunate antecedents had made potential buyers wary. Assembly was discontinued in 1952, after about 450 models had been produced.

Due to the small volume of big twin production, however, the motorcycle division did not show satisfactory profits, and Titeflex ordered the operation to be closed down in August 1953, after about 3,400 of these units had been manufactured during its time of ownership. This news created much consternation among Indian enthusiasts, both riders and dealers, who had been hoping that by some miracle a revitalized company might somehow arise Phoenix-like from the ashes of its once glorious past.

Small groups of riders and dealers in various parts of the country subsequently held numbers of informal meetings, the cumulative objective of which was to explore the possibilities of forming syndicates for the purchase of Indian's remaining assets, in order that manufacture might be resumed.

The most promising of these came from an association between Hap Alzina and Floyd Clymer, who reportedly claimed that they could raise $200,000.00 from their own personal funds and through additional private sources with which to purchase the Indian operation and inaugurate production in Los Angeles.

From what next transpired it became apparent that neither of them was aware of the true state of affairs in Springfield since the resignation of Rogers and the separation of the company into two separate entities.

Clymer wrote a number of letters to Brockhouse Limited at their home office, offering to purchase Indian's manufacturing rights and suggesting that negotiations be initiated. As Brockhouse was no longer concerned with motorcycle manufacture in Springfield, and in fact had not been for some years, its management did not see fit to answer Clymer's communications.

The upshot of the matter was that in the May 1954 issue of *Cycle* magazine, Clymer published a rather hostile letter to Brockhouse, accusing them of deliberately destroying the Indian company and of the sabotage of a long established American industry, and otherwise upbraiding them for their lack of courtesy in not answering his letters. Brockhouse refused to rise to this bait, however, and Alzina's and Clymer's proposal came to naught.

It is generally believed that 1953 was the last year of Indian motorcycle manufacture. But in a little known footnote to Indian history, a small number of Chiefs were assembled as a special order for the New York Police Department in 1955, and this episode came about in the following manner: As has been seen, this law enforcement body had been loyal to Indian since the early Hedstrom days, and it was an apparent tradition that no other make of machine was ever purchased for traffic patrol duties. In 1948, during the height of Indian's troubles with the Torque models, the Department purchased a number of Chiefs. In addition, it was decided to refurbish and repair a number of well worn prewar Four models still in service, at a time when the factory's supply of Four parts was almost exhausted. To supply parts for these overhauls, the factory was forced to enlist the aid of a number of larger dealers, such as Hap Alzina in Oakland, Indian Motocycle Supply in Kansas City, and Edward Nichols in Chicago, in order to round up the necessary spares. During the subsequent period of Titeflex manufacture, the Department purchased two large orders of Chiefs.

By Federal, state and municipal statutes, most types of equipment must be purchased by calling for competitive bids which are advertised in legal publications. In practise, however, when items supplied by specific manufacturers are desired, the specifications may be enumerated in such a way as to cover the possible acceptance only from the desired makers. Learning that Titeflex still had a comprehensive stock of component parts on hand, the Department decided to publish a bid that could result in a final order of Indians. The specifications, in part, called for "fifty American made V-twin motorcycles with 80 cubic inch of engine displacement, with foot controlled clutches, right-hand controlled gear shift mechanism, left-hand twist grip throttle controls, the machines to be painted Indian red".

The next part of this somewhat amazing story consists of a number of bizarre developments which the author has never been able to verify by any known documented facts. However, so many veteran Indian riders, dealers, and factory employees have recounted to the author their own versions of the matter, that it has been decided to include a composite review of these legends and allow the reader to draw his own conclusions.

It was alleged that after the assembly of the final Chief order was undertaken at Springfield, the Harley-Davidson Company got wind of the matter and built up two 80 cubic inch side valve twins to the specifications published, including the Chief control configuration and

the Indian red finish. When the news reached Indian, Titeflex's attorneys were said to have immediately threatened Harley with legal action, charging patent and design infringement. The ultimate resolution of the matter is at this writing still a mystery, but it is reported that Harley-Davidson cancelled their plans to enter the bidding and settled the matter with Indian out of court, by payment of substantial monetary damages. This could also be true, as the author has never been able to discover any legal records regarding any formal court action in the matter in either New York, Springfield or Milwaukee. Whatever the truth of the matter, the story remains as a typical incident of the two-fisted days of American motorcycling.

After the New York Police order was completed, it was discovered that enough parts remained on hand to assemble five more machines. Three of these are said ultimately to have reached Indian dealers in Pennsylvania, the other two being shipped to Texas. One of the former machines was purchased by Robert E. Stark, the son of Charles L., one time pioneer dealer in Akron, Ohio, who at this writing conducts an Indian restoration shop in Fullerton, California. As a life-long Indian enthusiast, this magnificently maintained Blackhawk Chief is Bob's most prized possession, and truly can be said to represent the very last of the old Indians.

Shortly after this final order was completed, Titeflex disposed of the tooling, jigs, dies and other equipment used in Chief manufacture. This was said to have passed through several hands and was ultimately purchased by a long time Indian dealer in Chicago, Edward Nichols, where it is said to be presently stored in a warehouse. In later years Sam Pierce has negotiated with Nichols concerning its purchase, with a view to reviving Chief manufacture on the west coast, but up to the time of this writing the matter has not been resolved.

Another little known sequel to Indian's final demise is that even though Titeflex apparently has abandoned the manufacture of motorcycles, it is still the legal owner of the Indian Motocycle Company and could initiate a resumption of manufacture when and if it ever desired to do so. This also means that the company is still in existence as a division of Titeflex, legally owned by the Atlas Corporation.

A favorite point of nostalgic discussion among older Indian riders to this day is the question of whether or not an updated postwar Sport Scout would have saved Indian. There is no doubt that such a machine, modernized with a spring frame and hydraulic forks would have had ready acceptance from many American riders. However, as a powerful machine still in the heavyweight class, with foot controlled clutch and hand gear shifting mechanism, it is certain that it would not have had the appeal to the new group of riders who were attracted to the lighter and more easily controlled foreign machines imported following the war.

While somewhat smaller than the Chief, the Sport Scout was basically similar, possessed the same number of parts, and would therefore have required almost identical machining and assembly operations in its production. This meant that its manufacturing cost and retail selling price would by necessity be nearly the same as the Chief, with the consequence that its market would have been strictly limited to former enthusiasts. It is, therefore, probable that as a high priced machine with a rather narrow market appeal, its low volume production could not have been profitable enough to warrant continued manufacture.

Large numbers of surviving Scouts were still in use during the decade following the war, augmented by even larger numbers of former military machines, both kept on the road through the availability of war surplus parts. Many old Scouts were seen in race meets and hill climbs as late as 1960.

The activities of the Indian Sales Corporation, while now totally separate from Indian motorcycle manufacture, are here included as a matter of historical interest.

Under the Presidency of Frederick B. Stote, the new organization took over a portion of the East Springfield factory for warehouse facilities, and the importation of the previously mentioned English machines commenced early in the Spring of 1950. An additional model was added to this line, the Corgi scooter, which was still manufactured by Brockhouse, but was now painted Indian red and was called the Indian 'Papoose'. As a small, underpowered machine, it was never accepted as anything other than a novelty by American buyers, and its importation ceased, after a few dozen examples had been distributed to dealers. Another Brockhouse manufactured machine, a small 250cc side valve machine with unit construction of engine and gearbox, also painted Indian red and marketed as the 'Brave', was introduced to both the English and American markets. This small capacity machine proved to be underpowered, was almost totally ignored by American buyers, was not well received in England, and its production ceased after a few hundred examples had been built during 1951 and 1952. In the Spring of the latter year, Stote was recalled to England and replaced by a new manager.

In the Spring of 1955, the Indian name was perpetuated by finishing certain Royal Enfield models in Indian red and affixing the old Indian script on the tank sides.

At the end of the 1955 sales season, the import rights to the balance of English makes were sold to individual US distributors and were no longer marketed through Indian. The Indian Sales Corporation continued to market the Indian-Enfields through the 1959 model year. On September 1st, the control of the Indian Sales Corporation was acquired by Associated Motorcycles Limited, who had lately purchased the Norton, James and Francis-Barnett companies. These records show that Brockhouse Limited, controlled the Indian Sales Corporation for about ten years.

Associated Motorcycles Limited, continued to operate the Indian Sales Corporation after 1959, during which time they marketed AJS and Matchless machines in the United States. A somewhat confusing situation existed during this period in that when AMC took control of Indian Sales, there was outstanding a separate contract with Royal Enfield for five hundred 700cc vertical twin machines that had to be fulfilled as a part of the transaction. Therefore, for a part of the 1960–1961 selling season, Matchless and AJS motorcycles were sold alongside Royal Enfield machines, which were painted Indian red and were designated as 'Chiefs'. After these machines were sold, Enfield machines were then handled under their own colors and name, by independent distributors.

The AMC group controlled Indian Sales for three years, after which time the distributorship of AJS and Matchless was acquired by the Berliner Motor Company of Hasbrouck Heights, New Jersey. The Indian Sales Corporation ownership next passed to Norton-Matchless Limited, who took over the then defunct AMC group. In due course, and during subsequent reorganizations taking place among the survivors of the ailing British motorcycle industry, the Indian name ultimately passed into the hands of a holding corporation called Metal Profiles Limited, where it still is at this writing.

After becoming acquainted with the many bizarre aspects of Indian's history, the obvious question comes to mind: How was the company able to survive through three decades of the most incredible misfortune? The answer most probably lies in the wide acceptance of Indian machines because of the general excellence of the product. The early Hedstrom models, through sound design and superior workmanship, were probably the best of their kind during the pioneer era. The later Franklin machines, while not directly descended from their forebears, reflected the genius of their creator and the inherited traditions of their immediate past. Added to these virtues were the simplistic functionality combined with an indefinably attractive styling that set the Indians apart from all other makes. Aside from appearance, the superior handling and performance gained through their racing heritage gave Indian a two-fisted advantage over its competition.

As the essence of motorcycling is inextricably combined with the emotion of personal freedom and surrounded with an aura of adventure, enthusiasts often come to view a certain make of machine as an extension of their own personality. With such deep-rooted affection, troubles at the factory or conflicts among its management fade into an impersonal remoteness that simply cannot tarnish the machine itself. So it was indeed the unswerving loyalty of so many really dedicated enthusiasts, whether riders, dealers, or certain individuals within the factory itself that made possible the production, sale and purchase of sufficient machines to ensure the survival of the company through many dark hours.

A fitting climax to Indian's last days was the outstanding sporting victories attained during the late 1940's and early 1950's, which many long time enthusiasts considered a memorial to Indian's fifty years of active competition.

In August 1948, Bobby Hill won the Ten Mile National Championship at Atlanta, Georgia. On May 10th, 1949 he repeated his victory in that category at Jacksonville, Florida. During the next three seasons he went on to win the 25 Mile dirt track National Championship at Springfield, Illinois, and the 15 Mile Classic at Milwaukee, Wisconsin. His final win was the 10 Mile Championship held in September 1953 at Syracuse, New York.

Bill Tuman scored a no less impressive string of victories during the same period. In September 1950, he won the 5 Mile National Championship at Des Moines, Iowa, and the 8 Miler the following month at Reading, Pennsylvania. In June 1952, he bested the field at San Mateo, California, for the 20 Mile National Championship, and came in first in the 25 mile event the following year at Springfield, Illinois.

These were remarkable victories considering the formidable competition from the lately improved WR Harley-Davidsons, which by this time turned out 56hp as well as from the potent postwar BSA, Norton and Triumph machines. Not to discount either Hill's or Tuman's superior riding abilities, the racing Scout's performance was further remarkable taking into consideration its basically ancient design. Much credit is also due to the tuning abilities of James Hill.

A year or so before the final termination of Indian production, the redoubtable Sam Pierce became of the opinion that the company's survival might be prolonged if a smaller V-twin model could be introduced to fill the void left by the loss of the Sport Scout. Working independently in his shop at San Gabriel, he devised a rather compact machine whose prototype included both Indian and postwar Ariel parts.

The basis of this interesting machine was a Chief engine unit with the lower edge of the cylinder spigots machined off to enable it to be destroked to a piston displacement of 61 cubic inches. A spring frame of Sam's own design was fitted, along with Ariel forks and shrouded headlight nacelle. Provisionally christened the 'Rocket', it was an interesting combination of American and English design and featured the latter's control layout. After investing about $20,000.00 in the prototype, Sam trucked the machine to Springfield for evaluation by Torque's engineering staff. While freely admitting its merits, the company decided that it did not have the funds available to develop a new model in the face of current conditions. The 'Rocket' is still stored in Sam's garage, another memento of both Indian's last days and the dedication of an Indian enthusiast.

Another and earlier attempt to launch an Indian-type motorcycle had occurred in 1948, the details of which are probably recalled today by only a small group of people.

During the height of the difficulties experienced during this time, Briggs Weaver decided to leave the company. The reasons given today indicate that he was not only under censureship from Rogers through his inability to produce an ultimately sound design in even the improved Torque machines, but he had come to disagree with Rogers over the latter's sales policies. At any rate, two other members of Indian's engineering staff resigned with him; a production assistant named Parrish and another engineer named Washburn, who has been described as a very able engineer.

These three men, with a common interest in motorcycle production, made tentative plans to produce their own line of machines, which were to include an improved and enlarged Torque-type vertical twin of 500cc (30.5cu in) and a big 500cc single. Parrish was said to have connections in New York City for financing the project which, by this time, had reached the blueprint stage.

Being well acquainted with Ted Hodgdon's sales and marketing abilities, they invited him to one of their initial meetings and offered him the position of Sales and Marketing Director of the proposed company. Hodgdon was presently employed by an oil heating firm in Springfield which was in process of expanding its sales activities nationwide.

With Parrish's assurances that he could obtain the necessary financial backing, the group began looking for an available manufacturing facility, and ultimately found an empty plant at Bethpage, Long Island, lately vacated by the Republic Aircraft Company. The New York financier, whose name is now forgotten, suggested in the meantime that the proposed new models should bear the name 'Cherokee', which carried on a pioneer American theme but which would in no way infringe on the name 'Indian'. For reasons now unknown, the promised financing was not forthcoming and a potentially interesting new make of American motorcycle died in infancy.

Carl Oscar Hedstrom passed away at the family home in Portland, Connecticut, on August 29th, 1960, when well into his ninetieth year, and was buried in the local Swedish Memorial Cemetery. During his long life he had witnessed the beginning of the Age of Science from the evolution of the safety bicycle to the complexities of the thermonuclear age and the inauguration of space travel and outlived all of his contemporaries of the pioneer motorcycling era.

An acknowledged mechanical genius, he was an innovator and an artificer rather than an inventor, yet he nevertheless possessed an early understanding of the practical aspects of industrial mass production. His efforts in this regard paralleled those of such distinguished contemporaries as Colonel Albert A. Pope, Henry Ford, Alexander Winton, and Walter P. Chrysler.

Not the least of his expertise in industrial management was his uncanny ability to incorporate excellence of mechanical detail into a mass-produced product. This was complemented by his unswerving conviction that only an honestly conceived and built product was worthy of public sale. When forces beyond his control within the company threatened this concept, he uncompromisingly chose to disassociate himself from it.

While his career with the company he helped to found was relatively brief, the solid foundations of mechanical excellence and quality of workmanship he left behind were an invaluable legacy to the company in an age when newly burgeoning industry produced questionable practises in both production and selling.

While it is known that he viewed with sorrow the ill fortune that later befell the great company that was once an integral part of his life, his stock comment was "Indian quit winning all the races". Perhaps this was his gentlemanly way of avoiding the personal complications of further fruitless controversy.

# Chapter 11

# INDIAN TODAY

As the once most popular and prestigious motorcycle manufactured in the United States, Indians of all models have become the object of great interest from antique enthusiasts, both at home and abroad. What with the increasing general interest in transportation nostalgia, attention to both Indian and other obsolescent makes of motorcycles has grown markedly during the past decade.

Due to their large production during the early years, relatively large numbers of Hedstrom designed machines are still about, many now restored to new original condition. Many of the Standard models with the later Powerplus engines also survive for the same reason. Lesser numbers of the early Franklin Scouts are to be seen, due to their smaller production and also because they were literally run to earth by a series of owners who rode them mainly for utilitarian purposes. Very few complete 101 Scouts exist, for, as a popular mount, they were usually ridden for fantastic mileages by a series of owners, and more often than not ended their days as stripped-down sports machines by a succession of impecunious boy racers.

Only about a dozen complete Motoplanes remain, due in the main to their very small original production and through subsequent hard usage by sports enthusiasts for whom they were essentially designed.

Larger numbers of Pony or Junior Scouts are still seen, due to their longer production run and because of the more sedate operation in the hands of utility riders.

Few Chiefs of the earlier years survive, due mostly to hard usage, as is also the case of the models of the 1930's. Larger numbers of post World War II models exist, due to

their later manufacture and the ready availability of war production parts that has kept them on the road.

Fair numbers of Sport Scouts are still extant, even from their initial production, due to the same ready parts situation, as they enjoyed a production run of six civilian and four additional war years as a military model. As primarily sporting vehicles, few survive with original mudguards and detail equipment due to succeeding modifications by speed enthusiasts. A few of these are still in use in various parts of the world for daily transport. Large numbers of the 640 Model 30.50 cubic inch machines also exist, but many of these have been stroked to 37 cubic inches.

In addition to the standard production types, many historic racing machines and hill climb models have survived. Many of these were recovered by enthusiasts or former employees or dealers when the State Street factory was dismantled. Others remained in the hands of dealers whose star riders borrowed them from the Racing Department. As the years passed, many of these riders and dealers conveniently 'forgot' to return them to the factory and now they happily exist as mementos of Indian's one-time competition supremacy.

Many interesting non-standard 'specials' are also about, created out of various components by enthusiasts. Some of these have incorporated parts from other makes of machine to include telescopic forks and rear springing. Included in this group are many competition machines

**Opposite:** *Close-up view of the engine details of the author's 1938 Crocker.* (George Hays)

THE IRON REDSKIN

273

of varying vintage concocted by private owners or mechanics working in dealers' shops.

The Blackhawk Chief models have a much better survival record, as most of them were purchased initially by enthusiasts during a time when it was generally well-known that Indian's days were numbered. Hence they were treasured and well maintained by owners who were usually loath to let them pass to other hands. It has been estimated that about one half of these models still survive in original condition. Most of the remainder have been resurrected and restored, either by enthusiastic new owners or by commercial shops. The current situation regarding the four cylinder models has already been discussed.

*A civilianized Military 841 model, as seen at the Classic and Antique Motorcycle Club rally in Visalia, California, 1973. (George Hays)*

Many of the Torque models are also preserved, and give reliable service if not subjected to prolonged high speed running. Most of these machines have been rebuilt with non-standard magnetos, to correct one of the most glaring early faults.

All in all, the survival rate of old Indians is truly remarkable, considering that the make has, at this writing, been out of production for two decades. There have been various estimates as to the presently existing number of Indians. Sam Pierce, who has over 21,000 customers listed, both at home and overseas, is of the opinion that a total of between 30,000 and 35,000 machines are still about, whether in museums, private collections, or in actual daily use. The author, after conducting his own exhaustive investigation, is inclined to agree with this estimate. It is also true that the number of machines tends to increase with each passing year. Old examples are still coming to light from out-of-the-way places, and

*An interesting Indian
Special by Dewey Bonkrud
with 249 cycle parts,
powered by a 45 cu in
Sport engine .*

several dozen more reappear as rebuilt machines, often being made up from spare parts by either private individuals or commercial establishments.

The Antique Motorcycle Club has been of signal benefit to enthusiasts in general by providing its members with a clearing house for the trading or sale of machines and spare parts. Many of the veteran motorcyclists of this group, such as co-founder Ted Hodgdon, have offered valuable assistance to younger members in their restoration projects by advising them of the correct detail, paint colors and finish and pinstripe sequences for various models of Indians and other makes of old machines.

The Classic and Antique Motorcycle Association, founded in 1967 by Frank Conley and based in Visalia, California, offers similar benefits.

Aside from Hap Alzina's and Floyd Clymers's abortive attempts to revive Indian manufacture in 1954, and Sam Pierce's later futile negotiations with Edward Nichols to purchase the Blackhawk tooling, the only actual serious activity in this direction was lately undertaken by Charles Manthos, a Springfield industrialist in 1972. Manthos, a long time Indian enthusiast, envisioned a modernized engine-gearbox unit that could be fitted as a replacement in later model Chief and Blackhawk machines. He leased a portion of the original East Springfield factory, and, with the assistance of James Hill and the advice of Erle Armstrong, prototype experiments were undertaken. One of the many problems encountered was reported to be the high cost of tooling up for the new units, which would naturally be reflected in future selling prices. At

this writing, however, no definitive results of this very fascinating project have been disclosed.

Since the final termination of the Indian motorcycle production, a number of machines have appeared on the market bearing the name 'Indian' which have no relation to the original product. The first of these was the Brockhouse 'Brave', as already described. Some time later Floyd Clymer had a prototype machine built in Europe which was labelled as a 'Scout', and which featured a modern lightweight spring frame into which was fitted a modernized 50° V-twin 45 cubic inch engine-gearbox unit, which was similar to the original Sport Scout. Clymer reportedly spent over $25,000.00 on the project in the hope of eventually marketing it in the United States, but its high retail price was said to have defeated the project. He later introduced a high performance single cylinder roadster machine, also with an Indian label, powered with a 500cc Velocette Thruxton power plant. As the retail price was fixed at $1,850.00, very few were sold, although the machine was an attraction to Velocette enthusiasts who were currently mourning the end of the company's motorcycle manufacture. Clymer also marketed a few small, two-stroke scrambler type machines with various proprietary engine-gearbox units that also carried the Indian transfer.

At this writing a range of small capacity two-strokes are currently being marketed in the United States but manufactured in Taiwan that also carry the Indian transfer. The legality of the use of the Indian name by these manufacturers is questionable, as the Indian Motocycle Company

Above: *Russell Harmon with an all original low mileage 1947 Chief.* (Ronald Mugar)

Left: *101 Scout enthusiast Johnny Eagles ready for a tour.* (George Hays)

**Right:** *Erle 'Pop' Armstrong (left) and Sam Pierce, examine a restored 1930 101 Scout at the 1973 Indian Day Rally held in Springfield.* (George Hays)

**Right:** *Bob Stark with carefully restored 80cu in 1955 Blackhawk Chief, one of the last Indians ever produced.*

is still owned by the Titeflex Corporation, and the Indian Sales Corporation is now said to be a part of Metal Profiles Limited. These firms, however, have not as yet challenged these interlopers in the courts.

The ownership of antique and classic Indians today has been facilitated by the activities of a number of commercial concerns who stock limited quantities of new old stock parts as well as used parts, and who also, in some cases, offer to rebuild, restore, or repair machines. In addition to Sam Pierce's activities in Monrovia, Robert Paulette in Midway, Kentucky, deals in Indians generally aside from his activities mentioned in connection with four cylinder models. Charles 'Chuck' Myles of Sloansville, New York, deals exclusively in Indian

work and is lately reported as having original casting molds for the manufacture of cylinder barrels and engine cases from Indian's original supplier, Brown and Sharpe. Robert E. Stark operates an Indian shop in Fullerton, California, as has been mentioned.

In addition to these and other commercial suppliers, many individual enthusiastic club members with specialized talents fabricate such small items as tank transfers and other small decals, tool boxes, chainguards, rubber footboard mats and handlebar grips, as well as the recovering of saddles with original type cowhide and magneto rebuilding.

Also still available are storage batteries adaptable to both antique and classic type machines. New ignition parts, such as distributors, coils, condensers, and similar items are also currently manufactured.

*Erle 'Pop' Armstrong, the beloved Patriarch of Indian.*

*Charles Vernon with his authentically restored 1936 Crocker.* (Ronald Muger)

The once numerous group of former Indian employees has dwindled rapidly with the passing years. Only a few of the executive and managerial personnel survive, most of whom are mentioned in the Acknowledgements. Ralph B. Rogers remains as the only living former President. James Hill still resides in Springfield, as does the patriarch of Indian, Erle Armstrong, now in his eighty-sixth year. A few surviving Springfield grandmothers spent a part of their girlhood as members of Indian's clerical staff.

A few dozen production workers still survive, some still living in the Springfield area, with others scattered throughout other parts of the country. Most of these men are now well past middle age, having spent a part of their youthful days as apprentices or journeymen at either the State Street or East Springfield factories.

The passing of two other of Indian's pioneer employees were noted in 1974. Arthur Constantine died early in the year at age 82. Arthur Lemon passed away in Florida in December, at the age of 87.

Arthur Rogers remained in Springfield after his brother, Ralph, resigned as Indian's last President, and conducts his law practise there.

Charles B. Franklin's widow, Nancy, is also reported as still living in the Springfield area.

Perhaps the oldest living survivor of Indian's earliest days is Edith Hendee Moriarty, who, at this writing, still lives in the original Hendee estate at East Haddam, Connecticut, and is said to be well over ninety years of age.

An added interest for old Indian owners has lately been the Indian Day held each summer in July in Springfield. The first meeting was organized by Chuck Myles in 1972, and it is hoped that these get-togethers will become an annual event. The 1974 meeting was attended by over three hundred enthusiasts, including many of the surviving managerial, clerical and production staff.

Through the passing of the years, the memories of the Indian Company's trials and tribulations have faded into the shadows of the past. The happier recollections are now kept alive for the present and future generations, through the viewing or fortuitous ownership of examples of Hedstrom's or Franklin's immortal motorcycles. During the more recent past some now-forgotten Indian enthusiast created a slogan which is now remembered by all Redskin devotees – "Old Indians Will Never Die".

# Chapter 12

# RESURRECTION OR REPLICATION

The anguish of Indian enthusiasts at the dismemberment of the Company and the cessation of manufacture has been mentioned, as well as the wide-spread speculation as to whether a reorganization of the operation might somehow come into being. The failure of a subsequent attempt to organize a company to produce a 'Cherokee' machine based on the Indian Chief model by a former production executive, Clarence Washburn, has been noted. The late Ted Hodgdon, who had been approached by Washburn to participate in the venture, subsequently told the author that the formidable problem of obtaining the necessary financing was also complicated by the consideration of acquiring the patent rights, a factor not of concern to those not wholly familiar with the complexities of industrial production.

At that point in time, however, the patent situation was in limbo. The British Brockhouse concern, who had obtained the logos through their taking over of the Indian Sales Company from the bankrupt Rogers operation, was itself dissolved with the sudden death of John Brockhouse. The remains of this operation, including the Indian logos, ultimately ended up in the control of another British firm, Metal Profiles Limited, which was an industrial holding company not itself directly involved in specific manufacturing activities. In this posture, it obviously had no intention of engaging in motorcycle manufacture on its own account, and in this context it would have been illogical for it to challenge other firms in the United States through the courts who might subsequently take over the trademarks, noting the potential complications of the time and expenses involved.

With the closing down of the Titeflex operation involving the assembly of Blackhawk Chiefs in the Fall of 1953, some of the tooling was acquired by a former Indian distributor in Chicago, Edward Nichols. This sale did not include a leftover supply of finished component parts, however, and Titeflex assembled a few more Chiefs as late as the spring of 1955.

In the meantime, and quite naturally, a number of individual Indian enthusiast mechanics, more usually as a part-time avocation, undertook the collection of both new and used parts from available sources and went into business servicing surviving machines. The foremost of these was the indefatigable Sam Pierce, who at times during the late 1950s and early 1960s criss-crossed the country, buying up all the surplus new and used parts and derelict or complete Indians of any and all years that he could find. He ultimately stated that at one time he had collected over fifty tons of such components. At his extensive premises in San Gabriel, California, a Los Angeles suburb, and under the registered title of Pierce Indian Sales, he restored and sold about one hundred machines during the next three or four years, some being of original specification, others being stripped down sport or 'Chopper' configuration. Aside from the resurrection of old Indians, Pierce's very important role in the preservation of the marque was his inaugurating the manufacture of replications of difficult-to-find or extinct spare parts to keep old Indians on the road. The fabrication of such

*Opposite: A 1947 Model Indian Chief built up from 85 per cent currently replicated components. Only the frame, fork, and engine cases are original. (Greer Engineering)*

items as transmission gear sets and their shifting mechanism, cam followers and cam gear, valves, oil pump components, and other small but important components were farmed out to local machine shops with facilities to successfully replicate accurate copies.

Contemporary to Pierce's west coast operation, similar activities were undertaken by Charles Myles in New York, the Paulatte Brothers in Kentucky, and George Hopps in Florida, who specialized in parts, restoration, and servicing of all four-cylinder models, and subsequently numbers of other enthusiasts were to engage in these activities. A young Robert Stark in Fullerton, California, contemporarily employed in aerospace work, began a part-time Indian service facility that was later to become an impressive full-service restoration and parts supply organization, featuring an ever growing number of replica components.

In again referring to Pierce's activities, in 1962 he endeavoured to conclude negotiations with Edward Nichols for the purchase of the tooling left over from the Titeflex operation. A price of $50,000 was tentatively agreed upon, but the deal fell apart when Nichols and his personal assets suddenly were tied up in litigation involving an unrelated matter. Pierce had hoped to obtain this original tooling for the fabrication of spare parts. He subsequently built up a prototype machine utilizing both Indian and British Ariel components, tentatively labelled as the 'Indian Rocket', but never as far as is known contemplated producing it. Instead, Sam had many Scout parts and 1949 to 1951 vertical parts, so he decided to build a Super Scout cycle.*

The author at this point in time was well cognizant of the problem of the ultimate ownership of the Indian trademarks and consulted with Pierce regarding his, as well as others, dealing in Indian restorations and parts sales and doing business using the official Indian logos and trademarks. Pierce stated that he had secured a legal opinion that if a bona fide manufacturer abandoned their trademark by suspending production and going out of business, the trademarks then reverted to public domain.

Pierce subsequently re-registered his operation as 'The American Indian Motocycle Company', and sold the business to another enthusiast, Charles Mathre, who moved it to Mokelumne Hill, a one time gold mining center in the Sierra Nevada foothills, and registered the business under Pierce's last designation. He later expanded the scope of parts replication.

In the meantime, other Indian enthusiasts entered the restoration and service field, more often than not on a part-time basis. The ongoing enthusiasm for old Indian machines appeared to be growing by leaps and bounds. The overall aspect and attractive lines of these classic machines blended in with the national preoccupation with nostalgic transportation subjects. The growing interest in antique automobiles was fostered by national organizations such as the Horseless Automobile Club of America, whose quarterly magazine became a clearing media for the sale or trading of needed spare parts. The Antique Motorcycle Club of America provided the same outlet for antique enthusiasts, with the added stimulus of regional swap meets that aided the exchange and acquisition of needed spare parts.

The initial extensive commercial application of the Indian trademarks was inaugurated by the late Floyd Clymer. In the early 1960s he purchased a number of 50cc two-stroke engine/gearbox units from Minarelli in Italy and fitted them to the frames of miniature motorcycles with 14in wheels, with the Indian script lettering on the tank sides. Clymer had registered the Indian trademarks under his own firm's name of Clymer Publishing Company in both the states of Colorado and California. It was later generally conceded that Clymer had simply appropriated the logos for his own purposes, but in any case there was at that time no bona fide Indian motorcycle manufacturer to challenge him.

Clymer's miniature motorcycles met with minimal sales success, as they were essentially overpriced impractical toys. Many Indian enthusiasts thought that the honoured name was being prostituted, similarly to the use of the trademarks on the ill-fated Brockhouse-built Indian Brave. Clymer's next venture with the Indian designation was his having built in Italy the cycle parts for a 500cc middleweight motorcycle fitted with MSS Model Velocette engines and gearboxes in the late 1960s. As practical and well-finished machines with proven power plants, they found a ready market, but most buyers scrubbed the Indian script off the tanksides and substituted that of Velocette, most buyers being Velo enthusiasts. The venture came to an end when Velocette phased out their classic singles in favour of lightweight machines and scooters, after about 150 units had been sold.

It must be emphasized that the United States Patent Laws are basically simple. Those applying for patent protection submit a working model or comprehensive working drawings or formulas, as the case may be, to the office in Washington. Then a search must be conducted to ascertain if the application does not cover a similar

*Indian built some prototype Scouts using the V-twin Scout power plants and the light vertical series chassis. Sam Pierce had many of these parts and in 1968 he obtained a manufacturing licence and built a number of cycles although no two were ever the same. This licence later formed part of Charlie Mathre's claim to the Indian trademark.

RESURRECTION OR REPLICATION

device or formula, or whether the details of the application infringe on an existing patent. This search is usually conducted through the services of a patent attorney, most of whom practise in the Washington, D.C. area. Once granted, a patent provides legal protection to its ownership and the trademarks and/or logos selected to identify it for as long as the owner is in the business of exploiting it commercially. But if the owner goes out of business without selling the patent rights, or simply ceases all activity, then after a period of seventeen years the rights pass to the public domain.

It was during this period that the author consulted an eminent California jurist, the late J. Harold Lauderback, then a sitting judge on the North Circuit Court of Appeals, concerning the legal status of indeterminant patent rights. (Lauderback may be recalled as the then young assistant Los Angeles District Attorney who headed an investigation of the allegations that Rich Budelier and J.F. Van Order were implicated in the suspected arson-induced fire that destroyed C. Will Risdon's Indian agency in Los Angeles in 1925.) It was Lauderback's opinion that the longer that the original patent rights remained in limbo, and the longer individ-

*A 1947 Model Indian Chief built up from 85 per cent currently replicated components. Only the frame, fork, and engine cases are original.* **(Greer Engineering)**

ual operators conducted business under the assumed patent rights, the stronger their individual claims to their use came about through eminent domain principles.

It was during the late 1960s that yet another potential application of the Indian trademarks entered the scene in the form of Charles Manthos. As a longtime Indian enthusiast, he had established a museum on the premises of the one-time Indian assembly plant in the east Springfield suburb of Hendeeville. He assembled a large collection of related artefacts from Indian history, including old machines, prototype models, together with some of Carl Oscar Hedstrom's personally built bicycles, tools and other mementoes. Like many other enthusiasts, Manthos envisioned a revival of Indian manufacture, and ultimately decided to explore the matter himself. Enlisting the aid of veteran Indian production employees still living in Springfield, Erle Armstrong and James Hill, as advisors, Manthos constructed a prototype Chief model. Utilising mostly standard components, the machine was upgraded with 12-volt ignition, electric starting, a four-speed gearbox with foot shifting, and other minor face lifting. Experimentation went on for some months, when, coincidentally, in January 1970, Floyd Clymer died suddenly of a heart attack. Knowing that Clymer was the most significant holder of the Indian patents, Manthos ultimately entered into negotiation with Clymers' widow, Meryle, who was then involved in settling his estate by disposing of his assets. An important part of these, aside from the Indian patents, was his publishing business that dealt with automotive and motorcycle repair manuals.

Manthos subsequently reported that later in 1971, he was able to negotiate with Mrs Clymer for the sale of the Indian patent rights for $10,000. But during the final stages Manthos learned to his dismay that Mrs Clymer had, without notifying him, finalised the sale to one Alan Newman, a Los Angeles attorney, for $10,500! Not being certain of the legal ramifications involved in the resurrection of an updated Chief model, Manthos regretfully abandoned the project, especially as he did not have knowledge of Newman's intentions, as he related to the author in an interview in 1984.

Alan Newman was a 42-year-old Los Angeles attorney who possessed considerable financial assets through inheritance, and who also enjoyed a successful legal practice. It was known that for some time he had entertained the desire of somehow entering the transportation field. In his articles of incorporation he had named his venture The Indian Motor Company.

As with many other manufacturing ventures, Newman established a factory in the Kao Hsung district in Taiwan, an area adjacent to the capital city of Taipei. This was a tax-free area which allowed foreign manufacturers a free hand unfettered by government regulations and income tax obligations on import and export operations, and at the same time was of economic benefit to the country by offering employment opportunities to the native workers. The intimate details of the financial structuring of the company were not at once available, but it was known that it was heavily backed by Bankers Trust International headquarters in New York, with an active branch in Beverley Hills, which was also the official corporate office location of the company.

Utilising initially Minarelli engine/gear units of 50, 70 and 100cc displacement the frames, wheels, and other cycle parts were fabricated locally by an adjacent bicycle manufacturer. Later larger units of 125 and 175cc made by Zenoah were fitted, who had formerly made these units for the Hodaka concern. This make had been briefly marketed in the US by the Pacific Basin Trading Company (Pabatco) located in Portland, Oregon.

Launched in 1972, the Newman Indian-badged lightweights were manufactured until 1978, when it is estimated that about 75,000 units were produced. These were mostly marketed in the US through a warehouse located in the Los Angeles suburb of Gardena. Sales efforts were initially directed toward the off-road market, and later to the owners of motor homes as auxiliary transportation. The presence of the Indian script on the tanksides was of indeterminate sales value on machines unrelated in concept to the originals, and Indian enthusiasts themselves usually looked with disfavour upon what was considered a prostitution of the name.

The operation was flawed by the poor quality of the frames and some cycle parts, resulting in product defect complaints from buyers, dealer expansion without adequate spare part supply, and a lack of firm control on costing procedures. With mounting financial problems, manufacture came to a halt early in 1976, ultimately leading to the filing of bankruptcy. The Indian trademark was advertised for bid in the *Los Angeles Times* newspaper as part of the company assets.

In the meantime, several additional enthusiasts in various parts of the country were offering repair and restoration services to Indian owners. One significant operation launched in 1956 was that of Robert Stark, the son of a veteran Indian dealer in Akron, Ohio, who had moved to California in 1962. With an ever expanding activity, he turned his part-time business into a full-time operation in Fullerton, and was soon to specialise in the replication of Indian components.

The aging Sam Pierce, now not in the best of health, went to work full time for motion picture star Steve McQueen, long a motorcycle enthusiast, and presently engaged in collecting antique machines. Pierce built an eight thousand square foot building in Oxnard, Ventura County, to house a growing collection, and undertook to inaugurate a programme to restore Indians for Steve's personal collection.

The increasing growth of the Antique Motorcycle Club, with the exchange of technical information and spare parts and the added advantage of regional swap meets was further facilitating the preservation of classic Indians.

Following the demise of the Newman Indian attempt, one Carmen D. DeLeone entered the picture*. An industrialist in Irvine, California, he imported lightweight 50cc mopeds and minature motorbikes assembled in Spain under the trade name of Derbi, competing in the moped boom that occurred in the late 1970s. The Derbi concern had for a few years previously been manufacturing various small-capacity two-stroke models in Barcelona. Its activities were somewhat indeterminate, as when the author visited the factory in 1982, only small 50cc units were being assembled using German-made Fichtel and Sachs and Zundapp engine/gear fabrications in frames and cycle parts furnished by Hercules, also a German firm.

At any rate, DeLeone had acquired the Indian trademarks and logos from the now defunct Newman operation during the latter's bankruptcy proceedings on January 28, 1978. To register the trademarks under his own name, DeLeone retained the services of Stetina and Brunda, a law firm specialising in patent matters located in nearby Laguna Niguel. In a letter of confirmation dated June 12, 1990, DeLeone was notified that he now had been awarded the rights to manufacture clothing, motorcycle parts, hand luggage, and retail items relating to the Indian trademarks. He had already assigned a one-half interest in the Indian trademark to Phillip Zanghi for vehicles on June 4, 1990.

Prior to this acquisition as confirmed, DeLeone had contacted the author in 1984 regarding his proposal to set up manufacturing facilities to produce replica Indian Chiefs. During our personal conferences we discussed the high cost and complications attendant to such a venture, not to mention the setting up of a dealership infrastructure were noted. After some consideration, DeLeone dropped his proposal, continuing to market the Derbi lightweights.

Another player in the drama now emerged in the person of one Philip S. Zanghi (also known as Philipo Salvatore Zanghi) a self-styled industrialist and financier

---

*Carmen D. DeLeone purchased the Indian trademark as an asset from Newman's bankruptcy following an ad placed in the *Los Angeles Times*. Stark, Pierce and McQueen bid between $2,000 and $4,000, while DeLeone bid $10,000.

with alleged connections in Europe and the Middle East. He initially set up temporary headquarters in a hotel in New York, and gave out press releases that he was organising a manufacturing company to revive the Indian Motorcycle Company and undertake production. He next moved to Boston and repeated the process, then moving to Springfield, this in the spring of 1990. He incorporated a new organisation with headquarters on East Elm Street in Springfield, and announced that motorcycle production was to be in place by 1993. He took out advertising space in local newspapers soliciting executive and production people to staff the new operation.

Just before setting up the proposed Springfield operation on June 4 1990, he had negotiated a partnership agreement with Carmen DeLeone in California to acquire the patent rights supposedly held by the latter in order to legitimise his intent to produce updated Indian motorcycles.

People in Springfield at once welcomed Zanghi and his proposal, as the state of Massachusetts was in serious economic decline due to the ongoing loss of manufacturing concerns. A combination of excessive taxation, unreasonable demands of labour unions, and stringent rules regarding environmentalism had driven industry to the southern states with their more hospitable business climate.

In the meantime, Zanghi was setting up what was described as a multi-million dollar dealer franchising program along with a licensing programme to use the Indian trademarks on unrelated diverse products. In addition, he was said to have made an offer to the city government to purchase the now vacant Tepley Street post office building for a reported $6 million.

Members of the Springfield city council, the local Chamber of Commerce, the US Postal Inspector's office, and the Federal Attorney located in Springfield became suspicious of Zanghi's intentions after no visible signs of actual motorcycle manufacture were forthcoming. A subsequent investigation into Zanghi's claims that he had several million dollars of available capital on deposit in banks located on the island of Jersey, Great Britain's income tax haven, was undertaken. This inquiry, which ultimately was reported to have involved New Scotland Yard, the French Surete and Interpol, turned up no evidence to back Zanghi's claims.

In the meantime, the author was contacted by one Wayne Baughman, a charismatic 51-year-old business man from Albuquerque, New Mexico, with claimed experience in sales engineering and retail management, who stated that he was in the process of forming a company for the revival of the Indian motorcycle. He stated that he had become interested in the make during a visit to the

Sturgis rally in 1948, and that he was convinced that American motorcyclists would welcome the presence of another make of heavyweight machine.

In a subsequent personal interview with the author, Baughman stated that he had incorporated a company in New Mexico under the name of Indian Motorcycle Manufacturing Incorporated. He also stated that he disputed both DeLeone and Zanghi's claims to the trademarks, citing Clymer's appropriation under the seventeen year ruling. Baughman went on to describe his plans to utilise an updated Sport Scout, based on original parts, but modified with 12-volt ignition, four-speed foot-shifted transmission, disc brakes, and other innovations. Baughman at this time was also contacting potential dealers for possible sale of franchises, but critics noted that as yet he had no real facilities in place, and only had a couple of original Sport Scouts on display in his retail establishment that featured leather products.

Meanwhile, Zanghi continued to issue bulletins to the local press, citing his plans to inaugurate motorcycle manufacture in 1993, and offering to award dealer franchises to qualified buyers. Along the way, he had contacted several small or individually operated engineering concerns regarding the designing of an updated Indian Chief model. Among those was Robert Stark of Fullerton, California, who by this time also operated a sizable warehouse facility in Perris. He suggested that Stark assemble such a model, and offered a written contract to bind the agreement. Stark, however, upon reading the fine print noted that in signing it he would give Zanghi control of his whole restoration and component part sales operation, and broke off the negotiations.

Zanghi registered an Indian patent in the state of Massachusetts as the American Indian Motorcycle Company in 1990, and, in addition to selling dealer franchises, was also sending out hand-written notices to both the firms and individuals throughout the country who were engaged in Indian transactions using the traditional trademarks, demanding varying sums as royalties. In some cases, he merely sent notification under a 'cease and desist' order. In all cases, the recipients ignored these communications.

In early 1991, Carmen DeLeone filed legal action against Zanghi aimed at dissolving their prior agreement citing the fact that Zanghi had been selling franchises without reimbursing DeLeone for his share of the proceeds. In his pleading, DeLeone also stated that Zanghi had breached their original agreement by withholding funds he accumulated through the sale of franchises. On this basis he demanded that Zanghi cease and desist any further use of the trademarks. Also cited was the fact that DeLeone had registered the trademarks

under his own name in 1983 (serial number 355,024).

The partnership between Zanghi and DeLeone had deteriorated, and they sued each other. Litigation was settled and as part of the settlement, Zanghi was awarded the remaining 50 per cent of the trademark that he didn't own, giving him full ownership.

Another action by Zanghi, allegedly to win public confidence, was to apply for a building permit from the Springfield city government in the amount of $150,000 for 'alterations and repairs' to an old long-disused two-storey building in a run-down section of the city. A sign on it read 'Home of the Indian Motorcycle Company', yet there was never any exercise of the permit or any evidence that the premises were ever occupied.

Meanwhile, Wayne Baughman continued to announce his intentions to inaugurate Indian motorcycle manufacture, and publicly disputed Zanghi's claim to the trademarks, citing the principle of eminent domain and pointing to the allegation that Floyd Clymer, who registered them under his own name, never had any legal right to their use. As it was, Baughman had in 1990 registered the Indian trademarks in both New Mexico and California.

An article promoted by Baughman and written by Lindsay Brooke in the British publication, *Classic Bike*, in the May 1991 issue, outlines an ambitious programme for the production of updated Sport Scouts utilising a mixture of second-hand, new old stock and newly fabricated parts. Baughman also stated that the project would involve a ten million dollar outlay, with $300,000 allocated for the next 18 months as a start up. He also announced the forthcoming acquisition of a 30,000 square foot factory. He added that dealer franchises were currently being awarded, together with a stock offering to the public that was being put in place by a prominent brokerage firm. Brochures were also circulated, showing both 1939 open fendered and 1940 skirted fendered Scout models that were to be offered, with projected retail prices of around $10,000. During this period, Baughman kept in touch with the author by telephone giving details of his current plans and hoping that he could enjoy the cooperation of Indian restoration individuals who could aid in supplying new or old stock Scout components. Interested observers, however, noted that Baughman's operation to date consisted of a Sport Scout on display in his retail establishment that featured sheepskin automobile seat covers and other like products.

Meanwhile, Zanghi continued his Springfield activities, promoting the sale of stock in American Indian Motorcycle Company and hawking dealer franchises, but without any visible signs of motorcycle production being evident, prototype designs being conspicuous by their absence. Zanghi claimed a prototype cycle was under construction by Pioneer Engineering of Dearborn, Michigan. He never paid for their efforts so he acquired no more than rough sketches. Zanghi, had in fact, engaged the services of several small engineering firms as well as individual engineers to work up preliminary designs of modernized Indians. Some of these individuals ultimately contacted the author, complaining that promised financial advances for their efforts had not been forthcoming. Confidence in Zanghi in Springfield was next undermined by his suggestion that the city government transfer the Tepley Street property to him as a gift. He had indicated formerly that the $6,000,000 purchase price was shortly to be made by a transfer of funds from his island of Jersey bank holdings (which an official investigation proved to be non-existent). His initial cycle offering was to be 100 reproduction original-type cycles built by Starklite Cycle. They were to be built from 90 per cent reproduction new parts and 10 per cent original parts, furnished by Zanghi, featuring a 12-volt electrical system, hand clutch, foot shift and other updates. One example was built, which still resides in Stark's museum.

With this disclosure, together with pressing inquiries concerning the ongoing activities of the new Indian company from now disenchanted stock holders, Zanghi hurriedly departed from Springfield and was next seen to surface in Hartford, Connecticut. From temporary office quarters he announced to all and sundry that he proposed to improve the depressed industrial climate of Connecticut by reviving the manufacture of the Indian motorcycle! Along with this pronouncement, Zanghi offered the opportunity for investors to purchase stock in the venture, and qualified candidates were urged to consider taking up dealer franchises.

Disaffected investors holding shares in the Massachusetts operation at once considered that Zanghi had moved to Connecticut in order to be out of reach of the Massachusetts courts, as matters had reached the point that a class action law suit against him was now the next proposed course to be explored.

Meanwhile, in the Fall of 1992, Wayne Baughman announced that the proposed plans for producing updated Indian Sport Scouts was temporarily put on hold in favour of undertaking prototype work on an entirely new model of machine. Designated the 'Continental Chief', it was described as a heavyweight V-twin of high tech design. An engineering team was described as being put into place. It was the Bollen Engineering Company, a prominent mid-western firm specialising in industrial design. The projected engine design was announced as featuring a 100cu in. displacement 60-degree V-twin with liquid cooling, fuel injection, and computerized control.

A new series of brochures were now circulated depicting a Chief-like machine with skirted mudguards, but with a simulation of a V-twin engine fabricated from wood! It was during this period that Baughman was also disputing Zanghi's legal claims to the sole ownership of the Indian trademarks. Baughman contended that the hiatus in trademark use strengthened the public domain issue, while Zanghi said that he had been granted a renewal early in 1993 by the Patent Office.

While the now aroused Massachusetts investors were contemplating ways and means to pursue Zanghi to attempt to settle their claims against him in Connecticut, it was suddenly noted that he had moved his operations to Raleigh, North Carolina, and had engaged the services of one Richard Rutherford as his attorney of record. It was then rumoured that Zanghi was attempting to move his proposed American Indian Motorcycle Company operations to North Carolina!

In a class action law suit a number of stockholders in the American Indian Motorcycle Company initiated a bankruptcy proceeding in Judge Henry Boroff's court, with one David J. Noonan appointed as Trustee. The latter presented a motion to have Zanghi apprehended in North Carolina and force his return to Springfield for an examination of both his American Indian Motorcycle Company and a retail motorcycle apparel and novelty store on Baystate West. Noonan, who was supervising the bankruptcy proceedings on both enterprises stated in his motion that Zanghi held a Spanish passport and was likely to flee the country. Also confirmed was that Al Dockus, a US Postal Inspector, and Andrew Levchuk, an Assistant US Attorney in Springfield, were currently looking at possible fraudulent dealings on Zanghi's part in relation to his ongoing multi-million dollar stock and franchise marketing.

According to articles appearing in Springfield newspapers, which had been featuring running accounts of Zanghi's activities ever since 1990, the latter closed his office on Avocado Street in August 1993. It was later that month that Hatchette Magazines and Conde Nast Publications, to whom was owed unpaid bills for advertising contracts, together with several engineering firms who had been engaged to produce prototype machines, forced the American Indian Motorcycle Company into an involuntary Chapter 7 bankruptcy liquidation. In September, Noonan reported that Zanghi had failed to respond to two summonses to appear in Springfield, but judge Boroff, for some reason, refused to issue an extradition order. It was then noted that Zanghi, from his Raleigh, North Carolina base, had lately been making forays into Atlanta and Athens, Georgia, in a sales campaign involving stock and dealer franchises.

Meanwhile judge Boroff had issued two court orders for Zanghi to appear in relation to the bankruptcy proceedings, which were ignored. A month later, in October, the US District Attorney in Springfield came into information that Zanghi had fled the US and was presently located in Spain. Judge Boroff then ordered the bankruptcy proceedings to continue, but with no bank accounts available, nor any tangible assets of the American Indian Motorcycle Company discovered, the plaintiffs in the action were left without further recourse.

The next chapter in this bizarre state of events involved press releases from Australia early in 1995 stating that a group of investors under the leadership of one Maurits Hayim-Landridge proposed to inaugurate manufacture of an updated Indian motorcycle. The latter was described as a disaffected Harley-Davidson distributor and dealer, with outlets formerly located in Sydney and Melbourne. It was further stated that this group had purchased the manufacturing rights and trade marks of the now defunct American Indian Motorcycle Company, and also had an alliance with Charles Mathre in California, who had registered the identical trade name in that state at the time he had purchased the rights from the late Sam Pierce.

It was further stated that the group had entered into an agreement with John Britten of Christchurch, New Zealand, a brilliant and innovative engineer who had built an enviable reputation with his racing engines. It was also reported that plans were projected to manufacture power plants in modular units of 250, 500, 750 and 1000cc for an updated line of machines. It was also stated that the Australian group was prepared, as a part of the agreement with Zanghi, to liquidate his alleged current indebtedness to shareholders and other creditors in the sum of two million dollars.

In the late Fall of 1993, Wayne Baughman informed the author that his newly organised engineering staff had completed prototype work on an updated Chief model, and that Bollen Engineering was perfecting a high-tech engine/gearbox unit. In the early spring of 1994, Baughman issued a public invitation to all interested Indian enthusiasts to attend an open house to be held on the grounds of the New Mexico State Fairgrounds in Albuquerque, this to be held during the first few days of June. The author, who was offered a special invitation, was in attendance. Several hundred interested parties attended, including about 50 individuals who were described as purchasers of dealer franchises. It was conducted on the lines of a country fair with outside vendors of motorcycle accessories present, along with refreshment stands, and entertainment featuring country and western bands.

The Bollen Company was represented by one of their engineers who superintended their proposed V-twin engine running on a test bed. At the initial public gathering, Baughman exhibited two prototype heavyweight V-twins, their design following the classic American style, highlighted by the skirted mudguards of the post WWII Chiefs. Following a lengthy address, in which Baughman elaborated on the difficulties experienced in putting his organisation together, he spoke in glowing terms of the financing now in place and the acquisition of a manufacturing facility in the industrial section of Albuquerque. As a climax to his remarks, the engines of both machines were started, but many in attendance were disappointed on being told that neither machine could be actually ridden due to certain unsolved difficulties with the electronic fuel injection system. However, a moving demonstration was promised at a proposed inauguration of a dealership in Las Vegas, Nevada to be held in September. A finale of the open house was a visit to the proposed factory location, the potential dealers being transported from the fairgounds in a fleet of limousines. The now vacant factory was an impressive 57,000 square-foot structure with adjacent office and meeting facilities.

It was estimated that the prospective dealers, some of whom were located in foreign countries, had paid Baughman about $800,000 for franchises. Many of them were disappointed when the promised moving demonstration of the Continental Chiefs was not forthcoming in September. It was subsequently noted in the trade press that a quantity of machine tooling had been moved into the factory facilities in October. At that point, all communications from Baughman's headquarters ceased, the telephones were disconnected, and it was then not possible to locate either Baughman or any of his associates. In February 1995, a press release by a local Albuquerque newspaper announced that the Indian Motorcycle Manufacturing Incorporated had but $22,000 left in its treasury! On April 7, 1995 Eller Industries (an investor in Baughman's company) filed a court complaint to appoint a receiver. On April 10, Sterling Consulting, with Richard Block as President, was appointed receiver.

Coincidental with this announcement, Hayim-Landridge's Australian group issued press releases stating that plans were going forward to manufacture a diversified line of updated Indian motorcycles, with power plants designed by John Britten, production to be undertaken in a factory to be secured in the United States. It was further stated that this group now owned the sole rights to the Indian trademarks, disputing Baughman's Albuquerque ownership, noting that their chain of title originated from Clymer's original acquisition. On a somewhat disturbing note, however, it was subsequently announced that John Britten had been diagnosed as suffering from cancer.

In the meantime, progress in the ever-growing numbers of restored and re-restored Indians had been proceeding, as evidenced by the growing numbers of individuals engaged in this work. According to the estimates of a number of knowledgeable individuals, the number of actively present classic Indians had increased from around 35,000 in the mid 1970s to well over 50,000 by the mid 1990s. This increase was due to the slow but steady increase in the number of individuals making replica components. Along the way it was noted that while large numbers of these items were not forthcoming from any one source, the substantial numbers of individuals fabricating one or more specific items had increased markedly. This included such components as rear chain guards, tool boxes of varying vintage, and latterly, mudguards in both open and skirted styles and fuel tank halves to fit both Chief and Sport Scout models from 1935 onwards. Much needed transmission gear sets applicable to 741s and Sport Scouts and Chiefs have been reproduced for some years, with the last critical items such as frames of various later years and forks being reported in 1996 as being considered for replication. On this basis, Sport Scout and Chief models by 1995 have been built with an estimated 85 per cent of replicated components. It was subsequently the opinion of many Indian enthusiasts that the Zanghi and Baughman fiascos have strengthened the resolve of most of the cottage industry exponents and that the continued fabrication of replicated components is the only assured course of preserving the Indian marque. It is also pointed out that old Indian enthusiasts are more interested in either restored or replicated examples instead of some modern concept that actually has but a nebulous relation to the genuine article.

By 1996, it was generally agreed among legal experts that it would be both legally as well as practically impossible for any firm or individual to both claim exclusive ownership and enforce the same in regard to the Indian logos and trademarks. Following the dismemberment of the original Indian Company, the use of the trademarks had been extended to the Titeflex Company under the Atlas group as well as the Indian Sales Company in the United States. Then such rights were extended to British firms Brockhouse, Metal Profiles Limited and, allegedly, Norton-Villers as well. At the same time, none of these firms had exercised their manufacturing rights, nor did they subsequently offer to challenge any of the other individuals who were dealing in or fabricating replicated Indian components. Thus through widespread and continuing usage of the trademarks, their presence on this basis reinforced the principle of possession by eminent domain.

In spite of class action legal actions filed against Zanghi's Massachusetts and Connecticut operations, the disaffected share holders and the disappointed franchise purchasers were now frustrated by the fact that Zanghi was now reported to have fled Europe, his exact location unknown. The matter was complicated by the difficulties of enforcing any extradition proceedings, which nominally did not cover civil legal actions. Those who had invested funds in the now moribund Indian Motorcycle Manufacturing Incorporated had also filed legal actions against Wayne Baughman, but with a now depleted treasury, there was little hope of any recovery.

In the meantime, John Britten passed away in August 1995, from the effects of cancer. This was a tragic end of a talented and innovative engineer at the young age of forty five, which also put paid to future prototype engine development for the Hayim-Landridge group.

At this juncture, a surprising press release on September 7, 1995, announced that a Colorado-based company known as First Entertainment Incorporated had taken over the trademark rights and logos of the American Indian Motorcycle Manufacturing Company held by the Hayim-Landridge group, which were still actually in dispute following the then current legal difficulties regarding the Zanghi fiasco. One Harvey Rosenberg, Chief Operating Officer of First Entertainment, announced that a new company had been formed based in Stamford, Connecticut, as the Indian Motorcycle Classic Kit Company. The plan was to offer component kits for the assembly of pre-1945 replicas of Sport Scouts, Chiefs and Fours. As a somewhat ambiguous statement, the advance literature stated that the classic designs would be adhered to, except that modern improvements would include electric starting, four-speed foot-shift transmissions, disc brakes – "1940s Indians with 1990s engineering".

In March 1996, another company, Evo Indian, was marketing the items to camouflage the modern Harley Dressers to look like Indian Chiefs, while at the same time a new 'Ace Advantage' motorcycle debuted at Daytona Beach. This was an Indian look-alike, powered by a 93cu in S&S motor and scheduled for production in Charleston, South Carolina.

In an opposing action, the Sterling Consulting Corporation of Englewood, Colorado, released a statement on February 7, 1996 that David J. Noonan and Richard A. Block would be available Thursday, March 7, 1996, at the Klassic Museum at Daytona to answer questions from the legitimate motorcycle press concerning future plans for a revival of Indian motorcycles.

Mr Noonan was noted as the Trustee in bankruptcy action known as Re: Indian Motorcycle Company, Inc, in Re: Indian Motorcycle Manufacturing Company and Re: Indian Motorcycle Apparel Company, Inc. Cases numbered 93-41354-HJB, 94-42288-HJB, 93-41955-HJB, in the United States Bankruptcy Court for the District of Massachusetts. These were all Zanghi's companies.

Mr Block was mentioned as the President of the Sterling Consulting Corporation, the Receiver in the action known as Eller Industries, Inc, versus the Indian Manufacturing, Inc, United States District Court for the District of Colorado, Case number Z-777.

It was also noted that pursuant to the actions in both Massachusetts and Colorado that the Trustee and the Receiver consolidated all material aspects of the Indian Motorcycle matter including trademark rights and any partially developed prototype motorcycles.

It was thought that the above action was instigated by First Entertainment, Inc., in order to convey the impression that they somehow had legal control of certain of the original Indian trademarks.

In subsequent press releases to the motorcycle trade, First Entertainment, Inc., announced that it held controlling interests in five distinct marketing segments including: Video, Radio, Film, Live Entertainment and Copyright Properties, and now claimed that they owned worldwide licensing rights to Indian Motorcycle logos and trademarks. They were to pay $2.3 million to Block/Noonan.

Mention was also made of First Entertainment rights to the design and manufacture of "Classic Indian Motorcycle Kits", which are described as precise operating replicas of classic pre-1945 Indians. First Entertainment was also mentioned as having established the rights to manufacture and market a full line of Indian motorcycle ancillary goods, such as apparel and novelties, as well as having franchise rights to Indian motorcycle cafes and dining establishments.

President Goldberg also announced that a firm called OTC Communications has been retained by First Entertainment to represent them to the investment community. OTC President Geoffrey J. Eiten was described as having 20 years experience in the investment field, as well as in marketing corporate trademarks for retail licensing. By February 1996, First Entertainment did not make scheduled payments, so Block/Noonan cancelled the trademark sale.

Motorcyclists in general who became aware of the intensive publicity put forth by First Entertainment were quite sceptical of their extravagant claims. They recalled the announcements of both Zanghi and Baughman that promised so much but produced no results. Then too, the problems facing any organisation contemplating indus-

trial production at the turn of the twentieth century are formidable. Several prominent experienced experts in industrial production have told the author that it would require a minimum of $30 million to complete prototype development and tooling facilities for a new motorcycle, with an additional $70 million for plant acquisition, setting up a dealer infrastructure, sales and marketing facilities, and sufficient capital for initial operations. Then there is the spectre of the legal implications of product liability.

The recent success of Harley-Davidson in reviving the popularity of the traditional heavyweight American motorcycle has prompted the thought that a revived Indian could benefit from this trend. But in the meantime, late 1995 and early 1996 saw announcements of replicas of this type from the leading Japanese manufacturers, offering formidable competition to the possible development of a new American machine.

In a review of the former ill-fated attempts to promote an Indian revival, a sad story of fraud and deceit is left for contemplation by investors and would-be franchise purchasers. Baughman has been reported as incommunicado, but with numerous law suits pending from disappointed investors. Zanghi was said to have collected $800,000 from similar sources and used the money to buy luxuries including a Ferrari automobile, Rolex watches, and fur coats for women friends. In addition, he gave about $42,000 of investors' funds to his daughter, and over $500,000 was funnelled into his personal bank accounts. In addition, after he fled the country, it was revealed that both the Internal Revenue Service as well as the Security and Exchange Commission had prepared warrants for his arrest.*

While there has been a great deal of interest within the motorcycle community regarding the possibilities of a revival of Indian through the years, the question remains as to whether old Indian enthusiasts would accept a latterly conceived concept that by necessity would be unrelated generically to the originals. The present viable market for original or restored machines, and the widespread interest in building up machines from replicated components illustrates a firm loyalty to the 'real' Indian example. In any case, and in spite of the scepticism sparked by the failure of responsible parties to actually produce an honest revival, the healthy extent of the building of replicated machines shows that this road is producing substantial results in keeping the Indian name alive. The present viability of the various large and small industries that support this trend is ample proof of its support from Indian enthusiasts.

*After 1996 Zanghi was back on US soil and served prison time. See the Postscript for this story.

# Postscript

Following the events of 1996, the Indian attempts did not stop. The old Indian slogan was "There is magic in the name Indian". The belief in this is shown by these continuing happenings.

In conclusion to one of the previous fiascos, by 1997 the law caught up with Philip Zanghi. He was sentenced to prison as evidenced by this account from the *Connecticut Post* on December 18th, 1997.

---

### Ex-state businessman jailed

SPRINGFIELD, Mass. – Philip Zanghi II is facing anything but an easy ride.

The former Connecticut businessman who bilked investors out of $830,000 with a scheme to reopen the Indian Motorcycle Co. was sentenced Tuesday to 7½ years in federal prison.

His sentence will be broken down into a term of 90 months in prison with three years supervised release. Zanghi was also ordered in Springfield District Court to pay $694,333 in restitution said U.S. Attorney Andrew Levchuk.

In August, Zanghi, formerly of Avon, Conn. was convicted of 12 counts of securities fraud, six counts of money laundering and three counts of tax evasion.

Zanghi, 50, who now lives in Mission Viejo, Calif., had maintained that he seriously attempted to revive Indian Motorcycle; which made its famous large motorcycles between 1901 and 1954.

Government prosecutors said while Zanghi claimed to want to open a Connecticut plant to resume production of the motorcycles, he did little but license T-shirts before moving to North Carolina.

Zanghi used the proceeds from stock sales and licensing agreements to finance a luxurious lifestyle with a Rolls-Royce, Ferrari, furs, Rolex watches and international travel, Levchuk said.

Zanghi's companies ended up in U.S. Bankruptcy Court.

---

By September 1996 the trustee for Zanghi's empire (David Noonan) and the receiver for Baughman's empire (Sterling Consulting Corp. – Richard Block) had agreed to set their differences aside. They joined forces to try and resolve the tangle of lawsuits and bankruptcies surrounding the effort to bring back the Indian.

First Entertainment, also known as Indian Motorcycle Classic Kit Company, was out of the picture by February 1996, since they failed to make the scheduled $2.3 million payments for the trademark. Noonan cancelled the purchase agreement.

Noonan and Sterling asked for the bankruptcy court approval to transfer all the trademark assets into a corporation they would jointly control. Once consolidated, they planned to issue the legitimate license agreements and then take bids on the portion of the company that wouldn't be held by current creditors. In addition they anticipated no problem raising $30 to $40 million to capitalize the company.

Eller Industries, whose president was Lonnie Labriola, was one of the major investors in Baughman's fiasco, and had fought Baughman in court, on various issues, for several years. Based in Niwot, Colorado, Eller now claimed trademark control and announced their plans to build a new line of Indian Motorcycles.

Eller was making attempts to pull all factions of the Indian community together. Various others also claiming rights to the Indian name (Charlie Mathre of American Indian, Jim Sutter of Indian Motorcycle Supply, amongst others) were causing more court problems. They were then 'bought out' to get them out of the trademark battle.

Eller, now renamed The Indian Motorcycle Company, came out with a corporate plan and overview.

Two prototype cycles were to be unveiled in November 1998. Roush Engineering was retained to do the prototype engine and chassis, with the design work being carried out by James Parker. Roush Engineering was responsible for many successful programmes with Ford, Harley-Davidson, Dodge and Chrysler. A prototype twin-cylinder was built and presented at a formal unveiling in 1998, but in the end they didn't get their legal rights through the courts to manufacture their Indian version.

A group of investors was formed who somehow obtained rights to the Indian name by court edict. They had a short time span to produce a prototype cycle, or give up their trademark claim. Starklite Cycle was approached with the possibility of purchasing the prototype built for Zanghi. In the meantime they also looked at a cycle company in Gilroy, California that was producing look-alike Harley-Davidsons, using S&S Power Plants. This plant was already producing cycles so an alliance was made.

In 1999 this company was called Indian Motorcycle of Gilroy and introduced the new Indian cycles. The first ones were the Harley look-alikes with Indian-type skirted fenders, Indian tank emblems (first 200 sets were not yet available, so they were purchased from Starklite Cycle), and miscellaneous Indian items.

This company expanded, building three models: Scout, Spirit and Chief. They all used S&S Power Plants through 2001. For 2002 and 2003 the Chief models had their own proprietary engine units, a 100 cubic inch V-twin motor.

In late 2002 a market survey revealed that riders wanted a cycle that looked more like the original pre-1953 Indians. Various parts were sent to Starklite Cycle to build a prototype. This prototype was used as the basis for what would become the last model that this company would build, the Vintage Chief.

By 2003 the Indian Company had established a fairly decent dealer network and extensive programme for their business plans. They were selling all the cycles that they produced, so sales were not a problem. The main problem was that their business development had a tremendously high overhead cost. I personally visited the plant and spoke with the employees, and I was told that the production rate needed to be 70 units per day to break even with the overhead costs. The production rate was approximately 25 units per day, so the company was losing money.

The main investor in the company was the Audax Management Company, LLC from Boston, Massachusetts. The investor company was represented by Jay Jester and Geoffrey Rehnert along with a few others, and when they saw that Indian was not on a profitable path, the financial plug was pulled. In September 2003 Indian Motorcycle elected to be liquidated through an assignment for the benefit of creditors process, managed by CMA Business Credit Services in Burbank, California.

The liquidation process resulted in the company being sold off in three categories. The first was the parts inventory, machinery, tooling, a few 2004 production cycles, which were due for release soon, and two prototype cycles being developed for future use. The second category was the buildings and property and the third was the trademark and all intellectual rights.

During this same time frame, another Indian production effort was in progress, to have a modern four-cylinder model based on the roots of original Indian Fours. This was spearheaded by Alan Forbes. Production was to take place in the United Kingdom and the cycle was to be sold as an Indian Four in the UK. Not wanting to get involved in the trademark wars, it would be marketed as the Dakota Four in the United States, beginning in 2004. There was a great similarity between this and the four-cylinder model that Eller proposed to build. Alan visited me during this time frame, along with one of these cycles. I got to ride it and was very favourably impressed.

Now, back to the final history of the Gilroy Indian Company and what has happened to bring us up to date.

The fate of the Indian factory is now a matter of record. On January 21st, 2004, a crowd gathered at the now defunct motorcycle maker's Gilroy, California factory. Bill Melvin, a retail liquidator, opened the building to buyers, who bought tools, storage items and miscellaneous motorcycle parts. The building itself was sold to Ken Gimelli, a developer and vineyard owner, for $3.35 million. Gimelli said he plans to rent the building to anyone who is interested, but would not play a role in encouraging a new owner to build cycles in Gilroy. Indian's liquidation broker say they expect to sell the Indian trademarks sometime soon.

The final chapter of the Indian saga to date begins with the announcement on July 26th, 2004 that Stellican Ltd, a London-based private equity firm, had just acquired the trademarks and intellectual property of Indian.

Stellican is the current owner of Chris Craft Boats, which they purchased in the year 2000 from the bankruptcy of Outboard Marine Corporation. They have now made Chris Craft a profitable company and plan to do the same with Indian. Other successful turnarounds by Stellican include the Italian boat builder, Riva, and the Italian premier league soccer team, Vicenza. Stellican is headed by Stephen Julius (Managing Partner) and David Wright (Partner).

It took nearly two years, but on July 20th, 2006, the new Indian Motorcycle Company announced that a new home had been selected. It was at Kings Mountain, North Carolina. This is 37 miles west of Charlotte in Cleveland county. The site consists of 11 acres of property and a 40,000sq ft manufacturing facility, which is expandable to 125,000sq ft.

To head up the product development team, Geoffrey Burgess, a renowned motorcycle engineer and product development expert was hired. He has a long history in many large motorcycle companies.

Another three years have now passed. There were many updated information sheets sent out in the interim, but now ads are beginning to appear in motorcycle magazines for the new 2009 Indian models, and the company is now displaying prototypes at the large cycle functions and prime locations.

The company claims they are aiming for a low-production, high-quality cycle, with projected prices of between $31,000 and $36,000 depending on model. At the time of writing, scheduled release is April 2009 and a few dealerships have been established and have 2009 models in their showrooms.

Now come the real questions. Is the trademark controversy over? Will Stellican succeed in successfully bringing back the Indian name? What will be the effect on the pre-1953 Indian community? It has been a long and complex battle with many versions of Indian showing up. When will the magic in the name Indian become ineffective for sales? These are the questions that the next generation will have to answer.

In conclusion, let's go back to where it all started, the original Indian factory. This is located in Springfield, Massachusetts and was abandoned by Indian in 1964. The structure is triangular with two sides being the length of two football fields, and the third side about one football field in length with an average height of six stories with an open centre section. Part of it has been torn down, part is still standing in poor shape, and part has been converted to apartments called 'The Indian Motorcycle Apartments'. The cycles are gone, but at least the building remains. For us of the older generation, this will always be the home of the Indian.

**Bob Stark**

# THE CROCKER

The story of the ill-fated Crocker motorcycle, while an entirely unrelated make of machine, deserves mention in connection with Indian history as its design was based on Indian lines and its originator and many of the people connected with its manufacture were at one time or another involved in Indian affairs.

Albert G. Crocker was born in 1882, and as a young man attended the University of Illinois, where he studied engineering. He left college after a couple of years to join the Aurora Automatic Machine Company in nearby Aurora where he was employed in the design section of the department that manufactured Thor motorcycles. He became a factory competition rider and won several contests on the old 'White' Thor big twins during the 1907 and 1908 seasons. In 1909 he resigned from Thor and secured a position in Indian's Engineering Department, where his work impressed both Hedstrom and Hendee. In 1911 the latter sent him to San Francisco, to manage the Parts Department of the newly-opened factory branch in that city under the direction of 'Hop' Hopkins, a pioneer west coast motorcyclist. One of Crocker's co-workers was a young competition rider named Hap Alzina, who had just joined the organization as a mechanic. The factory opened a branch in Denver, Colorado in February 1919, and Crocker was appointed as its manager. He resigned from this position in 1924 and took over the Indian dealership in Kansas City, Missouri which ultimately became a distributorship for several midwestern states.

In 1925, Crocker married Mrs. Gertrude Jefford Hasha, the widow of Eddie Hasha, a member of the Indian factory racing team who, among several other riders, was killed in a spectacular crash when several of them went over the banking of the board track at Newark, New Jersey in 1912. Mrs Hasha, a native of Denver, had returned to that city and was employed in the Indian factory branch as office manager, where the two met. The Crockers later had one child, a son, who today manages a machine shop.

Like many another midwesterners of those days, Crocker felt the urge to move to California. In 1928, he negotiated the purchase of the Freed Cycle Company of Los Angeles, which firm had briefly held the Indian distributorship for southern California since the recent death of C. Will Risdon, the pioneer Los Angeles dealer. He sold his Kansas City dealership to Earl Harding, and moved to California that August. He moved the business to a large building at 1346 Venice Boulevard, where, in addition to handling Indian machines, he also entered into a contract with the factory to supply them with crankpins and other small parts fabricated in his machine shop. His shop foreman was Paul A. Bigsby, a pioneer motorcyclist and competition rider who had also been a race promoter. A gifted mechanic and practical engineer, Bigsby at one time had devised a proprietary overhead valve and hemispherical combustion chamber arrangement for fitting to Indian Chiefs and Scouts. The business prospered under Crocker's experienced managership and, as this was the heyday of the 101 Scout, large numbers were sold or distributed in the southern California area. Bigsby formed a motorcycle club for Scout enthusiasts which was called the Los Angeles Forty-Five Inch Club, and catered to sporting and competition enthusiasts.

As a paradox to the general decline in motorcycle sales in the depression years of the 1930's, there had developed a lively interest in flat track racing, which originated in New Zealand and Australia a few seasons before. In order to give the American riders something better to compete with than converted 45 inch Scouts and WL Harley-Davidsons that were usually a poor second to the more potent English Douglases and Rudges, Crocker planned the limited manufacture of a special speedway machine. During this transition he maintained his contract work for the Indian factory, but sold his distributorship to a rehabilitated Floyd Clymer in 1934. Clymer had come out west since his recent incarceration in Leavenworth Prison, following his conviction for mail fraud in Denver.

With the assistance of Bigsby, Crocker designed and built about forty special speedway machines, which gave a good account of themselves on the local tracks until the advent of the more potent JAP engined speedway machines from England, which put an end to the project. The Crocker factory continued on with its contract machine work for the Indian Company. It was during this time that Crocker formulated plans to realize another of his long-standing dreams, that of manufacturing a high performance, heavyweight V-twin in the American tradition for the experienced competition and high speed touring rider. Again with Bigsby's collaboration, he began work on this project in the Summer of 1935, and early in 1936 the first prototype was ready for testing.

The machine was designed along Indian lines, with a low saddle position on a 60.5 inch wheelbase. The frame was fabricated from heavy gauge tubing and was of the diamond pattern, the lower engine plates connecting the down tube with the seat and chain stays. The gearbox case was cast integrally with the frame, the access to which was by a heavy plate bolted to the left side. The forks were of the girder type, similar to contemporary English machines, and were of heavyweight pattern as used in the newly introduced Indian Sport Scout. They carried heavy double compression and dampening springs of the barrel type. The rake and trail was laid out for quick and accurate steering, the motion being controlled by adjustable dampers. Many of the cycle parts, such as the fuel tank halves, footboards, generator drive case, countershaft sprocket cover, instrument panel and tail lamp nacelle were aluminum castings, made in the factory's own foundry.

The engine was a massive 45° ohv V-twin, with a nearly square bore and stroke, in contrast with the traditional American practise which up to that time had featured long stroke dimensions. The heavily finned cylinders were cast with thick walls, to allow for overboring, and

were deeply spigoted into a heavy, vertically-split crankcase. The primary drive consisted of an inner and outer casting, as in traditional Indian practise, and contained a four row Weller-type tensioned chain. The generator drive was by a gear wheel over the clutch housing, again similar to Indian design. The three-speed close ratio gears were massively oversized, and Crocker could rightly boast that as these were capable of transmitting over 200hp, no rider was ever able to blow up his gearbox! The large clutch was a massive multiplate affair, activated by a large central coil spring.

The overall result was a lithe and graceful appearing machine weighing about 475lbs that was rough running, dirty, noisy, and rather difficult to start, even with a specially adapted Splitdorf magneto that was fitted as standard. Once on the road, however, nothing else could catch it, and, after initial road test results were published, the Crocker was an overnight sensation.

Each machine was especially assembled to the buyer's option as to color combinations, degree of chrome trim, and final gear ratios. The thickness of the cylinder walls enabled optional bores to the extent that a Crocker could displace anything from the standard 61 inch configuration up to 90 inch. About half a dozen intrepid lady riders ordered Crockers with coil ignition for easier starting, as it took a hefty rider to crank over the massive engine and no girl rider could possibly start one with the standard magneto ignition. The cruising speeds of any Crocker were between 90 and 100mph, with top speeds well above the 100 mark.

The main drawback to volume sales was the necessarily high selling price, which was usually $75.00 to $150.00 over that of contemporary 74 inch Harley-Davidsons and Indian Chiefs. This factor also precluded any other than direct sales by the factory, as any dealer markups would have priced the Crockers out of sight.

The first five machines were built with exposed valve rockers, but excessive oil loss called for a redesign. All machines built from No. 6 on featured full tappet enclosure. There was no change in the basic design of the machines until 1940, when a larger and more bulbous fuel tank was fitted to increase the former limited cruising range of less than 100 miles on the original two gallon types, as the Crocker was not designed for economical running. This change began with engine number 81.

As is the case of most low production makes now long redundant, the actual number of Crockers ever built has been most difficult to determine. It was once thought that they were produced in batches of twenty-five, this being based on some hearsay evidence and some available engine numbers. These figures indicated that 197 were built between the Spring of 1936 and December

1941. The author's original estimates, together with those of Ernest Skelton who had been conducting his own research into the matter with the help of the late Elmo Looper, were based on these figures.

However, subsequent investigations by Skelton, with the aid of another enthusiast named Charles Vernon, who painstakingly traced the one-time owners of both available machines and resurrected engine cases, now indicate that the original estimates were far too high.

Gene Rhyne, one-time Excelsior and later Indian hill climb star who was the Crocker shop foreman later revealed that the engine cases were not numbered consecutively, most probably to conceal that fact of the make's extremely limited production.

Further evidence along these lines was later supplied by the discovery of an aged auto painter who had been engaged by Crocker to finish the completed machines. It was his recollection that less than 100 were built during the prewar years, and that about ten or eleven were clandestinely built up from spare parts and sold to favored customers when civilian sales were supposedly forbidden.

Later estimates by Rhyne, together with Skelton's and Vernon's continuing investigations, now indicate that about 95 pre-war machines were built, and include the fleet of ten sold to the Arizona State Highway Patrol in 1940. With a now well confirmed total of 105 or 106 Crockers ever made, the presence of over thirty machines, half of which are fully complete, gives the make the highest survival rate of any of the old-time classics!

The introduction of the Crocker was a great source of embarrassment to the Harley-Davidson Company, who concurrently had announced the introduction of their 61 inch ohv model in 1936. Herbert Fagan, an early Crocker enthusiast, reports the first ten machines produced were entered by their owners in the informal speed trials held each Spring on the old Lake Muroc dry lake. Nearly all the Crockers turned in times at least 10mph faster than the competing 74 inch side valve Harleys and Indian Chiefs. Due to teething troubles, the new Harley 61s were nowhere in the running.

In later years, Crocker told intimates of threatened legal action from Harley-Davidson regarding alleged patent infringement, although the Crocker scarcely resembled Harley-Davidson in any noticeable detail. There was also the story that Harley-Davidson threatened to boycott the Budd and Kelsey-Hayes Companies, manufacturers of stock motorcycle wheel rims, if they continued to supply the infant Crocker Company with any more units. Whether this story is true or not, Crocker buyers in later years were advised to supply their own rims, these being purchased from some nearby sympathetic Harley-Davidson or Indian dealer.

Financially, the Crocker machines were a disaster for their maker. The late Floyd Clymer, who was at one time interested in handling Crockers as a dealer, told the author in 1965 that Crocker lost at least $2,500.00 on each unit sold, due to high production costs and low sales volume. The make was not revived after the end of World War II for this reason, but Crocker recouped his losses during the war by undertaking extensive subcontract production of precision aircraft parts for the Douglas Aircraft Company in nearby Long Beach.

The small stock of remaining spare parts was acquired by a Crocker enthusiast, the late Elmo Looper, in 1952. These passed into the hands of his brother, Murray, after Elmo's death in 1969. The current Crocker exponent is Ernest Skelton of La Mirada, California, who owns several machines, restores various models owned by others, and who recently came into possession of most of the shop blueprints drawn by Paul Bigsby. In all, about thirty Crockers survive today, about half of which possess enough original parts to make them authentic. The author's machine was built in 1938 and carries engine number 31. It is of 68 inch displacement, and was restored by Skelton and Looper in 1969. It is typically Crocker, and for the novice rider is a thoroughly frightening vehicle.

Many legends grew up around the Crocker, most of them untrue. The most persistent one was that the machines were hybrids built up from Indian and Harley parts. This is, of course, untrue, although certain proprietary parts such as saddles, lighting sets, magnetos, wheel rims, and other minor fittings were common to all three contemporary makes.

As a highly specialized motorcycle designed for a very limited market, built to an ideal rather than to a price, the Crocker was foredoomed to failure, especially as it appeared at a time when interest in motorcycling in general was very limited. Nevertheless, the Crocker represented a milestone in motorcycle design and presaged the current type of today's popular superbike by nearly forty years.

Motion picture actors such as Randolph Scott and Clark Gable, who were experienced riders, had more than a passing interest in the make, although it is not known whether or not they actually owned one. John Payne was known to have owned a 1936 model, and several old photographs of him riding one are known to exist. Most of the Crockers quite naturally were owned in California, although a few found their way to the midwest and two travelled as far east as Massachusetts. The author's machine was unearthed in an old automobile repair garage in Chicago.

While the Crocker was anathema to Harley-Davidson, Indian officials usually encouraged its maker, mostly out of old-time acquaintanceship as the make was never produced in sufficient numbers to be a market threat to anyone. In 1940, Crocker approached the Indian management concerning their possible purchase of the manufacturing rights, either as a complete machine or for adaptation of the engine to the Chief frame as a super-sports model. Due to high production cost factors during a difficult time for motorcycle sales generally, the matter was never seriously considered by Indian.

Crocker retired shortly after the end of World War II and passed away after a brief illness at his home in Pasadena in May 1961. Paul Bigsby deserted the motorcycle business to manufacture electric guitars in Downey, California, and passed away in 1965. The sole survivor of Crocker's manufacturing days is the one-time Excelsior and Indian competition star, Gene Rhyne, who was Crocker's shop foreman and supervised machine assembly during the last years of the company. He is presently retired and living in Pasadena.

In the meantime, Skelton, Vernon, and the author continue to moniter the ongoing Crocker situation. By the late 1980s it was determined that of the fifty-odd survivors, about thirty machines now exist in fairly original condition, due mainly to the limited production of such replica parts as mudguards, footboard platforms, carburetor intake covers, generator drive cases, secondary chain covers, steering dampers, and tail lamp nacelles, the latter all being aluminum alloy castings.

The remaining machines consist mostly of incomplete items such as frames and engine cases, sufficient to indicate that the models once existed as such. Even at that, there are undoubtedly more parts somewhere about, but the tracing of the exact number is today a doubtful proposition.

Of the speedway machines, about a dozen are now known to survive.

The exact number of machines clandestinely assembled during the war years is still in doubt, and the whole investigation is clouded by the inconsistent numbering of the engine cases following their assembly. In any event, the number of survivors contrasted with the original numbers produced is still greater than that of any other make of the classic period.

# TECHNICAL DETAILS
## and Serial Numbers of Indian Motorcycles

**Indian Motorcycle Engine and Year Identification Numbers**

*Diamond Frame Models*

| Year | No. of Cyls. | HP | Motor No. |
|---|---|---|---|
| 1902–3 | 1 | 1¾ | 151–620 |
| 1904 | 1 | 1¾ | 621–1167 |
| 1905 | 1 | 2¼ | 1168–2349 |
| 1906 | 1 | 2½ | 2350–4048 |
| 1907 | 1 | 2¼ | 5000 up |
| 1907 | 2 | 4 | T100–T499 |
| 1908 | 2 | 5 | T500–T1200 |
| 1908 | 1 | 3½ | H100–H702 |

*Loop Frame Models*

| Year | No. of Cyls. | HP | Motor No. |
|---|---|---|---|
| 1909 | 1 | 2¾ | IA01 up |
| 1909 | 1 | 3½ | IOA001 up |
| 1909 | 1 | 4 | 40A001 up |
| 1909 | 2 | 5 | 20A001 up |
| 1909 | 2 | 7 | 70A001 up |
| 1910 | 1 | 2¾ | 1B01 up |
| 1910 | 1 | 4 | 40B001 up |
| 1910 | 2 | 5 | 20B001 up |
| 1910 | 2 | 7 | 70B001 up |
| 1911 | 1 | 2¾ | 1C001 up |
| 1911 | 1 | 4 | 40C001 up |
| 1911 | 2 | 5 | 20C001 up |
| 1911 | 2 | 7 | 70C001 up |
| 1912 | 1 | 4 | 40D001 up |
| 1912 | 2 | 7 | 40E001 up |
| 1913 | 1 | 4 | 70E001 up |
| 1913 | 2 | 7 | 40F001 up |

| Year | No. of Cyls. | HP | Motor No. |
|---|---|---|---|
| 1914 | 1 | 4 | 40E001 up |
| 1914 | 2 | 7 | 70F001 up |
| 1915 | 1 | 4 | 40G001 up |
| 1915 | 2 | 7 | 70G001 up |
| 1915 | 2 | 7 | 50G001 up |
| 1916 | 1 | 2½ | 20H001 up |
| 1916 | 2 | 7 | 70H001 up |
| 1917 | 2 | 2½ | 30J001 up |
| 1917 | 1 | 4 | 40J001 up |
| 1917 | 2 | 7 | 40J001 up |
| 1917 | 2 | 7 | RX001 up |
| 1918 | 2 | 2½ | 30K001 up |
| 1918 | 1 | 4 | 40K001 up |
| 1918 | 2 | 7 | 70K001 up |
| 1918 | 2 | ? | KRX001 up |
| 1919 | 2 | 2½ | 30M001 up |
| 1919 | 1 | 4 | 40M001 up |
| 1919 | 2 | 7 | 70M001 up |
| 1919 | 2 | 7–9 (Big Valve) | MP001 up |

*Both Hedstrom and Franklin 4-valve per cylinder racing engines were either unnumbered or numbered with no sequence.*

*The four dual-carburetor side valve racing engines were numbered 1, 2, 3, 4.*

**Engine Numbers of Chief, Ace, Scout and Prince**

| Year | No. of Cyls. | Model | Motor No. |
|---|---|---|---|
| 1920 | 2 | Scout | 50R00 up |
| 1920 | 4 | Ace | AMM00 up |
| 1921 | 2 | Scout | 50S000 up |
| 1921 | 4 | Ace | AMM100 up |

| | | | |
|---|---|---|---|
| 1922 | 2 | Scout | 50T000 up |
| 1922 | 2 | Chief | 80T000 up |
| 1922 | 4 | Ace | BMM00 up |
| 1923 | 2 | Scout | 50V000 up |
| 1923 | 2 | Chief 61 inch | 80V000 up |
| 1923 | 2 | Chief 74 inch | 90V000 up |
| 1923 | 4 | Ace | CMM000 up |
| 1924 | 2 | Chief 61 inch | 80X000 up |
| 1924 | 2 | Chief 74 inch | 90X000 up |
| 1925 | 1 | Prince | 30X000 up |
| 1925 | 2 | Scout | 50Y000 up |
| 1925 | 2 | Chief 61 inch | 80Y000 up |
| 1925 | 2 | Chief 74 inch | 90Y000 up |
| 1926 | 1 | Prince | AL 100 up |
| 1926 | 2 | Scout 37 inch | AL 100 up |
| 1926 | 2 | Scout 45 inch | AGF100 up |
| 1926 | 2 | Chief 61 inch | AZ100 up |
| 1926 | 2 | Chief 74 inch | AH 100 up |
| 1926 | 4 | Ace | EMM00 up |
| 1927 | 1 | Prince | EL100 up |
| 1927 | 2 | Scout 37 inch | BG100 up |
| 1927 | 2 | Scout 45 inch | BGP100 up |
| 1927 | 2 | Chief 61 inch | BZ100 up |
| 1927 | 2 | Chief 74 inch | BH100 up |
| 1927 | 4 | Ace | VF100 up |
| 1928 | 1 | Prince | CL100 up |
| 1928 | 2 | Scout 37 inch | CGI 00 up |
| 1928 | 2 | Scout 45 inch | CGP100 up |
| 1928 | 2 | Chief 61 inch | CZ100 up |
| 1928 | 2 | Chief 7 4 inch | CH100 up |
| 1928 | 4 | Indian Ace | CA100 up |
| 1928 | 2 | 101 Scout 37 inch | DG100 up |
| 1928 | 2 | 101 Scout 45 inch | DCP100 up |

## Technical Details of 37 inch Indian Scouts

**1920** Model R. Motor numbers 50R001 up. Chrome plated handlebars and luggage rack. Compression release trigger on handlebar. Dixie magneto ignition standard. Springs on saddle. Flat bar gear shift lever was chrome plated

**1921** Model S. Motor numbers 50S001 up. Design unchanged except that an electrically equipped model was offered as an option

**1922** Model T. Motor numbers 50T001 up. Handlebars and luggage rack painted black. Electrically equipped as standard, with Klaxon horn and ammeter in the switch box. This model had a spring seat post

**1923** Model V. Motor numbers 50V001 up. The luggage rack was no longer standard, and flat steel stays supported the rear mudguard. The compression release was now activated by a rod

supported by a small bracket fitted on the topside of the fuel tank

**1924** Model X. Motor numbers 50X001 up. New design front fork of trailing link type with spring rods outside the outer edges of the mudguard. The gear shift lever was now a chrome plated rod

**1925** Model Y. Motor numbers 50Y001 up. Design same as above except spring seat post was deleted and the saddle carried its own springs. Ricardo type detachable cylinder heads with increased compression ratio

**1926** Model AG. Motor numbers AG 100 up. Design as above except that all machines after May were fitted with low pressure 25 inch x 3.85 inch tires

**1927** Model BG. Motor numbers BG 100 up. Wide D section mudguards replaced previous ribbed type. Deep valance on front mudguard. Compression release rod extended through hole in outer edge of fuel tank

**1928** Model CG. Motor numbers CG 100 up. Flat handlebars substituted for swept back touring type

**1928** Model DG 101. Motor numbers DG 100 up. From April all Scout models had new low frame with smaller tear drop type fuel tank. This 37 inch model was the first 101

**1928** Model Scout 45 inch. Motor numbers CFD 100 up. This series started the famous 101 45 inch model first produced in April

### Colors And Gold Striping

All early Scout models were painted Indian Red with black wheels, brake assemblies, and spokes. Footboards, brake and clutch pedals were black, as were the horn, headlight, and tail light. Domestic color options were either white or dark blue.

The rib type mudguards fitted from 1920 through 1926 had two fine gold stripes about one inch out from the central rib on either side. The fuel tank also had a double gold stripe outlining the sides as shown in the illustrations.

### Technical Details of 37 inch and 45 inch Model 101 Scouts

The first 101 models whose production began in April 1928 were fitted with a compression release mechanism on the timing case which was activated by a rod which extended upward through a tube through the right side of the fuel tank.

The early 1929 models did not have this rod fitted, the compression release mechanism then being activated by a foot operated trigger.

The first 101 models were fitted with a small diameter 'bullet' type headlight. A larger type with greater diameter and a larger capacity bulb was fitted to the early 1930 models. Most owners of early machines subsequently fitted the later type which gave much better illumination.

In the Fall of 1930, the 1931 101 model appeared. An improved rear brake was fitted with an internal expanding band in place of the former compression type which was more susceptible to slipping when wet.

This model also dispensed with the two prongs or 'horns' that held the headlight, which was now moved slightly backward and downward to bolt to a flange cast in the forward part of the handlebar head lug.

The 1931 models also carried a vibrator type horn fitted to the front of the upper fork, in place of the Klaxon type formerly attached to a bracket on the left front frame tube.

In 1931 a wide variety of optional colors were offered.

## How to Identify Factory Racing Frames

From time to time racing type frames come to light. These are mostly of the single speed type with a round bracket behind the engine loop for the fitting of a countershaft drive.

Many of these were built up by private owners or dealer mechanics conversant with brazing, and are often so skilfully executed as to appear as a factory product.

These latter, however, were built up mostly from standard Hedstrom or later Standard frame components.

The factory built frames may be identified by their thicker fork jaws in the rear axle lugs, which may be up to ¾ inch thick. These heavy forgings were built in to counteract the torque reaction of the powerful four and eight valve racing engines, and were never fitted to standard production type frames.

## Technical Details of Indian Four Cylinder Motorcycles Manufactured from June 1927 through March 1942

### June 1927
Basic Ace design painted Indian red with gold decal Indian-Ace on gasoline tank. Motor number VF 101 up

### January 1928
Basic Ace design as above. Motor numbers CA 101 up. After motor numbers CA 209, a new sequence of EA 101 to EA 776. Two hundred and twenty-five machines after motor numbers EA 226 built with model 101 Scout type front and rear wheel and brake assemblies, fuel tank, upper and lower tank rails, and mudguards. Fork as in 101, except for one or two added lower spring leaves.

Lower frame with single down tube to oval motor mounting as in original Ace. Tires 18 inch x 3.85 inch clincher type. Five bearing crankshaft

### April 1928
Motor numbers EA 226 up. Double down tubes to engine mountings

### October 1929
Motor numbers EA 776 to EA 1509. Larger headlight replaces small bullet type of previous models. Tires 18 inch x 4.00 inch with drop center rims

### September 1930
Motor numbers EA 1510 up. Headlight now mounted on handlebar with center bolt. Detachable rear wheel with internal expanding brake. Circular vibrator type horn mounted under headlight

### September 1931
Motor numbers DOC 101 up. Shape of cylinder heads and manifold changed slightly. Square cylinder fins. Two piece fuel tanks now cover top frame rail. Saddle slightly larger. Rear mudguard hinged behind top of arc. Front mudguard shows deeper valance and contour follows arc of wheel. Heavier frame of new design

### September 1932
Motor numbers DCD 101 up. No visable changes except fish tail type exhaust pipe drops slightly lower

### September 1933
No changes

### September 1934
Motor numbers DCE 101 up. New streamlined type fenders with slight upward curvature in tips. Many optional color combinations offered, and handlebar grips now of greater diameter

### September 1935
Motor numbers DCF 101 up. A new engine design announced in July 1935. Exhaust valves in overhead position, with side fitted intake valves. Exhaust manifold on top of engine, with twin exhaust pipes. Updraft carburetor fitted. This was popularly known as the upside down four

### September 1936
Motor numbers DCF 609 up. This engine was slightly altered from the above but with dual updraft carburetors. Was known as the Sport Four

*September 1937*
Motor numbers DCH 101 up. A completely redesigned engine with cylinders and heads cast in pairs. All exhaust tappets enclosed in aluminum cases. Aluminum cylinder heads. Chrome fishtail type exhaust pipe. Enclosed aluminum instrument panel with switch and ammeter on forward tank top. 18 inch x 4.50 inch tires

*September 1939*
Motor numbers DCI 101 up. Motor design unchanged from above. Plunger type rear springing. Mudguard valances shrouding wheels. Tires optional in sizes, either 18 inch x 4.50 inch or 16 inch x 5.00 inch

*September 1940*
Motor numbers DDA 101 up. No changes from above except chrome strip along fuel tank sides. Last of fours built from January 1941 through March 1942 are similar

**Model Designations for Machines Manufactured before 1926**
Various letters were inserted in the middle of the motor numbers. An example is 50R001

| | | | | | |
|---|---|---|---|---|---|
| 1909 | A | 1915 | G | 1921 | S |
| 1910 | B | 1916 | H | 1922 | T |
| 1911 | C | 1917 | J | 1923 | V |
| 1912 | D | 1918 | K | 1924 | X |
| 1913 | E | 1919 | M | 1925 | Y |
| 1914 | F | 1920 | R | | |

**Motor and Serial Numbers of Indian Military Models from 1940**

| | **45 cu. in Scout** | **74 cu. in Chief** | **30.50 cu. in** | **Shaft Drive** |
|---|---|---|---|---|
| *Motor Number* | FDO 101 up | CDO 101 up | GDA 101 up | HDA101 up |
| *Serial Number* | 640 101 up | 340 101 up | 741 101 up | 841 101 up |

The first military models built in 1940 were designated as Model 640 for the 30.50 cu. in. and Model 741 for the 45 cu. in.
In subsequent factory literature and parts lists, the 30.50 type was designated as Model 741 A and the 45 cu. in. type as 741 B.

**Motor Registration Data from 1926 to 1948**

| **Model name** | **Motor model letters** | **No. of Cyls.** | **Bore** | **Stroke** | **Displ.** | **SAE rated** |
|---|---|---|---|---|---|---|
| Prince | AL - BL - CL | 1 | $2\frac{3}{4}$ | $3\frac{7}{64}$ | 21.25 | 3.02 |
| Junior Scout or 30.50 | EOC - ECC - ECD - ECE - ECF - ECG - ECH - ECI - EDO - EDA | 2 | $2\frac{1}{2}$ | $3\frac{1}{16}$ | 30.07 | 5.0 |
| Military 30.50 | GDA | 2 | $2\frac{1}{2}$ | $3\frac{1}{16}$ | 30.07 | 5.0 |
| 37 inch Scout | AG - BG - CG - DG - EG | 2 | $2\frac{3}{4}$ | $3\frac{1}{16}$ | 36.38 | 6.05 |
| 45 inch Scout Motoplane Sport Scout | BCC - BCD - BCE - BCF - BCG - BGP - CGP - DGP - EGP - FCD - FCE - FCF - FCG - FCH - FCI - FDO - FDA - FDB | 2 | $2\frac{7}{8}$ | $3\frac{1}{2}$ | 45.44 | 6.61 |
| 45 inch Military Shaft Drive | HDA | 2 | $2\frac{7}{8}$ | $3\frac{1}{2}$ | 45.44 | 6.61 |
| 61 inch Chief | AZ - BZ - CZ | 2 | $3\frac{1}{8}$ | $3\frac{1}{32}$ | 60.88 | 7.81 |
| 74 inch Chief | AH - BH - CH - EH - COC - CCC - CCD - CCE - CCF - CCG - CCH - CCI - CDO - CDA to CDH | 2 | $3\frac{1}{4}$ | $4\frac{7}{16}$ | 73.62 | 8.45 |
| Indian 4 | VA - CA - DA - EA - DOC - DCC - DCD - DCE - DCF - DCG - DCH - DCI - DDO - DDA - DDB | 4 | $2\frac{3}{4}$ | $3\frac{1}{4}$ | 77.21 | 12.1 |

# Bibliography

The Archives of the Hendee Manufacturing Company
The Archives of the Indian Motocycle Company
The US National Museum, Dept. of Transportation
The United States Congressional Record
The United States Department of Commerce
The Reports of the US Senate Committee on Money
    and Banking
The US Department of Justice, Dept. of Prisons
The Federal District Court, Denver, Colorado
The Detroit Public Library
The El Paso Public Library
The Los Angeles County Public library
Bibliotica Nacionale, Mexico City
*Motor Cycle Cavalcade*, by Ixion (Canon B.H. Davies),
    Iliffe
*Vintage Motorcycles*, by James Sheldon, Batsford
*The World's Motorcycles*, by Erwin Tragatsch, Temple
    Press
*Motorcycles*, by Victor Page
*Vintage Motorcycling*, by M.A. Bull
*The Golden Age of the Fours*, by Theodore Hodgdon,
    Bagnall
*The Story of the TT*, by G.S. Davison, TT Special
*Standard & Poor's Corporation Index*
*Moody's Corporation Index*
*The Motor Cycle*
*Motor Cycling*
*The Motorcyclist*
*Motorcycling Illustrated*
*Motorcycling and Bicycling*
*The Western Motorcyclist and Bicyclist*

*Cycle World*
*Automotive Illustrated*
*Motor Age*
*The World's Automobiles*, by G.N. Georgano
*The New York Times*
*The Los Angeles Times*
*The Wall Street Journal*
*The Journal of the Antique Motorcycle Club*
*Official Journal of the Vintage Motor Cycle Club*
*The Journal of the Antique and Classic Motorcycle*
    *Association*
Kuhn Loeb and Company
Merrill, Lynch, Pierce, Fenner and Smith
The First Boston Company
Hornblower and Weeks, Inc.
Francis I. du Pont & Company
*The du Ponts of Delaware*, by William H.C. Carr
The Atlas Corporation
Arnold Schwinn and Company
The Baldwin Chain Company
E.I. du Pont de Nemours
Delco, Incorporated
The Harley-Davidson Motor Company
General Motors Corporation
The Firestone Tire and Rubber Company
The Goodyear Tire and Rubber Company
Texas Industries, Inc.
Titeflex Incorporated
The Delaware Historical Society
The Massachusetts Historical Society

# Index